# PRAISE FOR TOUCHING HISTORY

Rabbi Sholom Gold grew up in America after the war. It was a time of religious awakening and he was fortunate to find his way into Yeshivat Ner Israel in Baltimore, whose *rosh yeshivah* was committed to Klal Yisrael, caring deeply for Torah learning as well as for the needs of the Jewish people as a whole. Rabbi Gold devoted his many talents to Torah education in America and Canada and built a successful *yeshivah* in Toronto, all the while looking forward to aliyah, so that he could take part also in the rebirth of the Jewish people in our ancestral home. The Almighty blessed him and enabled him to fulfill his dream of participating in the Divine drama of Israel's growth and development. In Jerusalem, he became a leading communal *rav* and built a modern congregation, which combines loyalty to Torah with responsibility to the Jewish people. Now he is telling his story, and there is much to admire and learn in this tale.

**HaRav Nachum E. Rabinovitch**, Rosh Yeshivah,
Yeshivat Birkat Moshe, Ma'ale Adumim

While reading Rabbi Gold's autobiography, two words said in the Shabbat Musaf service, which encapsulate the Golds' aliyah to Eretz Yisrael, came to my mind: ותטענו בגבולינו (May You implant us in our borders).

The blessing of being *implanted* in Eretz Yisrael, where even children and grandchildren are active participants in all walks of life, is a merit which not all *olim* enjoy.

This book can serve as a road map for *olim* to follow and reach the level of ותטענו בגבולינו.

**HaRav Nachman Kahana**, *rav*, Old City of Jerusalem;
author, *Mei Menuchot: Elucidations of Tosafot*

Rabbi Sholom Gold brings the Torah to life. His passion, love and dedication to Am Yisrael, Torat Yisrael, and Eretz Yisrael are unmistakable, and his unwavering stance as a proud Torah Jew inspires everyone who comes into contact with him. We are honored to have Rabbi Gold as Dean of OU-Israel's Avrom Silver College for Adults, and pray that he continues to educate, motivate, and inspire us for many years to come.

**HaRav Avi Berman**, **Executive Director, OU Israel**

The *baalei mussar* muse that everyone is born into this world as an "original" but with rare exceptions ends up as a "copy."

As one will quickly discover in the pages of this memoir, Rabbi Sholom Gold is the exception that proves the rule.

His life journey from Williamsburg to Jerusalem was nurtured by an exemplary family and *gedolei Yisrael*, enabling this passionate *talmid chacham* to become one of the outstanding pioneering rabbinic and community leaders of the last half of the twentieth century and into the present day.

His story is the unfolding drama of the Jewish people in the last seventy years. It is an inspiring and uplifting book that will hold your interest from beginning to end.

**HaRav Boruch Taub**, Rabbi Emeritus,
Beth Avrohom Yoseph of Toronto

Rabbi Gold provides his readers with an exciting, informative work, highlighting many areas of Jewish history of the past seventy years. As an important player himself in this saga, he gives us an intimate picture of this extraordinary period. He is uniquely qualified through his own experiences and achievements in America, Canada, and Israel to give insights into the developing communities. He does this through personal recollections and anecdotes and presents us with a highly pleasurable reading experience.

**HaRav Meyer Fendel**, founder, Hebrew Academy
of Nassau County (HANC) and Young Israel of West
Hempstead; author, *Nine Men Wanted for a Minyan:
Bringing Torah to Long Island*

# Touching History

# TOUCHING HISTORY

## From Williamsburg to Jerusalem

### Rabbi Sholom Gold

Copyright © Sholom Gold
Jerusalem 2015/5775
www.rabbisholomgold.com

All rights reserved. No part of this publication may be translated, reproduced, stored in a retrieval system or transmitted, in any form or by any means, electronic, mechanical, photocopying, recording or otherwise, without express written permission from the publishers.

Cover Design: Leah Ben Avraham/Noonim Graphics
Typesetting: Irit Nachum
Photos of demonstration in Kikar Zion taken by Mordechai Benita

ISBN: 978-965-229-639-9

3 5 7 9 8 6 4 2

| Gefen Publishing House Ltd. | Gefen Books |
|---|---|
| 6 Hatzvi Street | 11 Edison Place |
| Jerusalem 94386, Israel | Springfield, NJ 07081 |
| 972-2-538-0247 | 516-593-1234 |
| orders@gefenpublishing.com | orders@gefenpublishing.com |

www.gefenpublishing.com

Printed in Israel

---

Library of Congress Cataloging-in-Publication Data

Gold, Sholom, 1935- author.
Touching history : the memoirs / Rabbi Sholom Gold.
   pages cm
ISBN 978-965-229-639-9
1. Gold, Sholom, 1935- 2. Rabbis--New York (State)--New York--Biography. I. Title.
BM755.G564A3 2014
296.8'332092--dc23
[B]
2014039577

To the memory of Avrom Silver, *z"l*, a man who had a heart for Israel,
a zest for life, and a love for his family

To the memory of Harold Vogel, *z"l*, a true survivor who had a special passion for
the well-being of Israel and his family both in Poland and Canada

לְמַעַן צִיּוֹן לֹא אֶחֱשֶׁה, וּלְמַעַן יְרוּשָׁלַם לֹא אֶשְׁקוֹט,
עַד-יֵצֵא כַנֹּגַהּ צִדְקָהּ, וִישׁוּעָתָהּ כְּלַפִּיד יִבְעָר.
ישעיהו סב-א


וְגַלְתִּי בִירוּשָׁלַם, וְשַׂשְׂתִּי בְעַמִּי; וְלֹא-יִשָּׁמַע בָּהּ עוֹד,
קוֹל בְּכִי וְקוֹל זְעָקָה.
ישעיהו סה-יט

# Contents

| | | |
|---|---|---|
| Preface | | xiii |
| Acknowledgments | | xxi |
| Prologue | | xxv |

## Part One: Foundations

| | | |
|---|---|---|
| 1 | Growing Up in Williamsburg | 3 |
| 2 | Spiritual Influences | 18 |
| 3 | Taking the Boy out of Brooklyn | 35 |
| 4 | My First Dalet Amos in Eretz Yisrael | 49 |
| 5 | Ponevezh | 65 |
| 6 | Spring in the Air | 80 |
| 7 | Things Turn Serious | 90 |
| 8 | Back in Baltimore | 104 |
| 9 | Toronto | 119 |
| 10 | Living in Benevolent Exile | 134 |
| 11 | Entering the Rabbinate | 145 |
| 12 | West Hempstead and the *Eruv* | 161 |
| 13 | The *Mikveh* | 177 |
| 14 | Great Men and Good Times | 193 |
| 15 | Decision Time | 207 |

## Part Two: Eretz Yisrael

| 16 | For Good This Time | 221 |
| 17 | Behind the Iron Curtain | 234 |
| 18 | Building the Shul and the Family | 251 |
| 19 | Oslo, or, What Were They Thinking? | 271 |
| 20 | Fighting the Good Fight | 287 |
| 21 | The Wages of "Peace" | 296 |
| 22 | Of Classes, Trips, and Traveling | 316 |
| 23 | Israeli Innocents Abroad | 334 |
| 24 | Dreams, Nightmares, and Memories | 343 |
| 25 | Family Reunions | 357 |
| 26 | Retirement | 367 |

| Epilogue | 375 |
| Index | 377 |

Photos appear after page 198

# Preface

There is a story that has haunted me for years. I have shared it with many people, both young and old. It has served as a warning and a wakeup call. This is it.

As the morning dawned it was obvious that this was going to be another cloudless day with a brilliant blue sky. It was the third day of the war (it didn't have a name yet). Israeli paratroopers burst into the Old City of Jerusalem. The city that had been fought over so many times in the past was now again experiencing the deafening sounds of war – but with a big difference. It was not an invading army, it was not the Assyrians, nor the Babylonians, Romans, Saracens, Crusaders, Mamalukes, Turkish, or British. Jerusalem's children were returning home. The city that had not been under Jewish rule for two thousand years was being redeemed from her captivity by her children.

The young soldiers made their way quickly through the narrow streets and serpentine alleyways of the Old City toward their objective. The Kotel and Har Habayit. For nineteen years Jews had not been permitted to pray at the Kotel – a right that had been an integral part of the ceasefire agreement with Jordan in 1949, that they had not honored – so the Israeli soldiers didn't know how to get there. Then they saw a young man cowering with fear in an alleyway. They assured him that they meant no harm. "Just direct us to the Kotel," they said. Trembling, he showed them the way. He remained standing, watching as they hurried off, until he saw them ascending the Temple Mount. Transfixed, he saw the Israeli flag being hoisted over the mountain.

Abraham Rabinovich, in his book *The Battle for Jerusalem*, tells us that this young man was Abdullah Schleifer, a New York–born Jew who had converted to Islam, married a Jordanian girl, and was working as a reporter in the Old City. Rabinovich's closing comment is so simple yet so insightful: *What a strange witness to one of the greatest moments in Jewish history.*

Totally distant and alienated from his people and his heritage, he didn't experience the holy thrill and the profound joy with fellow Jews worldwide. Schleifer was culturally and religiously orphaned, Jewishly blind. What a pity. A Jewish soul wandering, confused, troubled, and then lost.

This story keeps coming back to haunt me time and time again over the past forty years, because I made a painful discovery. One can be a fine Jew who observes *mitzvot* and studies Torah; he can be Chassidish, Litvish, Ashkenazi, Sephardi, and all shades in between and also be blind. I have spoken to hundreds of people who simply don't see the majestic divine process unfolding before our very eyes here in Eretz Yisrael. Their vision is blurred, their ability to comprehend the meaning of events severely limited. They just don't get it. They are suffering a severe form of historic blindness: the Schleifer Syndrome.

The present can have meaning and significance only if it is connected to the past. Without the past, the present simply pales into a series of lackluster, mundane events, eliciting a reaction that is equally lifeless. This might very well be the reason the story of the exodus retold on Pesach night must be inextricably intertwined with the past. *"Matchil bi'gnut u'mesayeim b'shevach"*: the story must begin with the sad and painful past and proceed to the great moment of the exodus.

Anticipation of future stages in history takes its vitality from past and present. A present that is not connected to the past is bereft of meaning. It is this Schleifer confusion and blindness that compels me to write this autobiography.

The events of the past seventy years have profoundly affected the way we should view the unfolding reality. The dramatic change that began with the establishment of the State of Israel should express itself in the way we think, feel, talk, read the news, and maybe most of all, the way we learn a passage in the Neviim.

For years I had been saying sermons elaborating or explaining and elucidating the first Rashi in Chumash. I wanted my students to be able to recite that Rashi even when awoken in the middle of the night. But one day in a flash of inspiration, I was struck by the real power of that Rashi and how it defines the radical change that has taken place.

My imagination took over and this is what I saw. The year is 1944, the place is Auschwitz – more specifically, the children's barracks. With great self-sacrifice, a *melamed*, a teacher of children, furtively makes his way into the compound and says, "*Kinderlach*, let's study Hashem's holy Torah." The hungry, cold, bedraggled children huddle around the *rebbe*. He says, "Let us begin with the first *pasuk* in Chumash: 'In the beginning Elokim created heaven and earth.'"

He proceeds to teach them the first Rashi: "Rashi tells us that Rabbi Yitzchak asked, 'Why does Torah begin with the story of creation? Since Torah is a book of G-d's law, it should have begun with the first mitzvah given to Klal Yisrael, which is only later on in Sefer Shmos in Parshas Bo, that Nissan is to be counted as the first of months. So what is the reason that the Torah began with Breishis?'" The answer, the *rebbe* tells the children, is to be found in a *pasuk* in Tehillim (111:6): "'The power of His acts He told to His people in order to give them the estate of nations.' Rashi concludes, 'So that if the nations of the world will say to Israel, "You are thieves for you conquered the land from the seven nations," Israel will say to them, "The earth belongs to Hashem. He took it from them and gave it to us."'"

Having finished teaching the Rashi, the *rebbe* pauses for a moment when he sees a little emaciated hand raised and hears the weak voice: "*Rebbe*, what is Rashi talking about? We don't know how much longer we are going to live. Our people are being exterminated and Rashi says, 'The nations will accuse us of having stolen Eretz Yisrael.' What kind of world of make-believe does Rashi live in?"

All the children are now focused fully on the *rebbe*. With tears pouring down his cheeks, he says to the children, "Since Rashi said it, then we have to believe that someday it will be true. It will be so."

For years I was angry every time Israel would be condemned at the United Nations – until that day. From then on I was overjoyed at every hate-filled condemnation and would shout, "Rashi was right! Rashi was right!"

For 850 years everyone who started the study of Chumash would have to take the great leap of faith: if Rashi said it, then someday it will be true. We no longer need a leap of faith – we are living the reality. Could it have been that this was Rashi's introduction to his commentary on Torah, that a great measure of faith will be needed to understand it?

No more! So many prophecies are now reality, visions are current events. What we longed for is taking on shape and form before our very eyes. Hashem's promises are being fulfilled.

Unfortunately, the *rebbe* didn't know that only four years later the history of the Jewish people would enter a glorious new phase.

What a pity that there are some who can't see it. Start from the beginning. Learn the first Rashi.

Something so seemingly mundane and prosaic as a visit to your local fruit and vegetable store can be an uplifting spiritual experience, provided you know what you are looking at. Some people will see nothing more than tomatoes and cucumbers, while others will be thrilled to watch the words of Tanach living, breathing, and exuding a message of salvation and redemption. The produce proclaims loud and clear the divine dimension of what has transpired here in the last hundred years.

Yechezkel, in one of his magnificent prophecies of redemption (36:11), speaks of desolate cities rebuilt, of the land being plowed and planted, filled with masses of Am Yisrael: "I will multiply man and animal upon you." One of the outstanding passages of all (36:8) states, "But you, O mountains of Israel, will give forth your branches and bear your fruit for My people Israel, for they are soon to come." Rabbi Abba says that there is no greater revealed end (the beginning of the Messianic era) than this. Rashi comments that when Eretz Yisrael gives out its fruit in abundance, you can be certain the Messianic end is coming and there is no more revealed sign than that.

The tomatoes are taking on greater significance. But there is yet much more. The land was desolate for nineteen hundred years. We are all familiar with Mark Twain's description of Emek Yizrael (in his journal of a visit to Palestine, entitled *Innocents Abroad*), as a place that is arid and dead. Nothing grows there, only dust and sand. Hundreds of years earlier, the Ramban had described the absolute and utter desolation that he found here.

Most significant of all is the fact that the land was so inhospitable that no other nation was able to settle it. The divinely ordained wasteland it became was a clearly stated blessing: "I will make the land desolate, and your foes who dwell upon it will be desolate" (Vayikra 26:32). In the very middle of the chapter of the *tochachah*, of admonition and rebuke, this *pasuk* of great consolation appears. The desolation of the land, which looks like punishment and destruction, is, in fact, precisely the opposite. Hashem is making certain that in our absence, no other people will be able to settle the land. Eretz Yisrael will wait patiently for her children to return and then give out her bountiful blessings.

The fruits and vegetables are proof that Hashem wants us here. The tomatoes and cucumbers broadcast a Divine message: "*Kinderlach*, come home." Some years ago, in a moment of inspiration, I said, "If you want to speak to G-d, go to the Kotel, but if you want to see Him, go to Shuk Machane Yehuda."

The produce of Eretz Yisrael is everyone's "Charlie." (You'll have to read the book to understand that.)

Why did I write this book? I neither made history nor influenced it, I have no intimate behind-the-scenes knowledge of great events, nor have I had the ear of the great players on the world stage. I wasn't an unfortunate victim caught in the jaws of human brutality. I am simply a witness.

The years of my life happen to span the most dramatic period in Jewish history and, for that matter, in the history of any people. It begins with the Jewish people's descent into darkness, enveloped in a tidal wave of irrational hatred unprecedented in its fury, and faced with the indifference of the whole world. One could hear the gates clanging shut, closing off all avenues of escape from the inferno that was Hitler's

Europe, marking the onset of the greatest horror conceived by man – that was when I was born. My earliest memory was when I was all of six years old, "the day that will live in infamy": the Japanese sneak attack on Pearl Harbor, December 7, 1941. I was in Yeshiva Torah Vodaath in Williamsburg, among the few children in school on a Sunday in America – just us *yeshivah* kids. It was my introduction to the decades that would follow. Historic events would follow on the heels of one another, creating a tapestry of black darkness, red blood – a world in upheaval.

And after the war the focus shifted to hundreds of thousands of Jews languishing in Displaced Persons camps: the Sh'erit Hapleitah. With nowhere to go, they began to walk across Europe in order to claw their way to the only place they could call home – Eretz Yisrael – and that too was closed.

Then the dizzying events, the United Nations vote on November 29, 1947; war breaks out; the establishment of the state on the fifth of Iyar, 1948, and all that followed.

The 1956 Sinai Campaign; the 1967 Six-Day War; the 1973 Yom Kippur War; the July 4, 1976, rescue at Entebbe; the Lebanon Wars; the Oslo Accords; the exile of Gush Katif; Cast Lead; Protective Edge; and many others.

All I did was walk with history dramatically unfolding beside me and was fortunate enough to appreciate the grandeur and the majesty of watching G-d's divine plan taking on body and form. Step by step, just as the rabbis described it, the sun rising *kima kima*, little by little. I ever so gently touched history and was in turn touched by history in a powerful way. I watched the brushstrokes – some thin, some broad, some black, some white, some red, some crimson – beginning to cover the canvas. The Jewish people were again taking their place on the world stage. No longer wandering, no longer homeless, no longer existing on the edge, no longer at the mercy of the whims of tyrants, no longer beaten and hunted. After two thousand years, Jewish blood was no longer cheap. No burning at the stake, no crusades, no pogroms, no Kishinev, no Kielce, no Damascus blood libels. Those who would lift a hand against us have learned that it is a costly endeavor.

The dramatic resurgence of anti-Semitism on an unprecedented global scale is certainly cause for concern and calls for decisive action. I believe that G-d is sending out a message to His children to come home.

In the past sixty-six years He has created a Jewish state that is a world leader in science, technology, medicine, and so many other fields. It defies all logic that a community numbering six hundred thousand reinforced by the survivors of the Shoah, a people that had not fought a battle in two thousand years, emerged as a military power of the first order with an air force that ranks with the best in the world.

The successful absorption of millions of *olim*, which would have taxed other nations to their ultimate limits, is nothing short of a miracle.

What Divine Providence it was that nearly a million Jews from Arab lands came on aliyah following the establishment of the state. I shudder to think what would have happened to them if they were still there.

The lessons of the past seventy years should guide and direct Jews to leave the places where the danger level has become very serious. Now begin the journey home.

The American Jewish community still has the option to come on aliyah of their own free will. They are not yet being pushed. Now is the time to activate the age-old pull to Eretz Yisrael. It's not an opportunity that should be allowed to slip away. It should be seized, embraced, and acted upon.

I have chronicled the drama of these seventy years in the hope that my grandchildren and great-grandchildren will see the outpouring of Hashem's kindness to His people.

I once heard Rav Avraham HaCohen Pam say in a public *shiur* that there is a rule in Jewish history that following a period of great suffering Hashem embraces His people, comforts them, and showers blessing and abundance upon them. He described four such epic eras of extreme suffering followed by Hashem's countenance shining on His people. The fourth period was the Shoah, followed by *hakamat* Medinat Yisrael. The state was Hashem's embrace of Klal Yisrael.

Rav Eliyahu Dessler wrote only three months after the establishment of the state, "What is happening now in Eretz Yisrael is Hashem's great kindness from the extreme of suffering of the destruction of the six million to the very opposite extreme, our people settled in their own state in the Holy Land. Woe to one who will arrive at the day of judgment and is still blind to something so real."[*]

For years the most prominent place in our house was held by a beautiful saying. Surrounded by invitations, notices of meetings, recipes, candle lighting times, Rosh Hashanah cards, pictures and more pictures, all held up by attractive and colorful magnets – on the fridge of course – it always grabbed our attention. The printout from the computer said, "He who does not participate in the passion of his time will be judged as not having lived." Eretz Yisrael is the passion of our time and, thank G-d, we have been living it for more than three decades now.

Come to think of it, we may have gone beyond touching history. We are living it and we are writing it, because here is where the greatest chapters of the incredible story of the Jewish people are indeed being written.

May all of Klal Yisrael continue to be the beneficiaries of the goodness of the Guardian of Israel.

A technical note about transliterations: It was a dilemma to decide how to transliterate Hebrew words in this book. I have traveled an interesting path in my life and changed my pronunciation from the Ashkenazic tones of my youth to a modern Israeli pronunciation after making aliyah. This is reflected in the book. For the most part, in part 1, which covers the time before my aliyah, the transliterations are Ashkenazic as, contextually, I would have said them then. Part 2 uses modern Hebrew transliteration. Exceptions have been made where contextually appropriate.

Rabbi Sholom Gold
Yom Yerushalayim
28 Iyar 5774

---

[*] *Michtav M'Eliyahu* (Bnei Brak, 1964), vol. 3, p. 352.

# Acknowledgments

I wish to thank those who assisted me in the process of producing this memoir. They include Rabbi Nachman Seltzer, who gave the book structure and became a friend as we worked together, and Yehudah Goldreich, my son-in-law, who reviewed, checked, and refined it.

I am grateful to my long-time secretary, Ruth Pepperman, who was always ready to do what had to be done, and to do it yesterday.

My thanks to Debbie Buckman of Beit Shemesh, who listened to and evaluated hundreds of my taped *shiurim* and seemed to feel that I had something to say.

I thank the staff of Gefen Publishing House: publisher Ilan Greenfield, projects coordinator Lynn Douek, senior editor Kezia Raffel Pride, and production manager Eitan Tenenhouse for their patience in working with me towards publication of the book. Their professional expertise has contributed much to the final product.

Avrom *a"h* and Bonny Silver of Toronto have been there for me for years with their friendship and generosity. I am deeply grateful.

My children and my brother-in-law Mendel Rubinoff urged, cajoled, motivated, and finally convinced me to undertake the sometimes painful, ofttimes pleasurable, always challenging task of getting my story written.

My wife Bayla has shared with me her wisdom, advice, and encouragement; I am unendingly grateful to her for always being there. As the model *ezer kenegdo*, she guided me through the whole process. In fact, without her there would be no story and no book.

I am thankful to the many people who have enriched our lives: to my Ner Israel *talmidim* who gave me and continue to give me so much *nachat*, and to their parents who had faith in me and trusted me with their young sons when *yeshivah* learning was not yet popular; to the board of Ner Israel of Toronto of 625 Finch Avenue West; to the dedicated members of Congregation B'nai Torah of Willowdale, Ontario, from the store front on Transwell Avenue to "the shack" on Bathurst Street to the shul building on Patricia Avenue; to the Young Israel of West Hempstead family, whose love of Eretz Israel contributed to our great journey home; and to the Torah Academy for Girls of Far Rockaway, who tolerated my "obsession with Eretz Yisroel" for ten years.

Above all I thank the very dedicated, idealistic people of Kehillat Zichron Yosef of Har Nof – from the lobby of 50 Shaulson to the shul perched majestically on the hilltop looking out over the Jerusalem mountains – and the many, many students of the Avrom Silver Jerusalem College for Adults, as well as the *chaverim* of Kollel Sinai, established by Max Weil, to whom I have delivered weekly *shiurim* for many years.

To the Ribbono shel Olam I express boundless gratitude for granting my generation the *zechut* to live through this awesome period in Jewish history and be active participants in it. I marvel every day as I look out upon Yerushalayim and compare it with the city I first saw in 1955. It was scarred by the presence of an ugly concrete wall cutting it in half and denying Jews access to the Kotel. That wall was like a knife in the heart of Klal Yisroel. Thank G-d that wall is down and we have *the* Wall – the Kotel. The growth, development, and expansion of the city and the country from infancy to world power is nothing short of miraculous. I have been privileged to watch Eretz Yisrael go from food rationing to prophetic abundance.

I feel humbled to bear witness to the ingathering of the Jewish people from all four corners of the globe to their ancestral home. What we prayed for and dreamt of for two thousand years continues to unfold before our very eyes. Watching from my *mirpeset* as Highway One is being widened yet again, walking through the inner city and taking in the vast construction projects in progress is breathtaking. Who would have imagined a light rail gliding through town?

There is so, so much that we have been privileged to see in our lives – Hashem fulfilling the promises He made so long ago. The absolute truth of Torah is evident to all whose eyes are open.

May He continue to watch over us and protect His people Israel from all harm and return His palpable presence to Yerushalayim Ir Hakodesh, speedily in our days.

# Prologue

*"The Rosh Yeshivah wants me to go to Toronto, to a community where I have never been, to work with people I have never met, to build a yeshivah and serve in a leadership capacity even though I am still so young? Eileich – I will go."*

*Just like that, my life had taken on a brand new direction. I was embarking on an awesome adventure to find myself, to meet my wife, and ultimately to build an institution of youth who would grow up to become sincere members of the Jewish community. I was nearly twenty-four. It was the real beginning of my life...*

# Part One
# Foundations

# 1

# Growing Up in Williamsburg

My childhood played itself out in the timeless neighborhood of Williamsburg. This was a community filled with life, pulsing with energy and a love for G-d. There were almost no other communities quite like this back then. Spirituality in America was considered by many an epidemic to eradicate. All across the width and breadth of the United States, Jews were falling by the wayside in droves. At the same time, thousands and thousands of them were arriving from across the ocean, intent on making a new life for themselves and their families in the new world, their sights set on becoming successful, and if possible, even wealthy. This was America – wasn't everything possible here?

Some, they say, threw their tefillin overboard the crowded ocean liners with disdain the moment they caught a glimpse of Lady Liberty. Others didn't even wait that long. This was the new world. Who needed the ancient practices of blood-soaked Europe? And so, when these masses of starving, pinched-faced Jews walked onto the soil of their new land, they made a determined decision to change almost everything about themselves. To remake themselves. To become American.

Chaim became Charlie.

Avrohom became Abe.

Shmuel became Sammy.

They were a new generation. They refused to live in ghettos. No. Concentration was not for them. Soon enough, Jews found themselves living all across the land. And the vast majority of them were not religious. Even those who were observant weren't able to transmit their beliefs, traditions, and practices to their children. That's the way it was.

And then there was Williamsburg. And there it was different. This neighborhood managed to defy the world around it. People who lived in Williamsburg swam against the tide and raised children who were proud to be identified as the sons of Avraham, Yitzchak, and Yaakov. The sound of learning filled the streets from early morning until late at night. Yeshiva Torah Vodaath planted its saplings in the Williamsburg streets. Many Chassidic courts had been uprooted from their European villages and replanted in the fresh soil of the *goldene medinah*.

Children filled the streets, their childish shouts and boyish exuberance giving a lively bounce to the soot-covered tenements. Men like Mike Tress would influence them to strive to change the world. Men like Chaim Gelb would stop them on the street and in the schoolyard to listen to them make a *brachah*. And men like Rav Shraga Feivel Mendlowitz would cherish every one of the thousands of students entrusted to his care.

On Friday nights, the streets were full. Everyone was rushing to a *tish*. There were many Chassidic Rebbes in Williamsburg, and every one of them led a gathering of his followers come Friday evening. The singing rose high and powerful; it was heard from every corner, from the tiniest clapboard shul to the grandest edifice. From a ramshackle room filled with one old man and five Chassidim to Stolin on Rodney Street; Vizhnitz on Ross Street; the Poilisher *shtiebl* on Division Avenue; Boyan on Marcy; Boston, Pirchei Agudas Yisroel, and the Young Israel on Bedford Avenue; and so many more bastions of Torah and fortresses of Yiddishkeit.

This was where I was born.

I was raised in a neighborhood filled with men who, while working extremely long hours, still managed to wake up at five in the morning to study for a few hours before davening. A place where hunched-over old men sat in the back of the shul with a Tehillim and a cup of tea, which they drank through the pleasurable sweetness of a square sugar cube clenched firmly between their two front teeth. It was filled with the quiet singsong of Torah and fear of heaven. This was the home of my youth and its memories will always remain with me.

My mother hailed from a town called Kolbishev and my father from Ropshitz. This was a special town due to the holy name of Rav Naftali of Ropshitz, whose memory will never be forgotten. My ancestors fled Europe directly after World War I with the entire continent in profound disarray, the social order of a thousand years having been overturned. They traveled through Holland, taking the SS *Rotterdam* over the Atlantic and finally docking at Ellis Island in the third decade of the twentieth century.

My wife was able to track down the manifest of the SS *Rotterdam*, where she discovered the names of the entire Sandhaus family: my mother Chava Bayla, her father Mordechai Duvid, and her mother Maryam Devora. She also found my father's name on the passenger list of the SS *Nieuw Amsterdam*, on which he had come over earlier with his three sisters – Chana, Feiga, and Tziviya – on July 1, 1923. On a later manifest she also found his parents, Yona and Pinya Rochel Gold.

We were never able to find out where the name Pinya comes from, so when we named our younger daughter after her, we added a *daled* to the Pinya and called her Daphna Rachel.

My paternal grandparents, Pinya Rochel and Yona Gold, had thirteen children, four of whom died in infancy. Of the remaining nine, seven came to America in the early 1920s. Two remained behind in Ropshitz: a son, Efraim Fishel, and a daughter, Sarah. They and their families perished in the Holocaust. Sarah, a daughter of Efraim Fishel, left Ropshitz in 1935 and came on aliyah; her brother Yehoshua fled eastward into Russia as far as Siberia and survived the war there. After Warsaw was liberated, he made the long trek home to Ropshitz to discover the tragic truth of what had transpired.

There, Yehoshua learned that his father and his brothers Naphtali,

David, Yaakov, and Yosef Mordechai had been taken to a camp in Pustkow where they all were killed.

"On Tisha b'Av 1942 the Ropshitz ghetto was emptied of the remaining women, children and the elderly. The young women were sent by train to the Belzec concentration camp. The train was carrying lime and all the women died of poisoning. Among them were Yehudit and Esther Gold, Fishel's children. The extermination of the Jews in the Belzec camp was carried out by Ukrainians, who were even more bloodthirsty for Jewish blood than their German commanders," writes Yehoshua. "My mother Gittel Leah Gold (née Bernbaum), together with my little sister Hindele, who was seven years old at the time, was sent to Ghetto Bovna. Their fate is unknown."

Yehoshua made his way to Eretz Yisrael, fought in the War of Independence, married, and raised a family here, as did the family of his sister Sarah (Gold).

My father's parents opened up a dry goods store when they reached America. Or more accurately, Bubby managed the store while Zeide sat with a *sefer* and studied, because that was what he knew how to do best.

A historian once told me that out of the many Jewish families that immigrated to America in the 1920s, there was only one that she knew of in which every single member remained religious until this very day, and that was the Gold family.

My maternal grandfather went into business and made a comfortable living for his family in Cleveland, Ohio. We spent quite a few glorious summers in Ohio with my *zeide* and *bubby* Sandhaus, and when they grew older they sold the business and moved into an apartment in nearby Crown Heights.

My mother had a number of siblings. One of them, my uncle Moishe, studied in Yeshiva Torah Vodaath under Rav Shraga Feivel and then, to the shock of his entire family, enlisted as a chaplain in the United States armed forces, left his young bride, Aunt Eunice, and was eventually shipped overseas for the entire war, where he provided comfort and succor to countless soldiers in countries across the European continent.

I'm sure Uncle Moishe could have written a book about his war experiences, but I only remember a few details from his sojourn across the ocean. (I was only a kid when he left.)

He told me that he once came across a few hundred Jewish orphans that nobody especially cared for. Moishe felt responsible. He managed to obtain blankets and pillows for all of them, fed them, took care of them, and loaded them all onto American army trucks, which he then directed to the nearest army base. He didn't relinquish control of the situation until he was sure that they would be well taken care of.

When the war finally came to end, Uncle Moishe signed on to remain in the army as a chaplain, eventually moving up in the ranks until he was appointed chief chaplain of the US Army Veterans Administration – the only time that the Veterans Administration's chief chaplain position was filled by a rabbi. He got used to receiving calls from across the United States from priests and pastors and reverends galore. He loved relating the following exchange that he had with one particular member of the Catholic clergy.

He answered the phone one morning and heard, "Is this Father Sandhaus?"

"Well, sir," Uncle Moishe replied, "I'm actually a rabbi, but I'm a legal father of two as well."

He was an extremely bright man who accomplished a lot of good in a career that spanned a few decades. His son Rabbi Samuel K. (Sandy) Sandhaus and his wife Sunny live in Scranton, Pennsylvania.

Here's a sharp memory. My first. I was six years old.

It was a very cold, bitter day in December. A Sunday. All across America, children were relaxing, drinking hot cocoa cozily at home. Only the Jewish kids were in school, studying Torah every day of the week, Sundays included. At about two o'clock in the afternoon the principal of the elementary school entered the classroom, his face more somber than I had ever seen it. He approached the *rebbe*'s desk and bent down close to him. He whispered in his ear but we could hear nothing. The worried frown and furrowed brow had now been transferred over to our beloved teacher's face. Still we knew nothing. But we could feel the danger, the worry and uncertainty in the pits of our stomachs. Something was very wrong. As soon as the principal left the room, our *rebbe* spoke.

"*Kinderlach*," he said gravely, "get dressed. Put on all your clothing – your sweaters and coats. We are going out right now."

Under normal conditions, such an announcement might have served as cause for rejoicing. But not that day. Not on that bitterly cold day in December. On that day we felt only fear. We slipped into our gloves. Boots on every foot. It took a while – even longer than usual because we were so nervous. And then the monitors began moving us out of the school building and out toward the street. Down the hallway we went. Down the staircase. It was a very wide staircase and we moved down in unison, like a herd of sheep being collectively corralled by their master. Down the steps, out the front doors of the building at 206 Wilson Street, we were led to the corner of Wilson and Lee Avenue. And then our teacher looked down at us from his great height and told us, "*Kinderlach, loif aheim*" (Children, run home)!

Filled with trepidation and overcome by a feeling of terror of the unknown, the entire student body of Torah Vodaath ran en masse down Lee Avenue as if being pursued by nuclear disaster. Little puffs of warm air escaped my mouth as I flew down the avenue, passing all the familiar stores and landmarks that I knew so well. The grocery store. The tailor shop. The delicatessen. The bakery. And everywhere we looked it was the same. Such fear in everyone's eyes. Why? What had happened?

I couldn't pause for breath. I had to know, to find out the news. My parents would know what was going on. I burst into my apartment, questions on the tip of my tongue, needing to know, to ask, to find out. My parents sat huddled around the old-fashioned radio, that gigantic wood-paneled radio that everyone had in their homes. They were listening intently to the tinny voices emerging from within the whiny box.

And then for the first time in my life I learned about a place called Pearl Harbor. It was December 7, 1941, and Japan had just attacked the United States in the insane move that would force America into the Great War across the ocean and end with America dropping two nuclear bombs on the Japanese mainland. But for now we had been rushed home, because the country was afraid that the Japanese were planning on attacking the American mainland.

That terrifying afternoon is my first really clear memory and along with it came an almost insatiable need to keep informed about everything happening in the world. To keep a finger on current events. To keep abreast of the historic flow of the last seventy-five years.

At first the citizens of America hadn't wanted another war, remembering all too clearly the millions of lives that had been lost over the grievances of countries far away. In short, America wanted nothing more to do with Europe.

"Why does America need to involve itself in other people's problems?" editorials across the country scrawled in black ink. "Are we the world's policeman?"

The people wanted France and England to get along without them. The general consensus was to let the Europeans solve their own issues without America's involvement. The country was content to remain on the sidelines, taking no sides, remaining utterly neutral in thought and deed. So what if millions of people were dying or being killed across the Atlantic? The United States gave a collective shrug and asked rhetorically why Europe hadn't learned anything from what had occurred just twenty years earlier. And that's the way it went, with America very clearly opposed to entering the war – until that fateful morning when the Japanese attacked without warning or provocation.

As the pilots of the Japanese air force descended from the skies to decimate the sitting ducks of the US fleet, something was unequivocally altered in the American mind. Suddenly it had become them against us. The evil Axis of Germany, Italy, and Japan had shown its true colors in America's backyard, and all traces of neutrality were gone, disappeared as if they'd never even existed in the first place. From one second to the next America was at war. The Japanese had made the mistake of a lifetime. They had awakened the sleeping giant and were now going to face the consequences. And those were brutal.

America mobilized for war.

Factories began churning out war goods. Weapons in the millions. Planes, tanks, machine guns, trucks, uniforms, canteens. The army went into overdrive. Overnight there were signs up in every neighborhood depicting a determined-looking Uncle Sam with white beard and top hat pointing at passersby: "I WANT YOU FOR U.S. ARMY." And the youth of America were being called up to war with the blast of the trumpet and the hurrah of the marching band.

We, the kids of Williamsburg, were encouraged to do our part for the war effort as well. This meant gathering as many tin cans as we could lay our hands on. Ditto for discarded newspapers. The tin cans were used to manufacture bullets. Millions of them. The newspapers were used in the production of parachutes so American planes could fly over enemy lands and drop our boys behind enemy lines to cause mayhem and blow up trains.

We were encouraged as well to bring fifteen cents to school every Sunday for which we'd receive a savings stamp to stick in the cardboard case given out to every one of us. When the amount of stamps totaled eighteen dollars, it would be traded in for an American savings bond. And these bonds, which people purchased in every denomination, helped to finance the war in a major way. Hundreds of little *yeshivah* kids were running around Williamsburg and the Lower East Side of Manhattan and the Bronx collecting. There was a feeling of feverish excitement in the air as everyone wanted to do their part to save the universe from the unspeakable evil emanating out of Berlin.

Back in those days I was a member of Pirchei Agudas Yisroel of America. I used to spend my Shabbos afternoons being entertained and inspired by some of the most top-notch talent ever to come out of the Jewish world. My leader was the much esteemed Mike Tress. In 1938 Rav Elchonon Wasserman visited the United States and that unforgettable visit became the high point of Mike Tress's life. You couldn't have a five-minute conversation with the man without him mentioning Rav Elchonon, such was the impression he made on the young Mike Tress.

Mike was a master storyteller and his mouth was like a fountain of stories and information about the great rabbinical figures of the day –

and Rav Elchonon in particular. Mike was also a master tactician when it came to rallying up the troops of Pirchei to get out there on the streets to help. The hours flew by as we sat spellbound, entranced by his colorful language and masterful oratory. The tears slid unnoticed and unchecked down our cheeks when he spelled out the magnitude of the disaster facing the world Jewish body at this exact second.

He told us of little children living in incredible terror of a knock on the door, the knock heralding the removal of their father from their lives. He told us about the atrocities occurring in every city and town, of the bloodthirsty Germans and their murderous intentions, and he told us what we, the children of Pirchei Agudas Yisroel, could do to help in this monumental battle. He loved us and we in turn loved Mike Tress. He was the pied piper of Williamsburg; we would have followed him anywhere and done anything he asked us to do, no matter how difficult, if it meant making this special man proud of us. His fire, his clear call for action, his absolute charisma were all legendary, all larger than life. That was Mike Tress.

We knew about the Agudah's life-saving attempts. We heard about the food packages that were being sent over to Europe. We learned of the thousands of dollars being raised for saving lives.

Jewish survivors began to surface in Williamsburg during and after the war. One glance into the eyes of a survivor was sufficient to tell you everything you needed to know. It was as obvious as the sun in the sky. Even before they rolled up their sleeves to put on tefillin, even before you saw the concentration camp numbers on their arms, the eyes revealed the unspeakable suffering they had experienced. The feeling of sympathy and helplessness that arose within our chests when we caught a glimpse of those numbers tattooed on those holy arms, of the awful suffering etched across faces timeless in their grief, made us catch our breath and beat us silent, as if all air had been snuffed out of the room and we were being suffocated alive. Sometimes we'd hear our parents talking about a new member of the community, a refugee who'd barely made it to Williamsburg alive.

We knew.

More than our parents thought we knew. Pretty much like all children through the ages. The bulletin board at 616 Bedford Avenue had all sorts of cables that were being sent to us from Europe posted across it, the cry for help emblazoned upon our consciousness.

Need food. Stop. Send money. Stop.

There was a constant stream of activity going on in that Agudah building. It was a group of Jewish activists teaching and guiding the next generation.

ר

Williamsburg was a beautiful community in every way. And that's a major reason why, aside from the war and the nightmares it caused, my childhood was a mostly happy one. I don't think there has ever been a community in the United States that has been able to duplicate the wonderful world that was Williamsburg.

Undergirding the neighborhood was the strong framework of the *yeshivah*. The Roshei Yeshivah of Torah Vodaath were royalty, every single one of them. I remember the funeral of Rav Shlomo Heiman at the end of 1944. The entire student body left the warm building and took to the streets in their sobbing sorrow. It was an absolutely frigid day in the middle of the winter. A listless sun peered down from a wintry sky and yet it felt like we were standing in the middle of Siberia. Rav Shlomo Heiman had been beloved by all who knew him. He was eulogized by the Torah giants of the time, accompanied by a storm of tears.

Williamsburg was a neighborhood populated mainly by Jews. The majority were religious, but there were plenty of individuals who were not. And some of those people owned businesses on the avenues of commerce – which they kept open on Shabbos. I don't recall exactly when the Shabbos parade was first established, but those parades are as clear in my memory as if they happened yesterday.

They were without pressure. They were dignified. It was all done with tremendous respect for the other person. A respectable assembly of a few hundred Jews in suits, ties, and hats – usually light-colored because this was a time when you could still get away with wearing a light gray suit and a white hat – would march up and down the avenue taking in the scene, deciding who they were going to attempt to convince this year. And while they walked they sang. Gentle, heartfelt songs of Shabbos and peace.

When they arrived at a Jewish store that was open on Shabbos, the parade's representatives would enter the store, with the multitudes waiting in respectful silence outside. The representative would take the owner of the business establishment to the side and explain to him, ever so gently and with so much tact and even love, why everyone was standing right outside his store, asking him to shut the grates. Complete change didn't occur in one year; it didn't happen in two. But after a number of years, you couldn't find a Jewish store still open for business on Shabbos in Williamsburg.

Williamsburg was filled with personalities who were larger than life, men of uplifted character and charm. Some of them wielded huge influence cloaked in utter simplicity. One such man was Chaim Gelb.

Which Williamsburg child didn't have a relationship with Chaim Gelb? It wasn't possible not to. Every time I'd walk into shul, there he was. He presented himself without fanfare of any kind, never looking for honor. He had only one thing on his mind: to increase G-d's honor in the world.

And how did he do that?

Well, he had a plan. And it involved the kids. The children of Williamsburg absolutely loved him. They adored him. The outer reason for this love was simple. Chaim Gelb gave them candy. On the surface that was sufficient to turn all the neighborhood kids into his fans. But there was tremendous depth to his charm. He'd hand them a piece of candy and before they could pop that delicious sweetness into their mouths, he'd order them, "*Mach a brachah*" (Make a blessing). Thank G-d for the wonderful creations that He makes for us in this world."

It's no wonder that an entire generation of children all remember him fondly, because his memory is intertwined with sweetness – the sweetness of candy and the sweetness that comes from constantly recognizing the One Above on a day-to-day and even minute-to-minute basis. And when you finished that *brachah*, he'd let out such a joyful "Amen!" in response, as if you had just made his day with your *brachah*.

And what did Chaim Gelb do to make money?

He owned a bakery. But that's only a surface answer, because Reb Chaim was never in that bakery. He was constantly running around the streets of Williamsburg searching for *mitzvos* to do. Many, many people received their sustenance and nourishment from Reb Chaim's bakery. Did Reb Chaim make money from his bakery? I don't know if he did, but many others sure did.

Looking back I'd have to say that we weren't truly aware of the measure of this man. It was only as we grew older and matured that we started to appreciate his uniqueness and glorious perspective. I mean, how many adults are willing to sacrifice their personal time on a daily basis, day after day, year after year, just to influence thousands of youngsters in the comprehension of what it means to make a *brachah*, of what blessing our Creator is really about. In his quiet, unassuming way, Chaim Gelb was a hero of my youth and someone whom I will always recall with a fond smile and a sense of lingering sweetness on my tongue. What a personality. What strength. He simply enriched my life with his presence.

My childhood was populated by many giants.

I was sick and home from school on the day that Franklin Delano Roosevelt (popularly known as FDR) died. And I'm not exaggerating in the slightest when I say that you could literally touch the *eivel*, the sense of mourning in the streets of America and even in the religious communities. FDR was like a larger-than-life myth of epic strength and character. America loved the president in the wheelchair with his fireside chats and his New Deal and the fact that he took the country out of the Depression. They considered him a notch above human. They revered him.

Nobody knew then that he was not a friend of the Jews; that he could have bombed the tracks leading to Auschwitz with ease if he so desired – and didn't. Like so many other world leaders, he just didn't care about the Jews of Europe.

A sense of gloom hit America and the country mourned for the man with the golden mouth and brilliant mind whom everyone trusted. FDR had been voted into office for four terms. That's how much the population loved and idolized him. But in the end, the curtain came down on the Roosevelt era. Harry Truman, his vice president, assumed the presidency and gave the executive order to drop the Bomb on Japan. The State Department was opposed to the creation of Israel from the start, and President Truman bucked his own State Department and did what he felt was right. Divine Providence was working overtime during those years.

May 14, 1948, the fifth of Iyar, 5708, I entered the main shul in Torah Vodaath on Wilson Street in time for Minchah. It was two weeks before my bar mitzvah. A terrible anxiety filled the air, hovering above us like a cloud. Every Jewish person felt it acutely because the fate of Eretz Yisrael was hanging in the balance right then. On the twenty-ninth of November, the UN voted to partition Eretz Yisrael, and directly following that decision, Arab terrorism – which had been simmering under the surface – broke out in full force. It was full-scale war in the Holy Land. Seven Arab nations began the attack on Eretz Yisrael. The state of the Jewish people was extremely precarious right then. People were being killed every day. And every single Jew around the world felt the direness of the situation and was davening that everything should work out for the good.

I'll never forget the scene. The shul was packed. There must have been five hundred people there, a somber look on every face. The situation, the situation… That was all people could think about. Would the US recognize the State of Israel or not? And if not, what kind of ramifications would they face? These were our brothers across the ocean and it was so short a time after the Holocaust. Was it going to happen again?

And then right before Minchah, someone came running into the shul and screamed out, "Truman recognized the State of Israel!"

Three years after the Holocaust, thousands of people still walking around with numbers on their arms, suffering the nightmares of the war every day and night all over again…and now this piece of news. It was nothing short of miraculous. Jews around the world celebrated like never before. And the five hundred Jews sitting in the *beis midrash* of Yeshiva Torah Vodaath were overwhelmed with a profound sense of joy and gratitude. They were so utterly happy, so proud, and so full of love for the Land we'd been dreaming about for millennia. You had to see it to believe it. We'd been granted a country. G-d in His infinite mercy and kindness had seen fit to give us back the Land of our forefathers.

I have little patience for those who trivialize Yom Haatzmaut. Their knowledge of Jewish history is already limited and flawed. The people among whom I stood on that great Erev Shabbos were experiencing the joy of generations past, who had hoped, prayed and sacrificed for this great day. Every time I think about that day I get choked up and tears begin to fill my eyes. That's precisely what is happening now as I write these lines.

༄

My bar mitzvah passed without making too many waves. This was a much simpler time, when nobody celebrated such events in fancy halls. They didn't do it even if they had the money, which almost nobody did. Ours was a modest existence. But even so, a bar mitzvah was a joyous occasion, especially after the war years when Williamsburg was full of refugees and every family's happy moments were keenly experienced by one and all as their own. Friday night after a *seudah* filled with much joy, merriment, and singing, my Uncle Moishe led all the family men over to Taylor Street and the *beis midrash* of the Bluzhover Rebbe. They had met in Europe, at the end of the war.

We entered the *shtiebl* in the middle of the *tish*.

"Moishe!" the Rebbe called out loudly, imbuing all sorts of hidden meanings in that simple word.

I stood there watching the interchange in silent wonder.

The Rebbe rose up in his place and repeated my uncle's name.

"Moishe, Moishe Sandhaus." Uncle Moishe had been very instrumental in getting the Rebbe out of Europe after the war and the Rebbe had not forgotten him. Not by a long shot. There was genuine respect and affection between the two of them. As for me, this was just another life experience to file away in my memory vaults – the Friday night of my bar mitzvah and a visit to the Bluzhover *shtiebl*.

There was no hall or evening affair, no band, no fancy napkins or centerpieces, but a Williamsburg *kiddush* was something pretty special.

Some schnapps, honey cake, and herring galore. And of course Cornell soda in those old-fashioned glass bottles. I read the *maftir* in Torah Vodaath and that was that. Back then bar mitzvah boys weren't expected to read the *parshah* out of the Torah scroll, but I had decided to teach myself the *maftir* and by the time my bar mitzvah rolled around, there wasn't a boy in my class who wasn't intimately familiar with every word, after all the times they'd heard me practicing.

Sunday afternoon was another big day because all of our relatives were invited to a get-together at our tiny apartment on Lee Avenue. This of course meant that the Golds were about to do some catering. Nobody had the money to pay a caterer and really what was the big deal anyway? All we needed to do was get on the trolley that carried you over the bridge from Williamsburg into the Lower East Side where Mr. Goldberg, who sat next to my father in shul, had his famous Goldberg's Deli. The trolley cost about a nickel. I sat next to my father and was secretly ecstatic at having him all to myself. Upon arrival at the bustling expanses of the Lower East Side, we ordered about fifty deli sandwiches from Goldberg's and lots of coleslaw and other salads. Nothing fancy. Just satisfying.

That was my bar mitzvah. Surrounded by close and extended family, by my brothers – one nine years older than myself, the other twelve years my senior – and by my parents, whom I adored.

A pretty good childhood, all in all.

# 2

# SPIRITUAL INFLUENCES

I was about fourteen years old when I finished elementary school and moved on over to Mesivta Torah Vodaath, which was then on South Third Street. The Gold family's apartment on Lee Avenue was not close to the *yeshivah*, and it took me a good twenty minutes to get there every morning. Those were tranquil days in an impressionable young man's life. This was where I first began to grow in learning, under the expert tutelage of Williamsburg's accomplished educators. They molded and guided me and my mind grew sharper and I developed under their care.

One *rebbe* with whom I was particularly close was Rav Avraham Pam, a man who showered those around him with love; his heart was large enough to carry every Jew inside it. Others were Rav Karp, Rav Avrohom Yeshaya Shapiro, Rav Moshe Duber Rivkin, and Rav Luzer Kahanov. Each one gave of himself with such *mesiras nefesh*, such utter dedication. Their sole thought and dream was to reestablish the Torah world in postwar America. True, the world of European Jewry had gone up in flames. But there was an entire generation of pure American children living in the United States and a community waiting to be rebuilt from the ashes up.

And I was lucky enough to be part of this generation of rebuilding.

I asked myself what my aspirations were then, during my early years. Was it just about the learning or did I have a desire for other pursuits? The decision was not a difficult one for me. Mine was going to be a strictly Torah life, probably in Jewish education. I thought I knew how to teach.

My two older brothers had attended Torah Vodaath before me. They went through the entire system and transferred to Yeshivas Rabbeinu Yitzchok Elchonon afterwards. Both of them were pretty brilliant guys. My oldest brother Yosef Yoel, known to one and all as Joe, was an actual genius (and I don't use that word lightly).

In fact my oldest brother after graduating Rabbeinu Yitzchok Elchonon with the highest honors went on to serve as the rabbi in Worcester, Massachusetts, for thirty-six years. He had become extremely close to Rav Soloveitchik, part and parcel of the earliest cadre of students, and he remained in close contact with his esteemed teacher for decades afterwards.

After my oldest brother passed away, I sat shivah with my brother Shmuel in Eretz Yisrael, while the immediate family – his wife Rochie and their children, Rabbi Shaul (Sholie), Chavi Sprecher, Esther Hammer, Rabbi David and Miriam – sat shivah in Worcester, Massachusetts. Today, Esther and Miriam live in Israel. My nephew Sholie brought his father for burial on Har Hamenuchos. During the week of shivah, there were of course numerous visitors who told stories and reminisced about the connection they'd had with him.

One of the visitors in Worcester was Rabbi Fabian Schoenfeld. Rabbi Schoenfeld was arguably *the* senior rabbi in the United States, serving as the *rav* of the Young Israel of Kew Garden Hills into his upper eighties. Rabbi Schoenfeld had known my brother for years, and he shared the following anecdote with the assembled. It's classic.

It seems that Yeshiva University felt the time was ripe to establish a medical school and they wanted to name it after Professor Albert Einstein, world-famous scientist and father of modern physics. Being that you can't just name a school after someone without his permission, YU's board got in touch with Einstein at his home in Princeton, New Jersey. Einstein listened to their request and informed the caller that before he agreed to let their institution use his name, he wanted to meet some of their students to get a feel for what type of young men attended YU. The result of that phone call was an invitation from YU to Albert Einstein to come spend some time at their *yeshivah*. Four students were selected to meet with the celebrated Einstein. I only know two of them: my oldest brother and Rabbi Fabian Schoenfeld.

There they were, all sitting amicably around the polished table, when the conversation between the world-famous scientist and the cream of Rabbeinu Yitzchok Elchonon began in earnest.

As Rabbi Schoenfeld related, "Soon after the conversation started, Rabbi Gold initiated a give-and-take with Professor Einstein on a topic dear to the great man's heart. What topic am I referring to? The theory of relativity, of course. There they sat, the two of them, and it was as if everyone else had gone and they were alone on a desert island. One wise old man and one eager young scholar. They went at each other for an hour and after engaging in this intense discussion without break or letup, Einstein glanced over at the heads of the *yeshivah* who were present as well and said, "I don't have to meet any more of your students. You can have my name."

Which they did. The Einstein Medical School is a famous institution of higher learning. And Einstein was proud to have his name associated with students of my brother's caliber. That was my brother – a man who was able at such a tender age to engage in debate with the likes of Einstein and hold his own. I don't know too many other people who can claim the same.

My second brother, Shmuel Yehoshua (Stanley), was no less of a personality. He was a man on a mission and every time I recall his determination and single-mindedness in the pursuit of his goal, I am filled with admiration anew. He spent at least thirty years in the intense study of fifteen handwritten manuscripts of Rashi's major work on Chumash and fifteen first printed editions of Rashi as well. And then he proceeded to correct any mistakes that he found in the version of Rashi that most people use, from Sefer Bereishis until Sefer Devarim. He walked around for years with pockets full of Xeroxed copies of the manuscripts.

He sat and studied in the Bar-Ilan library.

He sat and studied in the Hebrew University library.

Sometimes I imagined him on a first-name basis with every librarian in the Land of Israel. He was completely engrossed in the world of Rashi for thirty years, to the exclusion of almost everything else. His entire focus in life was the clarification of Rashi's explanation on the Bible. There were many mistakes in the transmission and printing of Rashi and he wanted to correct them all and put together one perfected version of everything that Rashi had written.

Rav Shmuel Yehoshua Gold, Rabbi Shlomo Yitzchaki – *resh, shin, yud*, the acronym for Rashi.

He ended up writing a scholarly original work on Rashi. It's one of a kind. His treatise tells the story of fifteen manuscripts and fifteen early printed editions of Rashi. Chumashim with Rashi's commentary were printed as early as 1482 in Italy, 1490 in Spain, and 1491 in Portugal. In the sixteenth century, five editions appeared in Venice and three in Soncino. The earliest manuscript, from the thirteenth century, is found in the Vatican. All the others are from the fourteenth or fifteenth centuries. Manuscripts are from Vienna, Oxford, Berlin, Leipzig, and elsewhere. Just being able to decipher the handwriting of those who lived hundreds of years ago requires years of study, because many of those handwritings are extremely difficult to read.

So my brother developed his reading and comprehension abilities to the point where he was able to compare the different manuscripts and make informed decisions as to where today's accepted version of Rashi is in error. And then he was able to fix those errors. Some mistakes are printer's errors. For example, ten Rashi manuscripts will have something written a certain way and then the eleventh either has a different word or has a word left out, and some of those errors have remained with us till today. All because a printer left out a word by mistake. Sometimes great rabbinical figures in the distant and not-so-distant past wrote erudite pieces of work based on printing errors. Some major Torah thoughts looked very different after my brother got through his major work of comparison, because sometimes one word is sufficient to throw everything off.

Other Chumashim have been published over the years whose authors have attempted to do what my brother did, and many of them are substantial works of greatness and erudition, but none compare to the comprehensive work that my brother did, to the depth and breadth of his knowledge and to the absolute brilliance he exhibits throughout. His children, Rav Doron Gold, Sandy Gold, and Chavi and Mordechai Adler, have published his life's work so that now Jews the world over have the opportunity to gain clarity about what Rashi actually wrote.

My brother and his wife Sara came on aliyah in 1971 to Petach Tikva.

I came to love Tanach and Ivrit because of my brother. In my teen years I remember him walking through our apartment learning Yirmiyahu by heart and then Iyov. He wrote a long poem about Yirmiyahu and he would read stanzas to me as it progressed. He tried to penetrate the soul of a prophet who bore the awesome burden of warning the people of impending doom. He described the pain of Yirmiyahu facing opposition from his own community of Anatot, his incarceration in the catacombs of Yerushalayim, pleading with his people not to go down to Egypt, and then being taken there with them.

For many years a Hebrew literary journal called *Hadoar* was published in the United States. He studied its issues from cover to cover to improve his knowledge of Hebrew, which was already on a high level. It left a lasting impression on me.

I also learned Iyov from him; my brother went over and over Iyov like I did my bar mitzvah *maftir* so that even I began to pick it up from listening to him.

Looking at my brothers, although I was much younger, I knew that I wanted to follow in their footsteps and go into the field of education. Maybe become a *rav*. I had a lot to live up to, being third in line after two such exceptional people.

Another strong influence was Rav Dovid Kronglass, who was the revered *mashgiach* of Ner Yisroel. When he taught us Mishlei the verses came alive with his power of description. He painted powerful verbal pictures in his *mussar* talks. A number were dedicated to the importance of learning Tanach, and then how to learn Tanach. Many of my own *shiurim* were the result of what I learned from him.

In an absolutely unforgettable talk about learning Tanach, he described a fictional great *talmid chacham* versed in Shas Bavli and Yerushalmi, Rishonim and Acharonim; the buildup kept going and we were left wondering, where is Rav Dovid going? And then came the climax, which I must convey in Yiddish as he said it: "The brilliant scholar has come to the end of his life. *Men leigt em arain in kever un kein Iyov hut er nisht oifge'efent in leben*" (He is being lowered into his grave and he never opened the book of Iyov in his life)!

Every time that line comes back to me I open a Sefer Iyov and learn.

☙

I must tell you about my parents.

For thirty-six years, rain or shine, snow, blazing sun, sleet or hail, my father delivered an in-depth Gemara *shiur* on Shabbos afternoon in the ground-floor shul in Yeshiva Torah Vodaath on Wilson Street. It was most probably the best-attended *shiur* in all of Williamsburg, a neighborhood with numerous *shiurim* and countless scholars who were familiar with all of Shas and *poskim*. Yet Mr. Gold's *shiur* was one of the most widely attended of them all. Though he was not an official rabbi and held no authoritative position, his weekly lecture was graced with an eclectic gathering of multitalented and charismatic individuals. They were an interesting bunch – rabbis and laymen, old and young, scholarly and simple. Everyone found something to relate to in that masterpiece of a *shiur*.

My father made his living cutting leather for ladies' shoes. He'd leave for work very early in the morning and arrive home in the evening. He ate supper and then he took out his Gemara and prepared his *shiur*. The *shiur* was eagerly awaited by his students. They knew there would be something to sink their teeth into and came geared up for battle. And my father didn't give his class on the easy Gemaras, either. No. I remember that for a couple of years he delivered the *shiur* on the challenging *sugyos* of *Eruvin*, legendary for their ability to confuse even the brightest minds. Yet my father was undeterred and rose to the occasion with masterpieces of beauty and wisdom.

This was pre-ArtScroll days, and there were no diagrams to use as an aid while studying *Sukkah* or *Eruvin*, so my father simply prepared his own for use while illuminating the more obscure concepts that came along. I remember his pencils, special pencils with which he wrote his *shiurim* and drew his diagrams. He didn't waste any part. He merely used the extremely sharp knife with which he cut shoe leather to whittle down each pencil until he had squeezed out every last bit of lead from within.

A pencil cost money; you used it to the very end.

Every night he learned. Every night he sat and prepared those *shiurim*. And then Shabbos came and he'd enter Torah Vodaath like a man on a mission. He had a class to give, his very life's blood, and he was prepared to share this with the people he loved so much. Eighty, ninety, even one hundred people came every Shabbos to hear what he had to say. It was an awesome experience to see.

We didn't converse that much. My father wasn't a big one for lengthy conversations; fathers just weren't like that back then. But I always knew that he loved me very much. I felt it instinctively, though he kept the words to a minimum. But look, I was the youngest child, and which father doesn't love his youngest in a special way?

My mother was an intellectual, constantly reading, constantly busy with something deep and satisfying to stir the mind and creative juices. She always had something intelligent to add, and a well-thought-out, well-presented opinion.

My parents, beautifully worthy people, taught by example, by the way they lived their lives. I internalized the vital importance of Torah learning just from growing up in their home.

Likewise I come by my love for Eretz Yisrael honestly. And I say this proudly. I love Eretz Yisrael! We'd be sitting around the Shabbos table on any given Friday night, enjoying our Shabbos meal, our chicken soup and *lokshen*, and my father would suddenly and without warning begin to cry.

"Poor Moshe Rabbeinu," he'd say, the tears rolling out of his eyes. "Poor Moshe Rabbeinu. How he longed to be in Eretz Yisrael. He wanted to make it across the border to Eretz Yisrael so, so much, and he couldn't go."

I remember one Satmar Chassid accosting my father, heatedly exclaiming how the State of Israel was *"maaseh Satan! Sitra Achra!"* (the work of Satan). My father looked the man in the eye and replied, "I never knew that the Jewish people had such a good and kind Satan."

Incidentally the fact that I love Eretz Yisrael is nothing exceptional. That was always a basic part of a Jew's emotional and spiritual baggage that he carried with him wherever he went. I wonder rather how so many people seem to have lost that fundamental component of Jewish consciousness. Where did the innate *ahavas Eretz Yisrael* go? Why are so many people indifferent and tuned out?

My father couldn't bear to hear a bad word spoken of Eretz Yisrael. He was just grateful that there existed a place where all Jews were warmly welcomed with open arms, no questions asked. And he was fire when someone said or did something that he felt was wrong. My mother on the other hand was the quiet one, yet one word of hers went a very long way. He listened to and respected what she had to say. They were the two greatest influences on my life, both of them equally – the fiery *lamdan*, the brilliant mind and stunning intellect of one, and the still waters, patience, and unquestionable depth of the other. I developed through watching them. They educated solely by their actions and I loved and respected them.

While my father raised money for Eretz Yisrael, my mother busied herself fund-raising for Yeshiva Torah Vodaath. In my early years in school, the Golds lived right around the corner from the *yeshivah* at 218 Division Avenue, which meant that I had a visitor every day at recess who came equipped with a jar of chocolate milk for me to enjoy. I was thin as a rail. Consequently she worried about me all the time and brought that chocolate milk every day without fail. I can still feel her caring and concern to this day.

※

There were tough times as well. Times when things did not work out the way my father wanted. Yet he stood up to the challenges with an *emunah* that inspired me and remained with me all the years of my life.

In the early thirties my father was out of work for two years. This was at the height of the Depression and people considered themselves lucky if they had something to eat. People were starving. Yet my father didn't give up hope. He never ceased actively looking for a job, for a way to support his family in a respectable fashion. And don't forget, he did this all without forgoing his Shabbos observance.

People today have no idea, no concept of the difficulties facing a man who was determined to keep Shabbos. Being *shomer Shabbos* meant returning home to your hungry family empty-handed. It meant being fired from a job week after week. It meant self-sacrifice of the highest degree. But a Jew's self-sacrifice only truly worked if after returning home to his wife and kids with no prospects, he didn't sigh. He didn't say with woebegone eyes, "*Es iz shver tzu zein a Yid*" (It's hard to be a Jew).

Not only were religious Jews fired time and again, but they had to return home with a twinkle in their eyes every time and say, "*Kinderlach, ez iz gut tzu zein a Yid!*" (It's great to be a Jew!). Those who managed to pull off this awesome feat watched their children survive those harsh and bitterly difficult years with their belief in G-d intact. They even watched them go on to become the backbone of religious America.

That was my father. He never wavered. He never looked back. He knew what life was all about and compromise was not a part of it.

And then one day he contacted a company and requested an interview. The company was located in Brooklyn and it was a relatively nice place to work, unlike the majority of companies back then which enslaved their workers for hours at a time, paying them pennies for backbreaking labor.

He was ecstatic when they agreed to meet him, but their next words ruined everything.

"Your appointment is at the company headquarters in Brooklyn this Saturday at three o'clock."

He stood there for a second stunned.

Then he said goodbye to the secretary. His hands shook. Now what? A long-awaited, long-coveted interview. How many people received interviews in these tough times? Was he supposed to give it up just like that? Maybe there was another alternative?

My father set his mind to coming up with a way out. In the end he decided that he would attend the davening in Torah Vodaath that Shabbos morning like he always did and that he would set off on the long walk to Brooklyn after davening. He would not take any transportation and would carry nothing in his pocket. He would do no work, and would certainly not transgress Shabbos in the slightest. Not even in matters of *techum Shabbos*, because there were buildings along the entire route.

He told my mother his plan. Maybe he was expecting her to react with pride at the lengths he was willing to go to keep Shabbos. To walk from Williamsburg to the factory by foot – how noble. But that wasn't the reaction he got from her.

Far from it.

"Yidel, you're not going to the interview," she told him emphatically. "If it's *bashert*, if it's meant to be, you'll get the job even if you go on Monday." Quietly, yet with steel under the silk. In tones that were still and unraised, yet with no doubt whatsoever.

My father looked at her puzzled and concerned and worried.

"I'll walk there, all the way to the factory..." he pleaded with her.

She was as firm as a stone.

"Yidel," my *Yiddishe Mama* said, "if the job is the right one for you, then you'll get it on Monday, but you're not going on Shabbos."

Those were her words, delivered without doubt or recrimination, without hysterics or finger pointing, but with a surety that made my father overcome that particular *nisayon*, sit up straight and say, "You're absolutely right, there's nothing to talk about. An interview on Shabbos is out of the question!"

My father went to the factory Monday instead. Despite his having turned down their first offer for an interview, they were willing to meet with him. Not only did they meet with him, they offered him a job, which he accepted gratefully and where he remained for over thirty-five years until he retired. This was true sacrifice on the part of both my parents, sacrifice of a caliber that can't even be described. People do desperate things when faced with starvation, yet my mother didn't waver for a second. And she strengthened my father's resolve to go above and beyond the letter of the law and treat Shabbos like a diamond demands to be treated.

❧

When I was growing up, my father was never at home for Rosh Hashanah/Yom Kippur. A *baal tefillah/chazzan* par excellence, he was always in high demand. As I have mentioned, we were not a wealthy family and my father needed the money he was paid for the three-day position to support us. This meant that I was on my own during those very auspicious High Holy Days.

This was the way it went. Every year.

He'd return after Yom Kippur, having just finished praying his heart out, check in hand. The next morning he'd arise, put on his Shabbos finest, and make his way down to the office at Yeshiva Torah Vodaath to pay our tuition for the year. He had three sons studying in the *yeshivah* and he was keenly aware of his responsibilities. The *yeshivah*'s office never bothered him during the year, because they knew that come the day after Yom Kippur, he would present himself at the office, check in hand, and they would receive the entire amount owed them. He saw nothing from that check. The *yeshivah* received it all.

❧

Friday night in Williamsburg was something out of this world. A person had a choice of *tishen* to choose from. The Klausenberg dynasty drew more and more followers into its fold, eventually purchasing an old movie house in much need of renovation called the Lee, where it flourished, under the leadership of the much esteemed and beloved Rebbe, Rav Yekusiel Yehudah Halberstam.

And then Rav Yoel Teitelbaum, the Satmar Rebbe, entered the scene with his charismatic, unstoppable energy, unbreakable drive, and millions of ideas for how to save what remained of our broken nation after the catastrophe of the previous decade. I was twelve years old during the Rosh Hashanah/Yom Kippur when the Satmar Rebbe took over the Stoliner *shtiebl* on Rodney Street for the entire duration of the Yamim Noraim and Sukkos. That was where the Chassidim hoisted their *lulavim* up to the sky; that was where they danced the *hakafos*, bouncing off the floor in a frenzy of holiday spirit.

Stolin was between leaders at that particular junction in time and allowed the Rebbe full usage of their facility. I was suddenly introduced to a new Rebbe, someone burning with a desire to serve G-d and a fierce love for every single Jew. Someone who knew what it meant to be a leader. A man who had lived through the most hellish of circumstances and experiences and emerged much the stronger for it. I was but a child when I met him for the first time – twelve years old, and young enough and skinny enough to be able to float around anywhere.

I loved the atmosphere in the Satmar community and presented myself in the kitchen as the perfect all-around helper. The Satmar Rebbetzin took an instant liking to me, and it wasn't long before I was appointed the designated waiter, privileged to serve the Rebbe his meals. All Sukkos I sallied forth between kitchen and *sukkah*, determined to make the Rebbe proud of me. Chassidim were standing and sitting everywhere and all the while, little Sholom Gold was serving the Rebbe his soup on a tray.

We were destined to meet up again, but more about that later. At that time I knew nothing of the Satmar position on Medinat Yisrael. It was a time of pristine innocence. That would change. Oh, did it change.

The previous Stoliner Rebbe, Rav Yaakov Perlow, had traveled frequently to Detroit to visit the large group of Stoliner Chassidim living there at the time. He passed away during one of those trips. Since he had always been careful to take his *tachrichim* (burial shrouds) along with him wherever he might go, it was decided by the elders of Stolin to bury him in Detroit. After his passing, he became known as the "Detroiter," due to the location of his final resting place. His grave is in a little house where people can pray.

About a year later Rav Yochanan was appointed Rebbe of Stolin. Today's Stoliner Rebbe is his grandson. I became very close to the Rebbe, Rav Yochanan. I davened in the Williamsburg *shtiebl* for about six or seven years. Sure, I was learning in Torah Vodaath, but Shabbos was my own and I was able to choose where I wanted to daven. And much of the time, I chose Stolin.

For a number of years I spent my Chol Hamoed Sukkos going through hundreds of *aravos* until I managed to put together a set of the most impeccably handsome *hoshanos* in all New York. And then, full of anticipation, I'd present my gift to the Rebbe on the night of Hoshanah Rabbah. The Rebbe not only used my gift, but actually came to expect my yearly offering on one of the holiest nights of the year. His saintly eyes would look up as I entered the room where he sat learning, a smile would crease his distinguished face, and he'd nod as if saying, "Look what Sholom brought me." I was giving him a gift, but the true present was the fact that he was willing to accept my meager offering.

There was such beauty to be found at the Chassidic courts of Williamsburg. I visited them all. To some I grew closer than others. But every one of them has a warm place in my heart. This was where I'd spend those dreamy, endlessly long Shabbos afternoons of my youthful summers, listening to the fiery words of Torah emanating from many a holy mouth, seeing the sparks of light flashing from their eyes.

But it was Stolin I loved. It was Stolin that stole my heart.

Years later, when I was studying in Eretz Yisrael, late in the afternoon on a gloomy day in December 1955 I was learning in the Ponevezh study hall when a man I had never seen before gave me a tap on the shoulder. I looked up, trying to decide if I knew who he was.

"The Rebbe passed away. We're going to Yerushalayim."

I closed my Gemara as if in a trance, put on my coat, and followed the man to Yerushalayim. From all sides Jews were streaming toward the Stoliner *beis midrash* in Meah Shearim. It was jam-packed, at least according to the standards of those days, with a few hundred people.

I don't know what I'd been expecting. Maybe some eulogies as were normally given at the funeral of a righteous man. But nobody spoke. Instead they sang. This was my goodbye to the Stoliner part of my early years. Goodbye, Rav Yochanan. You inspired me more than I could ever put into words. In fact, words weren't going to do the job. Not at all. So we sang. Because sometimes, that's all you can do.

෴

Yeshiva Torah Vodaath was a mixture of all types. Cold Litvaks of distinguished lineage sat and learned *b'chavrusa*, in study partnership, with the scions and cream of the Chassidic world. One of my close friends in Torah Vodaath went by the name Zishe Heschel. His father, Rav Avrohom Yehoshua Heschel, was known far and wide as the Kopycznitzer Rebbe. The Rebbe's son Zishe had an engaging personality around whom a group of us gathered, which led us to become close to his father, the Rebbe. The group of young men, myself included, left the much quieter confines of Williamsburg on many a Shabbos afternoon, destination the bustling Lower East Side via the Williamsburg Bridge to Henry Street and the Kopycznitzer *beis midrash* for Minchah and the third meal of the day.

Crossing the bridge for spiritual reasons was something of an imperative for us at Torah Vodaath. Rav Nesanel Quinn, legendary *rebbe* in Torah Vodaath, would exhort the *bochurim* to attend the *yeshivah*'s all night *mishmar sedarim* on Thursday nights. "Those who live on the Lower East Side," he was in the habit of saying, "*zollen ibberhippen der brik*" (should jump across the bridge). That became a catch phrase, a byline, in our world. "*Ibberhippen der brik, men. Ibberhippen der brik!*" Till today, I can close my eyes and picture Rav Nesanel standing there, so earnest, so sincere, so loving. "*Ibberhippen der brik*, men. Across the bridge!" I've tried to keep doing that my entire life.

The Kopycznitzer Rebbe had a warm place in his heart for Zishe's *chevrah* and used to call us "Zishe's Chassidim," a title we acquired by general consensus. Yes, we American *bochurim* were Zishe's followers and proud of it.

Zishe might have been a quiet, unassuming leader, but he never became Rebbe. His brother Moshe took over after Rav Avrohom Yehoshua passed away, but he had a weak heart and passed away in his fifties. Zishe's son-in-law is today's Boyaner Rebbe, but Zishe himself chose never to don the mantle of official leadership. He didn't want to be Rebbe. Sometimes I think how much we might accomplish as a nation if we each knew our respective roles and didn't covet what we instinctively know isn't right for ourselves.

Those were great days in Williamsburg, in the shadow of Torah Vodaath and the rabbinical leaders of the times. Rav Shlomo Heiman.

Rav Reuven Grozovsky, son-in-law of Rav Boruch Ber Leibowitz. So many role models, so much wisdom concentrated in the minds and bodies of a few. We thrived on our exposure to those brilliant minds and were privileged enough to recognize it.

In Williamsburg scholarly men lived quietly on every block. Our teachers were outstanding, always molding us with an eye toward the future. Klausenberg. Satmar. Stolin.

I learned by Rav Pam, who had a tremendous impact on me, and by Rav Avrohom Yeshaya Shapiro. Rav Moshe (Duber) Dov Ber Rivkin was another person whose influence was imprinted on me. Rav Rivkin was the man who sat immediately behind the Rayatz, Rav Yosef Yitzchok Schneerson, second to last Rebbe of Chabad.

I was still in high school when the Lubavitcher Rebbe, the Rayatz, passed away and I remember that the entire *yeshivah* attended the *levayah* en masse. And not just Torah Vodaath. It seemed every single institution in New York had arrived to pay their final homage to a great leader in Israel. They simply closed the schools. In fact, the New York City transportation system sent out countless trolleys to ferry all of us to the funeral. Trolley after trolley filled with young and old, to Eastern Parkway, Crown Heights.

೭

There was a period in my youth when I immersed myself in the *mikveh* every single morning before davening. This was all well and good, but after exiting the *mikveh*, I had to walk along Rodney Street and here I ran into my daily challenge. The Doliner Rebbe's house of worship was located on Rodney Street, and this became something of an issue in my life. Most mornings found the Doliner standing out on the street on the lookout for a *tzenter*, a tenth man for his minyan. The reality of the matter was a little different. I came to this belated conclusion after I entered the *shtiebl* as the prospective *tzenter* a couple of times and realized that for the Doliner, *tzenter* was a loose term, which usually indicated that three to seven men were gathered in the *shul*. I ended up waiting quite a while on quite a few days until the Rebbe managed to gather himself a minyan. But who could refuse the Doliner Rebbe's request for a *tzenter*? Not I. And so, I somewhat forlornly ended up as that "tenth" man a few times too many for my *mashgiach*'s liking. My tardiness to *yeshivah* on those days was not appreciated.

Still I continued to frequent the *mikveh*, which was located at the Poilisher *shtiebl*. It was a classic sort of place, forerunner to such landmarks as Shomer Shabbos in Boro Park which would only become famous much later on. It was a full-steam operation. *Mikveh* downstairs in the basement. A study hall on the first floor constantly filled with people learning. High caliber learning. And there were even those individuals who felt the need to hide from the rest of the world and studied for hours on end in the women's section upstairs.

There was a brief interlude in my teenage years when I had a private session in Tanya with a man named Shlomo Carlebach. I still recall our first lesson together. "*Tanya sof perek gimmel d'Niddah…*"

I remember the fledgling Agudas Yisroel movement. Today, the Agudah convention draws thousands, but in the early fifties they had no supporters yet. They decided to make a convention at one of the many hotels on the New Jersey coast. But they didn't have anyone to come. Nobody was interested in Agudas Yisroel. What to do?

Someone contacted the boys at Mesivta Torah Vodaath and four cars filled with young men drove out for the convention. For our part we said, "Why not?" We were getting a free weekend. But when I describe the people who attended that free weekend as guests of honor, you'll quickly realize that we *bochurim* were in for a treat. It was a Shabbos to remember and savor for the rest of our lives.

Rav Elya Meir Bloch of Telz.

Rav Moshe Feinstein.

The Kopycznitzer Rebbe.

Rav Aharon Kotler.

It was a star-studded cast. There were probably more rabbinical figures present than laypeople. The fiery speeches, the lengthy meals, the fine food all combined to make it a weekend to remember. Late Friday night, Shlomo Carlebach led all the boys down to the beach on the edge of the hotel property. He had a handsome long winter coat, which he removed and spread with a flourish onto the sand.

"We're going to sit down," he said, "and we're going to be *mekadesh* [to sanctify] the entire eastern seaboard."

We sat until one or two in the morning singing songs. There weren't any "Carlebachs" yet. Shlomo was still a student at the time and had not yet begun composing. He studied in Lakewood under Rav Aharon Kotler, with whom he was purported to be extremely close.

So what did we sing for four hours?

The tunes of Modzitz, what else? All of us were into Modzitz. All Torah Vodaath was into Modzitz. Who didn't know, didn't listen, wasn't familiar with the music of Bentzion Shenker? I'll never forget how he came to the Mesivta one Motzaei Shabbos and sang a famous piece called "Ezkarah," a production some half an hour in length. "Ezkarah" is legendary for having been composed by the Modzitzer Rebbe while undergoing a complicated operation during the First World War without the benefit of anesthetics. The Rebbe was unaffected by the pain of surgery and retreated into his outstanding brain, where he composed one of his most superb musical pieces.

*No anesthetics? Big deal. I'll sing instead.* And so he did.

I can still sing part of it today. The musical notes and chords of a person's youth remain with him forever.

૨૭

And so I grew up with parents who served as role models and brothers who seemed to me to be the epitome of brilliance. I had teachers whom I revered and Chassidic Rebbes whom I cherished, synagogues where I felt at home and the *mikveh* in which to immerse myself in the early mornings. Chaim Gelb and Shlomo Carlebach. The Roshei Yeshivah of Torah Vodaath and the music of Bentzion Shenker. Daily life in Williamsburg was a wonderful way for a young man to begin a future of service to his people.

# 3

# TAKING THE BOY OUT OF BROOKLYN

I didn't know this, but my life was about to take a sharp and very interesting turn. I was now in the highest *shiur* in Torah Vodaath, well on my way to becoming one of the older students in the *yeshivah*.

Let me tell you about a day that would come to cause major upheaval in my life. It was Thursday afternoon and one of the *bochurim* sitting nearby in the study hall gave me a look. His name was Ronnie Greenwald and he grew up to become a major activist with connections to everything worth being connected to. Even as a young man, he was an activist.

He turned to me. "Let's go away for Shabbos."

"Away? Where exactly do you want to go?"

You have to understand, there really weren't that many places to go, back then.

"Let's work this out," he said. "The way I see it, there are two possibilities – either Telz in Cleveland, or Ner Yisroel in Baltimore."

We were obviously talking about reaching these far-away locations by a method known as hitching. This was how people got around back then, although it is a frowned-upon means of transportation nowadays. Going by train was not an option. Trains cost money and we had none to spare. Now what?

"Let me think about it," Ronnie said, and went off to try to work out the details. I turned back to my Gemara and waited to see what plan of action Ronnie Greenwald was going to come up with. That he would fail never even entered my mind. The term *failure* did not exist in Ronnie Greenwald's lexicon.

Ronnie returned a short while later with the travel plans.

"Listen," he told me excitedly, "one of the Ner Yisroel fellows is getting engaged tonight, and not only is it a mazel tov for him, but it's a mazel tov for us as well. This fellow hails from Williamsburg and the engagement party is taking place right here. A station wagon full of Ner Yisroel boys is coming in for the *vort* and returning to Baltimore eight o'clock sharp tomorrow morning. We can get a ride with them if we don't mind sitting in the station wagon's trunk."

I looked at Ronnie. Ronnie looked at me.

We shrugged. "Why not? Let's do it." Another adventure in the offing.

We met the station wagon bright and early the next morning. It was full of students waiting for us. The guys gave off a pretty *shtark*, serious impression. I hadn't imagined that the boys from Baltimore would look so determined and preoccupied. There was a distinguished gentleman with a long black coat and rabbinical hat sitting up front beside the driver. I didn't know who he was, but he appeared to be quite the impressive Jew. And so we were off, Ronnie and I, squashed like sardines in the trunk.

We stopped somewhere along the way and somehow (I was never quite sure how it occurred) I found myself undergoing a comprehensive test from the bearded man in the front seat. At the time I didn't know who he was, but I discovered soon enough that I had just been tested by the *rosh yeshivah* of Ner Yisroel, Rav Yaakov Yitzchok Halevi Ruderman. Some of the boys in that car would go on to become prominent educators and *roshei yeshivah* in the future. One of the students was Naftali Kaplan, today one of the foremost *mashgichim* in Eretz Yisrael. Another *bochur*, Gershon Weiss, is today the *rosh yeshivah* of Yeshiva of Staten Island.

After driving for hours we finally arrived in Baltimore, where we were graciously provided with sleeping quarters and made ourselves comfortable. It was a relaxing and beautiful Shabbos, made all the more enjoyable by the change in scenery. The singing was festive, the food superb, and the speeches at the meals inspirational. And I'm not even discussing the third meal of the day. The atmosphere during Seudah Shlishis was electric and intense, because that was when Rav Dovid Kronglass gave his weekly *mussar shmuess*. And what a talk it was. Direct, cutting-edge reproof and rebuke.

But through it all, through the entire Shabbos, Naftali Kaplan wouldn't stop talking to me about coming to study in the *yeshivah*. Obviously he'd made up his mind that Ner Yisroel was the right place for me, and he wasn't going to allow anything to get in his way. Every time he saw me, he stopped in his tracks and began trying to convince me anew.

"Forget it," I told him. "I'm a Torah Vodaath boy and you should know better than to try and convince a Williamsburg Torah Vodaath boy to come learn out here in the sticks."

But with a relentless persistence and single-mindedness, Naftali Kaplan just went on attempting to persuade me that Ner Yisroel was the best choice for me.

"I love Torah Vodaath. What do you want from me?" I protested.

He remained unimpressed. Undaunted. He knew that this was right, that we were a match. I just needed to arrive at this realization as well. But he did not succeed in convincing me to remain. No. I was going back to Williamsburg and that was that!

We got a ride back sometime Sunday afternoon and I walked into the *beis midrash* at the Mesivta bright and early that Monday morning, straight into the arms of Rav Nosson Elya Gertzlin, the *mashgiach* of Torah Vodaath. He was standing at the *bimah*, presiding over the study hall like he always did at that time of day.

"Gold," his deep voice boomed thunderously, "you weren't here yesterday. You weren't here on Friday. Where were you?"

With head hung low, in mortified tones, I admitted that I had hitched a ride to Baltimore with the *rosh yeshivah* of Ner Yisroel and had spent Shabbos at that institution. Needless to say, he was not mollified.

"You know something," he said to me, his eyes meeting mine

piercingly, "maybe you should go there. To Ner Yisroel. Maybe leave here and go learn there. That's a pretty good idea, no?"

He had thrown me out in the past due to morning timing issues on my part. I understood him. Here I was dipping in the *mikveh* at the Poilisher *shtiebl* every morning and making up a minyan for the Doliner Rebbe. I was a good boy but I was living on my own clock and that was not acceptable. In the past I had always managed to claw my way back in after being shown the door. But this time was different. Rav Naftali Kaplan's words were still ringing in my mind.

"Come learn at Ner Yisroel," he'd repeated countless times over Shabbos. Well, maybe he was correct. Maybe it was the right thing for me to do. I had one hesitation. Being that I had already reached the *shiur* of Rav Elya Chazan, I was in line to spend some quality time out in Spring Valley.

What was Spring Valley?

After building Torah Vodaath into a massive citadel of Torah with over one thousand *talmidim*, Rav Shraga Feivel decided to pursue another dream as well. Not one to allow dreams to atrophy, he went about the establishment of a *kollel* in Spring Valley. Learning in the *kollel* served as a reward to *bochurim* who had given their all in learning. Those students were privileged to hear daily classes from luminaries such as Rav Reuven Grozovsky, who based himself in Spring Valley, only traveling in to the Mesivta one day a week. For years I had been looking forward to learning at Spring Valley, and I wasn't about to relinquish that dream.

I went to the *rosh yeshivah*, Rav Yaakov Kamenetsky, and laid my dilemma out on the table.

"Sholom," he answered me, "I think that Ner Yisroel may be the perfect idea. You'll be forced to prove yourself again. It will be challenging for you. It's not a bad idea at all."

"But what about Spring Valley? I've been dreaming of learning in Spring Valley since I'm thirteen."

"Don't worry," Rav Yaakov told me, smiling his uniquely beautiful smile. "I'll make sure your place is waiting for you whenever you want to return from Baltimore."

"It won't be for more than a few months," I said.

"Whenever you want, Spring Valley will be waiting for you."

With dreams still intact and put on hold, I was content and ready to move on to the next stage of my life. And that was how it came to be that the following Wednesday found seventeen-year-old Sholom Gold moving his luggage into the dorm of Ner Israel Rabbinical College.

"I'll be staying until February," I told Rav Naftali Kaplan, who simply nodded and went about his business, confident that I was now ensnared in his *yeshivah*. Because he knew. He always did.

The fact was that I would never have the opportunity to learn at Spring Valley and I would never even return to Torah Vodaath at all. Rav Naftali didn't bother trying to convince me otherwise. He didn't have time for that. He just let nature take its course.

Ner Yisroel of Baltimore was an oasis of Torah in the midst of non-Jewish America. Religious teenagers traveled to Ner Yisroel from across the United States.

The staff was outstanding. And although the *yeshivah* allowed its student body to pursue a college education in concurrence with religious studies, the atmosphere in the *yeshivah* was one of Torah. How could it not be with a *rosh yeshivah* like Rav Yaakov Yitzchok Halevi Ruderman – may he be remembered for the good – and a *mashgiach* like Rav Dovid Kronglass, a saintly individual who demanded much from the student body but not nearly as much as he demanded from himself. It was my good fortune to hear *shiurim* from this man, and what I gleaned from his impressive presence has accompanied me and guided me at crucial moments in life. Rav Dovid was one of the Shanghai Mirrers and his entire essence was permeated with memories of Rav Yeruchem Levovitz and Rav Leizer Yudel Finkel.

Although I had originally planned on returning to Torah Vodaath in the winter, February came and went and I was still in Baltimore, with no plans to go anywhere else.

I loved Ner Yisroel, but I also made my own way. At one point I had a *seder* in Tanach between supper and night *seder* in the *beis midrash*. I had always felt that it was very important to not only focus on the regularly studied tractates of Talmud, but on the other parts of Torah as well. And that's why I set aside some quality time every day for Navi and Chumash. Not everyone was happy with my decision to focus on Tanach. One of the *yeshivah*'s advanced students, today a famous *rosh yeshivah*, approached me and informed me in no uncertain terms that this was not the way things were supposed to go.

"Sholom," he said in tones that tolerated no argument, "you should be learning Gemara now, not Navi."

I paid absolutely no attention to him. To me one part of Torah was as important as the next and I intended to devote a portion of time to mastering Navi.

∽

It was May 1955, about two and a half years after I'd first arrived at Ner Yisroel, when the pay phone rang in the hallway outside the dormitory. A student answered and the caller requested to speak with me. Wondering who could be calling, I made my way out of the *beis midrash* and over to the phone.

It was one of my friends from Torah Vodaath, and he had a very exciting and interesting proposition for me.

"Sholom, how'd you like to go to Eretz Yisrael for the summer?"

The idea struck me with tidal wave force. Eretz Yisrael! My father had gone around Williamsburg with a blue and white *pushke* in his hand collecting money for Eretz Yisrael. All my life I had grown up hearing – no, drinking in – stories about Eretz Yisrael. Was it really possible that I would be granted such an opportunity? Of course I wanted to go.

Rabbi Linchner was then English principal of Torah Vodaath while simultaneously building Boys Town in the Bayit Vegan neighborhood of Jerusalem. Then occupying one building only and going by the name Merom Tzion, it had yet to develop into the sprawling campus of the future. But Rabbi Linchner had big plans and the ambition and drive to carry them out. He was also a man with a host of brilliant ideas. This trip to Eretz Yisrael was his latest brainstorm.

Rabbi Linchner wanted everyone to know about Boys Town. He wanted people to talk about his groundbreaking endeavor everywhere. That was why he decided to open up a summer camp to be located at Merom Tzion where American *yeshivah* boys would travel to Yerushalayim to serve as counselors for the Sephardic youth from Morocco who were newly arrived *olim*. He wanted to reach out to a community that had been uprooted from North Africa and transplanted in Eretz Yisrael. They needed guidance, help, and warmth. It was a wise move and it did in fact generate a lot of publicity.

But all this meant little to me. I didn't care about publicity. I didn't care about people talking. I cared about going to Eretz Yisrael. If this was my chance, then I was going to grab it with both hands. After all, who received such an opportunity back in those days? We would be among the first American students to have the privilege.

Five friends of mine had already been selected from Torah Vodaath and they told Rabbi Linchner that they wanted me to come along with them.

Rabbi Linchner agreed.

I didn't tell the Rosh Yeshivah that I planned on remaining in Eretz Yisrael after summer's end. I merely told him about the camp and the job and asked his permission to spend the summer months working with the poor, neglected Moroccan children. Deep in the back of my mind, however, I knew that once I had stepped foot onto the pier at Haifa, I would be in no rush to return. I was going to stay and learn for a while. How could I not?

In the end, Rav Ruderman gave me his permission and I informed Rabbi Linchner that I would be joining the "Torah Pioneers." That's what all the public relations brochures called us.

The preparations for the trip were fascinating in themselves. Traveling to Eretz Yisrael meant having to obtain a passport, and that in turn meant a trip into New York City for the day. As the train roared into the city I said to myself, "Sholom, one of those underprivileged kids is going to look you in the eye and ask you what the Empire State Building is like. What are you going to answer him? You have never even been inside the Empire State Building in your life."

How would it look if their American counselors couldn't tell them of the grandness and glory of the *goldene medinah*? No, that wouldn't do. And so I walked the busy avenues, soaking up the frenzy and fast pace of the busiest city in the world, enjoying the sights, sounds, and colors of the Big Apple, until there it was – the Empire State Building, tallest building in the world at the time. Quick as a flash I entered the building, and then exited right back out. Now I could claim in good faith to have visited the famous landmark. I craned my neck all the way back and took a very good look at the majestic edifice, making sure to memorize every possible detail for a credible description later on.

And yes, my intuition proved correct, because my little campers did ask me about the Empire State Building and I in turn was able to satisfy their curiosity in an honest and descriptive manner. They were very impressed to be talking with someone who had been in the Empire State Building.

ॐ

What a group we were. Six great guys altogether. Each a real personality. Every one possessing an abundance of talent in a different area. Nosson Scherman, Chaim Libel, Avrohom Landesman, Yosef Weinstein, Yankel Goldberg, and me.

Getting there was a story in itself. The first leg of our journey was via KLM to Prestwick, Scotland. Don't forget that flying was a major event in those days. People didn't just get on a plane and fly around the world. Certainly for six sheltered *yeshivah bochurim*, it was a journey to remember and cherish. But the vigorous and rigorous joys of takeoff were soon a pale memory, because only hours later we found ourselves boarding a train bound for Gateshead, England. Our itinerary called for spending Shabbos in the *yeshivah* there. To tell the truth, I never knew what an itinerary was until that trip.

Those Gatesheaders had never seen American *yeshivah* boys in their lives. It was a memorable Shabbos as we submerged ourselves in the warmth and old-fashioned delight of the Gateshead community. What a special and insular world they had created. We met the *rosh yeshivah* and the *mashgiach*. It was an unforgettable experience.

During the course of our time in that tiny little world, we heard that Rav Leizer Silver was coming to visit Gateshead as well. This was important news. What were the chances of our having arrived for a visit at the same time? Rav Leizer Silver was slated to arrive at the Newcastle train station and when the Gateshead Yeshiva flowed out en masse to greet the *gadol*, we went along. We boarded a train from Gateshead, drinking in the splendid scenery along the route. England is a country of greenery. Sloping hills filled with lush green grass stretched off into the distant horizon, while cows grazed peacefully behind white picket fences. What a wonderful adventure this was becoming. Six young men off to see the world. Scotland. England. And soon Eretz Yisrael!

The conductor, a man with a fierce scowl and an accent so thick as to be almost impossible to decipher, kept passing through our car yelling out, "Newcastle upon Tyne, Newcastle upon Tyne."

"What on earth is he going on about?" we wanted to know. "New castles on time? What does that mean?"

In the end, our confusion was cleared up when we learned that the city of Newcastle had been constructed on the River Tyne, hence the name "upon Tyne."

We enjoyed it all – the Gateshead *roshei yeshivah* and even the English *yeshivah* students. Everything was worth remembering, every detail a story to tell my grandchildren. What a summer this was turning out to be.

Unfortunately every good thing comes to an end and soon enough it was time to leave Gateshead for the next stop on our journey, London. In London, we Torah Vodaath boys had a friend who had studied with us back home. His family resided in that sprawling metropolis, and they invited us to stay with them while we were passing through. They were Chinese Jews, a family named Avraham. Our friend's name was Avraham Avraham. The Avraham family lived in Whitechapel along with most of the other Jews in London at the time, and we were welcomed graciously with true English/Chinese hospitality.

In a matter of days our whirlwind trip had taken us through Scotland, Gateshead, and London, and now it was time for us to cross the channel to Paris, the city of lights. The Channel Tunnel was but a future dream; we took a ferry over the channel to the French port. We remained there for a day and a half, seeing the sights and buying sufficient provisions for the remainder of our voyage.

Paris was an enchanting city filled with graceful architecture and ancient stone buildings, tiny mock balconies, and cobblestone streets called Rue this and Rue that. The Parisian streets were filled with the laughter of six *yeshivah* boys exploring the world. We found a kosher bistro that carried the brand of salami that remains fresh forever and other stores that sold all types of interesting merchandise. There was a certain magic that was literally hovering in the streets of the world-famous capital. I could have remained in Paris for another week and been perfectly happy. It is such a beautiful city. But there was someplace else that I desired to be even more, and we still had another leg of the journey to go. After leaving Paris we traveled overland to one of Europe's most exquisitely breathtaking cities.

Venice. A place of true beauty. City of crisscrossing canals filled with murky water. Much of the traffic takes place by boat. There is much to see in Venice from a tourist's point of view: the royal palace of the Doge and the ancient Jewish ghetto of Venice. There are museums galore and squares filled with breathtaking artful sculptures. It is a city that caters to the arts.

Evening arrived.

The city's lights turned on and the streets were illuminated in a way that turned even seemingly prosaic walkways into magically secret paths. Soon after our arrival, we heard that the Satmar Rebbe had arrived in Venice along with fifty Chassidim. They too were on their way to Eretz Yisrael, and we would all be traveling together on a seaworthy vessel called the *Messapia*.

We were embarking on the final leg of our journey the following day, so we booked ourselves into a simple rooming house to catch some sleep and conserve our strength for the morrow. However, it was not meant to be a restful night. At eleven o'clock that evening, Venice was treated to a sight it had never seen in its long and eventful history. All fifty Satmar Chassidim came charging through the cobblestone pathways with no warning.

Why?

The Rebbe "*geit arois oifn vasser.*" The Rebbe was going out on the famous Venice canal waterways. The Italians' mouths were hanging open as they watched fifty grown men chasing after some regal-looking Jew. They had never seen anything even remotely close to this kind of spectacle and they contented themselves by pointing, laughing, and enjoying the show. All was well and good until the Rebbe actually boarded the boat, at which point the majority of the Chassidim threw themselves off the pier and onto the boat as well, causing the Italians to jolt themselves out of spectator mode and into the role of guardians of the law.

"Get off!" they roared at the Chassidim in Italian as they began pulling and shoving the Chassidim off the boat. "It's going to sink if you all stay on. Get off!"

It took a while, but in the end a much safer number of passengers was allowed to remain on the boat, much to the chagrin of those followers who were forced onto additional boats that soon joined the Rebbe's canal convoy. We also felt it was incumbent upon us to try out the local mode of transportation. We found a gondola and we were a sight Venice had never seen before. Young men bedecked in light-colored hats and jackets, hands trailing in the water, singing a tune which came to be known as "The Gondola Niggun," moving alongside a group of much larger boats ferrying dozens of Chassidim along the canals, all intent on watching their Rebbe.

At the end of that outing on the water we returned to our boardinghouse, caught a few exhausted hours of sleep, and presented ourselves at the *Messapia* on time at noon the following day for the start of the five-day voyage to the shores of Eretz Yisrael.

I, of course had been a favorite of the Rebbe since the Sukkos when I was twelve and serving as the Rebbe's personal waiter, and that meant that the Rebbetzin was very happy to take care of us boys during our time together. I was informed by the Rebbe's *gabbai*, Rav Yossele Ashkenazi, that we didn't have to worry about an *eruv* on board, because the Rebbe had purchased the entire boat.

"You bought the boat?" I asked him incredulously, not fully comprehending what he meant. I didn't know much about *eruvim* at that stage in my life, though I would come to know very much about them later on.

"Of course," he replied. "Not only that, but when we crossed the Atlantic I purchased the entire *Queen Mary* as well!" A few dollars, a halachic acquisition, and the *Queen Mary* had reverted to Rav Yoel's ownership until the Rebbe and his entourage disembarked in Europe.

There was a truly beautiful Chassidic gathering on the *Messapia*, with the Rebbe sitting at the head of the table, a look of otherworldliness on his face. The Chassidim sang and we sang along with them, accompanied at all times by the silent rocking of the boat. A *tish* on a boat – who ever heard of such a thing? It was a novel experience. The singing, the Torah, the atmosphere – everything was simply *me'ein Olam Haba* (from the World to Come). To this day I'm not sure how I managed to retain my connection to the Litvish world when I was so inspired by and full of love for the Chassidim, their rabbinical leadership, and the uplifting spirituality of their lives.

The Rebbetzin made sure that each one of the "Americanisher" boys received a bowl of soup and a piece of chicken. We were treated royally, turning a simple boat voyage into a five-star cruise.

The *Messapia* moved smoothly, making good time in its haste to reach the shores of Eretz Yisrael. The final port before reaching Haifa was at Limasol, Cyprus. Cyprus was under British control at that point in history, as was much of the civilized and not-so-civilized world. At the port in Cyprus, British soldiers boarded the craft, Tommy guns at the ready, and proceeded to give the *Messapia* a thorough searching.

Our captain lifted anchor and before we knew it, we were inching away from the port and heading out to the open sea, destination Haifa, Eretz Yisrael. The utter joy that filled my heart when I heard those words was not to be described. I was finally about to step onto the holy soil I had heard so much about. We were one night away from the Land of Avraham, Yitzchak, and Yaakov.

And of course, that was the night that everything exploded.

As our boat left Cyprus, vehement arguments broke out among the passengers, a cacophony of shouts and bitter rhetoric the likes of which we boys had never seen. Chilonim versus Dati'im. Tzionim versus Chassidim. I had never seen such bitter debating in my life. It was raw and vocal and went on and on and on at decibel levels that could probably be heard back in Cyprus. The people of Israel were returning to the Land and the arguments were as loud as they had been throughout history, to the point that it felt like the boat was on the verge of blowing up right then and there.

And then something awesome happened.

At about five or five thirty in the morning, I watched as everyone on the boat took a place by the railing. Waiting, looking, watching. Everyone. Chassid, Tzioni, Mizrachi, Chiloni, Litvak. Men, women, and children. Every single Jew on that boat found a spot from which to watch our long-awaited approach. They all wanted to see Eretz Yisrael for the first time. And then at about seven o'clock in the morning everyone was on deck, all silent, all eyes focused straight ahead. You couldn't buy that moment for a million dollars. You can't imagine the surge of feeling that resonated through the hearts of the assembled. Such heartfelt emotion. Such intense, incredible joy.

As the Haifa shoreline became clearer and more visible and the Carmel mountain range was silhouetted against the early morning sunlight, three tugboats left Haifa harbor and proceeded to approach the *Messapia*. Each of those tugboats held a band of musicians on its deck playing joyous songs of greeting to the Satmar Rebbe. The little tugboats surrounded our boat and the Chassidim on board were singing "*Yamim al yemei melech tosif*" (Add days to the days of the king)... The music and singing merged together with the dancing and happiness on board that seemed to embrace the entire boat.

Nobody was left unmoved. You couldn't possibly feel unmoved at the sight before your eyes. Every mouth sang, even those who had been arguing so vehemently just a few hours previously. It was positively awesome. That's the way we entered Eretz Yisrael. With three tugboats filled with Chassidim and music and dancing and song. Welcomed into the Holy Land in a royal manner guaranteed to ensure that we would never forget our entry. I know that I didn't.

The shore was filled with black-coated figures, all waiting anxiously to see the visage of the Satmar Rebbe, and their singing mixed with ours and wafted along the early morning wind as everyone from old man to child savored the touching moment of our arrival in Eretz Yisrael. It didn't matter who you were – Chassid, Chiloni, Zionist, or anti-Zionist. Every single person felt privileged beyond mere words to have been granted the opportunity to step foot onto the holy soil of Eretz Yisrael. It was not to be believed.

Huge banners hung at the port: "*Bruchim habo'im moreini v'rabbeini*" (Welcome, our rabbi and teacher).

And why in fact was Rav Yoel visiting the land of the Zionists?

He'd arrived to spread the message that it was completely forbidden to vote in the upcoming elections. Interestingly enough, Rav Aharon Kotler arrived not long after and his message was exactly the opposite: everyone had to vote, voting was imperative, every vote counted. Gimmel, Daled. Agudah was *gimmel*, Poalei Agudah was *daled*, and they were all one party. It was a heady time, full of choices.

Within minutes the *Messapia* had brushed against the dock with an almost silent thud and we were escorted off the boat, toward the Israeli customs officials.

"*Ibberhippen der brik, ibberhippen der brik!*" Rav Nesanel had ordered us, entreated us, cajoled us, and here we were, having done just that.

The Satmar Rebbe's Chassidim were provided with a special train by the Ministry of Transportation which ferried them smoothly from the dock at Haifa all the way to Yerushalayim. We young men did not merit such service and had to make do with the *sherut* (group taxi) that Rabbi Linchner sent to transport us to the camp facilities in Bayit Vegan.

And that was my voyage to Eretz Yisrael. I recall it all as if it happened yesterday. What an entrance, what a land, what a people we are! The next thing I knew, we were being shown our quarters at Rabbi Linchner's *yeshivah* in Bayit Vegan where camp was about to begin. My stay in Israel had commenced.

# 4

# My First Dalet Amos in Eretz Yisrael

I walked the streets of Yerushalayim in silent joy, contemplating my good fortune and thinking of the Ramban. Rabbeinu Moshe Ben Nachman traveled to the Holy Land in 1267 and while here, wrote letters to his son back in Spain. In them, he describes the ancient land with love and adoration, though it was difficult for a Jew to reside in the Yerushalayim of those times.

At the time of the Ramban's visit to Yerushalayim there were a grand total of two Jews living within the Old City walls. They were dyers by trade and lived there by special order of the local rulers who needed their craft. The Ramban didn't have a minyan to daven with.

In Yerushalayim Ir Hakodesh, the holy city of Jerusalem, two Jews and no more!

Rav Ovadia MiBartenura arrived two hundred years later and found two or three hundred Jews living here, a far cry from the bustling metropolis of today.

Rav Yehudah Hachassid came here in 1700 and found five thousand Jews living in Yerushalayim.

In 1955 I arrived in Yerushalayim and there were 146,000 Jews living in the city, yet it was divided by an ugly, ominous-looking concrete wall topped with barbed wire like a knife passing through its heart. The Kotel was inaccessible despite the fact that Jordan had agreed to permit Jews to pray there. Little did anyone know then what would happen twelve years later in six miraculous days.

Today there are five hundred thousand Jews proudly calling the City of Gold (pun intended) their home – half a million Jews of all kinds, of every background and religious affiliation. From every country around the world. Young and old, men, women, and children. How fortunate we are. Don't you see the miracle that took place here?

I have a recurring dream (usually when I'm awake). In the dream I'm standing at the Gesher Hameitarim, the harp-shaped bridge proudly standing guard at the entrance to Yerushalayim. Suddenly, the street is enveloped in a mist that blocks my vision and surrounds me on all sides. A man emerges from the cloud and fog and enters my line of vision.

I approach him. He is dressed as if he's still living in another century, another day and age.

I extend my hand. "*Shalom aleichem*," I say to him. "My name is Gold. What's yours?"

"Moshe Ben Nachman," he replies.

I look at him shocked beyond mere words. "The Ramban?" I manage to whisper in disbelief.

He nods his distinguished head in the affirmative.

And then more great men from our distant past step out of the mist. The Bartenura. Rav Yehudah Hachassid. Rav Menachem Mendel of Shklov. Rebbe Nachman of Breslov. And we're standing there all together under the bridge. And then slowly, the mist begins to evaporate and their eyes open wide and they start taking in the sights around them. The endless traffic, both mechanical and pedestrian, people coming and going in a never-ending stream of humanity. Jewish humanity.

The Ramban turns to me. "Where am I?" he says.

"Yerushalayim," I answer proudly.

He can't believe it.

"You can't be serious?"

"I've never been more serious in my life," I reassure him. "This is Yerushalayim, filled with more Jews then at any time since the Churban, the destruction of the Holy Temple, two thousand years ago."

"Are the Crusaders here?" That's his next question. "Where's the Crusader garrison?"

"There are no Crusaders anymore, Rabbeinu. They are long gone. They've disappeared into the pages of history."

"What about the Tartars, the Mamelukes?"

"No. It's a Jewish country now."

"A Jewish country," they all chorus, overcome by shock. "How can it be? Is such a thing even possible?" The shock gives way to the beginnings of comprehension, which then develops into an inner joy reflected in the light that shines from their faces, and then – they get it. What they could never have imagined has happened. No Babylonians, no Greeks, no Romans, no Muslims, no Saracens, no Crusaders, no Tatars, no Mamelukes, no Turks, no British. Jews rule Eretz Yisrael.

Silence descends on the whole entrance to Yerushalayim. Everything stops, an eerie yet holy cessation of sound. The mist intensifies, the clouds around us thicken, and then there emerges a figure of clear spiritual stature whose countenance bespeaks greatness. He approaches us and I ask him who he is. "Akiva Ben Yosef," he says. A gasp escapes from all the assembled. With great reverence and respect I introduce us all.

"Where am I?" he asks.

"You are in Yerushalayim Ir Hakodesh," I respond proudly.

Looking furtively around, he inquires, "Where are the Romans? Where's the garrison of the 10th Legion, stationed at Nebi Samuel? Where are they? I don't see any Legionnaires…"

And this is the answer I want to tell him – to tell all of them, really.

> Israel, my people,
> G-d's greatest riddle,
> Will thy solution
> Ever be told?
>
> Fought – never conquered,

Bent – never broken,
Mortal – immortal,
Youthful, though old.

Egypt enslaved thee,
Babylon crushed thee,
Rome led thee captive,
Homeless thy head.

Where are those nations,
Mighty and fearsome?
Thou hast survived them,
They are long dead.

Nations keep coming,
Nations keep going,
Passing like shadows,
Wiped off the earth.

Thou an eternal
Witness remainest,
Watching their burial,
Watching their birth.

(Philip Max Raskin, "The Eternal Riddle,"
*Songs of a Wanderer* [Philadelphia:
Jewish Publication Society of America, 1917])

And the dream sort of melts into another scene.

A few years ago, my wife and I began spending time up north in Migdal, a few kilometers north of Tveria. We were there as the holiday of Lag b'Omer arrived and hundreds of thousands of people began to converge on Meron – about a half hour's drive north from Migdal – for the traditional Lag b'Omer visit to the grave of Rabbi Shimon Bar Yochai. I told Bayla that the whole world can travel north, but I want to go to the grave of Rabbi Shimon Bar Yochai's Rebbe, Rabbi Akiva.

For a while we were hopelessly lost in the winding Tveria streets. Eventually we found our way to his grave, where I found a Tanach sitting peacefully, waiting for me. I flipped open to Zechariah and found the verses that Rabbi Akiva told the wise men of Israel in *Makkos* 24b, the tale of the rabbis standing on Har Tzofim and seeing a fox come running out of the Holy of Holies. The rabbis cry. Rabbi Akiva laughs.

"Rabbi Akiva," they ask him, "why do you laugh?"

"Why do you cry?" is his response.

"What do you mean?" comes the indignant response. "A fox has just come bounding out of the holiest place on earth, a place that even the Kohen Gadol was only allowed to enter on the holiest day of the year, on Yom Kippur – and we shouldn't cry?"

"That's exactly why I laugh." Rabbi Akiva explains, "When I witness how Uriah's prophecies of *churban*, of destruction, have clearly come true, how the Temple lies desolate, a shambles, then I know, *I am sure*, that the prophecy of Zechariah will come true as well!"

I stood at Rabbi Akiva's *kever* and recited that *perek* straight out of Sefer Zechariah from the beginning to the end: "Thus said Hashem: 'Old men and old women will once again sit in the streets of Yerushalayim each with his staff in his hand because of advanced age. And the streets of the city will be filled with boys and girls playing in its streets (Zechariah 8:4–5).'"

I spoke to Rabbi Akiva from the heart. "Rabbi Akiva," I told him, "if I had a can of spray paint, I would go throughout the country and spray-paint it from top to bottom: *'Rabbi Akiva tzadak!'* Rabbi Akiva was right!"

And then my dream transports me back to the bridge and once again I find myself surrounded by the elders of yesteryear and I turn to Rabbi Akiva and I motion with my arm at all the people and the buildings and the beauty of our city and I say to him, "Rebbe, you were right. This is what you foresaw so clearly thousands of years ago."

And I'll make one additional point. If the thousands of *yeshivah* students and seminary girls who flock to study in Yerushalayim for a year or two don't manage to accurately appreciate the awesomeness of this city, then what have they accomplished here? They need to know that when the Ramban arrived here in 1267 there were all of two Jews living here and now there are half a million. This is an awesome fact of life and should be recognized as such, because this is the reality that Rabbi Akiva never doubted.

☙

And so, the six of us arrived in Bayit Vegan.

Bayit Vegan was a tree-lined residential neighborhood whose handful of streets were full of apartment buildings covered with Jerusalem stone. Today, Bayit Vegan is comprised almost entirely of religious families. Back then that was not the case. The vast majority of the inhabitants were traditional but not particularly religious, and for the most part, everyone got along with one another.

Rabbi Linchner was keen to provide us with some grand experiences to begin our trip on the right foot. We had only been in Eretz Yisrael a few days when Rabbi Linchner managed to get us in to visit the Brisker Rav. The Brisker Rav, known as Rav Velvel, resided off Rechov Yeshayahu in an extremely simple and modest apartment in the Geula section of Yerushalayim, right around the corner from the infamous Edison movie house (the scene of many a demonstration by Yerushalmi Jews, led by Rav Amram Blau).

The Brisker Rav was sitting at the table when we entered his home.

We were introduced to him as "the *bochurim* from America," and found to our shock and dismay that he was not in the least impressed with our status and the fact that we hailed from so far away.

"What is this?" he thundered at us, eyes boring straight into our souls.

"*Vos tut zach in Torah Vodaas? Es iz in mitten zman – mi geit arois in der velt in mitten zman? Mi lernt nisht! Es iz Tammuz!*" (What's going on in Torah Vodaath? It's the middle of the semester. Why are you running around the world in the middle of the semester? No learning? As if it were summer vacation!) And so on. He simply could not fathom that the month of Tammuz was in fact considered to be vacation for American *bochurim*.

He was going on and on about Torah Vodaath and I of course was smiling because I was now a talmid of Ner Yisroel and as such not responsible for Mesivta boys. The Brisker Rav yelled at us, let us have it. It was quite embarrassing, to say the least. All six of us stood there feeling as if we had let down the entire world of Orthodox Jewry. But then a little voice piped up inside my mind. "Sholom," it said, "this will be another good story to tell your grandchildren someday. The day you were given a tongue lashing by the Brisker Rav. After all, how many others can boast of the same thing?"

By the time we filed white-faced and visibly shaken out of that tiny apartment and onto Yeshayahu Street, we needed a good breath of fresh air to regain our composure. What power that man possessed!

Thus ended my first encounter with the Rav.

～

It was during that exhilarating summer of awesome experiences and beautiful moments that the Kopycznitzer Rebbe came to visit Eretz Yisrael. He utilized this precious opportunity to meet with many holy personages and to visit the gravesites of the kabbalists and *tzaddikim* scattered around the Land. One of the most poignant visits of all was to the Belzer Rebbe, Rav Aaron Rokeach, a holy, holy man. Of course the Rebbe needed someone to accompany him to the elderly *tzaddik*, and somehow, from our group of six, it was Shloima Yosef (Joey) Weinstein and myself who were chosen to attend the historic meeting. Being "Zishe's Chassidim" probably had a lot to do with receiving this privilege.

To see this man was to meet an angel in the flesh.

The Rebbe was shrunken and gaunt, known as someone who fasted way more than he ate. He was more "there" than "here," his body hanging onto the earth by the most tenuous of threads. It was a steamy evening in Tel Aviv when we arrived at the Belzer Rebbe's home. The house was surrounded by *chassidishe bochurim* in their long black coats and velvet hats. You couldn't get near the building unless you were someone important. Alone, Joey and I would never have managed to get within fifty feet of the Rebbe's place of residence.

I looked around in wonder.

So many young men. Why were they all standing around the building? What were they waiting for? And then in a flash I understood. Someone had obviously leaked the news that the Kopycznitzer Rebbe of America was on his way to visit with Rav Aaron, and the *bochurim* had come running to catch a glimpse of the famous Kopycznitzer.

Joey and I were classic American *yeshivah* boys, which meant that we were clad in light gray hats and light-colored suits. That's what people wore back then. In other words, we stood out in that gigantic group of Chassidim like extremely sore thumbs – two light suits in a crowd of seven hundred black jackets. As the Kopycznitzer approached the building, the sea of black parted for the distinguished personage from the States, and closed up behind him from one second to the next, leaving us stranded behind, unable to reach the Kopycznitzer and unhappily adrift in the Tel Aviv night.

The Rebbe had reached the door to the building when he realized that "his boys" were no longer walking behind him. In a second he took in the picture and realized what had occurred. He turned around and said in his firm and powerful voice, "*Vi zenen di Americaner?*" (Where are the Americans?). And then again even more powerfully, "*Di Americaner?*"

The sea of black parted once more and the two of us walked through the throngs. The Rebbe hadn't forgotten us for an instant, and we were eternally grateful to be granted the opportunity of a lifetime on that steamy evening in Tel Aviv. It was eleven o'clock at night. The table was set very beautifully there in the home of the Belzer Rebbe, with delicious-looking cakes and cookies, fruits and nuts galore, and bottles of cold drinks. The Belzer Rebbe waved us to some seats around the table and motioned us to help ourselves, though we were hesitant to do so.

The Kopycznitzer didn't help himself at all. Instead he turned to the Belzer and said, "*Der Rebbe hut shoin gegessen pas shacharis?*" (Did the Rebbe eat breakfast yet?).

The Belzer wouldn't answer.

He was the kind of righteous man who subjected his diminutive body to all manner of afflictions. He cared not a whit for the physical delights of this world.

So the Kopycznitzer gave the Belzer an ultimatum.

"*Mir vellen gornisht essen biz der Rebbe est*" (We will eat nothing until the Rebbe eats), he said, and you could tell that he meant it.

In the end, the Belzer Rebbe ate.

As did we.

Just to be in the presence of that spiritual giant was an experience that was somewhat out of this world. And to be there with the Kopycznitzer was to take things up to the next level. I knew that night that I would never forget being in the presence of those two great men. And I didn't. Ever.

ஒ

Then there was my visit to the Tchebiner Rav, Rav Dov Berish Weidenfeld.

The Tchebiner Rav was a phenomenal scholar, but it wasn't even his knowledge or brilliant grasp of so many facets of Torah study that impressed me most. It was something else completely: his alarm clock.

They let me into the room where he received people. I waited for him to put in an appearance. From what I understood, the Rav was learning in his study upstairs. He descended soon enough. He looked like every elderly Jew, his face glowing with the shine of decades of Torah learning. But there was something in his hand, an object that didn't belong. What was it? I peered a little closer, craning my neck to catch a better view, and was shocked to see an alarm clock clenched tightly in his fist. Why was he carrying an alarm clock? It didn't take me long to understand. The alarm clock was set down on the table between us where it sat ticking away the time. Three minutes, four minutes…and then *brrringgg*. The alarm had gone off and the meeting was over. The Tchebiner, I later learned, used his alarm clock at every meeting. When the clock rang and the allotted time was up, the Rav said goodbye and left the room to return to his *sefarim* and solitude.

I've never met anyone else who guarded precious time quite like him.

ஒ

My year in Eretz Yisrael would leave me replete with memories and stories of time spent among the giants of the previous generation. It would also provide me with a wealth of positive life experiences on which I would draw for strength and inspiration in the years that lay ahead. It was in those narrow streets that I would meet many of the people who would influence me profoundly, as well as others who were slated to become friends for life.

One of these friends was the son of the *rosh yeshivah* of Marom Tzion, the forerunner of Boys Town. His name was Tzvi Kushelevsky, and he would later go on to become a highly respected *rosh yeshivah* himself with thousands of students around the world. His father had been the *rav* in Patterson, New Jersey, before they moved to Eretz Yisrael. (My own grandson, Ariel Gold from Afula, today learns in his *yeshivah*.)

While the rest of my friends would return home at summer's close, I remained in Eretz Yisrael for the next year and a half. The Kushelevsky home in Bayit Vegan became my second home, its door wide open to me anytime I needed anything at all. I spent my *yamim tovim* and many Shabbosim there, and they made me feel I had a family that would welcome me unconditionally anytime I needed them.

I recall accompanying my friends, the ones I had grown up with, to the airport when it was time for them to leave, and the feeling of loneliness that swept across my soul even though I knew with complete clarity that remaining behind was what I needed to do. I was in Eretz Yisrael. There was no way I would ever be willing to leave her shores so soon. Still I couldn't help thinking, "*V'yivaser Sholom levado*" (and Sholom remained alone).\*

And then I turned around and returned to Yerushalayim because that's where I truly wanted to be.

☙

The summer had flown by, its sweltering temperatures tempered by the coolness of the Jerusalem night, even at the height of August. My friends had left. It was time to find a *yeshivah* for Elul zman. The options were limited. It wasn't like today where *yeshivos* abound like mushrooms on

---

\*   My takeoff on "*Va'yivaser Yaakov levado*" (Bereishis 32:25).

the forest floor after a good rain. No, things were different back then. A handful of *yeshivos*, a couple hundred *yeshivah bochurim*. How things have changed!

I decided on Yeshivas Chevron in Geula. Its huge room, with a ceiling that soared off into the distance, was filled with about two hundred young men all gesturing wildly. Chevron's distinguished *roshei yeshivah* and *mashgichim* were famous personages – Rav Chatzkel Sarna, Rav Meir Chodosh… The roar of Torah filled that room from morning till night like a giant tidal wave never ceasing its pounding of the shore. The *yeshivah* had experienced trauma in the past when they were still based in the ancient city of Chevron, not far from the Me'aras Hamachpelah, where our forefathers are buried. In the 1929 massacre, sixty-seven people, including twenty-three students of the *yeshivah*, had been brutally slaughtered in cold blood. Yet they had managed to rebuild. And now Chevron was a force to be reckoned with. This was where I decided to go.

The first *shiur* that Rav Chatzkel Sarna gave in *Pesachim* at the opening of the *zman* was an experience.

The room was packed, not an empty seat to be found. There was a sense of electricity in the air. He stood at the front of the room, his forehead creased, *sefarim* piled up on all sides.

Then he uttered three opening words: "*Or l'arbaah asar*" – the first few words of the first *mishnah* in *Pesachim*. Pandemonium erupted. It was as if a volcano had been lying dormant beneath the Chevroner building in the middle of Geula. A frenzy ensued. All at once everyone was screaming at one another, everyone fighting with everyone else. I'm looking around, not understanding what on earth is going on, and the whole time Rav Chatzkel is banging on his shtender. "*Rabboisai*," he's yelling, "*ich hub noch gornisht gezugt!*" (I still haven't said anything!).

I had never witnessed such a sight in my life. When the *rosh yeshivah* entered the *beis midrash* back home, a hushed silence filled the room, with everyone straining to hear his every word. America was light years away from the boys in Chevron and their tumultuous exuberance.

I threw myself into my learning, immersing myself in the sea of Torah and reveling in the age-old arguments of Abaye and Rava.

And then one day I met someone who sat and learned in Beit Harav on Rav Kook Street. I was subjected to a barrage of questions regarding my intention to remain in Eretz Yisrael.

"I'm here for a year, a year and a half. All my friends left before Elul *zman*, but I needed to stay here longer. I'll probably go back to the States in the middle of next year."

The next thing I knew I found myself sitting at a dining room table in a room right off the *beis midrash*.

*This looks like someone's private home*, I mused to myself. And indeed it wasn't long before a saintly-looking gentleman sat down beside me, opened a *sefer*, and began learning with me. It was the Sefer Hamitzvos of the Ramban and we were studying mitzvah *daled*, the fourth mitzvah, the one that the Ramban authoritatively states should have been mentioned by the Rambam but wasn't. It was the famous Ramban that discusses every Jew's obligation to conquer Eretz Yisrael and come live in the Land, and how the mitzvah applies at all times.

I didn't realize at the time – actually it took me thirty years to understand – that the saintly Jew with the luminous light on his face was Rav Tzvi Yehuda Kook, and it was he, of all people, who taught me about our obligation to live in and fight for Eretz Yisrael.

౿

My second encounter with the Brisker Rav took place before Sukkos, just a few months after the first. Being that I was planning to return to the States at the end of the year, I needed to know what to do regarding keeping the second day of *yom tov*. The Chevron Yeshiva building was located close enough to the Brisker Rav's home that I decided to just run over and ask my question.

I knocked on the door and someone let me into the house.

The Rav was learning at the table, obviously deep in thought, when I arrived. I waited patiently for him to realize that someone was there and eventually he looked at me with his sharp, penetrating gaze.

"Yes? What do you want?"

"I'm an American boy learning in Chevron," I began, "and I want to know what my halachic obligations are regarding the second days of *yom tov*."

This was his response: "*Vos fregstu mir shailos? Ich bin nisht kein posek; ich pasken nisht kein shailos. Gei fregst Hirsh Pesach*" (Why are you asking me halachic questions? I'm not a halachic decisor; I don't give decisions on such questions. Go ask Hirsch Pesach).

This was a reference to Rav Tzvi Pesach Frank, chief rabbi of Yerushalayim and one of the more esteemed *poskim* at the time. That was it. The audience was over. I nodded at the Rav, thanked him, and left the house.

Looking back at the incident, I seem to recall smiling inwardly to myself and saying, *Well, that's twice.*

I'd gone to the Brisker Rav for an answer but had instead received a directive to go to Rav Tzvi Pesach Frank. *Well, then*, I told myself, *I'd better heed the order and find out where the rabbi lives*. Yerushalayim of old was a hodgepodge of courtyards and *yeshivos*, cobblestone market squares and overgrown hedges. It was a simple world where luxury and ostentation were frowned upon. Everywhere one turned, one saw the little Yerushalmi boys in their black pants and white knitted *koppelach* playing and shmoozing on the corners and congregating in the entranceways of the shuls. The young girls all sported braids in their hair and walked primly alongside their mothers.

Rav Tzvi Pesach Frank resided on one of the Geula streets – Amos or Micha – and he received me graciously and with tremendous warmth. He then heard me out with infinite patience.

"Are you unmarried?"

"Yes."

"Here in *yeshivah*?"

"Yes."

"For how long?"

"About a year."

In the end he gave the "day and a half *psak*." This is how he put it: "If you found a *shidduch* here in Eretz Yisrael," he asked me, "could you conceivably remain here?"

"Yes," I replied. I was not opposed to settling down with an Israeli girl.

"In that case, you should keep a day and a half. The first day of *yom tov* you should act just like everyone else. On the second day, daven a weekday davening, but do not do any *melachah*, any work. And on the last day, put on tefillin in the privacy of your home. Do you understand?"

I nodded, thanked him for his time, and retraced my steps out toward the bustling Geula streets, at peace with my halachic status and full of admiration for the *rabbanim* of this incredible city. Here was the Brisker Rav, a scholar beyond belief, head and shoulders above the vast majority of Yerushalayim, yet unwilling to answer a halachic question because he "wasn't a *rav*." His humility was acute and I appreciated it in a way that never allowed me to forget my two encounters with him.

The children were still playing outside the apartment building when I left, and they moved aside as I passed through their ranks, closing naturally behind me, paying me no heed. I was merely an outsider invading their turf. Little did they know that the outsider would one day return for good.

I loved every inch of that neighborhood, every alleyway, courtyard, kiosk, *shtiebl*, and *mikveh*. This was Yerushalayim and the boy from Williamsburg felt as much at home in those narrow roads as he did back on Lee Avenue.

☙

Of learning there was much in Chevron Yeshiva; of food quite the opposite. Not that anyone went hungry, but there was no such thing as an abundance of anything back then.

I remember once searching for one particular student in the *yeshivah*, only to find that nobody knew exactly where he sat. Back then, students took up residence in *batei midrash* all around the Geula neighborhood and still called themselves "Chevroners." But I really needed to speak with this particular individual.

"What should I do?" I asked a veteran Chevroner for advice.

"Come to the dining room on Rosh Chodesh for lunch," he advised me. "He'll be there for sure."

"How do you know?"

"Just trust me on this."

I arrived at the dining room that Rosh Chodesh and found that the Chevroner had been correct; the entire student body was there. But what was so special about Rosh Chodesh? Simple: the *yeshivah* served chicken for lunch on Rosh Chodesh. One chicken for about sixteen people. And everyone made sure to put in an appearance for lunch on that day. In general there were only three foodstuffs that appeared with any regularity on our dining room tables: tomatoes, cucumbers, and watermelon. That's what made Rosh Chodesh so irresistible.

When I transferred to Ponevezh not long after, I was shocked to find that they were serving meatballs three times a week. Meat was still being rationed at that time. Back in Chevron, meat was nonexistent, while in Bnei Brak, they were serving it regularly. Someone finally took pity on me and explained the truth about the "*meatballim*" emerging from the *yeshivah*'s kitchen.

"*Atah Amerikai; atah lo meivin*" (You're an American; you don't understand how it works).

"So tell me."

"If you honestly want to comprehend these meatballs, you must take a good look at Bircas Hamazon."

"Why?"

"It says in benching, '*Hu nosen lechem l'chol basar*' [He gives bread to all flesh]."

"So?"

"The *yeshivah*'s cook puts leftover challah into the meat mixture and you have unlimited meatballs. *Hu nosen lechem l'chol basar*" (He puts bread in all meat). Those Ponevezhers were creative.

This was back in the fifties. Israel was struggling then – with everything. The security situation. A perilous economy. The lack of goods. Rationing. But despite the hardship and utter simplicity of life, the *yeshivah* boys thrived and eventually took their places as the *roshei yeshivah* of the future.

On a different occasion one of the older *bochurim* in Ponevezh approached me in the dining room. He grabbed my arm, looked me in the eye, and said, "*Atah poshut lo yodeia eich le'echol agvania*" (You simply don't know how to eat a tomato). Then he proceeded to show me exactly how one was supposed to do just that.

He selected a plump, red, ripe, juicy tomato with care.

Then he picked up a knife. Then a fork. He was all seriousness.

I watched as that Ponevezher began dissecting that poor tomato. He cut it in half and showed me both sides. Held them up to the light. He described the tomato to me as if it were a steak – the bones, the veins, the sinews and the meat. And then he consumed that vegetable with the same delight with which one consumes the most expensive cut of meat. That was how it was back then – barely any meat or chicken, one or two eggs a week for each student, and vegetables. That was the extent of our culinary adventures. And yet, we managed to learn with diligence and the *beis midrash* was packed day and night with students young and old.

The *bochur* I was searching for in Chevron was in fact there on Rosh Chodesh, having arrived for his sixteenth of chicken the same as the rest of the student body. Back then, the Torah world was poor, penniless, and poverty-stricken. Nobody possessed any wealth worth talking about. And today, look how we've grown and what we've managed to build: a Torah empire and a world of *yeshivos*. And all this despite the fact that we live in a secular state that is constantly being accused of waging war against Torah. It is precisely here that the greatest explosion of Torah study in history has taken place. It's a miracle, plain and simple.

# 5

# Ponevezh

Since I knew that my stay in Eretz Yisrael was to be brief, I felt the need to experience not only the wonders and quiet joys of Yerushalayim, but the simple life of the Bnei Brak Jew as well. It was for that reason that I decided to transfer to Ponevezh for the winter term and then to cap off my time in Israel back at Chevron. Chevron, Ponevezh, Chevron. There were many giants of the spirit in the *yeshivah* building on the hill and I wanted to meet and learn from them all.

The religious community in Eretz Yisrael of those days was not into materialism. Not even slightly. They lived the words of Chazal, "You should eat bread and salt, drink water in small measure and sleep on the floor" (*Pirkei Avos* 6:4), and exhibited genuine joy as they made their serene way through life. Many homes did not have real heaters, relying on portable ones instead, and while the Bnei Brak winters were nothing compared to the frigidness of a real, full-blown New York January, their summers more than made up for it with a blazing heat unlike anything I had ever felt. And just to be clear on the issue, the concept of air conditioning had not yet reached Israeli shores and certainly had not yet put in an appearance in modest Bnei Brak.

Fortunately, I was arriving to those hallowed halls after Elul and would not have to deal with the worst of the heat. But the mere thought of what the average Jew from Bnei Brak had to deal with…

Ponevezh was the jewel in the Bnei Brak crown. It sat perched on the top of the hill like the king of the city, and all its citizens paid it homage. The Bnei Brak apartment buildings were four stories tall and built on stilts, or two stories high and sat on the ground. Many of them were water stained from the Israeli winters, when rain gushed down endlessly, turning the narrow streets into swirling pools of oil-streaked water. Every home was a simple affair. The same speckled *balatot* (floor tiles). The same drab furnishings. Every neighborhood had its quota of shuls and leaders.

From the Chazon Ish to the Steipler to Rav Shach, it was a town of men who were larger than life. There were countless *yeshivos* and *batei midrash*. Work-hardened men with callused hands shared the benches in the corner shuls with soft-skinned scholars who had never held a tool in their lives. Their love for Torah brought them together.

It was at a crucial juncture in history, when Rommel's Afrika Corps were preparing for the invasion of Egypt and Eretz Yisrael, that the Rav purchased the hill where he eventually built his royal *yeshivah*. The British had completed plans to withdraw into Mesopotamia and leave the Jewish community in the hands of Hitler. The story is told that someone approached Rav Kahaneman and asked why he was building now when the Germans were knocking on the gates of Eretz Yisrael. The Rav asked, "How much longer until the Germans enter?" He was told, "Ten days."

So he said, "Then I have to build even quicker."

At the end of October 1942, the great battle of El Alamein began and at its conclusion Germany had suffered her first defeat of the war. Churchill ultimately declared, "Before Alamein we never had a victory. After Alamein we never had a defeat."

The Rav continued to build the *yeshivah* to completion and he carried on building for the rest of his life. All this after having lost his entire family in Europe. And this was where I wanted to go. To Ponevezh, one of the most critically acclaimed *yeshivos* in the world.

And so it was that I came to be walking down the street just adjacent to Yeshivas Ponevezh a few days after Sukkos. Bnei Brak was a tiny city, hemmed in by orange orchards on all sides. The air was calm and warm, a hint of summer still in the air, and mothers sat with their children in the parks as I approached the campus. I strode past dormitories to my right and dormitories to my left, and entered the main building on the wide marble staircase that was worn smooth by countless treading feet.

I found the office with little trouble.

Behind the desk sat a man with a harried expression on his face and mounds of paperwork to address. He had no time for me; that much was clear. I stood there in silence waiting uncomfortably, the boy from America in his gray suit and light-colored hat.

Eventually he glanced my way.

"Yes?" His tone was not encouraging.

I ignored the less than cordial welcome.

"I would like to come and learn in Ponevezh."

"No room. I'm sorry, we can't accept even one more boy."

"But I've come here from America and I really want to learn in Ponevezh."

"There's no room. I can't help you."

I had lasted in Ponevezh all of five minutes. Things were not looking good.

I exited the office without a plan of action. Boys were milling around outside the office and before I knew it I had made friends with one of them and was telling him my problem.

"Go outside," he instructed me, "and if you see a man walking down the street so immersed in his learning that he can bump into a street lamp and say '*Slichah*' (Excuse me), then you know you have the right person, the man you need."

"And who is he?"

"Rav Shach. He's the one who can help you get into Ponevezh."

So I went to find Rav Shach.

Rav Elazar Menachem Man Shach lived in a nearby apartment building, which I found after getting directions from a helpful passerby. The city was in a perpetual state of construction and the apartment was surrounded by sandy lots. I walked up the few flights of stairs and gave a confident knock on the flimsy door. A few moments later the door opened and I found myself face-to-face with the man who would go on to become the undisputed *gadol* and leader of the Israeli *yeshivah* world. He invited me into his home and offered me a seat. Then he asked me to tell him why I'd come.

I explained the entire situation.

"I see," he said. "Why don't we talk in learning for a while."

I agreed.

Rav Shach sat in his shirtsleeves and plunged into a *sugya* with complete familiarity, navigating the complex highways and byways as if he'd been there just a few minutes before. I joined in. Questions were asked; answers were suggested and mulled over. I was astounded by the depth and breadth of his knowledge. We spoke for a while, engrossed in the give-and-take.

All of a sudden Rav Shach arose. Grabbing his frock, he began slipping one arm into the long, black outer garment, while motioning for me to accompany him with the other hand.

"*Kum mit mir*" (Come with me), he said, and I dutifully followed him out the door and down the stairs. As we walked, Rav Shach was still slipping his other arm into the frock's second sleeve, motioning me to follow him to the apartment directly below – the home of Rav Dovid Povarsky, one of the other *roshei yeshivah* of Ponevezh. Within minutes we found ourselves sitting with Rav Dovid. Rav Shach said to him, "Accept this boy into the *yeshivah*."

And I was in. As simple as that.

I guess I did well on my test.

Rav Dovid notified the office and things moved very quickly after that. I was assigned a dorm room and soon enough I had a seat in the dining room and a chair and *shtender* in the cavernous *beis midrash*. I felt that I had done well for a day's work, if you know what I mean. Not only did Rav Shach get me into Ponevezh, he also told me that he wanted me to sit next to him in the study hall. I spent a lot of time in his proximity and had the opportunity to speak in learning with him.

For a period of time I was even his designated "cigarette lighter," lighting the cigarettes that he used to chain smoke until he was eventually informed that it was a health hazard. The Dubek tobacco company in

Bnei Brak manufactured about fifty brands of cigarettes, all terrible. Rav Shach favored two brands – Knesset Sheish or El Al. He'd usually cut the cigarette in half and save the second part for later. They were unfiltered. When he found out how bad they were, he stopped smoking. He quit just like that, because he was a man with iron self-control.

When at the end of that year I left Eretz Yisrael, in my luggage were the first two copies of his brand new *sefer*, the *Avi Ezri*, to reach the States. Of course the moment my Einstein-like older brother caught sight of them, he removed them from my care and put them under his protection, as older brothers are wont to do.

༒

Ponevezh had a large campus filled with many dormitories. Rav Shach had insisted that I be accepted to the *yeshivah*, but he hadn't said a word to Rav Povarsky about where he wanted me to sleep, so I was not granted accommodations in the main building. Instead I was provided with a bed in another out-of-the-way building which was called "Los Angeles." My guess is that someone from that city donated the funds for the building, but I never managed to verify that assumption.

I shared a room with a fine young man from Manchester named Leo Fulda, and we became fast friends over the next five months. He was a lovely person with wonderful *middos* and we really hit it off. There were three additional American *yeshivah* boys in Los Angeles besides myself. One of them, Avrohom Golombeck, later went on to serve as *mashgiach* in the Talmudical Yeshiva of Philadelphia for decades until his passing in 2008. He prepared himself for being the *mashgiach* by becoming the *vekker* – the boy whose job it was to wake up the students – of the Los Angeles dormitory. Every morning, you could hear him going from room to room, banging his stick on the doors, calling, "*Shtei off, shtei off!*" (Get up!). It was obvious even then that the vocation of *mashgiach* was in his blood.

The other Americans from LA ended up exchanging Ponevezh for Lakewood in the middle of the semester, and this allowed me to sleep a little more peacefully in the morning and left me as the sole American residing in LA.

As one of the few Americans learning in Ponevezh, I didn't exactly have a natural social group. I found the boys of Ponevezh to be sharp-minded, youthful gentlemen who were serious and focused in their pursuit of growth in Torah knowledge. But I was unhappy with the fact that the majority of the boys didn't go out of their way to befriend newcomers such as myself who had come from overseas. Almost nobody came over to say hello or to introduce himself, and that disturbed me. I decided to do something about it. One morning I stood at one end of the giant study hall and began introducing myself to every member of the *yeshivah*, one at a time.

"*Shmi Sholom Gold*," I'd begin. "My name is Sholom Gold. I came here from America to learn in Ponevezh. I studied in Torah Vodaath and Ner Yisroel. What's your name?"

And I did this over and over again.

By the time I went through half of the first row, the entire hall was silent, watching my every move through intent eyes.

By the time I had finished the first row, the message had spread throughout the entire study hall: here was one American who was not content to do his time and leave without getting to know the boys. No. I wanted to know them all. And from that day on, everything changed, the atmosphere thawed, and the inhabitants of Ponevezh became much friendlier.

During that year, I had a friend who was also learning in Ponevezh – Elazar Mayer Teitz, presently the *rav* of Elizabeth, New Jersey. We had been classmates in elementary school through the beginning of high school. Elazar Mayer had a good friend of his own in Ponevezh, Berel Povarsky, later to go on to become the *rosh yeshivah* there. At the year's end, Rabbi Teitz would join me at Ner Yisroel.

༄

Bnei Brak in general and Ponevezh in particular were filled with personalities. One such force that defied nature on a regular basis was the Ponevezher Rav, Rav Yosef Shlomo Kahaneman, the driving power behind the *yeshivah*. And although the Ponevezher Rav had to travel the world on a constant basis, his heart remained behind, in the study halls, hallways, dining room, and dormitories of his awesome institution. Whenever the Rav left Bnei Brak for some distant country around the world, he had a beautiful tradition, which makes me nostalgic even now, sixty years later.

The entire student body lined up in front of him. Hundreds of *bochurim* stood humbly, like children before their father, all waiting to be kissed goodbye. I can't even describe the intensity of his love for each and every member of his *yeshivah*. And when he returned, the same scene replicated itself. Everyone stood outside his apartment waiting for his arrival and then once again, every *bochur* received a kiss from the Rav. Such tenderness and warmth in that simple act.

When I decided to leave Ponevezh, I couldn't make my departure until I bade farewell to the Rav, who was abroad, in *chutz la'aretz,* at the time. When he returned, everyone lined up to greet him and receive a kiss. After all the *bochurim* had gotten what was coming to them and had returned to their seats in the study hall, I went in to see the Ponevezher Rav to inform him that I was leaving. The Rav wished me well and then he kissed me again. I had received two kisses in one day. I think I hold some kind of record in this area. Five kisses from the Ponevezher Rav — four when he came and went and one when I left the *yeshivah*.

But the most exhilarating kiss of all, the sixth one, only came later after I returned to Ner Yisroel. Suddenly, one day, there he was, the Ponevezher Rav, walking into the Ner Yisroel *beis midrash* on a visit to the States. He entered the packed room, a luminous smile on his shining face, and every single person in that room stood up for him.

And then he caught a glimpse of me.

Our eyes met, locked on to one another like a magnet.

And then he walked over and hugged and kissed me in the middle of Ner Yisroel, with the love of a father for a long-lost son coming home. I wouldn't have sold that kiss for a million dollars. The Ponevezher Rav knew me, he remembered me. I was a student of his. The utter joy, the bliss I felt at that moment, to know that I had managed to acquire a personal relationship with the Rav during my time in Bnei Brak.

☙

The years 1955–1956 were difficult ones for the tiny population of Eretz Yisrael. It was a poor – almost penniless – country, struggling to absorb hundreds of thousands of Jews from around the world, most notably from the Arab lands. The millions of neighboring Arabs, still having trouble coming to terms with the Zionist intruders, made their displeasure known by sending in the fedayeen from Gaza to kill and maim everywhere they could.

The daily news was horrendous. Absolutely terrible. Vicious Arab terrorists smuggled themselves into the children's dormitories on kibbutzim, murdering tiny children in cold blood. For the most part the Arab murderers arrived from the Gaza Strip, then under Egyptian control. (As you see, the more things change, the more they stay the same.)

It was a frightening time for everyone, and especially if you were a young naive America boy learning in *yeshivah*, in which case you hadn't grown up with this kind of life and didn't necessarily know how to handle the feeling of vulnerability, of living unprotected. A number of times during that fateful year, the American consulate notified their citizens spread out around the country that vessels from the Sixth Fleet were approaching Haifa shores to evacuate all Americans from Israeli shores due to the extreme danger.

The American students had a halachic query. What were we supposed to do in such a situation? Was it a situation of *pikuach nefesh* (danger to life) for us to remain in the country? Were we obligated to leave? Needing an answer, a delegation of Americans approached Rav Yechezkel Levenstein (known as Rav Chatzkel), the Ponevezh *mashgiach*, to ask his advice.

"I don't know what to tell you," Rav Chatzkel said to our concerned group, "but one thing I can say with complete clarity and assurance. If the Chazon Ish were still alive, he would tell you clearly, 'Stay here – don't leave Eretz Yisrael!'"

Everybody stayed. End of discussion. All urgent warnings by the American government with their navy boats were forgotten by one and all. Rav Chatzkel had spoken and the doubts had disappeared.

It was a year of wondrous learning and of delightful adventures as well. Some of them I experienced by myself, others in the company of a friend or two. This particular adventure began during one afternoon session in Ponevezh.

A good friend approached.

"The *zman* has been going on for a while and I'm feeling a little burned out."

I nodded thoughtfully. I couldn't deny feeling the heat myself.

"What do you say we leave for a day and get some fresh air, just to, y'know, recharge our batteries. A day off will give us the drive to carry on for the rest of the term."

It sounded good to me. Off we went.

The train station in Tel Aviv was crammed with a colorful array of individuals heading in every direction, up and down the country's coast. When the train came into the station, I caught a glimpse of the manufacturer's name and found myself slightly shocked.

The train had been built by a German firm.

It hit me and I stood there taken aback. At first I didn't understand what a German train was doing in the middle of Tel Aviv. After giving it some thought, I understood. Hadn't I read in the newspaper that Ben-Gurion had been holding meetings with the Germans regarding the concept of reparations? Germany had agreed to take responsibility for the evil it had perpetrated against the Jewish nation, and as a result the streets of Israel would soon be flooded with Mercedes automobiles and other German goods. But right now, the sight of a German-made piece of machinery was still foreign and distasteful to anyone who had suffered under their jackboot.

I wanted to know how the people of Israel would react to this. I arrived at the conclusion that the Israeli people – including the people on this train – had the right to know that German vehicles were transporting them to their destinations.

I fashioned some cardboard into a little square on which I wrote the word "Press." I then proceeded to stick that piece of cardboard into my hatband. In one instant, armed with just a piece of cardboard, I had in fact become "press."

I stood up and began to let the public know.

"Excuse me," I said to a group of older men sitting together, conversing quietly. "Did you know that you are currently riding on a German train?"

Their faces registered complete shock and dismay at the information I had just imparted. It took them a few seconds to comprehend what I was saying.

One of them spoke up. "Do you mean to say that this train," he said, his eyes roving around the cabin at the fine upholstered seats and well-made end tables, "this train was built by Germans?"

I heard pained outrage in his tone. "Yes," I confirmed. "How do you feel about that, sir?"

"How do I feel about that? I'll tell you how I feel about that. I spent time in a concentration camp not too long ago as a guest of the German government. I was transported there against my will on a train that was probably built by the same company that built this one. How do you think I feel about this?"

The more he spoke, the louder his voice was becoming.

Soon more people from the other side of the coach joined in.

"You mean to say I paid money to sit in a German train?" one middle-aged woman with glasses and a Magen David around her neck asked me heatedly. The news of the German train was greeted by a mixture of anger and scorn. The majority of the people on the train were very unhappy that their government would even consider allowing the Germans to make amends with money.

"It's blood money!" they shouted. And it was.

"But our economy is weak," someone interjected. "This will help strengthen it."

"But not by allowing them to ease their consciences with a payoff."

"Why not?" someone else screamed. "Let them pay, I say. Let them pay. Why not? They murdered us and gassed us and burned us. The least they can do now is pay us back; at least they'll be returning some of what they stole!"

The argument raged throughout the train. I had wanted to see the people's reaction. Well, I saw it, all right. It was fierce and powerful.

Most of the passengers wanted nothing to do with anything German; not their money or their goods. And to prove it, many disembarked at the next station in protest of the information they had just heard. I would not have been surprised if this incident made the news. I had not been trying to create such an uproar, but I did feel that the people had a right to know. They had been the ones to suffer under German rule and they deserved to know that they had been riding on a German train and were going to be deluged by German goods from now on.

I returned to my seat shocked by the emotion that roiled through the carriages and swirled upwards. Eventually things quieted down. Those who had elected to remain on the train retook their seats and fell asleep. It was late afternoon by the time we pulled into the station at Zichron Yaakov. We disembarked and made our inconspicuous way into the town. The government might have been intent on accepting money for repentance, but the people would have something to say about that. That much had been made clear on a journey one day to the Galil.

☙

Eventually we arrived in Tveria, a sun-baked city located on the shores of the harp-shaped Lake Kinneret, the Sea of Galilee. We walked through the busy streets, a warming sun on our backs, and the glistening blue waters of the lake a constant backdrop. We saw some black coats, incongruous among Tveria's mostly nonreligious population. On closer inspection, I was able to recognize the leader of the Charedi gathering.

It was Rav Amram Blau, chief anti-government protester.

I approached the assembled and inquired as to why they had come en masse to the holy city of Tveria. I was told that the city's municipality had approved a plan to move the Rambam's grave or to have some sort of highway going through the cemetery area, and Rav Amram and his *chevrah* had arrived to ensure that such a travesty did not come about. At the moment they were demonstrating right outside the *kever*, their shouts filling the afternoon air, intensely serious faces lending credence to their protest. Moving the Rambam's *kever* was no joke and nobody was laughing.

Since we were there, we decided to join the demonstration.

Two Americans from Ponevezh stood shoulder to shoulder with the black-coated gentlemen from Meah Shearim, protesting the local government's decision to move the Rambam's grave. There was much yelling and shouting from one side to the next, the chanting of Tehilim, the sight of the workers attempting to get ready to dig, the media cameras flashing – all in a day's work for Rav Amram Blau, the man whom the nonreligious considered the most fanatic firebrand of all.

Many people question whether these types of demonstrations have a purpose. But the fact remains that the Rambam's *kever* was never moved. We returned to Bnei Brak the following day, our wanderlust assuaged and our hearts and minds ready for more learning.

It had been my first meeting the soft-spoken Rav Amram and his firm convictions, but there would yet be another meeting, in Yerushalayim later on that year, after I had already returned there from Ponevezh. I was officially back in Yeshivas Chevron, but in reality I was studying for my *smichah* (rabbinical ordination test). The eighteen-hour days were making me bleary-eyed and causing my head to spin.

It was late Shabbos afternoon and I had been learning since noon that day. I suddenly felt I couldn't sit inside the confining walls of that room for even another second. Grabbing my jacket and hat, I left the premises and went for a little Shabbos stroll to clear my mind. The halachic concepts followed me right out the door and as I walked through the middle of the Geula neighborhood, my mind wouldn't cease replaying the *sugyos* of *nat bar nat, batel b'rov* and *nosen taam lifgam* (halachic terminology from the laws of milk and meat). The streets were filled with families heading in various directions, and I followed my feet, allowing them to lead me anywhere they wanted to go.

Inexplicably, they decided they wanted to take me toward the Brisker Yeshiva off Yeshayahu Street adjacent to Rechov Strauss. I strode forward, my mind whirling with thoughts, a feeling of Shabbos calm pervading my entire being. And then I caught sight of the protesters from Meah Shearim.

What was going on now?

What had occurred to rile them up and make them take to the streets?

And then I took another look around me and I knew. They were standing outside the Edison movie theater, which was preparing to sell tickets even though it was still Shabbos. And there stood my old friend Rav Amram Blau in line at the ticket seller's window to prevent it. The line surged forward, the ticket people accepting payment behind the windows, and then Rav Amram took his spot in front of the window and suddenly he was grabbing on to those bars and he wasn't going to move no matter what. *Chillul Shabbos* was taking place in the streets of Yerushalayim and Rav Amram Blau wasn't going to stand for it. He would protest even if they hit him. Even if they tried to kill him. No matter what. He would close down this house of idol worship if it was the last thing he did.

And then there they were: the police had arrived and they were descending on the demonstrating Yerushalmis as if they were the worst terrorists the State of Israel had ever seen. Out came the billy clubs, which the officers wielded with a kind of ferocious intent to harm. *Makkos retzach* – murderous, indiscriminate beatings. Everyone standing in the vicinity was fair game to be beaten. A scene out of a nightmare. Jewish police in a Jewish country, beating up the religious people who were protesting against Shabbos desecration in their neighborhood streets.

I stood there watching, overcome with sadness and pain.

Amid the Chassidim and Yerushalmis I stuck out like a sore thumb. Taller than most of those surrounding me, clad in my American suit and gray hat, my eyes unfocused from my intense studying and from the brutality that was taking place before my eyes, I must have been easy to identify as an American. So while Rav Amram and his Chassidim were being beaten, a painful message they absorbed with genuine *mesiras nefesh* (self-sacrifice), I was left alone. No policeman harmed me and no stick-wielding madman beat me. I was merely a spectator, there to bear witness to the unfairness of it all.

Rav Amram fought the battle for Shabbos and against the desecration of the graves and the autopsies and anything else that he deemed appropriate. As a result, he was beaten along with many of his followers.

Rav Amram is long gone, and it's been decades now since the Edison went out of business. For a long time it just stood there, silent testimony to the mayhem and wild battles that had taken place right outside its doors. And then one day recently the bulldozers rolled up to the ancient building and within a day it was nothing more than unidentifiable rubble, torn down, to be replaced with a development that would house young Satmar couples.

Looking back, it doesn't seem like Rav Amram lost the war.

Not at all. Poetic justice.

☙

I had come in contact with the Brisker Rav twice already and had been on the receiving end of some fiery reproof on both occasions. Firstly because I was out of *seder* during the month of Tammuz and secondly because I had approached him regarding a halachic query when he wasn't a *rav*. But I strongly felt that I needed to see him again. The Brisker Rav was one of the most righteous men of the generation, no question about it, and I wanted to recite the blessing one makes when beholding a truly wise individual.

It was obvious that the Brisker Rav, who had no time for anything other than learning, davening, and serving G-d, wouldn't stand for someone coming into his home to gaze at him long enough to recite the blessing. There was no question that such a thing was not going to happen. But there is always a way when you want something enough, and this was something that I wanted to do. I considered the matter and came to the conclusion that although I almost certainly wouldn't be able to recite this particular blessing in his home, there were other places to see him and say it. The only question was where.

Ponevezh had plenty of Yerushalmi students, and it didn't take me long to track down someone who lived near the Brisker Rav's home and was happy enough to impart his life wisdom to me.

"If I wanted to see the Brisker Rav," I asked him, "how would I go about it?"

"You mean to see him without entering his home?"

He scratched his chin and pondered the question for a minute, then suddenly snapped his fingers with excitement.

"The Brisker Rav leaves his home every night at about eleven o'clock for a walk."

There it was. I had received the information I needed and knew exactly what to do. All that was left for me to do was to board a *sherut* on a day that wasn't too cold or rainy and stake out a position down the block from the Rav's home. And that was exactly what I did.

I left Ponevezh at nine in the evening. That gave me sufficient time, in case there were delays or something went wrong. But the traffic was smooth that evening, the roads unclogged. Before long we were driving through the narrow streets of Yerushalayim, the stone buildings staring down at us. It was ten thirty when I descended from the taxi and strode forth into the darkness of Rechov Malchei Yisrael. I hadn't been away that long but it was good to be back, even though the street was lacking its usual hustle and bustle with all the people home or learning in shul.

I made my way through the serenity and peacefulness of the Yerushalayim night and turned right onto Yeshayahu Street, whose steep incline led toward the Edison, the Brisker Yeshiva, and other famous Yerushalayim landmarks. When I reached the corner of the Brisker Rav's street, I found a spot to wait for the Rav's approach. I had traveled for more than an hour for the privilege of reciting the blessing on his saintly face, but I still didn't know if the Rav was actually going to appear.

As I waited in silent reflection, the words of the *brachah* reverberating through my mind, my eyes scanning the street before me, carefully keeping the entrance to his house in my line of sight, I did not lose focus on my mission. At eleven o'clock, right on time, the Brisker Rav did indeed leave his apartment and passed close enough that I felt comfortable reciting the blessing.

As he entered my space, I concentrated deeply and recited the *brachah*, "*She'chalak mi'chochmaso l'yireiyav*" (Who imparted of His wisdom to those who fear Him). By the time I was finished, the Rav had already walked past me and was off on his nightly walk, never knowing that an anonymous student from Torah Vodaath and Ner Yisroel, whom he had strongly cautioned for being out of yeshivah during the summer months, had just recited a *brachah* over him, chalking up yet another experience in a year that he would never forget.

# 6

# Spring in the Air

Rosh Chodesh Adar. Happy days were upon us. Celebration was in the very air, and a feeling of festivity blanketed the *yeshivah*. But it wasn't enough for me. I missed the Purim atmosphere of Torah Vodaath, the vitality and merry liveliness of Ner Yisroel. Something had to be done and it was up to me to do it. These Bnei Brakers needed to be enlightened. They needed to be taught some appropriate music, and I was just the man to provide them with that. Hadn't I been the *baal menagen* (singer) of Ner Yisroel, after all?

On the Shabbos prior to Purim, I entered the dining room of Ponevezh with purpose in my gait. I strode forth to the center of the room and stood between two tables. And then I spoke up in a loud voice, gaining the attention of all the diners, who became quiet and filled with curiosity, no doubt wondering what that American wanted now.

"Purim is almost here," I proclaimed, "and I need to teach you something."

They stared at me as if I had fallen off the moon. What on earth was the American doing? What did he want from them? What on earth could he possibly teach them?

I ignored the looks.

"It's time for you to learn a very important song," I said. "The Modzitzer 'Shoshanas Yaakov.'"

I taught the entire *yeshivah* "Shoshanas Yaakov." I sang it once and then again. And before I knew it, the entire dining room had caught on and the sounds of song burst forth from hundreds of the Ponevezh students. Over and over again, until the very walls of the dining room seemed to be dancing to the tune. It was out of character, but that moment would never be forgotten by anyone who had had the good fortune to be present for the debut of the Modzitzer "Shoshanas Yaakov" in the building on the hill.

Years later I told my wife the story of how I stood in the middle of the dining room during the third meal of the Shabbos day and taught that beautiful song. She listened to the story and I thought she might have considered it an exaggeration. Rollicking song in Ponevezh? Almost impossible! And yet I knew it had taken place. Did she really believe me?

Decades later we were attending a rabbinic convention at a hotel in Yam Hamelach. There we were on the silent shores of the Dead Sea immersed in conversation when a man sitting nearby looked up at me. An impressive-looking individual. Our eyes met; nothing ignited. Then he did a double take, turned back to me, and looked at me again, with interest in those wise eyes. "*Atah Gold, nachon?*" (You're Gold, aren't you?).

"I studied in Ponevezh in 1955. I remember you were there that year."

I nodded, corroborating his timing, memories of that long-ago time flooding my mind in an intense rush of recollections.

"I'll never forget how you stood up in the middle of the dining room in a way that nobody had ever done before and taught us a new 'Shoshanas Yaakov' just in time for Purim. We'd never heard anything like it before and certainly never met anyone like you."

We shook hands. And I smiled at my wife as we walked away because finally I had proof for my version of events.

That wasn't the only time I taught a *yeshivah* the Modzitzer "Shoshanas Yaakov." I did it in Ner Yisroel as well. It wasn't as big a deal because in Ner Yisroel people liked to sing. They were used to singing. This was no Bnei Brak. This was a *yeshivah* where people sang and hummed and loved music. No. The big deal was the fact that I taught them that beloved *niggun* during the third meal of the Shabbos directly prior to Purim.

And why was that such a big deal?

Because the third meal of Shabbos was Rav Dovid Kronglass's hour and most certainly not a time for festivity. It was an hour of introspection and *mussar*, reproof and self-examination and reproach for the stains on one's *neshamah*. All was still as the holy Rav Dovid opened his pure mouth and spoke his soul. But that Seudah Shlishis was different. Because that's when I taught the boys the song.

Should I, shouldn't I? What was the right thing to do? This was a time for self-improvement, after all, not festive song. And yet, Purim was right around the corner. Then I made up my mind. In the middle of all that third meal solemnity I raised my voice to the rafters and sang "Shoshanas Yaakov" with all the enthusiasm and joy I could muster. Within moments a contagious and delightful spirit pervaded the Ner Yisroel dining room as every single mouth sang along full voiced and every heart leapt with the joy of the upcoming Purim miracle. Rav Dovid enjoyed the song. I had made the right decision.

There was one more time when I taught Ner Yisroel a song. Not before Purim that time. A completely different time of year. You could almost call it the opposite of Purim. It was during the month of Elul. The third meal on a Shabbos during the month of Elul, right before Rosh Hashanah. If Rav Dovid had us in tears on a normal Shabbos afternoon, imagine the intensity of the moment, the serious atmosphere of late Elul. Imagine the awesomeness that replaced our natural boyish exuberance as Rav Dovid quoted Chazal and explained to us with brilliant precision how our lives were meant to be lived.

I had composed a song, entitled "Palgei Mayim." I knew that it was the perfect musical score to precede Rav Dovid's talk. And yet how dare I sing at a time like this? Try as I might, however, I couldn't control myself, and I asked his permission to sing a tune. Permission was granted, and I sang "Palgei Mayim," my *neshamah* quavering with the majesty of the moment and the sanctity of the time. And the boys picked it up like a snap and soon enough the entire student body of Ner Yisroel was singing my song with every fiber of their beings, caught up in the emotion of that late Shabbos afternoon in Elul.

Once again Rav Dovid Kronglass appreciated my song.

"Whose song is that?" he asked me.

And I, too shy to tell him the truth, blurted out, "I think it's Carlebach."

He accepted that.

I guess having your song mistaken for a *niggun* by Carlebach is compliment enough.

༄

There were two Purims for me during that memorable year in Eretz Yisrael. The first was celebrated in Bnei Brak, to the sound and sight of intoxicated *yeshivah* students rowdily racing through the streets singing songs while balancing bottles on their cap-clad heads.

But the next day was Yerushalayim's turn.

How did one get to Yerushalayim on Purim in those days? One took the train, of course – a Purim train, filled to the absolute brim with boys in high spirits, singing, dancing, and telling each other Purim Torah thoughts about Haman, Mordechai, and Esther Hamalkah. That train was a sight to behold. I have never witnessed another train even remotely similar. The train began its upward climb into the foothills of Yerushalayim. Someone played a fiddle, another banged a drum, and a third serenaded his unwilling audience with his saxophone. And then we arrived at the old Jerusalem train station and everyone disembarked and dispersed to celebrate, each toward his own address and destination.

I had a friend in Ponevezh, Zalman Druck, who invited me to spend that Purim afternoon with him at a very special Purim *seudah* to which only select individuals were invited. It was to take place at the home of the chief rabbi of Israel, Rav Yitzchak Isaac Halevi Herzog.

The house was a prominent one located at the corner of Ibn Ezra and Keren Kayemet Streets, in a stately building that still stands to this very day. It was a well-furnished home with a very large living-dining room sporting a table that hosted at least fifty people. When we entered the room, almost every seat had already been taken by celebrated *talmidei chachamim, rabbanim* and businesspeople from Israel, South Africa, London, and many other places around the world. Rav Herzog was sitting at the head of that exclusive table, and he motioned Zalman and me to sit beside him, granting us the perfect spot to view the scene before our eyes. Politicians, talented people, writers – you name it, they were there. We feasted our senses on that elegant room filled with such powerful men.

And then, all of a sudden, a man entered the dining room and a hushed silence descended on the assemblage.

Chaim Herzog.

Rav Herzog's son was one of the most important, imposing, and famous men in Yerushalayim at the time. Handsome, charismatic, and effortlessly influential, Chaim Herzog was the British-trained Israeli military commander of Yerushalayim at a time of great danger to the state. The fedayeen, Arab terrorists, were infiltrating the young state every chance they had, night after night, in the buildup before the war with Egypt in 1956. With time, the IDF created a special unit tasked with the role of preventing the fedayeen from entering Israel's cities and towns. This unit was headed by the fabled Ariel Sharon and was called Unit 101. They went on the offensive and paid the terrorists visits in their own homes in their villages in Gaza and even across the border in Syria and Jordan.

At any rate, Chaim Herzog came into the room in full battle dress, wearing what was then called an Eisenhower jacket. He was an impressive presence without meaning to be. When he entered a room, people's heads turned. That was Herzog, future president of Israel. He took a seat at the middle of the table, between the rabbi of some foreign city and a famous manufacturer.

The father met the eyes of his son halfway across the endlessly long table.

"Chaim'l," Rav Herzog said, his voice warm and fatherly, his demeanor welcoming. "Come here, Chaim'l." Rav Herzog motioned his son to join him across the room.

And Chaim'l Herzog arose from his place and made his way around the backs of some of the richest and most powerful men then living in the country, until he reached his father who was waiting for him at the head of the table. Chaim Herzog stood before his father with tremendous respect and *derech eretz*, and Rav Herzog was all love for his son.

"Chaim'l," said the Rav, and now he was pointing at me, "do you see this young man?"

Chaim'l listened intently to his father's words with the utmost respect, like a student before his master.

"He came all the way from America," his father went on. "Say *shalom aleichem*."

The famous Herzog reached over and gave me *shalom aleichem*.

Rav Herzog spoke, and I could hear his longing and anguish for the son who had broken ranks and become great in another world, on a road that should never have been chosen.

"Chaim'l," he said again, "this young man came here from across the ocean because he wanted to learn Torah in Eretz Yisrael."

He was sending a message to his son. The message was clear. Torah was the most important thing. Not politics, not the military. My heart aches when I recall that story, because here was a father, one of the most influential *rabbanim* in the world, showing his love for his Chaim'l while trying to impress upon him the unspoken joys and delights of Yiddishkeit. How sad it was. Yet on the other hand, the love he showed his son, despite the fact that he hadn't chosen to follow in his father's path, was moving in its depth and poignancy.

Chaim Herzog went on to an illustrious career in the State of Israel, culminating with his service as president. Yes, he did great things, but not great enough for his father, the Rav. I never forgot that Purim *seudah*. That wasn't my final meeting with Rav Herzog either. I'd still have another much more significant encounter. But that would only happen later on that year.

֍

P'eylim. This was *the* organization in those days. Every *yeshivah* student was either a member of P'eylim or wanted nothing more than to be a member. P'eylim did things that no one else could. P'eylim's goal was to make contact with the hundreds of thousands of *olim* from all over the world. The Israeli government had spared no expense populating their country. In fact, one entire department of the country's fledgling intelligence apparatuses was devoted solely to the goal of transporting hundreds of thousands of Sephardic Jews from Morocco, Yemen, and Iraq. These were legendary operations performed by courageous spies. In the end, the government succeeded in ferrying a huge number of Jews from around the world to the State of Israel, a development that allowed the government to bulk up the army and populate the land.

Many of these mainly Sephardic Jews ended up in the *maabarot*, the transit camps. These were development towns that were built overnight for mass resettlement of the penniless Mizrahi Jews. Unfortunately the secular forces saw a golden opportunity to turn these naïve, innocent Jews into their version of the new Jew, which meant ensuring that they shed their religious practices. There was no funding for shuls or *mikvaos* for these communities, or anything Jewish for their youth. Instead the government attempted to entice the Sephardic children toward the kibbutzim and the army, and along the way to those places, all vestige of religious life almost always fell to the wayside.

Here began to unfold before my eyes the tragic mistake made by religious Jewry in not coming en masse to Eretz Yisrael in the fifty years prior to the establishment of the state. If the religious Jews of Europe had come to Palestine along with the nonreligious Zionists, things would have been different, because we would have acquired more power and had more of a role to play in government politics. The vast majority of Europe's Jews unfortunately remained behind, and the State of Israel's power was consequently concentrated solely in the hands of a few, who were almost to a man secular and certainly not friends of the religious world. We continue to pay for that fatal historic error. What is even more unfortunate is the fact that the *frum* community has not yet risen to the challenge of Eretz Yisrael.

The time has come for the American Torah-observant community to board Nefesh B'Nefesh* flights in their tens of thousands every year

---

\* We owe a great debt of gratitude to Rabbi Yehoshua Fass for establishing Nefesh B'Nefesh. Coincidentally, he was born and raised in West Hempstead.

on their way home. The steady but modest flow of *olim* should become waves and waves of Jews, leaving the *galus* behind and taking their place as active participants in the great passion of our time. What a supreme *kiddush Hashem* it would be for the world to behold: masses of Jews choosing to leave comfort and affluence and embarking on the great journey that began four thousand years ago when Avraham Avinu left Ur Kasdim. I pray to see it in my days. The time has come.

In any case, in Eretz Yisrael in 1956 P'eylim entered the picture to help counter the leftist agenda that was being forced on new immigrants. P'eylim had no problem recruiting volunteers to assist in the organization's myriad activities, because what young man didn't want to be involved? I too wanted to take part in this magnificent mitzvah and volunteered for P'eylim, offering to do whatever they needed of me. And that's why I ended up, along with another student who'd serve as my partner, in the P'eylim office in Tel Aviv on Erev Shabbos Hagadol 1956.

Our contact at P'eylim informed my partner and me that we would be traveling to Dimona – of all places – for that year's Shabbos Hagadol. At the time we were sent by P'eylim to visit Dimona, there was nothing in that tiny town amid the desert sand dunes but a few rows of small houses that served as pitiful dwelling places for the refugees from the Arab lands. Other than that, the place was devoid of life and as empty a landscape as I would ever lay eyes on.

The main office in Tel Aviv had outfitted us with the standard P'eylim kit provided to its volunteers: a tin can of sardines, a box of matzah, and a bottle of red wine. It wasn't much but it would have to last us. We traveled down country to Dimona and when we alighted from that rickety bus, I shaded my eyes from the glaring sun and thought how I had never seen such a forsaken place in my life. The people of Dimona were almost all from North Africa, had been religious back in North Africa and were still trying now. But it was extremely difficult for them here, with no support.

They welcomed us as honored guests and offered us all manner of delicacies. We davened in their makeshift shul among the windswept dunes. The tunes they used might have been unfamiliar to us, but the undeniable warmth emanating from each and every one of them was contagious and made me smile.

And of course the volunteers from P'eylim were given the grand tour. Along the way, I noticed a nearby ditch that had been dug into the rocky ground and I asked our guides what it was for.

"Well," they replied, "we started digging that ditch so as to construct a *mikveh*, but the authorities stopped us from completing it."

Talk about religious coercion!

Coming from the United States, I was of course most indignant about the lack of religious acceptance that was being exhibited on the part of the local officials and suggested that come Sunday morning, we make a demonstration championing the cause of the Dimona *mikveh*, to take place right outside the Dimona *beit knesset* at the open hole of the *mikveh*.

And a demonstration did indeed take place.

I would have loved to have been able to alert the media to our immediate intentions. But alas, there were no cell phones in those days and no landlines from Dimona either. National telephone dialing between Israel's three major cities, Jerusalem, Tel Aviv, and Haifa, was introduced only in 1957. We were light years away from civilization, with no way to tell anyone what we were about to do. So why hold a demonstration at all? To alert the local authorities to the idea that the game had changed and that they would now be held responsible for their reprehensible actions. It would also serve as encouragement for those poor immigrants to keep fighting for what they deserved.

Sunday morning dawned bright and warm. It is always bright and warm in Dimona that time of year and the majority of the rest of the year as well. We gathered everyone together at the *mikveh* ditch where my P'eylim partner and I proceeded to deliver some inspirational speeches regarding those who dared stand in the way of building a *mikveh* and what they would have to look forward to.

In the middle of my speech, who should show up? None other than a local group of toughs-for-hire. The kind of guys I would not have wanted to meet in a dark alleyway. They began to approach us with murder in their eyes. They did not take kindly to some American

P'eylim activist from Bnei Brak coming to Dimona and disturbing the equilibrium they'd been working so hard to lay in place. In fact they wanted to rip me limb from limb. I found myself at a loss right then. They were going to beat me senseless and leave me lying bloody and half dead on some far-off sand dune.

But suddenly a light bulb turned on and I knew what I needed to do. I reached down to my front shirt pocket and quickly removed my American passport, which I proceeded to hold up in the air for everyone to see. The famous green (it was green then) passport of the United States of America. The moment the Dimona mafia caught sight of that little green book held aloft in my hand, the dangerous look in their eyes abated and they backed off, leaving me with bones intact and the people of Dimona with the feeling that they would live to fight another day.

And that, my friend, was my adventure in the desert city of Dimona.

☙

I spent Pesach that year at the home of Rav Elya Kushelevsky in Bayit Vegan. I enjoyed myself immensely as I always did at the home of my adopted family. I of course had to celebrate a second Seder, but Rav Elya made sure that I wouldn't be celebrating alone. He joined me for much of that Seder, watching with a smile as I drank my wine, ate my *maror* and matzah, sang my songs, and recited some Torah thoughts on the Haggadah. As always Rav Elya wasn't content to merely provide me with a home and bed where I could rest my head, he guided me through the Seder, telling me what I had to do and what not to do. The Kushelevsky home was warm and welcoming, the perfect place to spend a Pesach far from family.

# 7

# THINGS TURN SERIOUS

In the months leading up to the war in 1956, the security situation in the country deteriorated by the week. Unit 101 was doing an admirable job, but even they couldn't prevent the increase in danger. Just when it seemed that things couldn't get any worse, they did.

One day I had to go to Tel Aviv. Back then when one wanted to get to Tel Aviv and wasn't in the mood for a bus ride that lasted forever, one took a *sherut*. The classic *sherut* was a limousine-style taxi that had three rows and seated three people per row, plus the driver. You simply showed up at the *sherut* stand, waited until you had enough people for a ride, and you were off. On that particular day I arrived at the *sherut* stand just as a *sherut* was leaving Yerushalayim, which meant that I had to wait for the next taxi to fill up.

We left the station and made our way through the neighborhood streets that would take us out of Yerushalayim and onto Highway 1 to Tel Aviv. Malchei Yisrael, Sarei Yisrael, the streets flashed past. Soon we were almost out of the city, but suddenly we ran into massive traffic. Nobody knew why. We looked at each other, the scent of danger in the air. Back then almost nobody had a car and the streets were usually empty, but today we were inching along bumper to bumper.

There were many soldiers, policemen, and emergency vehicles at the entrance to Yerushalayim when we arrived. Crowds were running everywhere trying to figure out what was going on. And through it all, our *sherut* kept inching forward, trying to nose its way out of the mass of vehicles and pedestrians. Finally we came upon a sight that chilled me to the very marrow.

It was the cab I had missed by about twenty seconds. The cab that had been pulling out of the station when I arrived, panting and out of breath. It was now a wreck at the side of the road.

It had been shot up by terrorists and lay on its side bloodied and destroyed, while the ambulance and the *chevra kadisha* went about their heartbreaking labor. I was hit by the knowledge that I had come this close to ending my life on the slopes of the heavenly city. But G-d had been looking out for me and I came through that day unharmed.

It was incidents such as these that were turning the country on its head and instilling fear in every heart. If a person couldn't even take a ride to Tel Aviv without the fear of being shot on the way, then the State of Israel had been completely compromised. Something was going to give; the only question was when.

That wasn't the only time I had a close call involving a taxi.

Another time during the year I had to leave Yerushalayim. Clearly not having learned my lesson, I once again took a taxi from Yerushalayim to Allenby Street in Tel Aviv. The trip passed uneventfully and we entered the seething streets of Israel's busiest city without having any idea that there was something seriously amiss with our taxi cab.

We eventually approached the taxi stand on Rothschild Boulevard.

I remember the scene like yesterday.

The station was deserted. Not a man in the vicinity. Empty. Forlorn. Most unusual for Rothschild Boulevard in the middle of the day, a street that normally teemed with people going about their business.

There were only a few soldiers, who appeared to be waiting for us.

The moment we pulled up at the station, the soldiers came running over and began yelling at us, "GET OUT OF THE TAXI! NOW! RUN! THERE'S A BOMB IN THE TAXI!"

We didn't waste time. It was the quickest exit I ever made in my entire life. I got out. I ran. I didn't look back.

And I never forgot the fact that though army intelligence had received reports that there was a bomb hidden in the taxi that was transporting me from Yerushalayim to Tel Aviv, we, the passengers, had no idea. Miraculously, nobody was harmed. Once again, I escaped with my life to *bentsh gomel* (the blessing recited upon deliverance from danger) and thank G-d for having granted me the opportunity to live and repay His kindness.

So when I say that the security situation was deteriorating, you can trust me on that. It was.

☙

Pesach was over. The new *zman* was slated to begin shortly when an announcement was made letting all *yeshivah* students in Yerushalayim know that the semester would be beginning a week late this year.

Every *yeshivah* student in Yerushalayim was being sent out to dig ditches around the city's perimeter by order of the leaders of religious Eretz Yisrael. Everyone was assigned another area to dig. Today as I attempt to pinpoint exactly where we dug I find it hard to do so, because it was all no-man's land back then and I have no point of reference. All I remember was that we were taken beyond the borders of Yerushalayim and made to dig for hours on end. It could have been Ramat Eshkol (now a neighborhood of Jerusalem), for all I know.

The problem was that the ground was all rock. Whereas today anyone digging through this kind of ground would be using earth movers and bulldozers, we, the scrawny *yeshivah* students, were digging by hand. Sometimes we came across a rock that was so deeply embedded, so utterly entrenched in the soil that it took us a few hours just to get under the stubborn boulder. And then, when we were finally successful in clearing away the earth, we'd need to actually move the rock and it could take fourteen men to hoist it up as if we were a human crane. And this was especially difficult considering we were not used to manual labor. We were white-collar people with soft, clean hands who were suddenly working hard and developing major muscles, blisters, and calluses from the physical exertion.

The purpose of the ditches was to provide a means of moving troops undetected around Yerushalayim in case of war. An entire network of ditches was dug by the *yeshivah* students of Yerushalayim who were anxious to do their part for the upcoming war effort.

In the midst of all the labor, tragedy struck. The Jordanians were obviously not overjoyed about the intense activity taking place right across the border, and they showed this by bringing in snipers to shoot at us and cause anxiety and mayhem. Most of their shots went nowhere, but one Jordanian sniper managed to shoot a *yeshivah* student named Glatzer, killing him on the spot. Glatzer was a *madrich* in Merom Tzion, and his death caused a hue and cry. His funeral took place that same day, and when his body was carried out to be buried, everything in the entire city stopped. All Yerushalayim ceased working when Glatzer was carried out to the cemetery. The entire city mourned in one collective, primeval outcry of deep sadness. He was a wonderful fellow, and that's the way he will remain in my mind forever.

༄

I returned to Yeshivas Chevron for my final *zman* in Eretz Yisrael. Ponevezh had been a once-in-a-lifetime experience and time well spent, but I was ready to return to the coolness of Yerushalayim, its ancient streets, stooped old men in flat velvet hats and busy *shtieblach* filled with a wide assortment of craftsmen, businessmen, and youngsters all filling the air with their endless singsong. The Chevroner study hall was as crowded as ever, but this time I was ready for something different. I had heard about a select group of fellows who were studying for *smichah*, and I thought to myself, *Well, why not me?*

Why not, indeed?

I had another reason for wanting *smichah* as well. I knew that if I were to receive ordination from a famous rabbi in Israel, it would make my mother – who was ailing at the time – a happy and proud woman. She'd be able to tell all her friends that her son had become a rabbi in Israel. In fact, one of the first things I did after receiving my ordination was to take a picture of it and mail it to my mother in the States to show all her friends. It would be the ultimate gift I could give her.

The process was as follows: study day and night until ready for the comprehensive test, and then present yourself to the chief rabbi of Israel, Rav Herzog, for his examination. There was an older student learning in Chevron at the time who was known as someone who was intimately familiar with all the laws of *basar v'chalav*, *taaruvos*, and *melichah*. His entire life – his complete existence – was *Yoreh Deah*. He was prepared to study with anyone looking to get *smichah*. He'd guide you through the labyrinth of material and provide technical support.

And so I made the decision and went for it. I began learning with the *smichah* expert. We studied together for about an hour a day, and the rest of the time was spent reviewing and going ahead by myself. And that was what I occupied myself with eighteen hours a day for the next three months until my head was exploding with *Yoreh Deah*. I rented a tiny room at 4 Ovadia Street and there I remained, living in satisfied bliss with my *Shulchan Aruch*. Just me and him. And I learned and learned and learned from morning till night, as the day dawned and children passed my window on the way to school, and in the afternoon as they came streaming past my humble domain, and deep into the night, as the streets became still and only the faint sound of Jews learning carried on the sometimes silent and decorous, sometimes harsh and unyielding winds of the holy city.

And learn though I might and learn as I may, I didn't step foot into Chevron, knowing that in the *yeshivah* world the object was about learning for the sake of learning, not for the piece of paper. I enjoyed this type of study very much. Learning practical *halachah* was a completely different style of learning from what I had been used to. I found it invigorating and challenging.

There were another five or six *bochurim* studying for *smichah* at the same time as I, all of us preparing for the moment when we would present ourselves to the chief rabbi and receive the documents attesting to our proficiency in Jewish law. This document was our license to practice, so to speak, and vital if one wanted to make one's living as a rabbi. But then crisis struck with a bang.

A certain American *bachur* had requested *smichah* from Rav Herzog, who had turned him down due to his lack of knowledge. The American, upset by the rejection, had reacted by yelling at the chief rabbi. The response was not long in coming. Rav Herzog decided that Americans would no longer be granted rabbinical ordination by him. This was a stunning blow to all those who had been diligently studying for their tests, only to be turned down at the zero hour. Nobody knew what to do. In the end after meeting and discussing the dire situation, the assembled came to the unanimous decision to send one of us in to Rav Herzog to convince him to change his mind. I was elected.

I had been a visitor at Rav Herzog's home not long before. I was recognized by those attending the Rav and allowed in to see him. But they let me in with misgivings, knowing as they did that I was an American and fearing that I hadn't just arrived for an innocent visit. In fact, the secretary kept the door slightly ajar, so he could listen to what I was saying to Rav Herzog and interrupt if need be.

"What can I do for you?" The Rav sat there stroking his beard, a kind smile on his face.

"I would like to be tested for *smichah*," I replied.

Immediately the door was thrown open and the secretary came storming into the room, executing his role of protector to the Rav.

"No *smichah* for Americans," he bawled, "no *smichah* for Americans!"

Rav Herzog calmed the irate secretary down and gently shooed him from the room. Then he told me what I needed to do to complete the ordination process.

"You must go to be tested by one of my rabbis," he explained. "A tremendous scholar. He'll test you. Rav Yosef Shalom Elyashiv," he continued, "tests every *smichah* candidate in the laws of *Yoreh Deah*."

He gave me directions to Rav Elyashiv's home in Meah Shearim, and told me what day to present myself and at what time. I wrote down all the information and returned to my tiny room on Ovadia Street to cram another thirty hours of learning into my already overcrowded brain.

The day of my *bechinah* finally arrived. I woke up early, my brain wired and too excited to sleep. This was the big day. The culmination of months of intense study, countless hours spent in that tiny room, my interaction with other humans cut down to the bare minimum. It had been a wonderful time in my life. I had absorbed a mountain of knowledge and was now ready to be tested on it all.

Unbeknownst to me, something totally unexpected was happening around Yerushalayim on that fateful day. A civil defense exercise was in operation. Who would've believed it? What this meant was that the Defense Ministry was treating the city of Yerushalayim as if it were under attack right then and there, and nobody was allowed out of doors while the exercise was going on. This was a catastrophe for me.

I needed to present myself at Rav Elyashiv's home today. Being an American meant it hadn't been easy for me to obtain an appointment for a test and I wasn't about to miss my chance. Not I.

But walking the streets was forbidden. In fact, not only were the city streets out of bounds for civilians, but any civilian caught outside was immediately considered a "casualty of war," thrown down onto a gurney, flung into an ambulance, and sent off to the hospital for observation, exactly as if they were treating real injured civilians. What to do? Should I risk taking to the streets? I thought it over and arrived at the conclusion that come what may, I was putting in an appearance at Rav Elyashiv's home, where he would test me and hopefully declare me sufficiently competent in Jewish law to become a rabbi in Israel.

But how to get myself there?

And so I discovered that I had what it took to become a spy, for that was exactly how I maneuvered myself through the tiny, curving alleyways of Yerushalayim. I set out moving forward a few small steps at a time. I could hear the sirens of war and the sounds of the loudspeakers warning the populace to remain inside. But that was not a luxury being afforded to me. I couldn't do that. I had to move. I slid through the alleyways, managing to avoid the eyes of a pair of neighboring guards patrolling nearby. The moment they passed me by, sharp eyes prowling further, I was on my way, moving forward to the next adjacent alleyway. I imagined myself in the middle of a war, bombs falling on every side, while I evaded them all and ran from ruin to ruin to learn Torah.

The children of Yerushalayim unknowingly assisted me with my scheme. For them it was as if the circus had come to town. Ambulance after ambulance traversed the narrow Geula and Meah Shearim streets, searching for "injured parties," and the Yerushalmi kids made sure they found them. Boy, did they make sure. Like a storm of locusts, the kids swarmed through the streets, laughing as the emergency crews swooped down on them. Even as one child was caught, another twenty ran off hooting and catcalling as the exasperated wardens tried to catch them all with little success. The poor fellows didn't know what they were up against. They never stood a chance.

The children they managed to snatch probably arrived at school on the morrow with a wonderful story to tell about how the wardens had caught them, strapped them down to a stretcher, and thrust them into the waiting ambulances, which sped off, transporting them on the greatest, most thrilling ride of their young lives, sirens blaring in the direction of the nearest hospital, where they were kept under observation for a while and then released. How can I ever forget the tinkling laughter of the Yerushalmi kids, their braying voices serving as camouflage for my slow advance, protecting me against the ever vigilant wardens who were searching for people just like me, outside in a time of attack. And yet, not one saw me.

I crouched down beneath a stairwell and ducked my head behind a wall while the kids sang and danced, merrily evading their pursuers. And eventually, creeping painstakingly from one alley to the next, I reached the alleyway that Rav Yosef Shalom Elyashiv called home and I entered the foyer of his simple apartment building with a sigh of relief at my good fortune. I had managed to evade the stretchers. I was here. I was about to take my test. That was when the butterflies returned in full force. The moment of truth had arrived.

I knocked on the door and found myself being invited into the house of the man who would go on to become one of the leading rabbinical authorities of his generation.

Rav Elyashiv sat me down at the table in his simple dining room. A crocheted cloth covering protected the table. *Sefarim* were everywhere. It was a house of Torah. Rav Elyashiv was ready for me. He allowed me to catch my breath and then the examination commenced. The Rav's knowledge was incredible, his grasp of the material all-encompassing. His eyes were sharp and his questions rapid. He gave me as much time as I needed to think things over. No pressure. All in all, I knew the material. I had been studying eighteen hours a day for months. I had all the information at my fingertips.

The test continued for about three quarters of an hour. He asked me thirty questions in total. I got twenty-nine of them right. One I got wrong. A question about soap. I knew I was wrong the moment I gave my answer. I berated myself inwardly, not comprehending how I had managed to forget something I had learned so many times. But there it was. I had made a mistake. I didn't allow my error to throw me off track and did not make another one. Still, my heart pounded even quicker now. Did the fact that I had made a mistake mean I would be denied my *smichah*? Had I lost the battle and the war? What was going to happen? Thirty questions. One wrong. Surely that wasn't so bad? I waited tensely to hear his decision. Now what?

Rav Elyashiv took out a pen and wrote a recommendation for Rav Herzog.

I waited silently, nervously. What had he written on that piece of paper?

I watched his every move with eagle eyes. It didn't take him long. Soon he finished. Then he removed an envelope from a drawer and slid his handwritten memo inside. I waited in tense anticipation. Would he seal the envelope or leave it open? If he left it open I would be able to read his decision. If he sealed it shut, I would not.

He left the envelope open.

I thanked him for his time. We shook hands and I left his home, my heart no longer pounding in my chest. It seemed to me that I had done okay. The envelope was open. I could have read his words if I so desired, but I passed on the temptation. I didn't feel comfortable reading his private letter to Rav Herzog, figuring if I was meant to know what the Rav had written, Rav Herzog would tell me. But my nervousness had disappeared. I had done well. I knew it. One mistake was no big deal. Surely I had received high marks.

The civil defense exercise was over by the time I exited his home. The streets had reverted to their normal everyday atmosphere. People rushed here and there, all intent on their business, none knowing or caring that a young student had just been subjected to the test of his life by the future leader of the generation. I ran through the alleys to the home of Rav Herzog. I needed to present him with the envelope, recommendation unread. I needed to see his face, to hear the answer.

I left the familiar confining alleys of Meah Shearim behind me as I reached the leafy stillness of Rechavia and the home of Rav Herzog.

I handed Rav Herzog Rav Elyashiv's letter. He slipped the letter out of the envelope and read it from beginning to end.

After he'd finished reading, he asked me a question.

"How many *masechtos* [tractates of Talmud] do you know?"

He was going to test me as well.

"Eight." The *masechtos* I had studied over the last few years. I was comfortable and familiar with their concepts, their *sugyos*. He asked me two questions on each of the *masechtos* I had learned. Then he took out his stationery and began penning his *smichah*. I was about to receive *smichah* inscribed on the stationery of the chief rabbi of Israel.

And then came a shock.

He had just finished writing the first sentence of my ordination, when he picked up the pen and scrawled a thick line through his opening words, effectively ruining what he'd already written.

"*Nein!*" he cried without warning.

I sat there stunned, utterly shocked. I felt crushed. Rav Herzog was a gentle, quiet man, who never raised his voice. What had caused him to act like that? Had he changed his mind? Was I in fact not going to receive my *smichah* in the end?

He looked at me. I was white as a sheet. He said the following thrilling words. "Rav Elyashiv described you with the words 'Harav Hagaon,' so I too must write 'Harav Hagaon.'"

Rav Elyashiv had written a glowing letter about me. I caught my breath, couldn't believe my ears. How had I merited such an honor? Rav Herzog began writing again and this time he carried through to the end.

The line Rav Elyashiv wrote that I was most proud of went as follows: "*Yesh lo yideah makifah u'brurah b'hilchos issur v'heter*" (He has a clear and all-encompassing knowledge in the laws of what is prohibited and permitted).

That was not a line one heard every day. Rav Herzog handed me my rabbinical ordination and I left his home, feeling like I had just won the hundred million dollar lottery. It had been a day to remember for the rest of my life and I still recall every detail.

~

By the time August rolled around I was already preparing to return to the States. As much as I would have liked to remain for a longer period of time, I simply couldn't. My mother was ill and it was clear to all concerned that I should go home. The fact is, I had stretched my time in Eretz Yisrael to the limit and now I felt a sense of urgency to get back to Williamsburg before it was too late.

With my heart full of emotion and already missing Eretz Yisrael, I packed my bags and bade my farewells to all the wonderful people I had had the good fortune to meet during my time in the Land of the Jewish people. When the day of departure finally arrived, I boarded a train along with all my luggage and rolled along the tracks to Haifa and the port from where I'd be reboarding the *Messapia* for my return journey. The train ride to Haifa passed way too quickly for me. Before I knew it we were pulling into the train station and it was time for me to alight along with all my luggage, my *sefarim*, and the precious *smichah* that Rav Herzog had written out for me and which I treasured with all my heart.

A short time later I found myself shlepping all my luggage onto the *Messapia* and into my cabin, where I tried to make myself comfortable within the small confines. But my heart was lonely and dismal at the prospect of leaving my beloved Eretz Yisrael and I felt an acute sense of loss. When would I see Yerushalayim again? Tzfas? Tveria? Kever Harambam? Meron? I looked around at the cabin walls and felt like they were closing in on me with claustrophobic tightness. I couldn't stay in that cabin a minute more.

Locking the door behind me, I returned to the deck and spent the next hour studying the Haifa skyline, trying to embed every detail in my memory. And then came a surprise. About an hour or two before the *Messapia* lifted anchor and exited the harbor, a group of my friends from Ponevezh suddenly materialized on the Haifa dock. Somehow they had heard that I was leaving and had come to say goodbye. All the way from Bnei Brak to Haifa. Who says Litvaks are cold?

I walked down the gangplank and was surrounded by the entire group, who wished me well and shook my hand and sang "Ki b'Simchah" for me. I was extremely moved by the show of brotherhood they were extending and knew that I would never forget these guys. We had learned together, sung together, and spent countless hours together in the sweltering Bnei Brak study hall and dorms. Now they had come to say goodbye. Their act of friendship had moved me more than I thought imaginable.

༄

I now retraced my original journey. Back through Cyprus and over the sea to Venice, where I disembarked and began the rest of my journey by train and eventually plane. All was uneventful except for one incident that was unexpected and stands out from the rest of trip.

It occurred while my Paris-bound train stopped for a few minutes at the station in Montreux, Switzerland. Standing there on the station platform was a very distinguished-looking Jew. I didn't know who he was, but instinctively understood that this wasn't a regular bystander. I didn't want the opportunity to pass without ever discovering his identity. I knew that if I didn't find out I'd be haunted by curiosity for the remainder of my life. I inquired as to his name from someone standing there, who informed me that this was Rav Yechiel Yaakov Weinberg, author of the noted halachic *sefer* of responsa *Sridei Aish* and famed halachic authority.

To my extreme regret I did not approach him or even talk to him at all, and I consider this to be on my list of lost life opportunities. Unfortunately, there are others as well. But to think that I had the chance to converse with the *Sridei Aish* and I allowed it to slip through my fingers. It irritates me, even now so many decades later.

༄

A train to Paris, a ferry to London. Another train ride up to Manchester to see my English friend from Ponevezh, Yehuda Fulda. Then a ride on a tiny propeller plane back to London and then, finally, boarding a plane for the ten-hour flight from London to Idlewild Airport in New York.

After being away for more than a year and a half, I had finally arrived home.

The first thing I did upon walking through the door of my home in Williamsburg was to take out my *smichah* from Rav Herzog and show it to my mother. It brought a wonderful smile to her pale face. I had already mailed her a picture of the document, but there's nothing like seeing the real thing.

I had sent letters back home to my parents at steady intervals throughout the year and had asked them to keep those letters for me. They were all there piled up in a corner of the room – a diary of my trip to read and treasure as they transported me back in time to the first moment I caught sight of the shores of Eretz Yisrael amid all those squabbling Jews, who stood still and silent the moment the Land of their ancestors came into view. I recalled masquerading as a member of the press on that German train and the Purim train ride from Tel Aviv to Yerushalayim. I remembered Rav Herzog and his son Chaim'l and how the Rav tried his best to bring him back into the fold. Rav Elya Kushelevsky and his family. Rav Shach assisting me to get into Ponevezh and the Ponevezher Rav and the kisses that I wouldn't have sold for a million dollars. The Belzer Rebbe and the Brisker Rav and my tiny room on Ovadia Street where I sat and learned eighteen-hour days until my eyes became bleary and my head swam with the complex laws of milk and meat.

The Satmar Rebbe and all his Chassidim in Venice and during the amazing *tish* on the *Messapia*, and Rav Tzvi Pesach Frank who was qualified by the Brisker Rav to answer my halachic queries, as opposed to the Brisker Rav himself because he "wasn't a *rav*." Rav Chatzkel Sarna and Rav Meir Chodosh and being tested comprehensively and exhaustively by Rav Elyashiv on a day where it was forbidden to leave your home and the wardens of Jerusalem were throwing all children into ambulances.

My *smichah* from Rav Yitzchak Isaac Halevi Herzog.

Learning about living in Eretz Yisrael with Rav Tzvi Yehuda Kook and demonstrating alongside Rav Amram Blau by the *kever* of the Rambam and the Edison Theater on Yeshayahu Street. Teaching the Modzitzer "Shoshanas Yaakov" to an extremely appreciative Ponevezh Yeshiva amid floor stomping and boisterous singing that took place in the packed dining room on the hill. The Tchebiner Rav and the wonderful surprise when the boys from Ponevezh traveled from Bnei Brak to say goodbye and wish me farewell.

All this came back to me as I read my letters and I knew that of all the decisions I had made in my life, spending the year in Eretz Yisrael had been the best one so far. And now I was back and it was time to board yet another train to return to Baltimore, to Ner Yisroel, where Rav Ruderman would no doubt be most unhappy with me for having disappeared for so long, but would in the end allow me to return after rebuking me soundly. Big things were about to happen; I could feel it in my bones.

What had Rav Nesanel Quinn told us, admonished us all those years ago?

*Ibberhippen der brik*, I said to myself. *Sholom, it's time to cross the bridge.*

A few days later, I was back in Ner Yisroel.

# 8

# Back in Baltimore

And so, the world traveler made his grand return. The Ner Yisroel campus was as well maintained as it had always been, the grass just as green, the flowers smiling. On the outside I was as cool as a cucumber. But my insides were shaking with nerves. How was the Rosh Yeshivah going to react to my return? I was never supposed to have left for such a long period of time. Rav Ruderman had granted me dispensation to leave for the summer, yet that summer had somehow become more than a year. I had written to him after the summer informing him of what I planned to do. What was Rav Ruderman going to say?

I put my suitcases down in the lobby and went to find out.

Rav Ruderman was in his office when I arrived. There was an open *sefer* in front of him, and he welcomed me in an extremely grudging way. The extent of his unhappiness with me was made clear when he basically refused to give me *shalom aleichem*.

"Sholom," he told me, "leave the *yeshivah* immediately!"

Wow, I hadn't been expecting such a reception. I'd imagined that the Rosh Yeshivah would be upset with me for being away for so long, but to the extent that he was prepared to throw me out? This was drastic.

I turned toward Rav Ruderman, knowing that what I said in the next few seconds would impact my future tremendously.

"The Rosh Yeshivah once told me, '*Kol she'omer lecha baal habayis aseh, chutz mi'tzei*'" (Whatever the master of the house tells you to do you must obey, except if he tells you to leave).

"I'm going to put my suitcases down in my dorm room and if the Rosh Yeshivah wants to throw me out, he can call the police to do it because I'm not leaving!"

The Rosh Yeshivah, needless to say, did not call the police.

My next stop was the dining room. The eruption that went on when I walked in was unbelievable. The entire room arose and began dancing and singing as they welcomed me back from Eretz Yisrael. If my welcome from Rav Ruderman was slightly less warm than I would have liked, I had nothing to complain about when it came to my friends.

☙

I was sitting in the study hall one morning a few months later when the summons arrived.

"Gold, the Rosh Yeshivah wants to see you in his office."

I hadn't done anything particularly outrageous in the last few days and couldn't for the life of me figure out what the Rosh Yeshivah wanted.

I entered his office and took a seat on the other side of the desk.

"Do you have *smichah* from Rav Herzog?" he asked.

I replied simply. "Yes." I had been found out.

"Do you have the *smichah* with you here in the *yeshivah*?"

"Yes."

"Go bring it to me right away."

I went and brought the precious document to him and waited while he read it. Then he began to smile. From ear to ear.

"It's very nice," he said, his voice filled with pride. "Sholom, it's very nice."

The Rosh Yeshivah was clearly very proud. Rav Herzog had been impressed with me and that in turn gave Rav Ruderman tremendous satisfaction.

☙

When we were at Ponevezh, I had invited my good friend Elazar

Mayer Teitz to join me at Ner Yisroel, an invitation which he accepted. Elazar Mayer eventually took over his father's rabbinical position and is still the *rav* in Elizabeth today. Both Elazar Mayer and I returned to Baltimore with a certain goal in mind. We planned on going for a college degree at Loyola University while pursuing our Torah learning at the *yeshivah*. During the mid-fifties there had been an uproar in the *yeshivah* world when Ner Yisroel signed a deal with Loyola University to the effect that a student's years at the *yeshivah* would count toward a BA, which would then allow him to continue on for a master's in education at Loyola.

I cannot describe Rav Aharon Kotler's reaction to this development.

College participation at a *yeshivah*? And with a Catholic college, no less! But Rav Ruderman went ahead with the plan despite many a detractor, and this allowed a sizable number of young men to remain in *yeshivah* while simultaneously pursuing their college degrees, satisfying their parents and their own ambitions in a safe and spiritually healthy Torah environment. My plan was a simple one. I wanted to obtain a master's in education and then go on aliyah. I hoped to be finished with my degree in 1959, after which I'd be moving back to Eretz Yisrael.

We threw ourselves into our learning and attended Loyola one or two nights a week. We wrote papers and studied together and our learning didn't suffer. It was good to be back.

ಶ

It was Elul when I returned to Ner Yisroel. The Yamim Noraim passed uneventfully. Sukkos on the Ner Yisroel campus was a wonderful experience, the weather cooperating, the food special, the atmosphere uplifting. When Simchas Torah rolled around, I came up with an idea that would contribute greatly to the festivities. Coming from Eretz Yisrael, I was used to people dancing in the streets pretty much whenever the mood struck them. I decided to transport that custom to Baltimore.

"I just had an idea."

"Let's hear it."

"When *yom tov* comes to Yerushalayim everyone simply dances in the street."

"So?"

"This year, we are going to leave the *yeshivah* before *hakafos* begin, go to Rav Ruderman's house, and dance the Rosh Yeshivah back to the *yeshivah* for *hakafos*."

After I finished speaking there was a thunderous silence.

"But won't that disturb traffic?" someone finally said.

"I'm sure the police will help us out," I reassured my reluctant friends.

In the end, a few hundred students surrounded Rav Ruderman's home on that memorable Simchas Torah night. We danced him back along Garrison Boulevard, the boys kicking up their heels, heads thrown back in ecstasy, voices ringing through the silent night, the Irish policemen clapping along to the beat, the Rosh Yeshivah smiling the entire time, "Toras Hashem Temima" being broadcast with power, block after block as the students allowed themselves to let go of their inhibitions and just dance the dance for the honor of the Torah.

It was such a success that it became the tradition for years afterwards to dance the Rosh Yeshivah from his home to Ner Yisroel on Simchas Torah night.

All because the life of Eretz Yisrael was still burning inside me giving my soul no rest.

Now you know how traditions begin. Just like that.

꙰

It happened during one of the hottest summers I can recall. I grew up on the steaming New York streets, in the tenements of Williamsburg, where the unforgiving sun glared off the metal bars of the fire escapes. But that was nothing compared to the unforgettable heat that descended upon us during one summer afternoon in Ner Yisroel. The humidity of Baltimore, situated below the Mason-Dixon Line, was legendary.

I don't recall exactly how it all began. A few guys were horsing around in the extreme heat. Someone sprayed someone else with a cup of water, someone else retaliated by getting out a hose, and the next thing we knew, the entire *yeshivah* found themselves embroiled in the most ferocious water fight ever to take place in the history of Yeshivas

Ner Yisroel. It didn't confine itself to one room, one hallway, or one floor. It encompassed the entire *yeshivah* and spread out over every part of the grounds. It seemed like every student in the *yeshivah* was involved, although there were of course those who gave it the impetus it needed to really get going. If I were to provide you with a list of those who participated in that water fight, you would find yourself most amused to note the names, because some of today's most esteemed *roshei yeshivah* and *mashgichim* took part.

And when it was all over we took a look around and came to the belated realization that not one spot had been left dry. Not one. The entire *yeshivah* was soaked through and through – the dorms, the hallways, the classrooms. It was a sight to behold.

Eventually the water fight came to its inevitable end and, it being summer, everything dried fairly rapidly.

I cannot claim to have had nothing to do with this epic battle. I can't make such a claim, and I won't. Because truthfully, I had something to do with the fight. I was involved and made the most of the situation; after all, this was something that hadn't occurred in all the *yeshivah*'s history before my time and would doubtless never happen again. It was an afternoon to remember.

The summons from the Rosh Yeshivah arrived the next morning. Rav Ruderman wanted to see me. I won't say I wasn't nervous, because I was. I couldn't deny my involvement. After all, I'd been a key member of those who had made it happen. Now what? Would the Rosh Yeshivah punish me? Would he throw me out of the *yeshivah*? Would he ask me to leave? My gut churning, I walked over to the Rosh Yeshivah's office.

I'm not sure what I was expecting. Maybe a fiery speech of reproof, laced with a couple of threats regarding my future at his fine institution. He was staring at me, a tiny smile playing on his lips, an expression that I could not fathom on his face.

And then he began talking with me in learning. He discussed with me the *daf* of Talmud that the *yeshivah* was currently studying. A Tosafos, a Rashi, a Ritva. We asked, answered, debated, and clarified. We argued and raised our voices and brought proofs for ourselves. And the entire time I was waiting for his reproach. When was it going to come? When would he start with the reproof? I'd done something wrong – wasn't he going to tell me off?

But as soon as we ended our discussion, he stood up and I understood that our meeting was over. He had said what he wanted to say and made his point. He knew as well as I did that the water fight would never be repeated. He also knew that I understood how wrong it had been to soak the *yeshivah* from top to bottom. Yet he told me off by talking to me in learning. That was the way he dressed me down.

When I returned to my seat in the study hall, the *chevrah* wanted to know what he'd said. A great tumult arose, a roar of voices as the student body converged on me.

"What did the Rosh Yeshivah say to you?"

"Did he yell at you? Was it terrible?"

"We spoke in learning," I replied simply. "That's what we did."

"Oh." They were a little confused. I just smiled because I understood.

I have never forgotten the Rosh Yeshivah's reaction to the whole water fight debacle. He knew that the chances of this ever happening again were slimmer than slim. But he needed to say something. And he accomplished that by speaking in learning. How brilliant a maneuver. What a master educator he was.

☙

Most people don't know this, but there was a time in the not so distant past that the activists for animal rights managed to make their case against *shchitah*, to the point where a law banning Jewish ritual slaughtering of animals was being bandied about as a distinct possibility.

In America, of all places!

Before Congress would go so far as to pass a law banning *shchitah*, they needed to do their homework about ritual slaughtering. That meant understanding its ins and outs, how it worked, who was allowed to do it, the level of pain it caused the animals, and so on. One of the people summoned to testify at a congressional hearing on the matter was Rav Eliezer Silver. Famous as the man who rescued numerous Jewish children from the monasteries of postwar Poland, Rav Leizer, as he was called, was a beloved and much respected figure in the early years of the second half of the century.

Rav Leizer would be subjected to a fierce barrage of questions and queries that would go on for hours at a time. The *yeshivah* world did not want him to be all alone when under oath. Rabbi Neuberger of Ner Yisroel came up with an inspired idea. Ner Yisroel would bus a few hundred *bochurim* into Washington to sit behind Rav Leizer in the congressional hearing room. Our presence would serve a twofold purpose. It would provide the Rav with powerful moral support in his role as spokesman for the Orthodox world, and it would show the government how seriously the Orthodox Jewish community of America viewed the issue.

And so it was.

Ner Yisroel bused us in and we sat in that exclusive room on Capitol Hill looking around in wide-eyed wonder and feeling extremely important, knowing that we were sitting in one of the most important buildings in the world. All this as Rav Silver sat and testified before the Senate panel.

I remember one amusing series of incidents from that historic day. I am referring to the stand up/sit down scenario. Whenever Rav Leizer had to exit the room, every single *bochur* sitting behind him rose in deference as the *gadol* made his way down the aisle. And then they rose in unison to stand up for him as he passed them on his way back to his seat. Up and down, up and down. The senators of America had never witnessed anything even remotely similar.

Ner Yisroel made a *kiddush Hashem* that day on Capitol Hill.

࿘

One day, a few months after I had returned to the *yeshivah*, I was in my dorm room in the afternoon when I should have been in the *beis midrash*. I most certainly had something incredibly important to do, but for the life of me can't remember what. It was my luck that the Rosh Yeshivah decided to make a surprise inspection of the dorm that day and sure enough he apprehended me. It was a bit embarrassing to say the least but I tried to maintain my dignity. He didn't say anything; finding me was enough. He began looking through the *sefarim* in my bookshelf. He removed a little bright red volume, scrutinized it, took it, and then asked me to come to his home that night because he wanted to tell me something.

I was quite curious, even mystified.

I arrived at the Rosh Yeshivah's home, where he invited me to sit down with him at the dining room table. He told me that during the late thirties and early forties, Rav Shraga Feivel Mendlowitz would visit Baltimore once a year in the interest of Torah Vodaath. The legendary "Mr. Mendlowitz," one of the master architects of Torah in America, never failed to spend some time with the Rosh Yeshivah during those visits. He always left a donation of five hundred dollars for Ner Yisroel, a considerable sum in those days, though the purpose of his journey was to recruit students and raise funds for Torah Vodaath.

On one of his visits he told Rav Ruderman that when he packed his suitcase to go out of town, the first thing he always put in was a little *sefer* called *Orot Hatshuvah* by Rav Avraham Yitzchok HaCohen Kook. He went nowhere without it. I of course was very moved by that story. The *sefer* had been out of print for some years. During my stay in Eretz Yisrael it was reprinted by Bnei Akiva in bright red binding. That was the *sefer* the Rosh Yeshivah had found in my room. I have since purchased a number of copies and have even learned to be profoundly inspired by it. It contains powerful ideas expressed in Rav Kook's unique, poetic Hebrew. It took me years to appreciate the greatness of that little volume.

Rav Mendlowitz was steeped in the world of Chassidus and Kabbalah; he was a very sensitive soul, deeply moved by nature and music. The more I read about him, the more I came to realize that he was a kindred soul to Rav Kook. His *ahavas Yisrael* and *ahavas Eretz Yisrael* were legendary. On Friday, 19 Iyar, 1948, the Old City of Jerusalem fell to the Jordanians, its inhabitants exiled and many taken into captivity. That Friday night as Rav Shraga Feivel was bentshing after the meal, he burst into tears when he reached "*rachem na*," and became overwhelmed by the pain of the tragedy that had befallen the residents of Yerushalayim. He felt that it was his personal loss and he collapsed. He had suffered a severe heart attack and was confined to bed until he passed away a few months later on the third of Elul. That day was the *yahrtzeit* of Rav Kook.

Coincidence?

Maybe not.

During the months of his illness he told his students that his wife thought they would be returning to Williamsburg from Spring Valley when he recovered. "But I say otherwise," he told his students. "From here we go straight to Eretz Yisrael and nowhere else."

Unfortunately Rav Shraga Feivel's dream of moving to Eretz Yisrael was not to be realized in his lifetime. He is however buried in Bnei Brak, in close proximity to Rav Dessler.

೭

One day, someone told me that a rebbe in the *yeshivah*, Rav Yaakov Moshe Kulefsky, was looking for me. If Rav Kulefsky was looking for me, I knew that it must be for something important.

It was.

"Sholom," he said, "I've just gotten off the phone with your brother Shmuel." His face was very serious and I waited for the bad news.

"He said that your mother is very sick. You need to take the next train to New York."

I rushed to the station and did exactly as he said.

There I was, sitting on the train, when I noticed a man I had never seen before. He looked like a man of substance, a man whom it seemed would be worthwhile to talk to. I wandered over to speak with him.

I asked him his name.

"Yisroel Gustman," he replied. It was the venerable *rosh yeshivah* of Netzach Yisrael. Rav Yisroel Gustman, the man whom Rav Chaim Ozer had stood up for as a youth of twenty-one. The youngest person to have ever served on the Vilna Beis Din. We began to converse and I'm not exaggerating in the slightest when I tell you that the four-hour train ride passed in what felt like five minutes. Questions, answers, a whole slew of original Torah thoughts. Listening to Rav Gustman was like being fed a royal meal on golden utensils. I couldn't get over him. His stories. His mind. I didn't even feel the journey passing, he was so fascinating.

I wish that I could recall exactly what we spoke about for those four hours, but alas I remember almost nothing from our conversation. If only I had taken the time to write down what we spoke about! If only. But isn't that what life is all about? Many chances, many opportunities and many "if onlys." This became a lost opportunity like the conversation I missed having with the *Sridei Aish* on my way home from Eretz Yisrael.

It could very well be that I would have written down our entire conversation if circumstances had been even slightly different. My mother had already passed away when my brother called Rav Kulefsky. But my brother was very perceptive and he knew how devastated I would be upon hearing the news and he understood that my pain would have turned that train ride into a sea of suffering. So he chose to hide the news from me until I arrived home.

And that could very well be the reason that I have almost no recollection of what we discussed or what Rav Gustman said.

Everything flew right out of my mind the moment I learned the truth about my mother. The only thing in the world of any import right then was the fact that I was ripping my jacket and taking a seat on a low chair near the floor, mourning along with my father and brothers for the woman who had been the cornerstone of the Gold family for so many years.

ය

It was late 1958 when the phone call came for me from New York. A very influential Jew, Rav Yaakov Griffel, noted activist and the Agudah representative in Istanbul during World War II, was on the other end. I had heard of him and was surprised that he was calling me.

He told me in his direct way. "I want you to travel to Poland."

"Poland? What for?"

"To save the Jewish children that have been stolen from us during the war and are currently hidden away in monasteries and private homes all over that accursed country."

"But I'm young. I have no experience in getting people out of Poland, and I don't even speak the language. How would I be successful?"

"You've been highly recommended by quite a few people," he told me. "I would like you to travel to New York for training and a passport."

My first passport was by then expired. "You'll meet people who can teach you what you need to know, because obviously this is not a simple thing, but we have confidence that you can do this."

You may be familiar with a song sung by Yaakov Shwekey called "Shma Yisrael," which chronicles the experience of a young child whose mother has no choice but to leave him at a monastery, hoping that this move will allow him to survive the war. Rav Leizer Silver traveled to Poland after the war to attempt to save as many children as he could from the clutches of the Catholic Church. Upon entering a church he was told that "there are no Jewish children here."

He persisted in entering the church's dining room during mealtime when all the children were there. Without warning, Rabbi Silver stood in the center of the room and called out, *"Shma Yisrael, Hashem Elokeinu, Hashem Echad!"* The clatter of dozens of spoons dropping in their places was the response, as every Jewish child in the room looked up at him, tears in their eyes, and repeated the words after him.

This was what Rabbi Griffel wanted me to do: to go to Poland and rescue as many Jewish children as possible. The idea intrigued and fascinated me; I related to the concept and strongly connected with the possibility of rescuing lost Jewish children. But before I consented to his request I needed to get permission from the Rosh Yeshivah. I explained the situation, detailing the offer I had just received, and asked him if he felt I should accept.

Rav Ruderman voiced his concerns.

"Poland is a freezing cold place in the winter."

"Sholom will survive the cold," said his son-in-law, Rav Shmuel Yaakov Weinberg, who was also present.

"But he won't have what to eat."

"Somehow I don't see Sholom Gold starving in Poland," came Rav Weinberg's calm reassurance to his father-in-law.

In the end, Rav Ruderman went over all the details and gave me his blessing. Since time was of the essence, he handed the mission over to Rav Naftali Neuberger, the man who almost single-handedly ran the entire Ner Yisroel operation and who more than almost anyone else knew how to get things done. Within the day he had arranged with the State Department in Washington to issue a passport for me. Rabbi Griffel was in such a rush to get me to Poland that he didn't even insist on my coming to New York. Instead many of the experts on the subject called me at the *yeshivah* and gave me instructions. I was given a lot of advice as to where I should go and who I should meet.

I was all set to go. I had already said goodbye to my *chavrusa*. My mind had left the safe confines of Baltimore and was hovering over Warsaw. A few hours before I was to leave, I received a summons from Rav Ruderman to come to his office immediately. I went. The Rosh Yeshivah was sitting at his desk waiting for me. Rav Shmuel Yaakov Weinberg was there, along with Rabbi Neuberger. The three faces were serious. Very serious.

"Sholom," Rav Ruderman began, "I just got off the phone with Rav Yaakov Kamenetsky. I asked his opinion about your going to Poland. He had one question for me. He wanted to know if you were learning well, and I told him that you were. 'Then he should stay in Ner Yisroel and learn,' Rav Yaakov advised. 'There are other people who can do this job.'

"If Rav Yaakov doesn't think you should go," Rav Ruderman concluded, "then it's best for you to remain here."

I didn't argue with the Rosh Yeshivah. I didn't hesitate. I said one line in reply.

"If the Rosh Yeshivah feels it's better that I stay, then I'm staying."

That was it. Not one word of argument, no attempts at changing his mind. Never mind the fact that I had already broken up with my study partner, or that I had been running around since Rabbi Griffel's phone call from morning to night, trying to organize myself for the trip. If the Rosh Yeshivah said no, it was no. That was that. I left his office and entered the *beis midrash*, walking down the aisle to my old seat where my *chavrusa* was sitting by himself.

"I'm back," I said, opening my Gemara to the right page.

"*Shalom aleichem*," he welcomed me, holding out his hand. "It's good to have you back."

And then we started to learn.

It was January 1959 and I was learning in Ner Yisroel in Baltimore.

Ner Yisroel was a quality *yeshivah*, filled with serious and sincere *bochurim* and staff. The Rosh Yeshivah, Rav Yaakov Yitzchok Halevi Ruderman, was famous for his greatness in Torah; his presence pervaded the sprawling green sloped acreage that Ner Yisroel called home. The summons arrived one morning during *seder*.

A student approached me. "The Rosh Yeshivah wants to see you in his office."

I stood up, closed my Gemara, and met my study partner's eye. "What do you suppose I did this time?"

He smiled.

I made my way through the crowded study hall with its crush of young men, all gesturing and contending forcefully with one another. It was a sight to behold. The give-and-take, the intense intellectual effort to dig deeper into a passage of Talmud, to mine the Gemara until one arrived at genuine clarity. The doors of the study hall swung open before me and my feet carried me down the familiar corridors I had trodden a thousand times before.

Rav Ruderman was waiting for me in his office. His manner was serious, but that came as no surprise. The Rosh Yeshivah was a serious person. If you merited a smile, it meant it was well deserved and left a glow long after you witnessed it. I waited tensely in front of him. What did the Rosh Yeshivah want? What could have possibly happened that he needed to talk to me about?

Rav Ruderman chose to prolong the agony. "Sholom," the Rosh Yeshivah said, his voice warm, his manner formal, "I would like you to come to my home this evening. There is something I have to ask you."

I left his office more curious than ever. Had I done something wrong? I would have to wait until the evening to find out what was going on. My curiosity didn't let me rest. My mind whirled with possibilities. What could it be?

The day dragged on endlessly. It was with a sigh of relief that I saw the sun beginning to set on the campus and knew that soon I would find out what he wanted of me. The moment it was time, I was gone. It was January and extremely cold, but weather was the last thing on my mind.

I reached the Rosh Yeshivah's home and rang the bell. Soon enough I was sitting in front of my master waiting to hear his directive. I'll be honest with you: nothing I'd imagined came close to the real thing.

"Sholom, I would like to open up a branch of Ner Yisroel in Toronto."

A bombshell had just been dropped out of the sky.

"I want you to go to Canada and start it. And make it happen."

My answer to Rav Ruderman recalled another reply, spoken millennia before.

Rivka Imeinu's family asked her, "Do you agree to go with this man? With Eliezer? To a place that you never saw before? To marry a husband you have never met? To experience a whole new world?"

Her response was "*Eileich* – I will go."

And that was my response to Rav Ruderman as well. "The Rosh Yeshivah wants me to go to Toronto, to a community where I have never been, to work with people I have never met, to build a *yeshivah* and serve in a leadership capacity even though I am still so young? *Eileich* – I will go."

Just like that, my life had taken on a brand new direction. I was embarking on an awesome adventure to find myself, to meet my wife, and ultimately to build an institution of youth who would grow up to become sincere members of the Jewish community. I was nearly twenty-four. It was the real beginning of my life.

Not three months earlier, I had sat in the Rosh Yeshivah's office a few hours before I was to leave for Poland, and he'd told me that Rav Kamenetsky – and therefore he himself – felt I should cancel my trip. And now, because I had listened to *gedolei Yisroel*, because I had unquestioningly accepted their sage advice, my whole life was opening up before me. Looking back, it's clear to me that if I had traveled to Poland to save those kids from the clutches of the Catholic Church, the Rosh Yeshivah would never have sent me to Toronto. *La'kol zman v'es*. There is a time for everything. I had been meant to travel – but to Canada, not Poland. And G-d was moving heaven and earth so that I would meet Bayla, the girl who would become my wife, in Toronto.

This was a huge vote of confidence on Rav Ruderman's part. There were between two and three hundred young men in Ner Yisroel at the time, and the fact that he had chosen me from among them all clearly showed how much he trusted me and felt that I could be relied upon. I was being handed an incredibly difficult job. Building a brand new institution from the beginning is never easy, but I had never shied away from anything worthwhile before and I wasn't about to start now. If Rav Ruderman was asking me to go, then I never imagined saying no. That simply was not an option.

So I set about to take Toronto by storm. If the Toronto community weren't sending their children to Baltimore, it was time for Baltimore to come to Toronto. They needed us. They just didn't know how much. It would be my job to tell them. And that was how I ended up spending the next twelve years of my life in Canada. I would have to convince parents whose sole desire in life was for their children to get accepted to a prestigious college, who most certainly did not want them studying in a *yeshivah* high school, that my fledgling new *yeshivah* was the right place for all their kids. It would be a hard, thankless job. But I was going to do it.

Soon after, Chofetz Chaim, Lakewood, and Telz would send out pairs of rabbis to establish new Torah institutions. I was being sent to Toronto alone to conquer the Canadian frontiers.

The *yeshivah* threw a goodbye party for me a few days before I left. We sang the songs we'd sung so many times before and people spoke. I was nervous and excited at the same time. And then the party was over and I had finished packing. Two days later, I stood outside the *yeshivah* with my suitcases, waiting for a taxi to drive me to the station. Toronto, here I come!

# 9

# TORONTO

I arrived in Toronto on the thirty-fourth day of the Omer, in May 1959. You only get one chance to make a first impression and it was a good thing that I had been able to shave the day before. I took a sleeper train from New York – first and last time in my life that I had the opportunity. I knew that I would have to deliver a *drashah* in Toronto that Shabbos, so I seized the moment to prepare. As the train hurtled down the tracks toward Canada, I sat at the tiny desk and prepared something I hoped would capture their hearts. Rav Ruderman was sending me to Canada to put together a *yeshivah* and I needed to justify his decision.

    I would be speaking at Congregation Torah V'Avoda at 86 Vaughn Road. The shul was learning tractate *Shabbos* at the time and they were up to a page full of *aggadata* – stories, parables, and explanations of assorted Torah verses. I utilized my time aboard the sleeper to the maximum and managed to craft a very nice *shiur* for the future parents of my student body. As an aside, they weren't the only important people who heard me speak; my future father-in-law was there in *shul* that Shabbos as well and he came home after davening and told my mother-in-law all about the young rabbi who had just arrived from New York to start a *yeshivah*, and that was the first time Bayla heard my name. The wheels began to turn in my future mother-in-law's mind. But that was to take place in the future.

I took a taxi from the train station to 16 Strathearn Road, the home of Meyer and Minny Lebovic, where I spent the next two weeks. Meyer Lebovic was one of the original group who had approached Ner Yisroel with the proposition of opening a branch in Toronto. This committee of dedicated activists had done their homework, searched out *yeshivos* around the country and decided that the Ner Yisroel approach was right for them. The original board had grand plans for a *yeshivah* and were not afraid of implementing novel decisions. One of those was the concept that every single boy would be dorming under the *yeshivah*'s roof – even those young men who lived a mere ten minutes away. The boys were to be under our supervision at all times.

The students would go home for Shabbos except for the fourth Shabbos of every month, when they'd remain in *yeshivah* as well. These were truly revolutionary concepts, yet men like Meyer Lebovic and his group were not afraid to be radical. The crucial question really, now that I had arrived and part of the original aim had been attained, was where to go from here. We needed students to fill the dorms and study hall. How were we to find them?

On my first Shabbos in Toronto, I ate the morning *seudah* at the home of Dr. and Mrs. Julius Kuhl. I entered their fashionable home on Richview Avenue after davening and right away I could see that the Kuhls were serious collectors of art. The real thing. The kind of artwork that you find in museums. The kind of paintings that are offered for sale at Christie's auction house in the city. Dr. Kuhl took my arm and we walked through the house. And then as we were passing through the living room something there caught my eye.

"Julius," I exclaimed to my host, "that's a Renoir." Implicit in my comment was the surprising little fact that I too had an eye and appreciation for the arts.

The painting was in fact a Renoir – my hunch had been correct – and with that tiny observation on my part, we became firm friends, Dr. Julius Kuhl and I. Just like that.

You might be curious as to how I did in fact know that the particular painting in question was a Renoir. This bit of vital trivia dated back to about a month and a half before I left for Toronto, when I was still at Ner Yisroel. I had entered one of the dorm rooms for something and happened to discover, sitting on one of the students' desks, a thick book on the subject of the French Impressionists. This particular book was devoted to scenes of flowers and nature. Maybe the student needed the book for a paper he was writing on the history of art – I don't know. I opened that book and found myself entranced by the splendid artwork displayed within the pages. It was as if the book had sucked me into itself.

I had never been exposed to genuine art before, and here was a treasure trove of material that made me take notice. I sat at that desk and went through the book on French art from beginning to end. By the time I pulled myself away from that book, it had become a simple matter for me to identify a Renoir. I had uncovered a part of me that had never been given any notice before. But the colors favored by that famous artist and the shades of light in the painting displayed on the Kuhls' wall made me certain enough of the artist's pedigree to venture an opinion.

I had often wondered in the aftermath of that hour spent poring over a book of art why I had needed to see the book in the first place, thereby wasting all that time. Why had I needed exposure to a world that didn't interest me or draw me? And even if I had discovered that I had a natural fascination for the world of art, it wasn't as if I was going to do anything about it. I was a rabbi and teacher, not an artist or art historian. So why the great art education? After that Renoir incident, however, I understood. Dr. Kuhl and I were now friends, all because *hashgachah* had seen fit for me to spend an hour with a book on the French Impressionists.

We spent many hours together after that. When it came time to make up the *yeshivah*'s stationery, it was Dr. Kuhl and I who did it together. He was a visionary who recognized the need for a *yeshivah* in Toronto and we saw eye to eye. The men who identified the need and worked to make it a reality were pillars of the community, men of stature and vision – Hershel Rubinstein, Meyer Lebovic, Julius Kuhl, Saul Sigler, and others. They would be joined by Avrohom Bleeman and Sandy

Hofstedter. These were people who were *moser nefesh* for fifty years, the families that helped build Yiddishkeit in Toronto.

The third meal of my never-to-be-forgotten first Shabbos in Toronto took place further down Strathearn Road at the home of Meyer Gasner, who at the time could safely be called the community leader of Toronto. A sophisticated and motivated individual, Mr. Gasner headed the establishment of the Canadian Jewish Congress, part of which dealt with *kashrus* and many other vital parts of Jewish life.

I davened that first Friday night at Congregation Torah V'Avoda and the next morning at the "Burnside" shul, where I met Rav Chaim Nussbaum, one of Toronto's great *mechanchim*.

"So you're the new *rosh yeshivah?*" he asked me with a smile.

I nodded.

"Wonderful. You only have one *chisaron,* one defect, and that will get better every day: you're young." Rav Chaim's opinion seemed to be the widely accepted consensus around town. Everyone agreed I was a worthy candidate. They also agreed that I was young for the job. But that, they felt, was not a matter of great concern.

It was around this time that the Ner Yisroel committee purchased the *yeshivah*'s eventual campus, thirteen acres of rolling green hills and whispering brooks. The estate's crowning glory was the big old mansion in its center. There were many stories, myths, and legends about that house and those who had inhabited it over the decades. It was known to one and all as the Tyrell estate.

We worked very hard over the course of that summer to turn the mansion's palatial rooms and suites into dormitories, the main dining/ballroom into the study hall, and the basement into the dining room. We created offices and a bedroom for me in the servants' quarters. It was incredible labor.

We needed floor tiles. I asked around town and was directed to a man who had arrived in Toronto not long before me, named Moshe Reichmann, who was president of a company called Olympia Tiles. He did in fact supply our tile needs and was a pleasure to deal with.

Transportation was another problem. At the time of the grand opening of Ner Israel Yeshiva College of Toronto, our campus was located at the farthest point north in Toronto, and there was no bus service to the *yeshivah*. Bathurst Street (the main artery of the Jewish community) was paved only until Sheppard Avenue. The *yeshivah* campus was further north at 625 Finch Avenue West. Back in the early days I used to have to ferry the boys from the *yeshivah* on Friday afternoon so they could catch a bus home for Shabbos. Toronto was a different world back then.

The up side was that once you were at the *yeshivah*, you were really there. It was an extremely innovative way to educate students, because there was really nothing else to do on that estate but learn.

The hardest part of the work began. I met with a number of day school principals and put together lists of the names of students who were just finishing eighth grade. And then I began the actual canvassing, knocking on doors. Nobody had ever heard of me – or of Ner Yisroel, for that matter. A more serious problem was that almost nobody wanted their children to move on to a religious high school and certainly not to a high school that required its students to dorm throughout the week and only return home for Shabbos. Don't forget that Toronto back then was a place where no one wore a yarmulke in the street. Convincing the parents of these boys just to agree to listen to me was a big challenge.

Selling the school and its curriculum took me through the month of June and carried me over into the dog days of July as well. I knocked on a lot of doors and met many fine and good-hearted people along the way. I also spent some time interviewing the young men who were possibilities for our institution.

But as many people as I met, and as many young boys as I interviewed, I had received no actual positive replies yet. No parents had agreed to entrust their precious sons to my school. At this rate, it seemed almost inevitable that I would be forced to return to Ner Yisroel at the end of the summer knowing that I had failed, that Toronto's caution, nonchalance, and plain disinterest had beaten me.

One Motzaei Shabbos in July, I was at Meyer Lebovic's house when the phone rang.

"Rabbi Gold, this is Ruth Gryfe. I don't care what anybody else is going to do, but I'm ready to send my Hershey to your *yeshivah*."

I will never forget Mrs. Gryfe. She was the domino that knocked down the line.

Hershey Gryfe was all I needed. Everyone else had been talking about the *yeshivah* and thinking about the *yeshivah*, but here was someone who was truly willing to take the step. And once Mrs. Gryfe had taken that first step, many others fell into line as well. Within a very short time our first year was full.

The truth is, Hershey Gryfe wasn't actually the first student to register at the *yeshivah*. Rabbi Rosenthal, who was the rabbi in Sudbury, of all places, in frozen Northern Ontario, had a son named Leslie, later to be known as Akiva Chaim, whom he had registered at the *yeshivah* as soon as he'd heard of its upcoming existence. Yes, Leslie had been the first *talmid* to register at the *yeshivah*, but it hadn't meant anything to Toronto since they didn't know the rabbi or his son. Mrs. Gryfe, on the other hand, was well known in the community and her vote of confidence shifted the balance completely.

During that memorable summer, I acquainted myself with the *rabbanim* of Toronto. If I was going to be an educational figure in their city (and that was what I intended), then I needed to get to know them all. There were many venerable rabbinic figures in the city: Rav Gedalia Felder; Rabbi Walter Wurzburger; a young Rav Mordechai Ochs and his father, Rav Dovid Ochs; Rav Berel Rosenzweig; Rav Moshe Gorelick, rabbi of the Clanton Park shul. And then there was scholarly Dr. Jakober, with whom I developed a relationship of mutual respect. He was principal of the Associated Hebrew Schools. The fact that I had been forced to study while in Eretz Yisrael with *chavrusos* who didn't speak English meant that I in turn had picked up Ivrit and was happy to converse in that tongue. This cemented my relationship with Dr. Jakober and other members of his staff.

֍

The few months before the *yeshivah* opened were filled with strenuous labor from morning till night. Either I was busy recruiting students, meeting prospective parents and staff, or I was overseeing the renovations in the *yeshivah* building, or I was taking care of all the red tape one needed to sort through if one wanted to run a fully accredited Canadian high school. But eventually, this stage was over at last and it was time for the *yeshivah* to open.

I didn't sleep the night before the first day. How could I? It wasn't possible. My nerves on edge, I found that no matter how I tossed and turned, sleep just wouldn't come. Finally I gave up the battle and looked around for something to do. My eye hit on a vacuum cleaner sitting innocently off to the side. Without further ado, I turned it on and went about vacuuming every one of the *yeshivah*'s carpeted surfaces. And there were many. I wanted to make sure that when those boys arrived at the *yeshivah* the next day, they would find a spotlessly clean and inviting building. And they did. Because I didn't sleep that night.

There was another reason why I wasn't able to fall asleep. It's a little embarrassing but true. The Tyrell estate was located in the middle of nowhere and it was pitch black outside and more than a little ominous. Okay, it was downright petrifying. There I was, attempting to overcome my fear by vacuuming the entire building from top to bottom, when there was a knock on the door. It was eleven o'clock and the knocking was loud and persistent. If I hadn't been shaking before, I was shaking after that knock. Who on earth could it be? Would I find some monster or murderer waiting to greet me when I swung open the door?

But no. I could hear whoever it was yelling my name. "Sholom! Sholom!"

It was Meyer Weinstock, a Torontonian who had studied alongside me in Ner Yisroel in Baltimore. He still resides in Toronto to this very day.

"What are you doing here?" I asked him, when my heart calmed down a little and my pulse was almost back to normal.

"I was doing a little thinking," he said, "and I kind of figured that it's probably a little nerve-racking for you out here in the middle of nowhere. So I decided to keep you company for a couple of hours."

"That," I rejoined, "was extremely nice of you. An act of supreme consideration."

He helped me get through that first night. I was truly grateful.

And so we began.

I shared with Rav Ruderman my vision for the *yeshivah*: he would send older students to the *yeshivah*, providing me with an older boy to mentor every one of my twelve students. I wanted to give my boys lots of solid role models.

In the beginning, I split the student body in half. I gave one class, another teacher the second. Rav Chaim Mintz, who had been my *chavrusa* in Ner Yisroel, taught for a while. Rav Gershon Weiss, today *menahel ruchani* in Staten Island, taught that second class for a few months.

By Chanukah he had left and returned to Baltimore. We hired someone who would go on to become very famous in his day, Rav Noach Weinberg. He remained with us until the middle of June, close to the end of that first auspicious year. We were fortunate to have him, even if it wasn't for long. And we had a whole slew of teachers for the afternoon secular studies as well.

Here lay our biggest challenge.

The high school curriculum in Canadian schools then was extremely rigorous. The examinations were more comprehensive and all-encompassing than the regents in America. It was hard for me to see how Torah could be taught the way it should be with a system like that. French. Latin. The sciences. Not only that, but Canadian high schools had an extra year – grade thirteen. And that year was even more grueling and demanding than those preceding it. It was too difficult for the boys. How could they be expected to study diligently with the copious amounts of homework they were given on a daily basis and to take standardized tests in secular subjects as well? It was too much to expect.

But the students were good, solid young men. They learned well. They kept the pace despite the hardships. We began our first year with a student body of twelve. By our second year, we had grown to seventeen. Our third year kicked off with thirty-seven *bochurim*. By the fourth year we were hovering somewhere in the region of seventy to eighty boys. This was incredible success by anyone's standards. By our fifth year, our student body consisted of 127 boys. The vast majority were from Toronto, but at some point we began getting students from Montreal, and once they started coming, the number swelled and rose higher and higher.

Ner Israel Yeshiva of Toronto was rapidly becoming an institution to be reckoned with. Rav Reuven Silver came to teach. Rav Asher Turin arrived, sent from the mother ship in Baltimore to assist. The staff and student body were growing exponentially.

I realized that we were outgrowing the Tyrell mansion.

We needed more room. Our board stepped up to the challenge. We built a classroom building. Not long after, we held a successful appeal for a brand new dining room/dormitory building to be constructed on campus. Things were happening at Ner Yisroel of Toronto. There was a lot of learning going on at the *yeshivah*. By the second or third year, the student body had swelled to the point where I had stopped teaching every day so as to focus on the actual running of the *yeshivah*. I hired more staff and did my best to ensure that the *yeshivah* ran as smoothly as possible.

Meanwhile, we were receiving many of our students from the Eitz Chaim School and from the Associated Hebrew Schools, which was also trying to start a high school. These were my two main feeder schools. Eitz Chaim was more religious. Associated was more modern. Both, however, provided us with students of a high caliber whom we accepted with open arms. Our school was an interesting mix from all types of homes and all levels of religiosity. And yet, despite the mix (or perhaps because of it) we were flourishing.

Recently I was back in Toronto for a visit. Someone introduced me to one of the current *roshei yeshivah* at Ner Yisroel. He asked me my name.

"Gold," I replied.

"Gold..." he pondered for a few seconds, then... "you were one of the earliest *roshei yeshivah* of Ner Yisroel, weren't you?"

"That's correct."

Then he asked me an unexpected question.

"Do you remember Joey Greenbaum?"

Sure, I remembered Joey Greenbaum. He studied at the *yeshivah*. He had six boys who all learned in the *yeshivah. Their* children are learning there today. And I recalled the summer of 1959 when I went to see Joey Greenbaum's parents at the candy store they owned on Saint Clair Avenue. I sat on a milk crate in the back of the store trying my utmost to convince them to send their precious Joey to my *yeshivah*. In the end, they agreed. He graduated our school and went on to become a doctor. He lives in Hamilton today and is one of the pillars of that community. He has a home in the Shaarei Chesed neighborhood of Jerusalem as well. And those six boys learned in the *yeshivah*, one after the other. All because of a conversation that took place on a milk crate at the back of a candy store – an entire family of *bnei Torah*, all from one conversation when I first walked the streets going from family to family, to convince, cajole, encourage, and beg for their boys.

I looked normal. I sounded normal. I did not yet have a beard. (A crucial point in my favor in those years.) They wanted to be reassured that their children were not going to be rabbis. I reassured them. And in the end, some of them did turn out to be rabbis. And their parents were proud.

The fact is, the *yeshivah* was responsible in a big way for a lot of change in many long-established Toronto homes. Even if they didn't know this at first, even if they hadn't caught on that things were going to be different, they soon found out, but by then it was too late. The seeds of Torah had been planted and the boys of Toronto were thirsting for more. If the *yeshivah* had not opened its doors, the Agudah families would have continued sending their boys to Telz in Cleveland or to the Mechina High School program in Baltimore. But the majority of Toronto's *bochurim* would have been registered by their parents in the local public high schools, which would have wreaked havoc with their Jewishness. By 1959, Toronto, with the leadership and guidance of great rabbis and dedicated educators, had laid the groundwork and planted the seeds of Torah. Toronto was ready for a giant step forward. Ner Israel was that great leap into the next crucial stage of creating a Torah community.

In preparation for the opening of the school year, I decided to study the textbooks the Province of Ontario syllabus required. I was in for a surprise. And now, looking back, it was even more significant than I had first assumed.

The text describes the establishment of the State of Israel by saying that the Arabs were dismayed and angered by the well-equipped Israeli army that was funded by world Jewry. That was quite a departure from the truth. It also had the stench of anti-Semitism emanating from it. Jews, survivors of the Holocaust, coming in on unseaworthy boats, given a minimum of training and a gun and sent off to the front. The United States had clamped an embargo on the shipment of arms to the new state, which was struggling to be born and surrounded by seven invading Arab armies who planned to abort the birth. Yet this text had a completely opposite narrative.

I read on and came to a sentence at which I knew I had these liars where I wanted them. When listing a litany of Arab grievances, the book concluded, "What angered the Arabs most was that Jews captured the Old City of Jerusalem and held it." This was July 1959. Jews had been expelled from the Old City in 1948. The city was held by the Jordanian Arab Legion, who proceeded to destroy its synagogues and wreck the millennia-old cemetery on the Mount of Olives, using headstones to build latrines.

I sent off an angry letter with a less than veiled threat that I would go public on this scandalous revision of history. The publisher responded by saying that he sat down with the author, and they studied the newspapers of the period (from ten years earlier) and it seemed that I was right. They assured me that they would reprint the book correcting the inaccuracies. For the school year the new text would be ready.

These fellows didn't seem to have a clue what was happening in Jerusalem in July 1959. Of course, I didn't bother using their textbook but found an alternative. I hadn't realized that history was being reversed while it was happening.

☙

During that memorable first year, word spread in the community that

Purim in the *yeshivah* was going to be something special. I had invited Rabbi Nota Schiller to join my team at the *yeshivah* so I would have someone with whom to share the burden of recruitment. He accepted and made a very welcome addition to our staff. Armed with an impeccable sense of humor, Rabbi Schiller charmed everyone who met him. Many evenings during the second part of the year, we'd put on our suits, shine our shoes, then go out and knock on more doors. He was a natural at this type of work, and I was grateful to have him along for the ride.

As Purim approached, Nota and I and a few others wrote a Purim play and assigned parts to the various staff members. It was to be a musical: *Men Tor Nisht Zein a Chicken* (You can't be a chicken). The president of the *yeshivah* was Hershel Rubinstein, a tremendous supporter of Torah and a close friend of Rav Aharon Kotler. He was in the chicken business, and the musical's theme song powerfully reflected that angle. Its message was that to do meaningful things one dare not be afraid.

It so happened to be that my future mother-in-law heard about the *yeshivah*'s Purim plans and decided that her daughter, my future wife, should take *shalach manos* to one of her cousins who was learning in the *yeshivah* at the time. My wife resisted and most adamantly did not want to go. Girls going up to the *yeshivah*? But her mother insisted. Bayla might well have had her way were it not for a few of her friends who had heard about the festivities at the *yeshivah* and wanted to go. Since Bayla was the only one of her friends with a driver's license, they urged her to take them.

In the end, Bayla agreed to go. She drove up to the *yeshivah*, *shalach manos* in hand, and delivered the package to her cousin, Meir Yechiel Zoberman. She unknowingly walked into my office with her friend Ruth Lebovic (now Weitz), who was looking for her father with whom I was meeting. That was the first time I saw her. I found myself suddenly interested in marriage. I had met with others before; I was already in my mid-twenties. Yet here, suddenly, I felt that this could be it. All from a five-minute encounter. I decided that it was well worth an initial meeting. But that would have to wait.

In the meanwhile, the show went on and it was a smashing success, with people coming from all over Toronto to see it. I had taught the entire *yeshivah* the Modzitzer "Shoshanas Yaakov," and they belted it out with all their might, the sound of their youthful voices reverberating through the frigid Canadian air. The dancing and singing, the shtick, the laughter… It was simply an amazing Purim for everyone.

It took until after Pesach to arrange a meeting with Bayla. We announced our engagement at the Motzaei Shabbos bar mitzvah of Avram Lebovic, Chanukah, December 1960.

‏ଚ

My father-in-law's parents emigrated from Belarus. Their original name was Rubanovitch, but the border officials at Halifax decided to shorten it to Rubinoff. My *shver*'s father, Menachem Mendel, was the third of eleven children, and the only one who continued to keep Shabbos. He was never able to earn a living because of Shabbos; every Friday afternoon when he left work he'd be fired. They were very poor and my father-in-law, Binyomin Rubinoff, would sometimes arrive home from school to find all of the family's possessions outside because they had been evicted yet again. At times they were evicted in the winter. And the Canadian winters were cruel. The younger children would often cry from hunger at night.

Eventually, his father became a fish peddler, using an abandoned baby carriage as his cart. In the winter the fish froze and in the summer they suffered from the heat. But he kept Shabbos and that was the most important thing.

As the oldest child, my Toronto-born father-in-law had to leave school at the age of fifteen to help support his family. His father needed his help. He was always to regret that he had been unable to finish his education. After his marriage to my mother-in-law, Sarah Grafstein, he hired a private teacher to learn with him, and paid him a dollar a week from his weekly salary of nine dollars. He dreamed of becoming a Torah scholar. Being that he too was unwilling to work on Shabbos, he also found it very difficult to hold a job, but eventually found work as a cutter in a cousin's tailor shop.

In those days apartments were expensive to rent, so young couples rented a flat in the upstairs of other people's homes. When my wife was born, the second of five children, the landlord gave them notice. Since they couldn't afford to buy a home in the religious neighborhood, which was the College-Spadina area, they ventured further north to Saint Clair and Oakwood in a non-Jewish neighborhood. It was a wonder how their parents kept them *frum*. This was a family where everyone was willing to sacrifice for Shabbos. It comes as no surprise to me that Shabbos protected them in return.

In addition to working as a cutter, my father-in-law was a *baal koreh*, reading the Torah in the local shul, Shaarei Shomayim. His father had hired a *rebbe* to teach him with the hope of it keeping him connected to Yiddishkeit. It worked. A few years later he was upgraded to official teacher for all the bar mitzvah boys in the local Hebrew school and their financial situation improved somewhat. He proved to be very successful as a teacher, but when he asked for a small raise in salary after a time, he was refused. He opened his own Hebrew school in response, which flourished and grew. It wasn't long before my in-laws had to hire more teachers and staff. My mother-in-law became the principal of the school and tried very hard to instill in these nonobservant children a sense of Yiddishkeit. After a while, my father-in-law was able to devote more and more time to learning Torah, which is what he really wanted to do all along.

My mother-in-law arrived in Canada at the age of six. She was the daughter of Yirmiya and Liba Grafstein. They were from near Ostrov in Poland. Before my wife's grandfather left Poland with his family, he went to speak with the Ostrover Rebbe, asking him for a *brachah* that his children marry religious Jews in the *treife medinah*. The Rebbe gave him a *brachah* that his daughters would merit to marry religious men. They all did. My mother-in-law went out to work to help support the family as soon as she finished eighth grade. That's the way it was back then. Her father became a *shochet* (ritual slaughterer) so he could be sure he ate kosher.

My wife's mother was very industrious, but she had one "problem." She wouldn't work on Shabbos either. (What a family!) But she wanted to work. She would find herself a job with a new company and work extremely hard, trying to prove how valuable she'd be to the firm, but in most cases, when Friday rolled around, they fired her anyway, hard worker or not. Eventually she was hired by one particular boss in a new company. They packaged dolls. It was hard work and long hours. She worked diligently that entire week and on Friday made her way into the boss's office to inform him that she didn't work on Shabbos.

She dropped the words on the table, sure of his wrath. She was not mistaken.

"How could you do this to me?" he yelled at her. "I would never have hired you if I had known this. You got yourself a job under false pretenses!"

She turned to leave the office, sure that she wouldn't be welcome in the company any longer.

She was almost at the door when the boss called out, "Make sure you're here on time on Monday." He wasn't firing her. She could keep the job.

Looking back at our roots, at my wife's parents and grandparents and my own, I am able to see and appreciate the rich tapestry of Jews who were ready and willing to give up everything for G-d and His commandments. Their self-sacrifice was of a very lofty nature and I'm sure that their merits have stood our family in good stead until this very day.

# 10

# LIVING IN BENEVOLENT EXILE

Rav Aharon Kotler, *rosh yeshivah* of Beth Medrash Govoha in Lakewood and chairman of Chinuch Atzmai and Torah Umesorah, passed away in 1962. The funeral was slated to take place in New York. As *rosh yeshivah* of Ner Yisroel of Toronto, I was hit with a major dilemma. On the one hand, one of the most esteemed leaders of the generation had just passed away. How could I not attend his funeral? On the other hand, were I to leave the *yeshivah* and travel to New York, I would be abandoning ship, leaving my vessel with no captain. I knew for a fact that with the authority figure gone, there would be very little learning happening on campus.

And so I fretted and pondered and swung back and forth. I had to go. I couldn't go. What was I supposed to do? What would Rav Aharon have wanted me to do? If I went to the funeral, maybe nobody would end up learning that day, but at least they would have some understanding of what their nation had lost. They would have learned that one should be prepared to travel for a day to give final honor to a man who had guided the Jewish people. That was a lesson in itself. What to do? What to do?

In the end I didn't go.

After the funeral was all over, I found myself very depressed. I felt that I had made the wrong decision, that I had made a terrible mistake.

I was beside myself with guilt, when I happened to meet an expatriate Yerushalmi, Rav Avraham Parshan, who lived a few blocks away from my home. Rav Parshan, a Torah scholar with a Chassidic Yerushalmi flavor, was the man responsible for putting out the *Shem mi'Shmuel*. He took one look at me and exclaimed, "Rav Gold, you're not looking good. What's wrong?"

"Today was Rav Aharon Kotler's funeral," I told him, "and I made all these calculations about why I shouldn't travel to New York, but now I can't help but wonder if I made a mistake."

I shook my head miserably, while he nodded in commiseration.

"I should have gone," I said, bereft.

"You know something? I also wanted to fly to New York for Rav Aaron's funeral, but my doctor forbade me to do so. He said that the trip would be dangerous for my heart. My doctor said no, it's no. He knows what he's talking about and I trust him. So you know what I did? I got into my car and I drove over to Malton Airport." Toronto's main airport, which featured wooden buildings, was called Malton back then. "I got out of the car," Rav Avraham continued his narrative, "and stood outside the airport. Then I got back in the car and drove home. And as I drove home, I looked skyward and said, 'Master of the world, driving to Malton was the most I'm able to do right now. Please accept this drive as if I flew all the way to New York.'"

I stood there stunned by his words, so impressed was I by his logic. *Ad makom she'yado magaas.* As much as a person is capable of, that's what G-d expects us to do. This concept became the cornerstone of quite a few future classes.

Take this one, for example.

The Torah tells us, "*Va'yelech Moshe,*" and Moshe went. Where did Moshe go? What's the Torah talking about? So we take a look into Rashi, who writes, "*V'gomer,*" roughly translated as "etc."

What's Rashi saying with the word *etc.*?

In the next *pasuk* Moshe Rabbeinu tells the Jewish people that he is 120 years old and that he will soon be taken away from them. He won't be going anywhere else ever again. And Rashi uses the word *v'gomer*, etc. Why? Rashi was telling us the following important message. Moshe

Rabbeinu was about to pass away. His life was going to end that day. Still the Torah says "*Va'yelech Moshe*," and Moshe went. As long as Moshe was alive, he was in a state of growth, of perpetual movement. Forward looking. Focused on the future. As long as he had any power whatsoever, he was going places, improving himself, always going, always growing.

That was the main thrust of my *drashah* on Parshas Vayelech one year. I gave over five different explanations and classes on this verse over the years.

Here's another one.

G-d told Moshe that he wouldn't be allowed into Eretz Yisrael. What was Moshe's response? *I'm going to keep on going, keep on walking, keep on traveling, so as to be as physically close as possible to Eretz Yisrael when I pass away. I may not be able to actually enter the Land, but at least I can stand beside it. Stop me when You want to, but I'm going!*

That was looking at things through Rav Avraham Parshan's eyeglasses. I may not be able to go to the actual funeral, but at least I can drive to the airport.

And another one.

A *malach*, an angel, is called an *omed*, something that stands in its place. A *malach* is a stationary object, because the state in which an angel is created is how he remains for the rest of his existence. Man is called *holech*, someone who moves, because he has the constant ability to choose to grow. "Moshe Rabbeinu," I told my congregation, "was a *holech*, someone who was constantly going places and growing, a true *adam*, until the last and final moment of his life."

Those were a few of my ideas on the subject.

Now I'm going to share something with you. Not about me. About my brother and why I admire him so much. You see, every year when I originated another brand new approach to this verse, I would deliver it over in *drashah* format to my congregation, who incidentally came to wait for my annual *va'yelech/v'gomer* speech. And I made sure to share my new idea with my brother Rav Shmuel Yehoshua as well. He was always very appreciative and would thank me for calling.

After he passed away, his family published his monumental work on all of Rashi. I, of course, went through the entire *sefer* cover to cover. This was my brother's legacy, after all. Somewhere in the middle of the *sefer*, I found a certain sentence that simply blew my mind away. It was as if my brother was talking to me from the grave.

The word *v'gomer* does not appear in even a single handwritten manuscript of Rashi.

In other words, my brother was claiming (with all the considerable authority at his disposal) that Rashi had never used this word.

My brother had listened patiently to all my ideas over the years, enjoying them, all the while never bothering to inform me that in truth, the word *v'gomer* really isn't part of the Rashi at all. The concepts I was originating annually didn't truly need the word *v'gomer* to work and he didn't feel like bursting my balloon. So he never said a word.

It so happens that I remain in good company regarding the word *v'gomer*, because both Rav Moshe Feinstein and the Lubavitcher Rebbe discuss the word *v'gomer* and the difficulty that it poses to the straightforward understanding in Chumash. Yet according to my brother it seems likely that *v'gomer* was inserted by a printer and not by Rashi at all.

All these Torah concepts came into being, inspired as they were by my conversation with Rav Parshan. I'd learned a vital lesson. The most important thing was to do as much as you could. Like Moshe Rabbeinu. If your best meant attending the funeral, flying to New York by plane, wonderful. On the other hand, if your best was a drive to the airport, that was more than acceptable in G-d's eyes. Every man according to his abilities.

Two years later, in November 1964, one of the Telzer *roshei yeshivah,* Rav Mottel Katz, passed away. This time I didn't hesitate for a second. I immediately organized two or three station wagons, packed with as many students as I was able to take along, and we drove to Cleveland, Ohio, for the funeral. It was a full-day trip and we were all exhausted when we returned to Toronto. But I had made up my mind to never allow what had occurred with Rav Aharon to happen again. When a man of such exceptional caliber departs this world, it is up to every single one of us to mourn.

❧

A few years after the *yeshivah* was up and running, Rav Ruderman decided to send his son-in-law Rav Yaakov Weinberg to become the senior *rosh yeshivah* of Ner Yisroel of Toronto and I would continue running the overall operation. I knew Rav Yaakov well. He was much older than me, but we had enjoyed a close relationship back in Baltimore and had even studied together *b'chavrusa* for a period of time. He was a truly brilliant man.

I proposed to him that I would run the technical aspects of the *yeshivah*, deciding the curriculum, overseeing the staff, and making sure that everything was running smoothly, leaving him free to serve as an example of Torah and *hashkafah*, to teach and inspire by personal example.

When I had been in Toronto for about two years I was approached by one of the pillars of the community, Shea Wortzman. He was a leader in Toronto and someone who contributed generously to charity.

"Rabbi Gold," he said to me in his heavy European accent, "we did something for the boys, now we must do for the girls too."

"Shea," I rejoined, "you are absolutely right. Let's call a meeting and get down to business."

We put together a list of Toronto *baalei batim*, called a meeting, and the Bais Yaakov of Toronto was born right then and there. The first principal we brought in was a young, charismatic rabbi, Rav Shloime Freifeld. One happening triggered another. The *yeshivah* triggered the Bais Yaakov. This in turn led to more and more Torah institutions opening their doors in Toronto. The little Bais Yaakov, the Lakewood Kollel, the Ulpana, Ohr Chaim, and other *yeshivos*. The first to follow Ner Yisroel was the Community Hebrew Academy of Toronto (CHAT), a school that caters to all shades of religious observance in Toronto. The city was well on its way to becoming a major Torah center.

❧

Yeshiva Yesodei HaTorah of Toronto held a dinner in the early sixties honoring Moshe Reichmann for his charitable benevolence. The guest speaker at the dinner was Rav Shneur Kotler, who was then serving as *rosh yeshivah* of Lakewood. Rav Shneur made a point in that *drashah* that resonated deeply within my soul, pertaining as it did to a thought I'd been working on.

The Gemara in *Megillah* relates that the students of Rabbi Shimon Bar Yochai asked their teacher why the Jews living in the days of the Purim story had deserved the threat of complete and utter destruction. Rabbi Shimon replied, *Why don't you tell me? You must have given some thought to this obvious question.*

Their response: *Because the Jews enjoyed King Achashverosh's royal feast.*

*That explains why the Jews of Shushan were slated for punishment,* their *rebbe* replied, *but that still doesn't explain why the Jews of the entire world were deserving of death.*

The students were at a loss.

*Tell us, our master. You tell us.*

His reply (in *Megillah* 12): "Because they bowed down to the statue in the days of Nebuchadnezzar."

Forty or forty-five years earlier, Nebuchadnezzar had erected a statue in the valley of Dura and had ordered all his subjects to prostrate themselves before it. Being that Nebuchadnezzar was king of the world at the time, he was basically including everyone in the universe in his command. Even the Jews. And the Jews bowed down. Only three men stood strong and firm: Chananiah, Mishael, and Azariah refused to give in to the pressure.

*Wait a second,* cautioned Rabbi Shimon's *talmidim, if the Jews actually bowed down to the statue, they should have been completely destroyed. For real. Why did G-d agree to drop the charges, as it were? Didn't they bow down to* avodah zarah, *to idol worship? One of the three cardinal sins. Why did Hashem rescind the decree?*

*They didn't really mean it,* Rabbi Shimon explained to his students. *They were simply pretending because of the danger of disobeying the king. So G-d took it to threat level but stopped there.*

What does the fact that the Jews bowed down to a statue some forty-five years earlier have to do with what's going on in Shushan decades later? What's the connection? What kind of answer is Rabbi Shimon Bar Yochai giving his students? And furthermore, if the Jews who bowed down to Nebuchadnezzar's statue didn't really mean it as idol worship, why did G-d threaten them with total annihilation forty-five years later?

In order to understand the perplexing dialog between teacher and students, we need to take a step back in time to the moment the exile began seventy years earlier. What did the Jewish people look like then? Fortunately, we have a poignant verbal portrayal that paints for us a vivid and accurate picture of Klal Yisrael at that most tragic moment in our history. Chapter 137 in Tehillim, "Al Naharos Bavel," is the moving description of a people on their way into exile who adamantly refuse to make peace with their forced estrangement from Eretz Yisrael: "By the rivers of Babylon we sat and wept as we remembered Zion. There on the willow trees we hung up our harps, for there our captors asked us for songs, our tormentors for amusement said, 'Sing us the song of Zion.'"

The people respond: *How can we sing the songs of Hashem on foreign soil?*

There you have it. Absolute refusal to come to terms with an alien land. It was at that great moment that Israel took the oath that has accompanied us through the exile. The promise that has become the hallmark of the Jew. "If I forget you, Yerushalayim, may my right hand forget its skill; may my tongue cling to the roof of my mouth if I do not remember you, if I do not set Yerushalayim above my highest joy."

A ragged, disoriented nation, engulfed by sadness and anguish over the loss of their beloved Temple, feared they had lost the love of G-d forever. They were in an alien place, not a home; they would never make peace with their newfound reality. Fast forward seventy years: Jews were now sitting and enjoying themselves at the party of Achashverosh.

And there was something peculiar about this party.

Achashverosh was celebrating because according to his calculations the seventy years of the Babylonian exile prophesied by Yirmiyahu had come to an end and the Jews were still in exile. The prophecy, he concluded, was false, and that's why he and Haman were celebrating.

Meanwhile the Jews, who had cried only seventy years earlier on the banks of the river of Babylon, were now enjoying a party meant to celebrate the fact that they would never return to Jerusalem. Look how their perceptions and yearnings had changed in a mere seventy years.

Rabbi Shimon's students weren't just referring to the Jews who lived in Shushan. No, the Jews of Shushan were representative of the Jews dispersed throughout the entire world. They had lost their connection to Eretz Yisrael and the Temple. Not only didn't they care, they were actually glorifying their current lifestyle and society.

They had made peace with their exile.

Rabbi Shimon Bar Yochai agreed with his students' interpretation of events. And he added the following.

*What you're saying is true. This was the cause for G-d's threatening them with complete destruction. But when did their disdain for the past begin? At what point did the Jews go from crying over the Churban to the insensitivity of enjoying such a party? What was the fatal error that began the process of alienation from Eretz Yisrael? What tragic compromise had set in motion the downward spiral that led from the rivers of Babylon to the halls of revelry in Shushan? What episode can we point at and say, "That's when it all began"? At what moment could we have predicted where it would all end? When was the right hand no longer raised in solemn oath?*

The students didn't know.

So he told them.

*The problem started – the shift in the Jewish mindset began – at the time the Jews bowed down to Nebuchadnezzar's statue forty-five years prior to the Purim story. If you're searching for the turning point, the fatal error, the tragic compromise, that is it!*

I want you to picture the scene. The edict emerges from Nebuchadnezzar's palace. Every citizen of the empire must bow down to the statue, prostrate himself before the idol. Immediately the Jews of Bavel turn to their rabbis and communal *machers* to ask them what to do. For instruction. For advice. Rabbis begin churning out halachic treatises by the dozen. The RCB (Rabbinical Council of Bavel) meets to discuss the challenge facing them. The Orthodox Union of Babylonian Rabbis comes together to address the crisis. The BJC (Babylonian Jewish Council) is convened to meet. A giant gathering of all heads of

Jewish organizations. An emergency plenary session is scheduled.

Jews around the world look to their leaders for guidance.

Out come the halachic rulings from the great rabbis of the day.

The RCB: "Bowing down to Nebuchadnezzar's statue is permissible. It is not *avodah zarah*."

The BJC: "The statue is a glorification of the king; it is most definitely not idol worship. On the contrary, the law of *dina d'malchuta dina*, 'the law of the land is the law,' applies here."

And so on and so forth.

What makes this even more intriguing is the fact that Rabbi Shimon Bar Yochai himself agreed with their halachic ruling that the statue really wasn't *avodah zarah*. But whether it was permissible to bow down to the statue was really not the point. There were three individuals walking around saying, *There is no way that we are ever going to bow down to this statue, whether it's called an "andarta"* (that's the term used in the Gemara) *or a "pesel" or an "idol." We don't care what it's called, we refuse to bow down, to prostrate ourselves in front of anything or anyone reminiscent of avodah zarah. All we care about and fear is G-d in heaven.*

These three do not compromise with "the realities of *galus*."

And I quote the Babylonian Jewish Press's words in response to their "fanatical" stance: *Those three are zealots and are as such not representative of the Jewish community. We do not agree with them nor concur with their judgment, nor condone their actions and behavior. They are fanatics, outside the mainstream of the Jewish people.*

But Chananiah, Mishael, and Azariah didn't listen to what everyone else was saying, not even for a second.

They didn't bow down.

And they were thrown into the burning furnace.

A miracle occurred and they were saved.

Said Rabbi Shimon Bar Yochai: *The moment the Jewish people made the collective decision to bow down to Nebuchadnezzar's statue, the mindset of "the rivers of Babylon" came to an end. They were succumbing to the reality of life in exile. We're allowed to bow down because it's not idol worship. The willingness to bow down to someone other than G-d means that you are accommodating yourself to a long stay in Bavel. And that's the beginning of the end. A fatal compromise. It meant that they had decided that Babylon was now their own and native land.*

Rabbi Shimon agreed with his students. But enjoying the party was the result and not the cause. He took it one step further by looking for the starting point. And that had happened forty-five years before the Purim story. Eretz Yisrael had receded from their consciousness. Return was no longer on the agenda.

I had been developing this thought for a while.

And then, at that dinner in Toronto, Rav Shneur Kotler uttered a line that exhilarated me.

"*In numen fun Tatten*" (in the name of my father [Rav Aharon]), he said, "*der yeshuah fun a dor ken nur kommen durch der vos hut nisht oiver geven der chet hador*" (the salvation of a generation can only come about through someone who did not commit the sin of his generation). He then continued and said, "*Un dus iz geven Mordechai Hatzaddik in Shushan Habirah*" (and that was Mordechai the *tzaddik* in Shushan Habirah).

Those were the words Rav Shneur said in the name of his father Rav Aharon Kotler.

When I heard that line, I broke out into a big smile. Because I realized then and there the secret of Mordechai's greatness.

"*U'Mordechai lo yichreh v'lo yishtachaveh*" (And Mordechai didn't bend his knee or bow down to Haman).

It was as if Chananiah, Mishael, and Azariah had returned. Mordechai was exhibiting the exact same behavior. He refused to even consider bowing down to anyone other than the Holy One blessed be He. There was nothing to talk about, nothing to consider. Only G-d. And that was why Mordechai was the only person capable of saving the Jews and leading them to redemption. Mordechai was the only Jew walking the streets of Shushan who had not compromised himself in any way.

And now let us go one great step further.

The Megillah introduces Mordechai Hayehudi with the famous line "*Ish Yehudi hayah b'Shushan Habirah u'shmo Mordechai Ben Yair, Ben*

*Shimi, Ben Kish, ish Yemini.*" There is an inherent contradiction in this *pasuk*. *Ish Yehudi*, a man from the tribe of Yehudah. *Ish Yemini*, a man from the tribe of Binyamin. Which tribe was he from?

The Gemara supplies a number of answers.

But I would like to resolve this obvious contradiction with the following suggestion.

Mordechai Hayehudi was an "Ish Yehudi," the one man, the sole individual in Shushan who remained faithful to the oath taken by the rivers of Babylon. "If I forget thee, Oh Jerusalem, may I forget my right hand [*yemini*]." Mordechai was the kind of person that were you to ask him how he felt, or if you asked him to perhaps sing for you, he'd reply that he could not even contemplate such an action, because how can a person sing when the Temple has still not been rebuilt? For him Shushan was nothing more than exile (a benevolent exile, perhaps, a comfortable exile, but an exile nonetheless), and he ultimately moved to Eretz Yisrael along with Ezra and Nechemiah. He was *"ish Yemini,"* the man who would rather forget his *yad yamin,* his right hand, than lose sight of Yerushalayim even for a second. Mordechai never made peace with the exile. If you wanted to know what an uncompromising "Al Naharos Bavel Jew" looked like, all that was necessary was to seek out Mordechai.

# 11

# ENTERING THE RABBINATE

As time went on and the years passed, I came to the realization that I didn't see myself remaining in Toronto for the long term. For the time being I continued at Ner Yisroel, while accepting a job as *rav* for the northernmost shul in Toronto at that time, which was located a mere ten-minute walk from the *yeshivah* campus in a neighborhood called Willowdale. When I first arrived at the *yeshivah*, we had been completely surrounded by forest land, but you can't stop progress, and soon enough a bridge builder, Joe Tenenbaum, began constructing a huge housing development called Tangreen Village. Other builders began putting up hundreds of houses as well.

A good friend, Rabbi Shlomo Jacobowitz, was the principal of Toronto's Eitz Chaim School and a wonderful individual. He was the brother of Lord Immanuel Jakobovits, chief rabbi of the United Kingdom from 1967 to 1991. He moved out to the new housing development north of the *yeshivah*, which was a courageous move at that time. It wasn't long before a group of families decided they needed a place to pray and rented a storefront to be used as a shul. Rav Shlomo had been serving as the de facto rabbi of this new congregation, but he was planning on moving elsewhere at the end of the year, which meant that the shul would be needing a new *rav* shortly.

"Listen, Sholom," he said to me one day. "I think you'd be perfect for the job. Are you interested in the rabbinate?"

I was. I knew I would enjoy the challenge of having to constantly originate new speeches and material. I knew that I would love giving classes to the members of my shul. I was also drawn to the unmatched opportunities for doing *chesed* – everything from counseling to comforting mourners to visiting the sick to answering questions and queries on halachic matters. There was no question in my mind that this was the right path for me to take. Next thing I knew, he'd invited me to come address the shul. I walked over on Shavuos and gave the *drashah* and found to my happiness that it was a *shidduch*. I liked them, they liked me, and it looked like Rav Shlomo's idea was going to work.

I met with the board several times in the summer of 1966, and by Elul I had officially been inaugurated as *rav* of Congregation B'nai Torah. The congregation had moved premises shortly before I arrived, from their storefront on Transwell Avenue to a wooden structure on the corner of Patricia and Bathurst Streets. The structure, affectionately referred to by one and all as "the shack," was used by the Eitz Chaim School during the week and by Congregation B'nai Torah on Shabbos. It was quite a large shack as shacks go, with a few classrooms and even an *ezras nashim* for the women, but it was nothing that could be considered permanent.

People fell in love with our fledgling operation. So much so that it wasn't long before we'd outgrown our humble origins. The only question was where to move. There was a bountiful portion of land nearby that had been zoned by the city for future usage by a shul and a school and was granted to Eitz Chaim Schools. I negotiated with my good friend Harry Korolnek and suggested that since we were the only shul in the area it was fair and logical that we should get the shul portion.

In the end, we got the land. I could already see the magnificent shul that we were going to build. However, I had a challenge on my hands. A large percentage of my membership were employed in the same profession, the upstanding field of accounting. And these competent gentlemen all wanted to know exactly how we would be able to pay for our dream building. I was ready to build a shul without a nickel to my name, but I had to harness all my powers of persuasion to convince them that we could do this. It was a tough sell.

After weeks of me trying to peddle my vision for the future, we had reached a major split right down the middle of the board. Everyone had taken a side and I had no idea whether those in favor of building were going to win in the upcoming vote.

Board meetings can get tense at times. This one sure was.

Each side was very serious about its position. The nays felt we were being irresponsible by taking on such an overwhelming financial obligation without knowing how we were going to manage to pay it off. The yeas were full of confidence that we would be able to carry the load. This vote was going to shape the future of our shul.

We sat around the conference table and you could cut the tension with a knife. Those against wouldn't meet my eyes. At some point during the voting, I made my own calculations and arrived at the conclusion that the way things were developing meant that it was going to take one vote to swing things my way. One vote. One vote to ensure a beautiful building for our growing *kehillah*.

I took the president of the shul out of the room.

"Please trust me," I implored him. "I promise you that we'll be able to pull this off. We need one vote and you're it."

He looked me in the eye. "Rabbi Gold," he said, "even if I vote your way and you win by one, I don't consider that a mandate to go ahead and build a shul."

I used every ounce of persuasion that I had left. "Let it pass," I cajoled him. "I promise you that it will be okay. You'll see, the community will rally behind us and we'll end up building a beautiful shul."

In the end he did it my way. The vote passed by one. A year later the building was up.

The first major donation came from a man who would go on later to establish a name for himself as a philanthropist of the highest caliber. He was a very wealthy man who had built himself up from scratch. Already then he sat on the board of the *yeshivah* and many other Jewish organizations. His name was Joe Tenenbaum, the real estate developer.

We knew one another and had always been friendly. Still, I had never asked him for money before.

I had nothing to worry about. He greeted me cordially, heard me out, and agreed with me that it was a very important cause. He gave a serious contribution. The shul's cornerstone is dedicated in memory of his parents.

*≈*

As the *rav* of B'nai Torah I developed a relationship with all the rabbinic figures in Toronto, and with two of them in particular. One was Rav Gedalia Felder, a major Torah scholar and the author of *Yesodei Yeshurun*, among other halachic works. My friendship with Rav Felder began soon after I arrived in Toronto. He was a good friend and very helpful to the *yeshivah*. Through his efforts a major endowment was made from an estate to a number of the Torah organizations in Toronto. We served on the Toronto *beis din* along with Rav Nachum Eliezer Rabinovitch (today the esteemed *rosh yeshivah* of Yeshivat Birkat Moshe in Ma'ale Adumim). Together we extended the Toronto *eruv*, which had been operational for forty years and needed to keep pace in a Toronto that was growing faster than anyone could have foreseen.

We extended the *eruv* to Finch Avenue, where the *yeshivah* was located, and included all the new housing developments that were along the way. Then we extended it to Steeles Avenue even farther north, encircling Tangreen Village and pretty much any place where Jews were living. My entire community was now included in the *eruv*. We Torontonian rabbis walked the streets, worked out distances, and discussed whether a particular telephone poll or wall could be included. I didn't realize it at the time but my exposure to the laws of *eruv* would stand me in good stead a few years later when I became *rav* in West Hempstead.

We were a *beis din* for divorces as well, and the better I got to know my fellow rabbis, the more I respected them. They were a group of sincere men who genuinely cared about the community. Toronto was fortunate when it came to rabbis. They even merited to host Rav Yaakov Kamenetsky as a *rav* before he moved on to become *rosh yeshivah* of

Torah Vodaath. And since his second wife was from Toronto, he visited the city fairly often. Rabbi Avraham Price and Rabbi Dovid Ochs were the community's senior rabbis, and they brought the taste of the European rabbinate to Canadian shores.

Being a shul rabbi was a wonderful experience for me. I enjoyed a warm relationship with my congregation and came to the realization that being a *rav* could very well be the career that I was searching for.

❧

1967. In the weeks before the Six-Day War broke out, all anyone talked about was Gamal Abdel Nasser and the massive buildup of the Egyptian army on Israel's border. From Cairo came the unending sound of Nasser's fearsome rants as he boasted of the damage he planned for "the blister on the skin of the Middle East." Egypt had been the recipient of abundant military and financial aid from their patron, the USSR. They were equipped with impressive weaponry, including the latest in tanks, artillery, and jets.

During the month of May, the sounds of war began to reach new heights. The cacophony of saber rattling from Arab capitals and the frenzied crowds calling for death to the Jews intensified alarmingly. When Nasser closed the Straits of Tiran, the noose began to tighten around Israel. Foreign airlines stopped flights to Israel. World Jewry was gripped with concern, which escalated to anxiety and then to outright fear. The situation became desperate. Israel prepared for the worst. Thousands of graves were dug in Israel's parks.

In May and early June, all we knew was what we saw: pictures of Nasser and the bloodthirsty Egyptian masses, arms waving in the air, voices bellowing for Israeli blood. The sight of those millions chilled our very marrow. Arab leaders made pacts between themselves even as the world remained silent and Israel isolated. Jews across the globe gathered in their synagogues to pray and cry for Israel's deliverance. At the *yeshivah* all the boys and staff walked around in a daze, the worry evident on their faces, the strain everywhere.

A man walked into his bank in Toronto and asked the manager for a loan.

"What do you want the money for, sir?"

"I want to send the money over to Israel."

"I'm sorry, sir," the manager replied, "We don't grant loans for that kind of thing. Loans are for someone who wants to purchase a home or improve on an already existing home."

The man looked the manager in the eye and said, "I want a home improvement loan."

The manager gave him the money.

There was a feeling in the air that our "home" was in grave danger. The unity exhibited by one and all was phenomenal.

And then it happened. All we knew was that war had broken out. But we did not know until later that the war was won in the first three hours. It began with a surprise attack by the Israeli Air Force. Using almost every single jet at their disposal (at the start of the attack there were only nine planes left behind to protect the country), they proceeded over the border to Egypt, where they destroyed hundreds of enemy aircraft on the ground.

In the next six days, Israel would be granted the heavenly assistance to not only demolish the enemy's air force, but to vanquish their ground forces as well. Egypt was completely routed, as was Jordan, in a stunning victory where Israeli troops recaptured the Old City of Jerusalem, the Temple Mount, and the West Bank from the Jordanians. In the final two days of the war, Israel turned its attention to Syria and captured the Golan Heights and other strategic areas. The Hand of G-d was clearly visible throughout those six days, and all Israel rejoiced.

The *yeshivah*'s executive director, David Cohen, called me that Monday morning.

"Sholom, it's war!"

The reports and misinformation from the Arab media had us tied up in knots. They swore that the Haifa refineries were burning; they claimed that Tel Aviv was being bombed and was already in flames. The fear was awesome. Many of us went down to the Israeli consulate and signed up for any job that the Israelis needed. We were prepared to go and fight if they wanted us. We would do whatever was needed to save our brothers. But by the end of the week it was all over and there was no reason for anyone to go anywhere. The war had been won.

Michael Oren, Israel's ambassador to the United States, is a historian who has written the definitive work on the Six-Day War (*Six Days of War: June 1967 and the Making of the Modern Middle East* [Oxford University Press, 2002]). Reading the book is a religious experience, with one chapter in particular that will turn an atheist into a firm believer in G-d. The chapter that describes "Day One, June 5" reads like Megillas Esther, where the name of Hashem does not appear yet His presence is pervasive. What follows are some of the stunning series of "coincidences" that punctuated the first hours of the war.

- Israeli planes started taking off at 7:10 a.m. and within twenty minutes there were two hundred planes on their way to Egypt, flying incredibly low to avoid radar detection.
- Egypt had assumed that any potential raid by the Israelis would be carried out at dawn. Having already flown early-morning patrols, the Egyptian air force had returned to base and nearly all the planes were on the ground.
- Two planes were taking off from Egypt's Almaza Air Force Base, carrying most of Egypt's army commanders. They did not notice the oncoming Israeli planes.
- Jordan had a highly sophisticated British-supplied radar facility at 'Ajlun, near Jerash, and it indeed picked up the massive concentration of Israeli planes. The Jordanian officer then in charge at 'Ajlun immediately radioed the code word for war to General Riyad's headquarters in Amman.
- Riyad promptly radioed the news to Defense Minister Shams Badraan in Cairo, but the message had no effect, because the Egyptians had switched to different encoding frequencies the day before, and no one had thought to inform the Jordanians.
- The Israelis had also changed frequencies, so the radar station at 'Ajlun could not be certain whether the massive concentration of planes approaching Egypt were Israeli, British, or American, leaving them uncertain as to the exact nature of the threat. They continued to cable their now indecipherable code word.

- Egypt's defense minister, after a late-night vigil, had apparently been satisfied that things were calm for the time being, and had retired to bed with a "do not disturb" order. Other key personnel such as chief decoder Colonel Mas'ud al-Junaydi and Air Operations Chief General Gamal 'Afifi were also unavailable.

Quite a fascinating series of "coincidences." Jordanian radar detects Israel's planes and sounds the alarm, but Egypt doesn't get it because they just happened to change the codes the day before and failed to inform the Jordanians. It just so happened that the Defense Minister had gone to bed a few hours earlier leaving instructions not to be disturbed. Most of the top Egyptian brass "happen" to be in two planes in the air, unaware of the approaching Israeli Air Force.

Weather conditions turned out to be just about perfect as the Israeli planes arrived. What jolly good "luck." The Israelis benefited from complete surprise: by the time they appeared on Egyptian radar, it was far too late for the Egyptian pilots to get into their planes. Within half an hour, half of Egypt's aircraft had been destroyed. Within less than two hours the extent of the damage to Egypt's planes, airports, pilots, radar, and support services was such that Air Force Commander Motti Hod could announce to Yitzhak Rabin, then chief of staff of the IDF, "The Egyptian air force has ceased to exist."*

The Israelis lost only eight planes to Egyptian fire in that first wave.** Incredibly, chief of staff of the Egyptian army Abdel Hakim Amer had given a no-fire order while he himself was in the air, to prevent his own plane being shot by "friendly fire." Imagine that just when hundreds of Israeli planes are on their holy mission, the enemy has ordered its anti-aircraft batteries to remain silent.

The most practical "down to earth" commentary on the Six-Day War was expressed by Commander Rafael "Raful" Eytan: "Apparently

---

* Cited in Michael Oren, *Six Days of War: June 1967 and the Making of the Modern Middle East* (London: Oxford University Press, 2002), 176.
** Ibid.

someone in heaven was watching over us. Every unintended action they took and every unintended action we took always turned out to our advantage."*

That's why I say Hallel on Yom Yerushalayim. Three million Jews saved in so miraculous a fashion. No words to describe it. "Amazing," "fantastic," even "miraculous" just don't do it. Only Hallel says it best.

Years later I gained a greater appreciation of the *mishnah* that describes the mitzvah to relate the story of the Exodus at the Seder: "*Matchil bi'gnut u'msayem b'shevach*," one must begin the story by relating the suffering, servitude, pain, and horror of the enslavement in Egypt and only then describe the triumphant exodus. To fully understand and appreciate the majesty of the Six-Day War one must relive the anxiety, concern, and fear of May 1967.

ه

A year later. Yom Yerushalayim.

I looked around the *yeshivah*'s dining room and mused to myself that it was only fitting for the *yeshivah* to celebrate this great day.

I turned to some of the staff.

"Don't you think the boys should sing and dance in honor of Yom Yerushalayim?"

They looked at one another. Finally one *rebbe* came up with a good reason to keep things quiet.

"It's *sefirah*," he said. And the rest of the staff echoed his statement. "*Sefirah. Sefirah*! No singing or dancing during *sefirah*."

They didn't want to dance for Yerushalayim's honor for fear of being branded Zionists. So they concocted a nonsensical, pitiful excuse: *sefirah*.

Suddenly the sounds of merriment filled the dining room. The *rebbeim* turned toward the doorway to see what was happening. One of the senior students entered the room, a gigantic smile on his face, offering cigarettes to anyone who wanted. He had just gotten engaged. The entire dining room jumped up. A roar of "Od Yishama" (a song

---

* Ibid., 179.

which ironically describes joy in the city of Jerusalem) filled the cavernous room as the boys jumped and danced. The entire staff joined the joyous dancing, except for me. I just sat there.

Eventually the dancing petered out. The *rebbeim* returned to the table sweating and out of breath, a smile on every face. I looked at them one by one, met their eyes. Then I smiled gently and uttered one word.

"*Sefirah?*"

There is no need to describe their utter shame.

And then I told the students of the *yeshivah* that if they sang in honor of Yerushalayim, they would not be marked absent for missing classes. And they did. For an hour and a half. All in all, it was a wonderful moment.

A similar incident happened to me a few years later after I'd assumed the position of *rav* of the Young Israel of West Hempstead. I had been invited to a dinner for Chinuch Atzmai and once there, found myself seated at a table with a bunch of old friends, some of whom I had known since childhood. We made small talk and then one of the guys piped up.

"So, Sholom, what did you speak about in your *drashah* yesterday?"

The Israeli government, intent on making peace, had just given the Sinai Desert to Egypt, and the dismantling of the beautiful community of Yamit had been part of the deal. Pictures of crying Jews being dragged from their homes by crying soldiers filled the pages of the world's media. It was a tragedy beyond belief.

"I spoke about the evacuation of Yamit and its being ground into the sands of Sinai. What else could I possibly talk about?"

Half the people sitting at the table had never even heard of Yamit.

Others looked at me suspiciously. I knew what they were thinking. Why had I wasted a Shabbos *drashah* on politics? *Drashos* were for Torah!

I ignored my tablemates and prepared to listen to the keynote speaker – but I admit that I was hurt.

I want you to picture the scene. Rav Moshe Feinstein was sitting on the dais, Rav Ovadia Yosef sitting by his side. The leaders of American and Israeli Jewry were all represented.

Soon enough Rav Avraham Yosef Shapira stood up to speak. At the time he was a member of Knesset from Agudas Yisroel and was known as "the director general of the *medinah*."

He waited for complete silence. "I've just arrived here from Eretz Yisrael," he began, "and I know that I'm supposed to speak about Chinuch Atzmai."

A pause.

"But how is it possible for me to speak about Chinuch Atzmai today without speaking about Yamit? I was the Gerrer Rebbe's personal messenger to see the situation in Yamit. Being his personal emissary gave me the clout necessary to get past the military lines while other civilians were stopped and sent away. We had heard about those who had threatened to blow themselves up in their homes rather than be sent into exile. The Gerrer Rebbe was extremely concerned and was waiting for a report."

Rav Avraham Yosef Shapira began describing the scene that had met his eyes and as he spoke, there was not a sound in the room. Suddenly, he just burst into tears, right in that fancy ballroom, surrounded by the elite of the Torah world. And he began crying like a baby, because *how could he talk about anything that day without talking about Yamit?*

I looked around the table at all my old friends. Nobody would look me in the eye as Rav Shapira cried his heart out in front of the world's most famous rabbinical figures and spoke with passion about a city in Israel that had been destroyed. I hope my friends matured a bit that day.

❦

In the summer of 1969 Bayla and I went to Eretz Yisrael for a visit. My in-laws moved into our house and took care of the children. Only now do I realize how difficult it must have been for them. But they did it for us. They knew that I had been working very hard and how important it was to me. It would be Bayla's much anticipated first visit, and my first time back since my student days. On the plane, I made the acquaintance of a truly gifted *talmid chacham* who said a *shiur* in one of New York's finest *yeshivos*. Our conversation got down to issues of the day and I discerned that my new friend had absolutely no use for Yom Haatzmaut.

I tried to convince him that a new *yom tov* of only two years' vintage,

Yom Yerushalayim, marking the miraculous victory of the Six-Day War, the liberation of vast areas of our biblical homeland, and the return of Yerushalayim to Israeli sovereignty was certainly of great historic significance. He didn't buy that either and was just opposed to it all. I never really figured out what he wanted. Should we bring the British back and renew the Mandate? Close Eretz Yisrael to all the world's Jews? Did he want us to hand the Kosel over to Jordan or the Vatican?

He was vague (or confused?).

Be that as it may, I suggested that when we arrived in Yerushalayim I would take him to a great Torah scholar who was not yet well known in the Jewish world, Rav Yosef Shalom Elyashiv, and present our respective positions to him. A few days later, we were wending our way through the alleyways of Meah Shearim as I retraced the steps I had taken thirteen years earlier. Much to my surprise I found it. The walk was far more calm and peaceful then the first time I had been there during the civil defense exercise in the summer of 1956.

We entered Rav Elyashiv's apartment and proceeded to present our positions. For me Yom Yerushalayim is a day of great historic significance, of thanksgiving for Hashem's awesome gift to His people, for the victory of the Six-Day War, the reunification of Yerushalayim, and the liberation of Yehudah and Shomron.

My friend made it clear that he saw no reason to celebrate.

Having presented our positions, we fell silent and waited to hear what the Rav had to say. He sat up tall in his chair, then bent forward facing my friend, his eyes boring into him, and proceeded to let him have it.

"You were in America for the nineteen years that we were here unable to pray at the Kosel. You obviously don't appreciate or understand the depth of our feeling for Yerushalayim and the pain of being separated from her. Well, for us here, it was and is a great day. Do you realize that the entire Yishuv was in grave, mortal danger and then saved by Hashem's miraculous intervention?"

Rav Elyashiv's reply was spoken with intense feeling and emotion.

I have reported what he said and how he said it with no embellishment of my own.

≈

During my twelfth and final year in Toronto, I had already left the *yeshivah* completely and while remaining *rav* at Congregation B'nai Torah, I took up teaching as the Gemara *rebbe* for the tenth grade at one of the other high schools in Toronto. The staff of that school was comprised of some old-time Mirrer alumni. These were men who had escaped with the *yeshivah* through Europe and over to Shanghai, eventually reaching the shores of North America, where they found to their chagrin that there weren't sufficient high-level teaching positions available for them all. With no choice, many of them became high school *rebbeim*, serving Klal Yisrael as best they could. I had the privilege of teaching alongside those giants of spirit. Sitting with Rav Shochet and Rav Gordon in the staff room was like an injection of adrenaline for me.

In that final year, I had a student in my tenth-grade class whose path was destined to merge with mine years later. I, who had never imagined teaching the tenth grade and who considered that year as nothing more than a stop along the way to much "bigger" things, found out later on that my tenth-grade interlude would end up serving as an extremely vital period of time in my life, because that was when I met Avrom Silver.

Thirteen or fourteen years later, he would reenter my life at a most crucial moment, just when I needed him most. He would dedicate the shul in Har Nof, Kehillat Zichron Yosef, in memory of his father, and help me make that dream into a reality.

During my last year in Toronto, G-d was laying the groundwork for the future. In retrospect, the *hashgachah* – the Divine Providence – was nothing less than incredible.

≈

Throughout my Toronto years, I went to a number of interviews for rabbinical positions. One was a most promising community in California that was growing exponentially. In addition, a friend of mine from Toronto set up another interview for me in an East Coast town as well.

I was to meet the board of the Young Israel of West Hempstead, which was actively looking for a new rabbi, and then after that meeting, I would continue my journey by flying on to California. To be perfectly clear here, I had no particular aspirations about the position in West Hempstead because the California job seemed perfect for me. And besides, there were many rabbis interviewing for the West Hempstead position and I really didn't expect to be the one they chose.

I met with the thirty-member selection committee in West Hempstead and then flew to California. When I got home I wasn't sure what to do next. West Hempstead had already called to let me know they were interested in me coming in for a follow-up Shabbos, and California had let me know that they were tentatively interested in continuing the relationship. What was I to do? What if both communities wanted me? Which was a better place? I was lacking direction. So I sat down and I wrote a letter to the Lubavitcher Rebbe outlining my dilemma and requesting his assistance and clarification.

My letter to the Rebbe was two pages long. I dedicated the first page of my letter and three quarters of the second page as well to a vivid description of the community in California. I devoted my last remaining paragraph to West Hempstead.

I figured out how long it should take for the Rebbe to receive mail from Toronto. When I was sure that the Rebbe had definitely received my letter, I called his secretary, Rabbi Chodakov, and asked him if there had been a response to my missive.

He replied in the affirmative.

"The Rebbe said that you should have written two pages about West Hempstead and one paragraph about California. And then the Rebbe said, 'Take a closer look at California.'"

This was a cryptic line if I'd ever heard one. Did the Rebbe know something that I didn't?

I called Rabbi Neuberger at Ner Yisroel. He had been the one who'd set up the interview for me on the West Coast, and if there was anything to know, he'd know it. I asked him to give me a very straight and thorough picture of what was happening out on the coast. I didn't stop my investigation there. I dug further. The more I dug, the more I uncovered. Soon enough I had a very clear picture about the California job and had learned that this particular town was full of infighting and arguments and jealousy and that it was not for me. In the end, a friend of mine assumed the position and left after a year. The Rebbe's insight was simply uncanny.

Meanwhile, West Hempstead invited me to come spend a Shabbos with the community so that we could get to know each other. But it was already late July, early August. If I went to West Hempstead now and they offered me the position and I accepted, that would mean leaving my Toronto congregation in the lurch right before Rosh Hashanah, and I didn't feel that was right.

In the end I called the West Hempstead board and said as follows: "Right now I have a commitment to my shul in Toronto and it wouldn't be fair for me to get involved anywhere else. Please take my hat out of the ring. I am officially removing my candidacy for this job."

That was the end of it, I thought.

And then, more than half a year later, just before Purim, I returned home from giving my weekly Gemara class, walked into the house, and my wife said to me, "Sholom, you'll never guess who called."

"Who?"

"West Hempstead. They didn't yet hire a *rav*" – this despite having interviewed many *rabbanim* – "and decided that they want to see you again."

She didn't sound at all surprised.

I called them back and Bayla and I were invited to spend another Shabbos in West Hempstead. I was put through the rigors of a *proba*, an "audition" Shabbos, and was ultimately offered the position of rabbi of the Young Israel of West Hempstead. This time everything was different. Willowdale, my Toronto congregation, had sufficient time to interview and hire another rabbi and they had more than a few months to adjust to the idea that their *rav* was moving on to a different locale. And so it was in August 1971 that the Gold family, five children and two parents (Menachem, born in 1962; Chavi, born in 1964; Libi, born in 1966; Daphna, born in 1968; and Yirmi, born in 1970), made their way out of Canada and over the border to the township of West Hempstead in the State of New York.

What was it Rav Nesanel Quinn had thundered at us decades before? "*Rabboisai, men darf ibberhippen der brik, ibberhippen der brik!*" One must cross the bridge.

It had taken me twelve years to cross the Canadian bridge, but I was finally reaching the other side. The United States was calling my name. It was time for the prodigal son to return.

I vividly remember saying to Bayla that West Hempstead is over five hundred miles closer to Eretz Yisrael and only half an hour from Kennedy Airport.

# 12

# WEST HEMPSTEAD AND THE *ERUV*

Our first Shabbos in West Hempstead. My first time officially addressing my new shul as their *rav*. This was my one and only opportunity to make a first impression, and I wanted to make it memorable.

The shul was located between two of the main streets in town, Hempstead Avenue and Dogwood Avenue. Those of you who are slightly older might recall two extremely popular comic book characters by the names of "Dagwood" and "Bumpstead." Standing there at the front of the shul, I described to my amused audience how confused I'd been since my arrival in their fair town.

"I'm new here," I began, "and I don't know whether I'm going from Hempstead to Dogwood, or from Dagwood to Bumpstead!"

When the laughter quieted down I began the *drashah* in earnest. In Parshas Re'eh, the Torah says that "when Hashem…will bring you to the Land…to possess it, you shall deliver the blessing on Mount Gerizim and the curse on Mount Eval" (Devarim 11:29). Then the Torah proceeds to give a precise description of where they are located. "Are they not on the other side of the Jordan, far in the direction of the sunset, in the land of the Canaanite that dwells in the plain, far from Gilgul, near the plains of Moreh?" (Devarim 11:30).

The location of Mounts Gerizim and Eval is clearly pinpointed, yet when the Torah refers to Yerushalayim, a veritable wall of secrecy – a consistent silence – appears throughout. More than twenty times the Torah talks about "the place that Hashem will choose from amongst your tribes," "the place where Hashem will make His presence dwell," and so on, yet not a hint of the name. Why the secrecy?

"What's the Torah afraid of?" I asked my congregation. "Just say the word – *Yerushalayim*! This is the Torah we're talking about. The very same Torah that stays far away from redundancy, that won't use an unnecessary word. When it comes to Mount Gerizim, no word is spared to fix its location, but when referring to Yerushalayim, utter silence. This is puzzling.

"The Torah didn't mention the name Yerushalayim," said I, beginning to answer my questions, "because if it had been mentioned, it might have left the impression that G-d is the one Who sanctifies Yerushalayim.

"This however is not so.

"Holiness in our universe is created by man. If I say this table is holy, it becomes holy. I have the ability to sanctify any object I want. You want some proof to what I'm saying?

"Consider this.

"The greatest event in our history, the giving of the Torah to the Jews at Mount Sinai, took place at a location that was not holy at all. That's right, Mount Sinai is not and never was a place of holiness. We don't visit it, we don't make pilgrimages there. It's not *kadosh*, not holy. Yerushalayim, on the other hand, is extremely *kadosh*, extremely holy.

"What's the difference between the two places?

"The reason Mount Sinai was holy at the moment of revelation was the Divine Presence. When the Divine Presence departed, the holiness left as well. Yerushalayim, however, became holy through man. Avraham Avinu offered Yitzchak as an offering to G-d in Yerushalayim. The holiness began right then and never left. But it always came about through humans. Later Klal Yisrael arrived and David Hamelech purchased the area from Aravnah using money given to him by the entire nation; this was an act leading toward the sanctification of Yerushalayim, continuing the chain of actions put into motion by our forefathers long before.

"G-d referred to Yerushalayim as 'the place chosen by Him' because He wants future generations to know that Yerushalayim's holiness comes about from the people, by the people, and for the people. Once His nation made it holy, then G-d contributed tremendous holiness to the city as well. But only after we took the first step."

My point was that as people, we're the ones that give a sense of purpose, sanctity, and future to any given place, to any community. It depends completely on us. I concluded by telling my congregation that we had a job to do. Together we would continue to build on the foundations established by Rabbi Meyer Fendel and Rabbi Zvi Dov Kanotopsky, my illustrious predecessors. I emphasized that West Hempstead had great potential to be a major Jewish community and that is what together we would strive for.

As a first speech, I found that it went over very well.

Our first week in West Hempstead passed uneventfully. We were settling in to our new home, getting acquainted with our new location, streets, schools, shops. A new town. The doorbell rang almost nonstop. People were coming by to say hello and introduce themselves and to drop off little gifts: bottles of wine, catered food, vegetables from their gardens, you name it. A wonderfully warm welcome. The second week I went about meeting people and giving classes. I was also spending time preparing for my teaching position in Torah Academy for Girls (TAG) in Far Rockaway, where my three daughters would go to school.

Things were progressing well, but Shabbos was quickly becoming a problem for us. Toronto was the first – and for many years the only – city in North America that had a citywide *eruv*. It was established by Rav Yehuda Leib Graubart, the author of five volumes of responsa called *Chavalim Ba'ne'imim*, who served as chief rabbi of Toronto for about twenty years until his passing in 1937. This means that Bayla had grown up all her life in a city that had an *eruv*. Now in West Hempstead with a baby (Yirmi was around a year old at the time), she was confined to the house on Shabbos. Something had to be done. So I decided to investigate the feasibility of making an *eruv* around the town.

About the third Sunday in West Hempstead, I got into my car and began driving. I circled the entire perimeter of the town in every direction. I stopped the car at times, got out and walked for blocks. My neck began to hurt from peering up at all the telephone and electric wires. But at the end of that Sunday excursion I knew one thing: building an *eruv* in West Hempstead was a feasible option and there was no reason to delay getting started.

Before I could take this *eruv* idea to the next level, however, I needed to discuss it with someone greater than myself. I had had the opportunity to get to know Rav Moshe Feinstein over the years. In fact, we had a pretty close relationship. I called him and asked his advice.

I told Rav Moshe all about my new job and the challenge facing my *eruv*-less community. Since he was the halachic authority of the generation, I felt that I needed his blessing to go ahead with my plan before embarking on such an ambitious and unconventional project.

Rav Moshe heard me out. Then he asked me the following insightful question.

"How many congregational rabbis live in West Hempstead?"

"One," I replied.

"Do you mean that there is one rabbi in addition to you, or are you the only one?" His tone was deliberate. Clearly this was an important question.

"I am the only rabbi in town," I said.

"If that's the case, Sholom, build the *eruv*. Build the *eruv*." And with that our conversation came to a close. It was clear from our little discussion that if there had been more than one *rav*, differences in opinion might have caused friction in the community. But since it was only me, there was no reason to hold back on my initiative. I was to build the *eruv* of West Hempstead and I was to build it now.

With Rav Moshe's blessing in hand, I set off on my mission. Although I had been in town for just a short while, there were a number of men who were already attending my classes on a regular basis. I approached this group of young men and, spelling out my intentions, requested their assistance. They wanted to know what building the *eruv* was going to entail so I explained the entire procedure to them. Before I knew it, the impromptu *eruv* committee (including Bert Pechman, Bernie Zivotofsky, Marvin Wachspress, and other dedicated individuals) had begun devoting four hours to Operation Eruv every Sunday morning.

My first move was to ask those who were good with a hammer and nails to pick up lumber so we could begin constructing the *lechi*s, the pieces of wood that would be used as poles.

The *eruv* committee went from pole to pole around the perimeter of the town. Since the Long Island Railroad abuts the town, its gate served as a natural wall for the *eruv* along one side of West Hempstead, making our job that much easier. Most of the utility poles in town were ready-made *eruv* material as well, and there wasn't that much that we needed to do. But in certain places the telephone wires weren't hanging straight enough or there was some other technical problem and then we were forced to build a *lechi* here and a *lechi* there to solve each individual issue that arose. It was slow going but we persevered, making steady progress on our community project. We tried to use what was already in place, turning to our "construction" experts only if we absolutely needed to. It wasn't long before our *eruv* really began taking shape.

I contacted two people to help facilitate the *eruv* committee work all the way to the finish line. Staten Island had already constructed an *eruv* a few years before, and the man who had made it all come together was Moshe Friederwitzer (today of Har Nof, Jerusalem). I still have his letters to me where he describes the *eruv* in Staten Island.

The second person I contacted would go on to become a respected halachic authority over the next twenty years. Rav Shimon Eider was still a relatively young man at the time, but already making a brilliant name for himself.

I welcomed Rav Eider into my home and before we could even begin discussing the *eruv*, he did a very strange and unexpected thing. I watched in surprise as he pulled a small copy of the *sefer Mesillas Yesharim* out of his pocket.

He handed me the *sefer* and motioned me to open the cover.

I did. There was an inscription written on the first page. I glanced at the handwriting. Then I did a double take. It was mine. Quickly I scanned the written lines.

"This *sefer* is a gift to my dear camper Shimon, from your counselor Sholom Gold."

I couldn't believe it.

I was suddenly thrust back to a summer in Camp Agudah decades earlier, when I'd met a little boy who was then attending public school. Over the summer I'd come to know the young man well and I recognized a potential inside that *neshamah* that bordered on the incredible. I studied with him over the summer, my efforts culminating with a gift to a special boy at the summer's end, a gift which he treasured and brought to me years later to show me how much it had meant to him at the time.

You just never know which action of yours is going to make a difference. I stood there in my house in West Hempstead recalling those wonderful summers back at camp, surrounded by religious youth enjoying the delightful weather and scenery up in the Catskills. I thought about the time Rav Yaakov Kamenetsky (who was then visiting the camp), scared the wits out of me when he dove into the pool and disappeared beneath the water for an inordinate amount of time. I recalled being beside myself with fear, trying to decide what to do. Maybe I shouted out in panic, maybe not. I don't recall. But a few seconds later, there he was, emerging at the far end of the pool with a smile on his holy face, having swum the entire length of the pool beneath the water. He was an amazing swimmer.

From Agudah, I moved on to Camp Kol Rina and spent a few summers there too, assisting Reb Yankel Greenwald back when he first opened his wonderful camp. It was a pioneering movement in America. I used to go there from Torah Vodaath and afterwards from Ner Yisroel. And it was never about the money. I didn't even request a salary from him. He was trying to run a successful camping enterprise and I was content to assist him in his endeavor, pro bono. But toward the end of the summer I noticed that I was having serious problems with my tefillin. They were not an expensive pair – far from it. My parents couldn't afford better.

I made up my mind to purchase my own pair of tefillin, a truly beautiful pair. There was a scribe in Williamsburg named Rav Spinner who was famous for writing special tefillin and I wanted his. But they were very expensive. Way out of my league.

You're probably imagining that they cost hundreds of dollars, right? No. They were eighty dollars. But who had eighty dollars back then?

Still, I wanted those tefillin desperately. Having no choice, I approached Rav Yankel Greenwald and asked him for back pay, for the salary which I'd never requested, but which I now needed. And he gave me the eighty dollars and I purchased a pair of tefillin from the best *sofer* in Williamsburg. Such well-made tefillin that I still use them until this very day. I was overjoyed when I donned those brand new tefillin for the first time.

I returned to reality from my camping days and saw Rav Eider standing in my living room, his *Mesillas Yesharim* clutched tightly in my hand. I handed it back to him.

"What do you have in mind?" he asked me with a warm smile. I could tell that it was a pleasure for him to be in my home, sort of a relationship coming full circle. We got into my car and drove around town, me pointing out to him every section of the *eruv* as we drove. He concurred with my judgment on almost every point, although there was one thing that needed immediate fixing before we could begin operations. In the end, Rav Eider became a firm and committed member of our *eruv* team, even calling Rav Moshe Feinstein a number of times with questions. He was our consultant and he discharged his task faithfully.

I am overcome with sadness as I write these last lines, memories of Rav Eider flashing through my mind. What a fine Jew. How sweet, kind, and real. What a mensch! And what a loss it was for Klal Yisrael when he passed away in 2007. He may be gone, but he is certainly not forgotten.

&

The building and construction part of the operation had come to an end. The *eruv* was ready for use. But there was still one more detail that needed to be taken care of before we could actually begin using it. According to *halachah*, the area enclosed by the *eruv* needs to be owned or rented to the community. This was a legal hurdle. I needed to explain to the town council that I wanted to purchase the township of West Hempstead for a small fee for a religious purpose.

I set up a meeting with the town representative, Mr. Francis Purcel to discuss the matter. I told him, "I need something that's actually very simple to do, but will probably sound a little crazy to you. I would like to purchase the town from you for a dollar."

The words hung in the air for a few seconds. Purcel stared at me, a bemused look on his face.

"What's that, Rabbi? Say that again. You want to what?"

"Buy the town for a buck."

He was full of questions. I tried my best to supply the answers. It took the council some time just to grasp the concept that Jews were not allowed to carry in the streets on Shabbos, unless one made a halachic delineation. Eventually we cleared it all up and they came to an elementary understanding of the concept.

There was a Jewish lawyer on staff at the municipality who realized the significance of the planned lease of the town to the Jewish community. He grasped what a story this was, the publicity angle that could be played up, and the extent to which this could enhance the town's image.

At the time, I was totally unaware of all this. I had never dreamed of the PR possibilities of our little *eruv*. All I wanted was to provide my congregation with the ability to keep Shabbos in the best possible way. What did I know of the media, of newspapers and radio?

*Erev bedikas chametz* 1972. My phone rang that morning.

"This is Francis Purcel from the West Hempstead municipality. I'm calling to invite you down to city hall for a meeting at one o'clock this afternoon."

One o'clock on the afternoon of *bedikas chametz*. Not the best time in the world. I still had many things I needed to do before Pesach commenced, but if town hall wanted a meeting with the rabbi, then we were going to have a meeting. My wife was busy with Pesach preparations, and so were the neighbors, and the kids needed to be kept busy. And that was why I drove down to City Hall with my station wagon filled with kids. All in all, a grand total of twelve kids came along with me for the ride.

We entered City Hall, all together. Twelve kids and one rabbi were ceremoniously ushered into the grand council meeting hall. All twelve kids took their seats in the row behind me. They peered around them curiously, taking it all in. Every member of the municipality was there. Every one.

They stared at the kids.

The kids stared back.

Without further ado, they handed me a copy of the document which clearly stated our agreement in legalese:

> Whereas the Jewish law dictates that one may not carry from one domain to another during the course of the Sabbath day…
> And whereas an *eruv* is a legal measure provided by the rabbis…
> And whereas it becomes necessary to purchase the town for this purpose…

There must have been fifteen "whereases" on that document.

They gave me a few minutes to peruse the document and then the town representative stood up to speak.

"We would like to welcome Rabbi Gold and all his children to City hall," he began. This statement was greeted by clapping, perhaps due to the council's admiration of my huge tribe.

The representative went on.

"The town of West Hempstead," he continued, "has decided to lease the grounds of the *eruv* to you, Rabbi Gold." Another outburst of clapping by the council greeted this proclamation.

"Thank you, thank you all very much," I responded, smiling broadly at one and all.

It was a powerful moment. The council members sat there beaming at me, gratified in their magnanimity, proud of having worked this challenge out, happy to be providing all the town's citizens with services needed.

"I would like to lease the land for a period of twenty years," I said, "and to retain the right to renew the lease at that time."

When the members of my shul asked me later why I'd specifically requested a twenty-year lease and not more, I explained that even though I was allowed to ask for fifty years according to the *Aruch Hashulchan*, I decided to ask for twenty because there was no doubt in my mind that we would be long gone from beautiful West Hempstead by then. Despite my fervent hopes, Mashiach still hasn't arrived, but my family and I had the good fortune to make aliyah before the twenty years ended. I still remember calling Rabbi Yehuda Kelemer, who succeeded me as *rav*, to remind him to make sure to renew the lease when it was up.

Meanwhile, the West Hempstead city council was amenable.

"Sounds about right to us," the secretary said. Everyone nodded. The feeling was amiable in the extreme. "We would really like to make this work in the best way possible."

I thanked the members of the council again and again, full of gratitude for their terrific attitudes.

Mr. Francis Purcel, however, was having some technical problems with what exactly to do with the dollar bill I'd presented to the council. They simply weren't equipped to deal with it and didn't know how to deposit it in the city's account. There was no procedure set up to put it through their books. They were at a loss.

I smiled inwardly at all the confusion and tension and merely suggested that instead of depositing the dollar into any city account, he should frame it and hang it on his office wall as a testimony to the wonderfully beneficial working relationship that the city had with all who lived in their boundaries.

By three thirty the party was over. I packed up my legal document, gathered together all twelve of "my" kids and proceeded to get them all back into the station wagon. Then, still smiling ear to ear, I drove out of the parking lot and headed home. *Bedikas chametz* was that evening and there was still much to do.

I entered the house with a spring in my step.

"I'm home!" I called out, brandishing the lease for my wife to see.

"It's been quite busy here while you were out," Bayla said, smiling mischievously. I knew that smile. Something had happened. I waited silently for her to tell me what it was.

"Someone called for you."

"Who?"

"A reporter," she said, stringing out the suspense.

"A reporter for which news publication?"

"A little newspaper called the *New York Times*."

Things were beginning to get interesting.

"The *New York Times*?" I repeated, stymied by the very mention of said newspaper in conjunction with my name. What on earth did the *Times* want from the rabbi of West Hempstead?

"Did they say what they wanted?"

"No, but the reporter said that it's very important that you call back as soon as possible. Here's the number."

Full of curiosity, I dialed the number. The phone rang and was answered almost immediately.

"This is Rabbi Gold," I identified myself to the man on the other end.

"Rabbi Gold? Rabbi Sholom Gold?"

"That's me."

"The rabbi that just leased West Hempstead for a dollar?"

"That's me."

"Rabbi Gold, I want to tell you something. You've just reached the newsroom in Great Neck, Long Island. We have representatives from the world press all sitting here in this room. All the media. Reuters. AP. BBC. *Time* magazine. Everyone. We drew lots and I was the lucky one who won. That's why I'm the one who gets to interview you. So tell me, is this really true? Did you just lease the city for a dollar?"

"I did, I really did."

"But what does that mean? And why did you even have to do this? And what's this whole *eruv* thing anyway? Readers around the world are going to be very interested in this story, Rabbi Gold, and I need to get my facts straight over here."

So I did my best to explain exactly what an *eruv* was and why West Hempstead needed one. I gave lots of credit to West Hempstead and to elected officials like Francis Purcel and the entire team from the township. It was a real eye opener of a conversation for the reporter, who had never even heard of the concept and was fascinated by the very idea of the symbolic purchase. The conversation didn't last very long and I was off the phone about ten minutes later. Four o'clock rolled around. WINS radio (famous for its slogan "You give us twenty-two minutes, we'll give you the world") was on in the house and suddenly we hear, "And in other news today, Rabbi Sholom Gold of West Hempstead purchased West Hempstead for a dollar."

The calls began coming in fast and furious. People were on their way home from work. Some were driving along the Long Island Expressway, others were on the Grand Central Parkway, some were even watching the four o'clock news, and the biggest story of the day was about some unknown rabbi who purchased a city for a buck. The phone was ringing off the hook. Suddenly everyone was talking about the *eruv* and trying to ascertain exactly what an *eruv* was. America had never even heard the word and now they were becoming experts on the matter. It was a big story for the next few weeks as well.

Erev Pesach, there was an article in the *New York Times*. The story was intriguing – a Catholic mayor doing his best to help an Orthodox Jewish rabbi and his community keep their Sabbath. The people were just lapping it up. And that Jewish lawyer who worked for the West Hempstead municipality was the one who got it, who comprehended the significance before anyone else. It was he, I believe, who alerted the press to what was going on and made something great out of it. The story in fact made the world press and was written up in many different languages.

The *Post* wrote about it. The *Times*. The *Daily News*. Each one of them made funny mistakes. I think it was the *Post* who wrote something to the effect that "Orthodox Jews will now be able to use umbrellas on their Sabbath." A different paper chimed in adding, "the *eruv* gave the Jews of West Hempstead the ability to drive to shul on the Sabbath." Every paper had its take on the situation.

The Seder finally arrived after a day and a half of tremendous excitement. Our phone rarely rang during Shabbos or *yom tov* meals. Everyone knew that a rabbi wouldn't answer his phone on a holy day. But during the Seder the phone started to ring.

One of my kids piped up.

"That's *Time* magazine," she said.

The phone rang again.

"That's *Newsweek*," yelled a different child.

After two days of *yom tov* when the phone rang numerous times and nobody answered, the media finally gave up trying to reach me. But though the media ceased hounding us, other Jewish communities began pursuing me. I was brought in to communities in many other cities that were trying to construct their own *eruvin*. I had become known as an *eruv* expert. I was asked to evaluate their streets to ascertain whether they fit the halachic criteria.

My good friend Rabbi Benjamin Blech of the Young Israel of Oceanside asked me to investigate the feasibility of an *eruv* in his community. Incidentally, as its name indicates, the community has the ocean along one entire side. I didn't really have the time to devote to *eruv* consulting, but for a friend and a neighboring community, I agreed. I asked a member of the community to take me out to sea in his boat, me carrying a stick ten *tefachim* long (a *tefach* is a measurement equivalent to a handbreadth, or about three and a half inches), and I had him stop the boat in ten or twenty different spots so I could measure the depth of the water. There were no beaches there. The water lapped up against the community houses and I needed to ensure that it was ten *tefachim* deep in every spot. Sure enough, I was able to help turn Oceanside's *eruv* into a reality.

These were the days before phone wires were underground. There were telephone poles everywhere, all equipped with wires that served as integral components in every *eruv* around the country.

There are always issues when something new comes along, and an *eruv* is certainly no exception. A few people in the Oceanside community weren't sure that my *eruv* was halachically good enough for them. So they went to Rav Moshe Feinstein to ask him about it.

"Who built your *eruv*?" Rav Moshe asked them.

"Rabbi Sholom Gold," they replied.

"If Rabbi Gold built your *eruv*," Rav Moshe said, "you can use it unquestionably. There's no question about it at all."

There was nothing to discuss when it came to this subject. He was behind me one hundred percent.

It didn't hit me until recently that my actions in building the *eruv* in West Hempstead ended up preventing millions of acts of Shabbos desecration. After the publicity about the West Hempstead *eruv*, community after community around the world decided to construct *eruvin* as well. And that adds up to millions and millions of acts of *chillul*

*Shabbos* that were prevented. I was even knighted with a nickname of which I was very proud, known far and wide as "the *eruv rav*."

I cannot take credit for the whole *eruv* idea because Staten Island had built one before me, as had Toronto, but through the West Hempstead community and our *eruv* team, the idea and the concept became accepted and famous and everyone wanted in on it – so much so that it truly became the norm all over the world.

In the Baltimore community, the man who decided to construct the *eruv* went so far as to put together something he titled the *Eruv List*, and he publishes an updated version of this book every year. It's something akin to a community phone book, which includes community services along with other specialized information, and it's filled with advertisements and the amazing tale of how Baltimore's *eruv* was born, uniting many halachic experts, including Rav Moshe Heinemann, to make this dream a reality.

Dr. Bert Miller, the publisher of the Baltimore book, came to my home in Eretz Yisrael years later to bring me a copy. Dr. Miller writes, "I got the idea to build an *eruv* in Baltimore after I read a *New York Times* article which described the successful *eruv* project of Rabbi Sholom Gold in West Hempstead, New York. I thought that since Rabbi Gold was able to build an *eruv* in West Hempstead, our Orthodox community in Baltimore, home to a major *yeshivah gedolah*, Ner Yisroel, a *yeshivah* filled with prominent *talmidei chachamim* and *poskim*, certainly could complete an *eruv* project also."

Reading through the history of the Baltimore *eruv*, the deliberations and the differences of opinion, I realized how wise Rav Moshe was.

☙

There were many details to work out with the advent of the *eruv*. The main question was how to let the community know when the *eruv* was kosher and operating and when not. There was also a need for the *eruv* team to divide the town into five or six sections, one per team member. Each member of the team was given a map of his section, and when he arrived home from work on Thursday he'd make sure that his entire section was in fine working order. Every part of the *eruv* was clearly marked, every detail noted: was there supposed to be a *lechi* in a particular spot, were we relying on existing wires and poles at any given location… Nothing was left to chance. The moment a member finished checking his section, he'd pick up the phone and call the general *eruv* coordinator, who was waiting to hear from every member of the crew that all was in order.

Diagonally situated across the street from the shul was the Hebrew Academy of Nassau County (HANC). My good friend Rabbi Meyer Fendel built HANC from the ground up, and along with the school, the entire West Hempstead community. I found a store that specialized in making flags and helped them design a beautiful flag of blue background and white lettering. The white letters spelled out the word *eruv*. The moment we were informed that the *eruv* was okay, the flag went up. People returning home from work, picking up their kids from school, driving down the street all kept a sharp lookout for the flag, and within a short while the entire community knew that the *eruv* was up and running. In addition to that, we set up an *eruv* information hotline to call. You dialed the number and if all was well that week, the recorded voice on the other end informed you that the *eruv* was intact.

There was one particular *lechi* that kept on coming down. It seemed like we were constantly repairing this *lechi*, which had been put up on the recommendation of Rav Shimon Eider to fulfill the opinion of the Chazon Ish. It so happened that right across the street from this *lechi* lived a non-Jewish man who couldn't help but notice a continuous stream of Jews constantly trying to repair a string and stick across the street from his house.

Finally he decided to cross the street and ask us what was going on. I explained all about our *eruv* and how it wasn't cooperating.

"Don't you worry, Rabbi," he replied. "I'm going to watch your *eruv* like a baby and make sure that it doesn't come down. You'll see – from now on, you won't have anything to worry about. Just trust me. Your '*leki*' is safe with me."

You know something – he gave us his word and it never came down again.

West Hempstead was the epitome of what one would call "suburbia." And that translated into an open-door policy for one and all. People were friendly and in and out of one another's homes at all hours of the day. Neighbors were considered family and children never felt themselves confined to just their own homes. A rabbi's home was a busy, lively place to live, and once the *eruv* committee came into existence, it became busier than ever.

I'll never forget the day Josh Lichtenstein came over.

He entered the house clutching something in his hand – some sort of creation.

"Something I invented for the *eruv*," he explained to me.

We got into the car, found a stretch of *eruv*, and he showed me his magic. An amateur inventor, this enthusiastic member of the *eruv* committee had originated a brilliant scientific tool for us *eruv* enthusiasts. How Josh ever arrived at what we termed the LEM (Lichtenstein Eruv Measurer) was beyond me. Suffice it to say that his tool became a component of our *eruv* construction. The device measured wires and could tell with precise mathematical accuracy where a wire would fall were it to be lowered to the ground, thereby showing us exactly where to place a needed *lechi*.

The LEM became part and parcel of our *eruv* team and was treated with deserved respect by one and all, as was Lichtenstein, the genius behind this monumental discovery. Many times we needed to determine whether a pole was straight, or whether something was sagging. The LEM came through for us every time. Every single one of that original group helped build and create our *eruv*, and its success was a credit to each and every one of them because they worked tirelessly to make it a reality.

# 13

# THE *MIKVEH*

The next big project that became my focus was the need for a *mikveh* for the community. The closest *mikveh* to West Hempstead called for a drive to Far Rockaway, which wasn't the end of the world, but things got problematic come Shabbos and *yom tov*. Something had to be done. West Hempstead, whose population was growing, needed its own *mikveh*. Step one was putting together the Mikvah Association, which included Bernie Kesselman, Sandra Sokal, and Sonia Swidler (who has since come on aliyah). Rabbi Stanley Wexler helped me design the *mikveh*'s first plan and assisted me in the earliest stages, as did many others.

As soon as I had something concrete in hand, I went to show it to my designated *mikveh rav*, a great scholar from Boro Park, Rav Moshe Stern, the Debreziner Rav. We spent many hours together going over the plans and ensuring that it was kosher according to the most stringent opinions. I wanted the West Hempstead *mikveh* to be accepted and usable by every single Jew.

Money, as always, was a serious problem. Despite our best attempts at fund-raising we hadn't been successful. *Mikveh* building requires some serious capital and we had come up short.

After giving the matter careful consideration, the Mikvah Association came up with an idea.

We asked the shul for a ten-year loan to finance the *mikveh*. Simply speaking, it would be taking money from one pocket and putting it back in another. It was a good idea and I had full confidence that the money would be repaid long before the ten years were up. It wasn't a question of having the money. The shul had the money. The issue was whether the board would be willing to lend us the money from their reserves. Unfortunately, there were a number of individuals who were not in favor of the project in the first place.

Still we forged ahead with our plans, while those who opposed us forged ahead with theirs as well. Everything hung on one fateful board meeting. On the agenda was the decision to lend the Mikvah Association the money it needed to make the *mikveh*.

The board was going to vote.

You can imagine how nervous I was. The *mikveh* was a matter of great importance to the community. But some were diametrically opposed to my view. It was all coming to a head.

One man stood up. He was most emphatically not in favor of the *mikveh*. And he had this shocking statement to make: "If the board votes to lend our shul's monetary reserves to this project, I will go into court and take out an injunction against the shul for misuse and abuse of shul funds."

Five seconds later I was on my feet, reacting like a mother lioness protecting her cubs. "If anybody goes into court in matters pertaining to the *mikveh*," I stated quietly, but with a dead certainty that left no room for doubt, "I will personally put him into *cherem*. He will not count for a minyan in this shul or be called to the Torah. He will not be part of this community in any way and nobody will be permitted to talk to him. No one goes to court."

I would fight this to the bitter end.

That was effectively the end of the issue. They voted us the money. And the *mikveh* paid it all back in five years' time, half the term agreed upon.

Building a *mikveh* was a priority of the highest order, and I would have done anything I needed to do to stop anyone who tried to get in the way of this vital mitzvah. Thank G-d, one showdown was all we needed. But I was utterly serious about my threat and would have acted on it with no compunction whatsoever. He would have become persona non grata and he knew it. There was never another issue with the *mikveh* again.

The Mikvah Association proceeded with the building. We purchased a house and dug out the basement, in the process turning our *mikveh* into a truly beautiful and comfortable place. It took a year to build, and after that we had a lovely, well-furnished *mikveh* in town, with much attention given to details. We found a religious couple to move into the house's upper floors, and their children became members of our community as well. It had been a battle, but a worthwhile one. And we won it.

ಞ

While still in Toronto I had joined the Rabbinical Council of America (RCA). I had even become the president of the Ontario region (consisting of around ten rabbis). Now in the United States, I became a bit more interested in doing something meaningful on the national scene. The RCA was involved in many vital projects for the wider American Jewish community. One of these projects was the RCA's *mikveh* committee, whose job it was to help build new *mikvaos* in places that had none. I volunteered to be on this committee and was accepted aboard. My partner in this worthy endeavor was Rabbi David Stavsky, of Columbus, Ohio, a *rav* who accomplished great things in his community.

I remember a man, Max Schreiber, who devoted his entire life to one cause – the *mikvaos* of the Jewish people. He breathed, ate, and slept *mikvaos*. That was his cause, his burning passion. He lived in Far Rockaway and involved himself in our committee and assisted in any way he could. He'd drive over to my house and we'd plan *mikveh* projects together. Anytime a new *mikveh* was being built, Max insisted on funding the architectural plans for the structure. Here was a wealthy man who knew how to use his money. I remember one particular year when Max Schreiber, Rabbi Stavsky, and I assisted in building a grand total of fourteen *mikvaos* together. He spent a fortune on his *mikvaos*.

They were like his children. Watching "Mikveh Max" in action was something amazing to behold. The man didn't rest. He just built another *mikveh* and another *mikveh* and another *mikveh*.

Another thing I did was to print up a thousand copies of a little *sefer* that had been published by the Organization for Taharas Hamishpacha (family purity) of Yerushalayim. The *sefer* was a handbook of the laws of building a *mikveh*. The halachic requirements were spelled out clearly so that a *rav* would be familiar with the procedure for *mikveh* construction. This helped people become conversant and fluent in the ideas and *halachos* of *mikveh*.

༄

West Hempstead had come a long way since we'd arrived. There was now an *eruv* that was being emulated by communities around the globe. We had built a state-of-the-art *mikveh* under the guidance and personal leadership of the Debreziner Rav.

Another project to which I devoted a considerable amount of time and energy was convincing our young people graduating from high school to travel to Eretz Yisrael for a year of Torah study and developing a love of the country. The example had already been set by Rabbi Fendel, who had sent his children to study in Eretz Yisrael even in their high school years. This was a groundbreaking concept, and it took a lot of work to condition people to the idea. Many of the boys went to Kerem B'Yavneh, others to Sha'alvim. And they did well and some remained for a second year, but most returned. Eventually "Israel for the year" developed into a movement and over time became an accepted fact of American Jewish life.

There was also a surge of Torah learning in the town. I delivered four classes on assorted topics during the week and others gave classes as well. This was all in addition to the *chavrusa* learning that was taking place both morning and night. There was a marathon Shavuos night set of classes in the shul for about four hours of enthusiastic learning and one on Tisha b'Av for over five hours that was very well attended. And the people tasted Torah and saw that it was good.

༄

Every rabbi can tell you that a Friday night knock on the door is the harbinger of trouble. Serious trouble. People don't want to disturb you on a Friday night. If they're knocking, it's because something has gone frightfully wrong.

One Shabbos we were celebrating a bar mitzvah in shul, and relatives had traveled into town from all over for the big event. My late-night knocker was one of the people in town who were hosting the guests. In this case, a doctor. A fine man.

"What happened?" I asked as soon as I opened the door.

"I'm sorry to bother you in the middle of the night, but as you know the uncle and aunt of the bar mitzvah boy are staying in my home, and a few hours ago the aunt became extremely ill. So ill in fact that I had to call an ambulance."

I sat there stunned, shock written across my face. The family's long-awaited Shabbos of joy was about to turn into something very different than they'd envisioned.

When I saw him out, I requested that he keep me posted. I knew that the hospital would call him if they needed something for the aunt. It was a matter of *pikuach nefesh*, saving a life. Later on that night, the doctor informed me that the bar mitzvah boy's aunt had passed away. Now I had another decision to make: to inform the family or not?

In the end, the president of the congregation and I elected to keep the matter to ourselves for the time being. There was no point in turning the bar mitzvah into a tragedy. I gave my Shabbos *drashah* as usual, wished mazel tov to the bar mitzvah boy, to his parents and grandparents; but the entire time I was thinking of this family who had no idea of the magnitude of the tragedy awaiting them come the end of Shabbos.

I was acting, plain and simple. I was acting the part of the happy, joy-filled rabbi, when in reality, I was being torn apart on the inside, filled with grief over a young woman of thirty-nine whose life had ended so abruptly. But I did my job and they never knew until Shabbos was over and the time had come to inform them of their loss. That was one of the most challenging Shabbosim of my life. But that's all part of what it means to be a *rav*.

It was early evening when the phone rang.

"Rabbi Gold, Yitzi ran away from home!"

"Are you sure?"

"Yes, he left a note."

"Did you inform the police?"

"Of course. They say more time has to pass before they can legally get involved."

"Please keep me posted if you learn anything more."

A few hours later the phone rang again. This time it was an old friend on the line, calling from Baltimore. We'd been study partners in *yeshivah* and gone to Camp Kol Rina together.

"Sholom, it's Chaim Wallin."

"What's going on?"

"Not much," he replied, "but I was walking down the street here in Baltimore a few minutes ago and I ran into some kid I never saw before. He looked a little lost and disoriented so I asked him his name and where he was from and he identified himself as someone who lives in your neighborhood and davens in your shul. I figured I'd better give you a call."

"Thank you so much," I told my friend. "Get back out there, find him, and keep him in your house for the next few hours. I'm on my way!"

The boy's father and I left West Hempstead in the middle of the night and drove into Baltimore, arriving at eight o'clock the following morning. We davened Shacharis, picked up the errant young man, and had some breakfast at my friend's house. And then we returned home, me, the father, and the runaway, sober and full of regret.

What an unexpected manifestation of *hashgachah pratis*. A fugitive from West Hempstead is found by a friend of mine a few hundred miles away.

All part of the job description.

༄

After attending a mid-winter conference of the Rabbinical Council of America in Washington, DC, I was on my way home. I boarded the shuttle flight to LaGuardia and made myself comfortable. An interesting-looking gentleman took the seat next to me. He was wearing a brown floppy hat with matching brown leather jacket and clutching a not-inexpensive briefcase. My curiosity was piqued but I waited. To me he looked like he had stepped out of Hollywood. When he opened his briefcase for a moment, although of course I didn't mean to intrude on his privacy, I saw that just about the only thing in there was a Gemara *Bechorot*.

I was sure I knew who he was. I turned to him and said, "You must be Herman Wouk." He smiled and acknowledged his identity. The great author of *The Caine Mutiny*, *The Winds of War*, *War and Remembrance*, and *This Is My G-d* was an avid devotee of *daf yomi* (*Bechorot* was the *masechta* being studied at the time). In his book *Will to Live*, which is sort of a memoir, he describes his struggles to keep up the pace. He leaves no doubt that it was of the utmost significance in his life.

I learned that he was flying to New York to participate in a *farbrengen* of the Lubavitcher Rebbe, Rav Menachem Mendel Schneerson. That night was Yud Shvat, the *yahrtzeit* of the previous Rebbe, his father-in-law, whose funeral I attended in 1950.

&

I used to deliver a Gemara *shiur* every Shabbos afternoon. Not such a huge crowd, but we had our regulars. At one point we were learning tractate *Sanhedrin* when we arrived at the Gemara dealing with *oso ha'ish* (that man), a euphemism for the Jewish founder of the Christian religion. It so happens to be that the non-Jewish censors of the past had chopped a large section about him right out of the Gemara. But I was able to track down a rare uncensored volume and began giving a series of classes devoted to an examination of the relationship between *oso ha'ish*, the Sanhedrin, and the Jewish people.

From there we moved on to other censored *sugyos*, which we examined in depth. It was fascinating learning. And of course with such scintillating classes, the numbers of those attending grew exponentially. The *shiur* doubled in size within weeks and kept on growing. By the time the series of seven or eight classes was over, we had a packed study hall.

After the final class was done, I looked around the room and met the eyes of man after man. And then I made one comment. "*Rabboisai*," I said to them, "for the last seven weeks you've been coming to learn for *oso ha'ish*'s sake. Now come learn for G-d's sake!"

The place exploded. Laughter hit the rafters.

It was one of my better lines.

~

As a student, when I entertained the thought (sometimes out loud) of entering the rabbinate, I was always shot down by a number of individuals who pooh-poohed the idea as involving a life full of brotherhoods and sisterhoods. "No," they insisted, "you should become a *rosh yeshivah*, a talmudical instructor, or a *mashgiach* at least." And I was all those things for a while. But somehow, the paths of life took me where I was supposed to go and that meant a life spent as a career rabbi. And you know something? I found that it wasn't just a lifetime spent in the company of the brotherhood and the sisterhood. It was a grand calling. A true opportunity to do real kindness for my fellow man. It meant answering endless halachic questions, it meant giving advice, and it meant doing *mitzvos* and teaching Torah all the time.

I used to say that looking at a rabbi was like seeing an iceberg – you only see about one-seventh of the entire mass. The rest is hidden underwater. The same is true of the community rabbi. People sometimes wonder what the rabbi does all day. How does he fill his time? They conclude, no doubt, that the rabbi is preparing his Shabbos speech six days a week to be delivered on the seventh. They are completely wrong. In fact the rabbi is visiting the sick and officiating at weddings and *brissim*, answering questions and burying the dead, counseling couples and youngsters, and comforting the bereaved. His job is never truly done and he makes himself available at all hours of the day and night. Truthfully, it's a wonder that he's able to find the time to actually prepare his Shabbos speech.

In the last thirty years, I have watched in silent joy as sincere Torah scholars have entered the rabbinate, intent on changing the face of America and the world with their warmth, earnest wisdom, and down-to-earth common sense.

Back when I was a rabbi in the RCA, you couldn't find a single rabbi with a beard. Everyone was clean-shaven and sporting names like Harry, Steven, Robert, or George. And these men spread out across America, usually by themselves, and built day schools and *mikvaos* and did their best to ensure the future of the Jewish nation. And they generated this incredible rebirth during the religious turbulence of the fifties, sixties, and seventies, as the Conservative and Reform movements underwent a surge of exponential growth, building gigantic temples and impressive edifices, while the Orthodox rabbis (looked upon by one and all as the poor cousins of the family) stood their ground and spoke with eloquence and sincerity to anyone willing to listen. How much reward will be waiting for these unsung heroes who built shuls, day schools, and *mikvaos* across America.

The rabbinate has a completely different face now. Literally. Today, a rabbi with a beard is a commonplace sight. These days they have names like Moshe, Chaim, or Yankel. Times have changed. But the contributions made by the earlier spiritual leaders set the stage for all who followed them.

༄

One day, I was walking along the street in Far Rockaway, having just finished teaching at TAG, when I heard a voice calling my name.

"Sholom, Sholom!"

I looked around but didn't see anyone. I wondered briefly if this was how a *bas kol,* a heavenly voice, sounded.

I heard it again.

"Sholom, Sholom!"

Soon I recognized the master of the voice. Rav Nachman Bulman was standing in the doorway of his home, motioning me over.

"Take a look at this," he exclaimed, motioning with one hand to a *sefer* that he was holding in his other hand. "I would like you to borrow it."

I flipped through it, noticing that Rav Bulman had penned notations alongside almost every page, in every available space. Obviously, this *sefer* was very dear to him.

In the end I had the *sefer* for two years. It was called *Em Habanim Smeichah*, and had been authored by Rav Yissachar Shlomo Teichtal, who was murdered in the Holocaust, may G-d avenge his blood. Rav Teichtal writes in the introduction to the *sefer* that he never involved himself in politics in any shape or form, and that he'd always subscribed to the view that it was forbidden to make aliyah and that it wasn't yet time to return to Eretz Yisrael.

"And then," he wrote, "I saw the troubles occurring on a frighteningly large scale all across Europe." (Rav Teichtal lived in Hungary where the atrocities only commenced at a much later date.) "And I sat down and gave the matter much thought."

And he came to a complete revolution in his mindset, to the point that he writes, "Our sin lies in the fact that we are not going to Eretz Yisrael despite the fact that G-d clearly wants us to go."

The *sefer* is simply remarkable. Rav Teichtal quotes Chazal, the elders of Chassidus, the Torah scholars of Lithuania – sources from across the vastness of Jewish literature – to make it clear that it's a mitzvah to live in Eretz Yisrael, to build it up and populate the Land.

I had always wanted to move to Eretz Yisrael and I have no question that this *sefer* pushed me one or two steps closer toward my lifelong dream. By the way, Rav Bulman ended up moving to Eretz Yisrael a few years later, where he established his own community in Migdal HaEmek. He was a builder of people and communities and a man I admired very much. My own daughter, Chavi Koenigsberg, and her husband Daniel lived there for seven years.

Rav Bulman did everything with passion and heart and feeling.

We once attended a rabbinical conference together up in the Catskill Mountains. On the drive up the scenic route, Rav Bulman read the *Algemeiner Journal*, perusing an article about clashes between Israeli soldiers and Jewish settlers. As he read the description of pushing and hitting and beating, of the struggles of Jew versus Jew in the ancient Land of Israel, I saw the man begin crying like a baby. Tears. Such tears. Such pure, honest tears.

By Yom Kippur 1973, the Young Israel of West Hempstead had grown to the point where there wasn't sufficient space for those who came to pray. We divided the shul into two separate locations. One minyan took place in the shul's main sanctuary and the second at HANC, located across the street. I davened Kol Nidrei and the nighttime davening at the main shul and joined the minyan at HANC for the daytime davening.

I remember the following conversation with crystal clarity.

One of the members approached me as I was entering the school building.

"I'm afraid something bad is happening in Israel right now, Rabbi."

"Like a war?"

He nodded, fright in his eyes.

"How do you know this?"

"I walked past the gas station on my way to shul and one of the men working there told me."

"Go back to the gas station right now," I told him, "and find out all the information you can."

He left. I waited tensely to hear the news. He returned a while later.

"Something very serious is going on. It seems that Israel has been attacked!"

The news hit me like a ton of bricks. The Arabs were attacking from the north and from the south on the holiest day of the year. From Egypt and from Syria. Jewish soldiers were being pulled out of shul all over the country to go fight a war that had taken them by surprise. The probable carnage was too horrible to contemplate.

I crossed the street in a daze. I could have been sleepwalking. A dread had descended on my soul. I entered the main sanctuary and trudged through the brightly lit room until I reached the *bimah*. I raised my hand like in a dream and brought it down with a hard clap on the velvet covering.

Everyone stopped what they were doing to stare at me.

"*Rabboisai*," I said, and they could hear the severity in my voice. "Eretz Yisrael is in grave danger. It has been attacked simultaneously by massive armies. From this moment on and until the end of Yom Kippur, we are not praying for ourselves and our personal needs, but rather for the safety of Eretz Yisrael and the millions of our brethren living there."

As I spoke, I grew very emotional. I then repeated my message at the second minyan as well. That Yom Kippur passed in a haze of endless worry, a state of profound concern overwhelming my very being as I tried to daven and concentrate on the words of the ancient prayers.

*Who will live and who will die?*

The age-old question had taken on new meaning now. And in fact my worst fears were realized with the news that came in after Yom Kippur. It was a catastrophe of the highest order. The Yom Kippur War dealt a huge blow to the morale of the country and its security forces and ended up causing a major shakeup in the army's upper echelons when the dust eventually cleared. Thousands of soldiers were killed and the State of Israel lost much of its newly acquired deterrence.

However, after the shock of the initial days of the war passed, Israeli forces began to recover, regroup, and ultimately go on the offensive, crossing into Egypt and surrounding the Egyptian Third Army. They routed Syria out of the Golan Heights in the north as well. Rav Yosef Shalom Elyashiv commented at the time that the miracles of the Yom Kippur War may have been greater than those of the Six-Day War.

಄

A few months after the war had finally been won, the Rabbinical Council of America organized a solidarity mission of rabbis to visit Israel. About 150 rabbis were traveling to Israel in an attempt at demonstrating that we stood with a wounded country that still had thousands of soldiers guarding the borders and hundreds in captivity. Two and a half thousand soldiers had been killed. The economy was a complete shambles. It was a period of introspection and soul searching.

I myself had received an unconfirmed report about a close friend who had been reported missing in action, and I intended to visit his wife to follow up on the matter. I decided to take my oldest son Menachem along with me for the trip, as I felt that it would be a trip that he would remember for life. He was just under twelve and a ticket for him was half price. Two of his close friends from West Hempstead were then living in Eretz Yisrael, Dovid Fendel and Robbie Bechoffer. Rabbi Meyer and Goldie Fendel had gone on sabbatical to Israel that year.

I was more than a little uncomfortable with the whole trip. We would be visiting a bleeding country, filled with people who would stare at our fancy cameras and our tour bus and might even smile at us and thank us for coming to see them but inside they'd be wondering where we'd been while they were being attacked and killed and maimed on the battlefields. But would it be better for us not to go? I was filled with mixed emotions.

The Shabbos before we left was Parshas Shmos. I spoke in shul that Shabbos and delivered one of the longest *drashos* of my life. I began by sharing a very puzzling episode from the portion of the week. G-d commands Moshe Rabbeinu at the burning bush to return to Egypt and take the Jewish people out of slavery. And what's Moshe's response? Truthfully it's a shocking one: Moshe Rabbeinu, Moshe our teacher, our prophet, refuses to go to Egypt. For seven long days he resists Hashem's direct order for a series of reasons. Moshe, the human being closest to G-d. G-d is telling you to go save the Jews – you should run to do His will. But no. He comes up with excuse after excuse.

We would have expected Moshe to respond immediately in the affirmative and prepare to leave for Egypt. Instead, we are confronted with a dialogue between Moshe and Hashem spread over thirty-nine verses that spans a period of a week – seven long days. Moshe refuses to go and raises a series of objections and excuses that restrain him from doing Hashem's bidding. G-d deals patiently with each reason in turn until the last, when He gets angry. After Moshe has run out of all excuses he says in Shmos 4:13, "*Shlach na b'yad tishlach*" (Please, send through whomever You will send). At this point Hashem's wrath burns against Moshe because now it becomes clear that Moshe's arsenal of objections is empty; he just doesn't want to go. While all of this is happening, Jews continue to suffer and fall before the taskmaster's whip.

Why indeed doesn't Moshe want to go and end the pain of Israel?

Furthermore, why doesn't Hashem simply tell Moshe that He will find someone else who is willing to save His people? Why does Hashem persist in His quest after Moshe?

I believe that Moshe's reluctance to go save his people is rooted in his profound respect for every other Jew in the world. Moshe fails to understand Hashem's choice. Why me of all people? This is not humility on his part. Humility is not an excuse for failing to act quickly and decisively at this most critical moment in the history of the Jewish people. Moshe is perplexed by Hashem's charge to him of all people, because Moshe is the only Jew in the entire world who is not in Egypt suffering with his fellow Jews. For many years now, only one member of the Jewish people was not in Egypt. Only one Jew did not suffer with them.

Moshe has been in Midyan, has married and raised a family, lived the pastoral and peaceful life of a shepherd who grazes his sheep in lush meadows and lays them down beside tranquil waters. He imagines himself arriving back in Egypt and people wondering where he has been all this time. What will he say to the widows, the orphans, the maimed, the crippled? Moshe is telling Hashem, send any other Jew in the world who was there and suffered with them, who experienced the same pain, fear, and terror. It was almost as if he were saying, *How could I go on a trip to Eretz Yisrael right after the Yom Kippur War? I wasn't in the war. I didn't suffer. Who am I to come show my face?*

*Who am I that I should go to Pharaoh and that I should take the children of Israel out of Egypt?*

The emphasis is on "I." Only I am unfit; all others are worthy.

It is told that when people came to the Satmarer Rebbe after the Shoah for a *brachah*, he said, "Go into shul and find a Jew with a number on his arm. Ask him for a *brachah*, not me."

When Moshe says, "But they will not believe me and they will not heed my voice for they will say, 'Hashem did not appear to you,'" he does not mean to cast aspersions on the Jewish people. They are believers; they will trust anyone else You send. It's only me. I haven't been there for them.

His final refusal, "Please, send through whomever You will send," evokes Hashem's anger. G-d replies in Shmos 4:14, "*Halo Aharon achicha Halevi – yadati ki daber yedaber hu; v'gam hinei hu yotzei likrasecha; v'raacha v'samach b'libo*" (Is there not your brother Aharon the Levite? I know that he can speak well; and behold he is coming toward you, and when he sees you he will rejoice in his heart).

This brings us to one more question. Why is G-d presenting Aharon with this long introduction?

G-d tells Moshe, *Aharon is coming.*
*You know which Aharon?*
*Your brother.*
*The Levite.*

It would have been sufficient for G-d to have merely said, "Your brother is coming toward you."

All in all, I ended up asking something like eighteen questions on this particular stretch of Chumash.

I concluded with the following ideas.

This was Moshe's problem – the worry that the people would look at him and say, *Why on earth are you here now, after we've suffered so much?*

G-d had this to say in response: *Moshe, you're wrong. The people remember. They remember that you were the first one who stood up for them and that the only reason you weren't there alongside them the entire time was because you had to run for your life.*

*Furthermore, do you know who the most beloved Jew in Egypt is?*
*Aharon, your brother.*

*He just happens to be a Levi, and as I'm sure you know, the Leviim were not obligated to work and were not enslaved. And do you know what Aaron has kept himself busy with for quite some time? He's been a true comforter to the people. And they accepted his comfort despite the fact that he was not someone who suffered alongside them. If Aharon Hakohen presents you to Klal Yisrael, they will remember who you are and what you did.*

And why did G-d want Moshe and only Moshe to be the one to rescue the Jews from their slavery?

Because Moshe of all people had the most awesome, staggering respect and love for each and every single Jew suffering in Egypt. He saw himself as being less worthy than anyone else. "*Shlach na b'yad tishlach.*"

*G-d,* Moshe begged, *send any other Jew, any Jew whose children were slaughtered by Pharoh; send any Jew whose babies were thrown into the Nile; send any Jew with a number on his arm to save the nation because each and every one of them is worthier than me.*

That's why Moshe Rabbeinu refused his orders time and again.

I looked my congregation in their collective eye and asked them, "Why am I telling you all this? Because I'll be leaving to Israel tomorrow, to bring comfort to the sufferers of Zion. But I myself did nothing. I sat on the sidelines while they suffered through a bloody war. Sure, we gave money and davened, but it's not the same thing and I have an uneasy feeling that I can now understand and relate to Moshe Rabbeinu like I never understood him in my entire life."

The next day our group of RCA rabbis flew off to Eretz Yisrael.

The first thing I did after arriving at the Batsheva Hotel in Yerushalayim was to go look up my old friend. I needed to know if he'd returned safely from the war. I got my son Menachem settled in the hotel room and then set out into the cold Jerusalem night for Bayit Vegan. It was a freezing night and the rain poured down without letup. The streets were deserted. Jerusalem was almost desolate in its mourning of lost children. The wind blew mightily and I struggled against its iron grasp.

I knocked on the door, my heart pounding with wary anticipation.

My friend's wife answered the door and I saw a huge smile on her face. And I knew that everything was fine, that my friend had come back from the land of the dead. He'd survived.

Baruch Hashem.

Standing on those steps in the midst of endless chilling rain on a foggy, stormy night in the Jerusalem of bitter wars, I knew firsthand what joy was all about.

We also learned that the visit of the rabbis sent a strong message to the people of Israel that fellow Jews the world over had not forgotten nor abandoned them. We spread out across the country and found a people that sought and appreciated the consolation and expression of solidarity from their brothers and sisters.

# 14

# GREAT MEN AND GOOD TIMES

West Hempstead was what people called a "bedroom community," because the majority of its inhabitants commuted to work. They used the Long Island Railroad to get to work in Manhattan, which was twenty-five minutes station to station. The majority of those living in West Hempstead were Brooklyn expatriates and many were highly educated. There were many doctors, lawyers, college professors, physicists, and teachers. It was a very laid-back, understated community. It was also a beautiful residential neighborhood with many dogwood and maple trees and even a duck pond.

A pioneering spirit hovered over the town. We were building a religious place to live and we were doing it together. A sense of camaraderie enveloped the doers. All this was begun by Rabbi Meyer Fendel, who had been sent out by Torah Umesorah in the early fifties to build an outpost in the wilderness. And he succeeded. Sure, it was pretty tough in the beginning (to the point where Rabbi Fendel took out an ad in the paper that read "Nine Jews needed for a minyan"), but things began coming together after a while. The *neshamos* that he and his devoted life's partner Goldie have created are too numerous to count. Their *zechusim* are awesome.

Years later while living in Israel, I was invited to a weekend retreat for rabbis that took place a short while after the signing of the Oslo Accords (I will say more about that accursed agreement in a later chapter). For some reason the event organizers invited Yossi Beilin to address the assembled. Yossi Beilin and his superior Shimon Peres had undertaken to secretly make a deal with the PLO at a time when negotiations with them were against the law. They hammered out the deal in Oslo, Norway, far from the center of the Israeli political arena. They agreed to relinquish Jewish rights to major parts of Eretz Yisrael to an organization led by the architect of modern terrorism, Yasser Arafat.

The Oslo Accords were most probably a classic example of a march of folly, a historic blunder, second to none in Jewish history. Being that the Oslo Accords accomplished nothing positive and even caused the deaths of many Jews, I did not feel Beilin was the right man to be addressing our gathering. In fact, in my opinion, he had a lot of Jewish blood on his hands and should have been treated as persona non grata.

From the moment I arrived at the Yam Hamelach hotel, I began raising a storm of protest against this terrible affront to all things sacred. This went on all Shabbos. By the time Motzaei Shabbos rolled around, things were getting pretty heated up in that hotel. Most of the assembled were against Beilin speaking, while a minority wanted to hear what he had to say. It was intense. The press had gathered at the hotel and they were interviewing one and all in anticipation of Beilin's speech. My protests were on record. Still it looked like he would be speaking after all.

When Yossi Beilin finally began approaching the podium to deliver his address, three people jumped to their feet in protest. I stood in the middle of the conference room shouting at him at the top of my lungs. Irving Maisel stood on one side of me and Rabbi Meyer Fendel stood on my other side, all three of us shouting our protest. One of the rabbis attending the convention was so incensed by my behavior that he stood up and struck me, at which point the hall erupted in a torrent of noise and shouting as the rabbis all began screaming at once.

One of the main memories I remember from that wild day was the undying support of my friends Irving Maisel and Rabbi Meyer Fendel.

Standing there beside me.
Shouting at Beilin.
My good friends.

☙

The West Hempstead community had a collective heart of gold. They genuinely cared about other Jews who needed their assistance. One cause that was extremely close to their hearts was the plight of Soviet Jewry. Once a year, an event was held in the city that gained more and more recognition by the people and press as time went on. It was called Solidarity Sunday.

On that Sunday, buses rolled out of every religious community in the tri-state area toward Fifth Avenue in Manhattan. Many buses full of West Hempstead's Jews left our community and headed over to the city, where we stood and protested in front of the UN, marching back and forth. The Soviet embassy was located in Glencove, Long Island, in those years, and who can forget the nighttime vigils held in front of that doorway to the Iron Curtain. Those were days to remember. And we were an important part of it, because we cared.

Later on when some of the most famous refuseniks were finally released, a number of them spent a Shabbos in West Hempstead. We had Herman Branover for a Shabbos and Rabbi Yosef Mendelevich as well. Great men both; we were privileged to host them, celebrating with them in the good times, after we'd cried with them through the years of pain.

West Hempstead was both beautiful and productive, and an all-around wonderful place to live. It served as a welcome respite of calmness between the tumultuous years I'd spent building Ner Yisroel of Toronto and the tumultuous years to come in Eretz Yisrael. West Hempstead was an oasis of peace and tranquility and I appreciated that very much.

☙

Simchas Torah in our shul was something to see. Everyone's kids were growing up and more families kept on joining the community. Before we knew it, there wasn't enough room for everyone to dance on Simchas Torah. This didn't really faze me, being that I recalled my *yeshivah* days in Ner Yisroel and how we'd danced Rav Ruderman from his home to the *yeshivah* and how the police even closed off the streets. I figured that we might do the same thing here.

My congregation understandably enough wasn't exactly excited about the idea of wild dancing in the middle of the neighborhood, but I insisted that it was a good idea and even brought in the police to officially close Hempstead Avenue to traffic while all the dancing was taking place. I led them all out into the street and did we ever dance. Like you wouldn't believe. They danced that year like nothing I'd ever seen. And the community ended up looking forward to Simchas Torah in a big way, with the kids discussing the outside dancing and the candy and the police, and it was a time of happiness and laughter and celebration with the Torah in a community that was coming of age.

જે

July 4, 1976. We were spending that particular Shabbos in the city of Worcester, Massachusetts. My oldest brother, Rav Yosef Yoel, was the Orthodox rabbi of the city.

The occasion was the Shabbos of my nephew David Gold's bar mitzvah. It turned out to be a Shabbos that many of us will never, ever forget.

There are certain moments in life that stand out in a person's memory and never leave it. Not only that, but you even remember where you were and what you were doing at the moment the event occurred. The JFK assassination is but one example of this phenomenon. Anyone then alive remembers in vivid color the trauma of learning that America's beloved president had been killed.

The Six-Day War.

The Rabin assassination.

More recently, 9/11.

The Entebbe raid.

On Sunday, June 27, 1976, Air France flight 139 left Tel Aviv, its ultimate destination Paris, with a scheduled stopover in Athens, Greece. A few moments after takeoff from Athens, terrorists on board with a bag of grenades hijacked the plane. Thus began a terrifying odyssey for the more than one hundred Jewish passengers on board, for the State of Israel, and for Jews worldwide. After a stopover at Benghazi, Libya, the plane continued on to Entebbe, Uganda. The terrorists demanded the release of many of their friends imprisoned in a number of countries. At first Israel refused to negotiate with them, but by Thursday of that week, word was out that Israel had changed its mind and was now talking to the terrorists.

Meanwhile, America's bicentennial was rapidly approaching. Americans across the wide plains of the United States made plans for what promised to be a memorable Fourth of July weekend. America was two hundred years old, and people were walking around humming "The Star Spangled Banner" to themselves. The entire country was abuzz with bicentennial fever. But things were about to get complicated.

July 3 dawned bright and sunny, but there was nothing cheerful about the news we heard. The plane that had been diverted by German and Arab terrorists to the city of Entebbe in Uganda had been welcomed by Idi Amin, Uganda's egomaniacal dictator. That in itself was pretty bad. What was worse, however, was that the terrorists had separated the Jews and non-Jews from one another, in a clear throwback to the Holocaust. The non-Jews had already been freed. This behavior evoked Nazi Germany in everyone's mind. The news rocked the world, causing a furor anywhere Jews lived, as they took to the shuls to storm the gates of heaven with tear-filled prayers.

Huge, insane demands were being made on the Israeli government: the terrorists wanted Israel to free hundreds of terrorists. And then came the ultimatum. Either cave in to the terrorists' demands by twelve o'clock on July 3, or they would begin shooting the hostages one by one. Terrible tension was building in every Jewish heart, as people across the United States busied themselves with the celebrations of America's freedom from tyranny.

The Israelis were negotiating, claimed some.

They were not willing to negotiate, insisted others.

Nobody knew the truth.

Motzaei Shabbos we were just arriving home from shul after Maariv when a member of my brother's shul came rushing into his home.

"Rabbi," he panted, "reports are coming in on the radio. Something is happening in Uganda right now!"

My brother turned on the radio. Info began pouring in. The picture was still vague. There had been some kind of raid on the Uganda airport. Everything was still fuzzy. And then, breaking news – an Israeli plane had flown across Africa to carry out a raid in the heart of Uganda. By the middle of the night, the earth-shattering story was out. Israel had managed to carry out a raid and rescue the hostages. This raid would go down as one of the most daring in all history. Jews around the world were euphoric. Israel's deterrence had been restored. Yet there was sadness as well because a brave and brilliant young officer, Yoni Netanyahu, commander of the operation, had lost his life in the raid.

We drove back to New York the next day. I listened to the radio as we drove down the highway. America's bicentennial had taken a backseat to the great news of the day – the Israeli raid on Entebbe. We passed the Hudson River as we drove into New York and watched all the action on the waterfront as thousands of boats – schooners, sailboats, thousands of old-time boats – joined the celebrations. Tens of thousands of people lined the shores of the Hudson to watch the festivities.

And then a small boat flying an Israeli flag sailed by – one of the smallest crafts in the harbor, just like the country whose flag she bore. The roar of the crowd was simply earsplitting. Outstanding. America was two hundred years old. Big deal. Let's talk about Israel. This became one of those moments to savor and recall when times get tough. Simply amazing! What a day. What a raid. What awesome, awesome heavenly assistance.

❦

July 1977. We're dreaming of aliyah, but it's not happening.

In May of that year, there had been a dramatic turnover, an earthquake, a seminal event in the world of Israeli politics. For the first time since the beginning of the State, the Left was out and the Right was in. The new prime minister of Israel was Menachem Begin, leader of the Irgun and erstwhile foe of David Ben-Gurion. Suddenly it seemed like anything was possible. Except aliyah. Somehow that didn't seem doable yet.

Our wedding, March 5, 1961, Torah Emeth, Viewmount Avenue, Toronto

My mother Chava Bayla (née Sandhaus), *a"h*

Uncle Sydney (Shaya) Rubinoff, *hy"d*, in his Canadian air force uniform. He fell in the War of Independence, 10 Tammuz, 1948

The family in the lobby of the Ramada Hotel before the Young Israel dinner where Bayla and I were honored, Sunday March 3, 1991 (three days after the first Gulf War)

Rabbi Shlomo Zalman Auerbach at the wedding of Libi Gold to David Nadav, Nof Yerushalayim, Bayit Vegan, December 24, 1987

Rabbi Mordechai Eliyahu, *ztz"l*, Sephardi chief rabbi, speaking with me at a Tzvi and Tamara Sand simcha. *In background*: Yirmi Gold

Eli-Har Nof twinning ceremony in support of residents of Yehuda, Shomron, and Aza after the Oslo Accords, fourth day of Chanukah, December 12, 1993. *Left to right*: Binyamin Netanyahu, then leader of the opposition; me; Rabbi Eli Sadan, Bnei David Military Yeshiva Academy

Eli-Har Nof twinning ceremony in Eli

Beginning of twinning ceremony in Kehillat Zichron Yosef, Har Nof

Twinning ceremony

Binyomin Rubinoff's parents, Matla and Mendel Rubinoff

My uncle, Rabbi Moshe Sandhaus, head chaplain of the Veterans' Administration, Washington, DC, during World War II

Torah Vodaath *yeshivah* high school graduation

Eretz Yisroel, 1956

The Golds at Disney World, July 1977. *Back row*: Menachem, Ima, Chavi; *front row*: Yirmi, Daphna, Libi (Abba took the picture)

1. Harav Yaakov Kamenetsky, *rosh yeshivah* Torah Vodaath
2. Harav Shraga Feivel Mendlowitz, founder of Yeshiva Torah Vodaath
3. Harav Moshe Feinstein, *rosh yeshivah* Mesivtha Tifereth Jerusalem
4. Harav Yaakov Yitzchok Halevi Ruderman, *rosh yeshivah* of Ner Israel, Baltimore
5. Harav Yosef Shlomo Kahaneman, *rosh yeshivah* of Ponevezh, Bnei Brak
6. Harav Dovid Kronglass, *mashgiach* of Ner Israel, Baltimore
7. Harav Yochanan Perlow, the Stoliner Rebbe
8. Harav Avrohom Yehoshua Heschel, the Kopycznitzer Rebbe
9. Harav Yissachar Shlomo Teichtal, Hy"d, author of *Em Habanim Smeichah*, the classic *hashkafah sefer* to emerge from the Shoah
10. Reb Amram Blau, religious activist in Eretz Yisroel, mid-twentieth century

Kehillat Zichron Yosef, dancing at a *hachnasat sefer* Torah

*Hachnasat sefer Torah. Left to right*: Yossi Engel; Kurt Rothschild; Meyer Weinstock, the donor, holding the *sefer Torah*; Rabbi Gold; Yirmi Gold; Rabbi Menachem Gold

Completing *sefer Torah* donated by Rabbi Shmil Halpern (left)

Congregation B'nai Torah, Willowdale, Ontario, Canada, late 1960s

Young Israel of West Hempstead as it looks today

In honor of
The Prime Minister of Israel and Mrs. Begin
The Ambassador of Israel and Mrs. Dinitz
request the pleasure of your company
at a reception
on Wednesday, the twentieth of July
five to six-thirty o'clock
Shoreham Americana Hotel            Regency Room

R.s.v.p.
(202) 483-4100 Ex. 223
(703) 920-3886

Not transferable
(Please present this card)

The invitation to the Washington reception in honor of Menachem Begin
that was given to the uninvited crashers

Groundbreaking for Congregation B'nai Torah, Willowdale, Ontario

Honorees at an OU Israel Center dinner, 2009

Speaking at a Yom Yerushalayim celebration in Los Angeles

Tanya and Yuli Edelstein, Melaveh Malkah, Moscow, December 1983

Pretending to be a tourist in front of the Hermitage Museum in Leningrad (now Saint Petersburg), December 1983

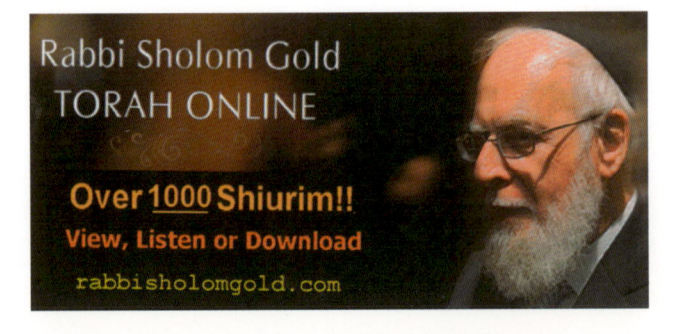

Rabbi Sholom Gold
TORAH ONLINE
Over 1000 Shiurim!!
View, Listen or Download
rabbisholomgold.com

A clandestine Talmud Torah, Moscow, December 1983

Old Chevron Yeshiva in Geulah

Rabbi Alexander Linchner and Chief Rabbi Yitzchak Isaac Halevi Herzog in front of Merom Zion (later Boys Town), Bayit Vegan, 1955

Rav Avraham Yitzchak HaKohen Kook, whose spirit pervades this book

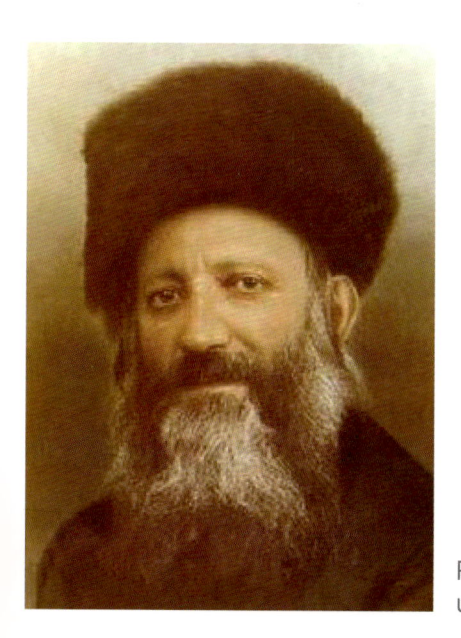

First annual Ner Israel dinner, 1961. *Left to right*: Reb Itche Meyer Koronek, Mr. Meyer Gasner, guest speaker Rabbi Ralph Pelcowitz, Rabbi Sholom Gold, Rabbi Ruderman, Mr. Herschel Rubenstein

Students of Ner Israel of Toronto, 1962

Students of Ner Israel of Toronto, 1962

Meyer Lebovic, one of the prime movers in establishing the *yeshivah*, with Rabbi Gold.
In the background the new dormitory building on the Finch Avenue campus

Rabbi Moshe Rose, director of Young Israel in Israel

Dov Rubin, a founding member of Kehillat Zichron Yosef, Har Nof

David Bruce, a founding member of Kehillat Zichron Yosef, Har Nof

Avrom Silver and me

Guests at the shul dedication dinner

CASE NO. 16879                      RESOLUTION NO. 1525-1976

Adopted: November 9, 1976

Mr. Cairo offered the following resolution and moved its adoption:

RESOLUTION AMENDING RESOLUTION NO. 702-1972, ADOPTED MARCH 28, 1972, SO AS TO EXTEND THE TERRITORIAL GRANT OF RIGHTS TO PROPERTY AT WEST HEMPSTEAD.

WHEREAS, in accordance with the Jewish Religion, the Laws of the Sabbath contain the Commandment:

"Let no man go out of his place on the Seventh Day."
(Exodus 17-29),

and a man's place is defined by (1) specifying certain natural or artificial boundaries, and (2) by mutual agreement, letting the use of the common domain; and

WHEREAS, pursuant to Town Board Resolution No. 702-1972, adopted March 28, 1972, the Town Board granted the petition of Dr. Sholom Gold, Spiritual Leader of Young Israel of West Hempstead, on behalf of those of the Jewish Faith who resided within the boundaries specified in their petition to grant for a period of twenty years at a rental of One Dollar, the rights to the public domain within the aforesaid boundaries for the purposes of "carrying" on the Sabbath and other Jewish holidays; and

WHEREAS, by petition of Dr. Sholom Gold, dated October 7, 1976, a request was made to extend the territorial area of the grant due to an expanded congregation, for the same purposes as permitted under the aforesaid Resolution No. 702-1972, adopted March 28, 1972; and

WHEREAS, the Town Board of the Town of Hempstead

STATE OF NEW YORK  }
COUNTY OF NASSAU   } ss.:
TOWN OF HEMPSTEAD  }

I do hereby certify that I have compared the annexed copy of **Resolution No. 1525-1976 (1 page) adopted by the Town Board on November 9, 1976** with the original, on file in the office of the Town Clerk of the Town of Hempstead, and that the same is a true and correct copy of said original and of the whole thereof.

IN TESTIMONY WHEREOF, I have hereunto set my hand and affixed the official seal of the Town of Hempstead on this day of **November 9, 1976**

NATHAN L. H. BENNETT, Town Clerk

*Joseph R. Mazza*
Deputy Town Clerk

The extension of the lease of West Hempstead for the eruv initiated on March 28, 1972

# ERUV
# WEST HEMPSTEAD

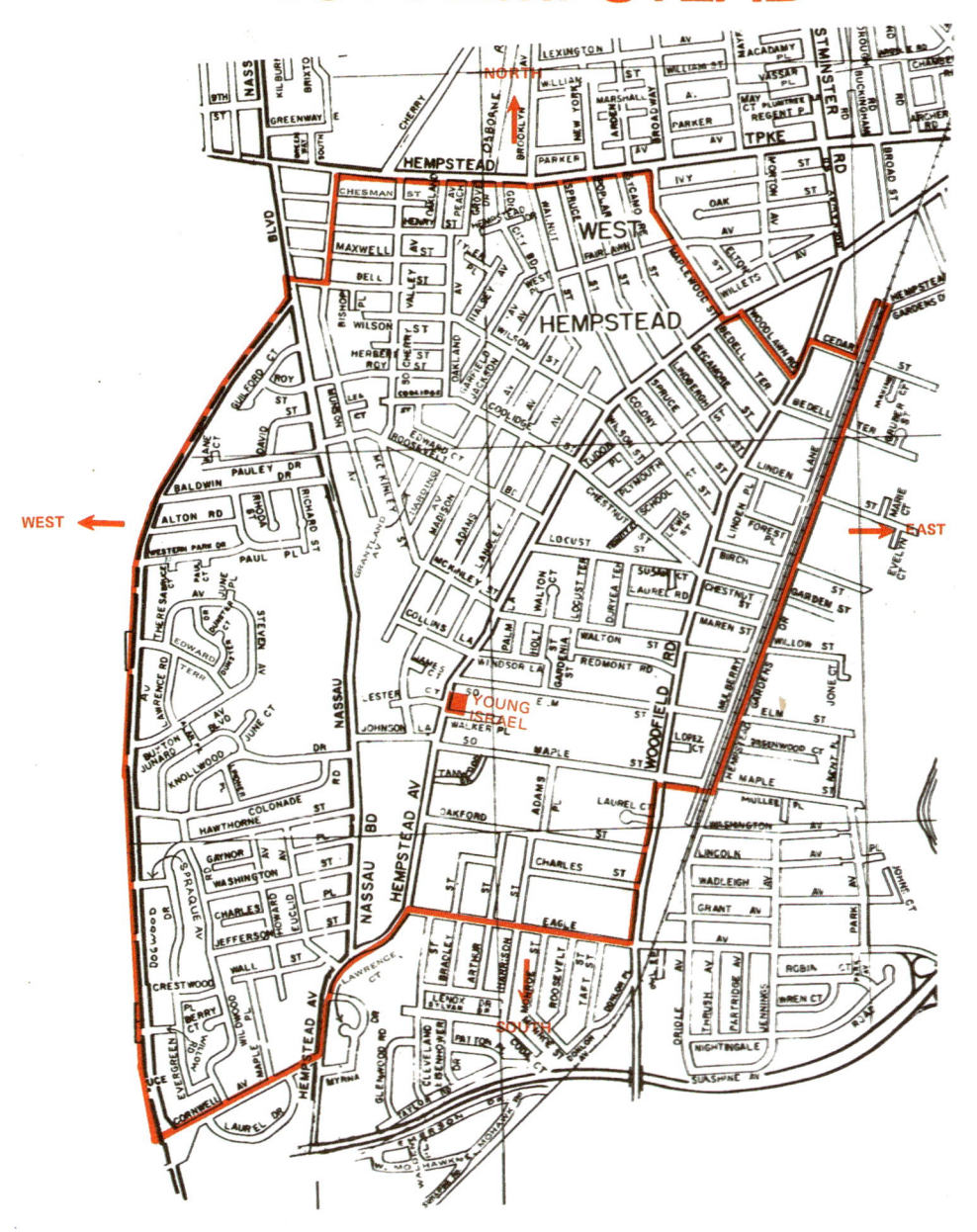

Map showing West Hempsted Eruv

Yehuda Gold and his three sons. *Left to right*: me, my father, Yosef Yoel (Joe), Shmuel Yehoshua (Stanley)

Ponevezh Yeshiva, Bnei Brak

Ner Israel of Baltimore, 4411 Garrison Boulevard

Ner Israel of Toronto, 625 Finch Avenue West, 1959

Procession through the streets of Har Nof for *sefer Torah* donated by Mr. and Mrs. Harry Tark, parents of Lizzie Rubin

Weinstock *sefer Torah* procession. Rabbi Simcha HaCohen Kook (*left*), Meyer Weinstock holding *sefer Torah*, me, Lou Benjamin from West Hempstead

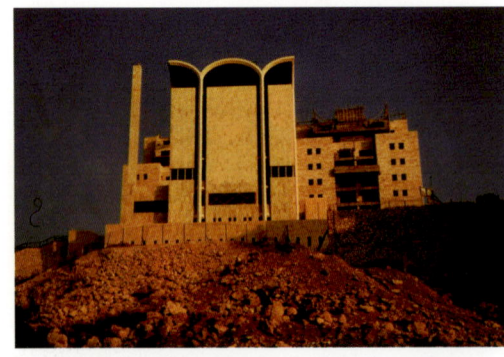

Kehillat Zichron Yosef, Har Nof (in memory of Yosel Silver, father of Avrom Silver), under construction, 1987

Another view of the shul

Rabbi Avraham Shapira, Rosh Yeshiva Mercaz Harav and Ashkenazic chief rabbi, at demonstration against Oslo Accords

Lighting Chanukah candles in a hotel room in Moscow, December 1983. Notice that the drapes are closed

Mark and Slava Shifrin and children, Moscow, December 1983. *In the back*: Rabbi Mallen Galinsky, z"l

Passport photo of my father's parents, Pinya Rochel and Yona Gold, 1923

Bayla's parents, Sarah (née Grafstein) and Binyomin Rubinoff, Toronto

Sarah Rubinoff's parents, Liba (née Brickman) and Yirmiya Grafstein, at Susie and Shimon Werner's wedding, 1951, Toronto

My mother's parents, Maryam Devora and Mordechai Duvid Sandhaus, in Cleveland

Twinning ceremony. *Speaking*: Dov Rubin. *Seated*: Rabbi Meyer Fendel, Rabbi Gold, Rav of Neve Nof Rabbi Yaakov Wahrhaftig

Rabbi Menachem Gold, who in addition to the educational institutions he has established in Afula, also provides food for the needy there for Pesach

## RAV AVRAHAM SHAPIRA שליט״א
FORMER ASHKENAZIC CHIEF RABBI OF ISRAEL; ROSH YESHIVA, MERCAZ HARAV KOOK

and the

## איחוד הרבנים למען ארץ ישראל
INTERNATIONAL RABBINICAL COALITION FOR ISRAEL

urge all Rabbis to participate in a one day mission to

## WASHINGTON, DC

### TUESDAY, JUNE 13, 1995

TO REQUEST CONGRESS TO DEMAND THE PLO'S FULL COMPLIANCE OF THE OSLO ACCORDS BEFORE $500,000,000 IS ALLOCATED TO THE PALESTINIAN AUTHORITY

Join

| | |
|---|---|
| Rav Hershel Reichman שליט״א | Rosh Yeshiva, RIETS |
| Rav Hershel Schachter שליט״א | Rosh Kollel, RIETS |
| Rav Moshe Dovid Tendler שליט״א | Rosh Yeshiva, RIETS |
| Rabbi Moshe Faskowitz שליט״א | President, Young Israel Council of Rabbis |
| Rabbi Avraham Hecht שליט״א | President, Rabbinical Alliance of America |

and with the urging, participation, and full support of the Rabbinical Council of America

as we meet with Senators and Representatives on this crucial issue.

Buses will leave from two locations:

| Young Israel of Queens Valley | Young Israel of Midwood |
|---|---|
| 141-55 77th Avenue | 1694 Ocean Avenue |
| Flushing, NY | Brooklyn, NY |
| Shacharit: 6:30, Bus Leaves: 7:00 | Shacharit: 6:20, Bus Leaves: 7:00 |

Buses are expected to Arrive Back in New York At APPROXIMATELY 10:30 P.M.

To reserve a seat, make arrangements to join us in Washington if not going on the bus, or for more information, please contact the ICHUD HaRabbanim
212-867-0577 (phone), 212-867-0615 (fax)

Travel arrangements, meals, and all costs associated with this mission have been underwritten by:
NATIONAL COUNCIL OF YOUNG ISRAEL

March on Washington, June 13, 1995

---

## KEHILAT ZICHRON YOSEPH קהילת זכרון יוסף
AN AFFILIATE OF ISRAEL COUNCIL OF YOUNG ISRAEL — מועצת ישראל הצעיר בישראל
7 RECHOV AGASI, HAR NOF, JERUSALEM, TEL. (02) 538 319 — רחוב אגסי 7, הר נוף ירושלים, טל.
RABBI DR. SHOLOM GOLD — הרב ד״ר שלום גולד

### DEDICATION DINNER

❖

Honoring
Mrs. Nancy Silver

and

Avrom and Bonny Silver
of Toronto, Canada

❖

Wednesday, 8th June 1988 - 23 Sivan 5748

Ramada Renaissance Hotel, Jerusalem

Inaugural Shul Dinner. Paul Shaviv, a member of the shul at the time, masterfully organized the entire inaugural shul dinner

Some of Rabbi Linchner's Torah pioneers, Eretz Yisroel, summer of 1955, together with some young Israelis. *Left to right:* unidentified, Chaim Libel, unidentified, Nosson Scherman, Yankel Goldberg, Shlomo Yosef (Joey) Weinstein, Avrohom (Bumy) Landesman, Yoav Elstein, unidentified

Tugboats with bands coming to greet the Rebbe of Satmar, June 28, 1955

My first view of Eretz Yisroel (Haifa) from the deck of the *Messapia*, June 28, 1955 – a very emotional moment

April 1956. Digging trenches around Jerusalem. *In the foreground*: Yehuda Leon Fulda from Manchester, my roommate

Charlie, the dog who made aliyah before us, with Suzy Cooperberg on Colonade Road, West Hempstead

Disengagement, 2005 – demonstrations in Zion Square

# כולנו מתגייסים
## הועד למען ציון-הר נוף, ירושלים

*Center:* Rav Mordechai Eliyahu;
*right:* Rav Avraham Shapira

*Second from right:* Moish Kempinsky, chairman of Vaad Lemaan Tzion, Har Nof

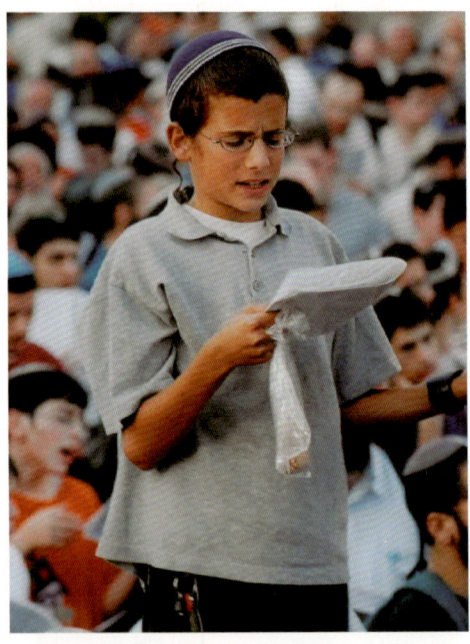

Sabbatical year, with my father at the Kotel, September 1980

Avrom and Bonnie Silver, with Jeffrey Saul Silver, Sherri Rosalie Silver, and Jeremy Aaron Silver

Teaching at Avrom Silver College

Avrom Silver Jerusalem College Israel Center

Rabbi Nachum Rabinovitch, then rabbi of Clanton Park Synagogue, at our farewell dinner, Toronto, 1971

Hempstead's presiding supervisor Francis Purcell presenting citation to Dr. Yirmiyahu (Herman) Branover following his release from the Soviet Union. He was hosted by Young Israel of West Hempstead. *Left to right*: Purcell, Branover, me, Norman Feiden

Dinner celebrating opening of mikveh in West Hempstead honouring author, 1981. Left to right: Robert Steinberger, unknown, Howard Kanowitz, Rabbi Sholom Gold, Bernard Kesselman, Stuie Milworm

*Right to left*: Steven Berger, Rabbi Daniel Korobkin, Dr Ernest Agatstein, Rabbi Sholom Gold (guest speaker at Yom Yerushalyim celebration in L.A.), Bayla Gold, May 2006

Rav Yosef Shalom Elyashiv, who tested me for *smicha*, 1956

The Lubavitcher Rebbe, Menachem Mendel Schneerson, whose advice I sought at life's crossroads

Rav Avraham HaCohen Pam, *rebbe* of the three Gold brothers in Torah Vodaath

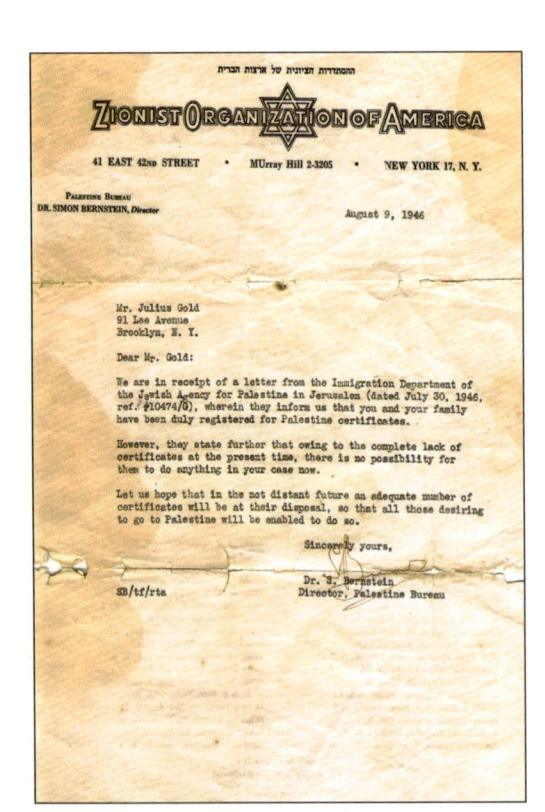

Letter of Zionist Organization of America to my father, August 9, 1946

*Smicha* I received from Chief Rabbi Yitzchak Isaac Halevi Herzog, August 1956

Our good friends Rabbi Meyer and Goldie Fendel had taken their family on a cross-country camper trip the previous summer. And they had had the time of their lives. We decided that this would be a wonderful adventure for the Gold family as well. And so in the beginning of July 1977, the Gold children and parents set off on our own cross-country summer trailer trip. There was always a fight over who got to sit beside the driver (me) because the air conditioning worked the best in that exact spot; somehow my youngest son Yirmi always seemed to be there. Don't ask me how he managed that.

Although he was all of seven years old, he learned how the whole trailer worked, the ins and outs of the entire apparatus, what to hook up where, and he'd show the rest of us what needed to be done the moment we pulled up for a stop at the trailer parks where we spent the nights along the way. The rest of the family was spread out through the very comfortable trailer, some reading, some fighting, some eating, but everyone was all set to have the summer experience of their lives.

And so, with much fanfare we left West Hempstead. Rabbi Neuberger had graciously given us permission to use the facilities of the campus of Yeshivas Ner Yisroel for the night. We plugged our trailer into the *yeshivah*'s systems. We connected up to the water pipes, the sewage pipes, and electricity.

Being in Baltimore was a nice trip down memory lane, and I was able to show my family all the places that held such fond memories for me. That was the last time I stayed overnight at Ner Yisroel.

We left Baltimore early the next morning and began driving further south, crossing into Virginia. It was very, very, very hot. I figured that since we were rapidly moving deeper into the south, it would just keep on getting hotter. What I did not know was that the entire country was experiencing one of the worst heat waves in its history. New York was crippled by a blackout. The heat wave lasted for about ten days – the length of our entire trip. We continued southward, stopping for a day at Orlando, Florida, to allow the kids to experience the magical world of Disney. They enjoyed the Magic Kingdom, and even Bayla and I found it a place of tremendous charm and wonder.

We enjoyed the scenery and beauty outside and suffered in the heat. At night we usually found ourselves a trailer park to rest in and then Yirmi supervised the hookup. Those days were the stuff family memories are made of.

And then one day during the trip I found out that Menachem Begin was making his first visit to the States and would be arriving at the White House on July 17. I decided that I wanted to be there and perhaps even get a chance to meet with him (he'd always been a firm favorite of mine). I decided to make a mad dash and head north to Washington, DC. Along the way, I also managed to find out that we'd be arriving on the very day when there was to be a diplomatic reception planned for Begin at a glitzy Washington hotel. And I intended to crash that reception. With the whole family.

The scene was fantastic.

One second, the hotel's driveway was filled with luxury cars discharging politicians, extremely wealthy individuals and famous movie stars, and the next minute, the Gold family pulled up in their trailer, by now covered in grime and dust from our road trip.

The hotel was absolutely elegant. Took your breath away.

Our ride was anything but.

The people streaming toward the front of the hotel were impeccably dressed.

We on the other hand were wearing sweaty clothes; since the Nine Days had begun and we couldn't do laundry we had sort of run out of clothing to wear.

They looked fantastic. We came across somewhat bedraggled. No matter. I opened the door and five dirty, sweaty, summer-vacationing children came stepping out, right into the glamour and glitz of a gathering of the Who's Who of Washington.

The entire way there, Bayla kept on asking me, "How are you going to get us in to see the man? This is an invitation-only kind of event."

"I'll figure out a way."

Now was the time to figure out a way. The moment of truth had arrived. With my wife and kids looking at me expectantly, I approached the door of the hotel, where the team of security guards looked me over suspiciously. I was not wearing a suit, I was sunburned, and I had a long beard. I did not seem to belong at this august and auspicious gathering.

"Can I help you, sir?" one of the security team asked me.

"I am the president of the Council of Young Israel Rabbis of the United States of America." (It was true.)

I waited while he chewed on that for a while, mentally reconciling my appearance with the position I claimed to fill. Then I asked if my five children could also enter. The security staff scrutinized them all standing there with that very cute "Oh, please…" look.

They let us in.

And so the seven of us came shlepping into the grand ballroom of one of the most exclusive Washington hotels.

We stood inside the ballroom and simply gawked at the scene before our eyes: the richest, most famous people in Washington were there. We just stood off to the side and were content to watch. Menachem Begin entered the ballroom and the place went crazy. Everyone jumped to their feet and began cheering for a man who had done the impossible, a man who had fought the British Empire, thrown the Israeli Left out of power and who wasn't afraid to say *"Baruch Hashem"* in public. A man who would go on to attack and successfully destroy the Iraqi nuclear reactor. A man who did big things. He had a Jewish heart and wasn't embarrassed to wear it on his sleeve.

Menachem Begin made his way farther into the hall and the next moment he was passing right beside our family. And then the prime minister of Israel caught sight of my son Yirmi, who was standing on a chair to get a good view of the whole shebang. The next thing I knew, Menachem Begin swooped over and picked up Yirmi, just hoisted him off that chair and lifted him up into the air and he held my seven-year-old son in his arms, saying all the while, *"a Yiddish boychickel, a Yiddishe yingele!"* Begin was so happy, smiling from ear to ear as if he'd just won the lottery, and then he bent down and gave Yirmi a big kiss on the cheek with the love of a benevolent, loving grandfather.

All this in front of the cameras of the world press.

Menachem Begin and Yirmi, caught on film for the entire world to see. For posterity. This was a moment to store away in our memories.

We spent Shabbos in a trailer camp in Virginia. While there, we had a very interesting experience. But first, a little introduction.

A short while ago, my grandson Yehuda Gold decided that since many of the boys in his *yeshivah*, Mercaz Harav, devote substantial amounts of time toward learning *halachah*, and since they were now about to begin the fourth section of Mishnah Brurah which deals with the laws of *eruv*, it would make sense for them to join Dirshu. This learning program, set up by Rav Dovid Hofstedter, stresses the importance of reviewing what one has learned and reinforces it by testing participants on vast amounts of material. About 150 boys signed up to join the program. It was very impressive.

The Dirshu inaugural program took place in the library of Mercaz Harav (the scene of a terrible terrorist attack in March 2008). A special guest joined my grandson and his friends at the event – none other than Rav Dovid Hofstedter himself, chairman of Dirshu. My grandson delivered a moving speech about the importance of learning *halachah* and being part of the Dirshu family, and then the *rosh yeshivah*, Rav Yaakov Shapira, delivered words of blessing to the assembled. The program was winding itself to an end when the *rosh yeshivah* suggested that Yehuda invite me to say a few words in honor of the occasion. I was unprepared and taken by surprise, but I walked up anyway, trying to think of what to say on the way up to the podium.

I took a look at the guest of honor and told my listeners that I had merited building a *yeshivah* in Toronto many years earlier and that the father and the father-in-law of our esteemed guest Rav Dovid had been two of the strongest pillars of the *yeshivah* for over fifty years – great builders of Torah. I spoke about his parents and his in-laws, whom I knew very well, and then I devoted a few minutes to Rav Dovid himself, whom I'm proud to say was a student of mine back at Ner Yisroel of Toronto. Rav Dovid was shaking his head in agreement and nostalgia throughout the speech.

I then turned to the idea of *Eruvin*, the section of *halachah* that the boys were about to begin learning. I related how I had merited extending the *eruv* in Toronto as the city grew northward, together with two of the other members of the city's *beis din*, Rav Gedalia Felder and Rav Nachum Eliezer Rabinovitch, both tremendous Torah scholars. And then I shared my *eruv*-building experiences in West Hempstead and my conversation with Rav Moshe Feinstein. The students listened raptly. I discussed the importance of learning the laws of *eruv* and how important it was to be part of such a select group of people who were all studying the same laws together.

And what does this all have to do with the Shabbos we spent in that trailer park in Virginia?

Because when we reached the trailer park, I realized that for us to have a real Shabbos experience, I was going to have to construct an *eruv*. This would allow the family to eat outside on a picnic table not far from where the trailer was parked and would allow us to carry outside. It was simply imperative for our wellbeing, because it would provide us with space to move around and to carry a siddur outside, a book, a game.

So I built an *eruv*.

A person can only construct an *eruv* on the spur of the moment if he has devoted real time to studying the laws of *eruv*. *Eruv* building is a very crucial and useful talent to have. It's something that every Torah Jew should learn.

In the middle of Shabbos, our immediate neighbor decided that he was in the mood for a BBQ and wasted no time in getting the grill up and running. There was one problem: he'd set up the grill almost adjacent to one of my *eruv* posts and I was afraid that he was going to burn my *eruv* down. The entire time he was busy with his grill, our hearts were in our mouths. We watched the flames from his grill dancing upwards, so, so very close to our wood and string. Thank G-d our *eruv* was spared. But it was a close one.

That trailer trip was something to remember and in fact, our children still have fond memories of it. Personally I'd recommend that every family take a trailer trip at least once in their lives. There's nothing like it. Completely cut off from the world (at least in the days before technology took over our lives), out on the road with nobody but one another for company, a family can reconnect and spend quality time with one another in a way that will never be forgotten.

March 26, 1978. A historic signing was taking place on the White House lawn, hosted by President Jimmy Carter and attended by President Anwar Sadat and Prime Minister Menachem Begin. As president of the Council of Young Israel Rabbis of America, I was invited to the White House for the event. It's always nice when a cable arrives at your door with the words "President and Mrs. Carter cordially invite you…"

I flew from La Guardia Airport to Washington, DC, took a taxi from the airport to the White House, showed the Marines at the entrance my invitation, and was shown into one of the most famous residences in the universe. I followed the crowds to the South Lawn, where a podium was set up for the big three. After taking my place among the thousand people attending the event, I looked around with interest. I had been at the White House before and found the place fascinating from a historical and architectural point of view.

Jimmy Carter was the first to address the assembled. He praised his two partners and spoke of their courage to withstand the pressures waiting for them at home, their moral clarity in a world filled with ambiguity, and so on. And he ended his speech with the following famous words, delivered in his southern drawl: "The prophet Isaiah said, 'Nations shall beat their swords into plowshares and their spears into pruning hooks: nation shall not lift up sword against nation, neither shall they learn war any more.'"

Anwar Sadat (who would be assassinated just two and a half years later) spoke next. He ended off his speech with the following now familiar words, delivered in his Egyptian accent: "Let us work together until the day comes when they beat their swords into plowshares and their spears into pruning hooks…"

Menachem Begin spoke last. And I had a sneaking suspicion we would hear the same words again. As he began his speech, I had a sinking feeling that he would reference the same *pasuk* from Isaiah and for a few fleeting seconds thought that he should have chosen some other *pasuk* – but I caught myself and knew that the prime minister was absolutely right.

Begin intoned, "Yeshayahu Ben Amoz...gave the nations of the world the following vision...: 'And they shall beat their swords into plowshares and their spears into pruning hooks. Nation shall not lift up sword against nation; neither shall they learn war anymore.'"

He's so right!

Here's a Christian, a Muslim, and a Jew (this almost sounds like a setup for a joke), and despite having millions of books to choose from, despite all the world-class literature at their disposal, and despite having three different teams of speech writers, the best quote all three men arrived at independently, and the quote that most effectively sums up the world's desire for peace, is straight out of the Prophet Isaiah, from the Jewish Tanach.

You know what Begin was probably thinking? *I, Menachem Begin, a grandchild of Isaiah, I have the right to use this verse. He's my prophet, not yours! How shameful it is that neither of you were able to come up with an appropriate quote from all your writings that would have been sufficiently representative of peace. Shame on you for once again having to rely on the Jews.*

And if you should happen to be visiting the United Nations building in Manhattan, your guide will no doubt point out the "Isaiah Wall" to you where the very same quote has been inscribed for posterity. All I can do is point out the incongruousness in the fact that the UN had to dip into Jewish wellsprings of literature for the perfect quote. How ironic is that? Here they are, constantly trying to teach us and preach to us about peace – to the People, the Nation, who actually wrote the Book on peace in the first place.

My only regret was not asking Begin himself what he thought of those two plagiarists. It would have been interesting to hear his response.

Only now, years later, did I learn that I understood Begin well. *Segula* magazine in February 2013 reported on the speech that Menachem Begin delivered upon receiving the Nobel Peace Prize in Oslo (a name that would come to describe folly and tragedy twenty-five years later). The following is my free translation of the first paragraph:

> I come from Eretz Yisrael, the land of Zion and Jerusalem, and I stand here with humility and pride as a son of the Jewish people

and as one of the children of the generation of Shoah and *geulah*. The ancient Jewish people gave to the world the vision of eternal peace, the mission of global disarmament, the end to making war. The prophets Yeshayahu Ben Amoz and Michah Hamorashti saw the spiritual unity of men under G-d as He comes forth from Zion and Jerusalem, and bequeathed to the world their vision in identical expressions, "And they shall beat their swords into plowshares and their spears into pruning hooks; nation shall not lift up sword against nation, and they shall no longer learn how to wage war." When we mortal men who believe in Divine Providence remember these holy prophetic words, we don't ask ourselves whether the dream will come true – but when.

꙳

I met Menachem Begin on a number of occasions and never failed to walk away with an appreciation for the man. One particular meeting took place between the prime minister, Rabbi David Hollander, and myself regarding the controversial issue of "*Mihu Yehudi?*" (Who is a Jew?).

When we arrived at the prime minister's office, Begin was running late. We were shown into a waiting room where we were joined by Begin's legendary secretary Yechiel Kadishai. The latter turned to us and said, "The story is told about the famous *tzaddik* Rav Menachem Mendel of Kotzk, who said, 'When Mashiach comes, Jews will flock to say *shalom aleichem* to the Mashiach. They'll line up in droves. Personally,' the Kotzker continued with his trademark sharp wit, 'I'm going to wait for a few days, until the crowds thin out. I will then approach the Mashiach and say, "*Shalom aleichem*, Mashiach." Mashiach will respond, "What took you so long?" And you know what I'm going to reply? "What took *you* so long!"'"

Menachem Begin was a special Jew and his secretary was pretty special as well. Those were the days.

# 15

## Decision Time

We went to Eretz Yisrael on sabbatical from the summer of 1980 until the summer of 1981. I had big plans for my sabbatical year. My father had been living with us for the past number of years and accompanied us to Eretz Yisrael. We rented an apartment on Uziel Street in Bayit Vegan and looked forward to a relaxing and enjoyable year. Unfortunately, our stay was not meant to be an uneventful one. Our sabbatical year strayed wildly from its course when I took sick shortly after we arrived. There I was, raring to learn, to do research on a number of assorted projects, and to teach classes everywhere I could, but in reality, I was too sick to do much of anything.

There was a doctor, Moe Weinberg from Toronto, living nearby in Bayit Vegan. I shuffled into his office and asked him to check me out. After a thorough examination, he proceeded to give me his professional diagnosis.

"Rabbi Gold, you have a severe bout of pneumonia."

This was the second time I had been stricken with pneumonia. It sucks the very life out of a person. The first time had been in West Hempstead. I'd been out of commission for five or six weeks. Simply speaking, I hadn't been able to move. I'd had the greatest desire to be up and about, but my body had betrayed me. And now it was happening all over again. My body was saying, *time for a break.*

I spent the first two months of what was supposed to be a glorious year in the Holy Land in bed. I couldn't move. I told myself that it was psychological, that there really was no reason for this type of behavior, but all to no avail. My body simply refused to cooperate. Finally I began feeling better. I was able to sit up and then stand and sure enough, it wasn't long before I was walking to shul and beginning to experience the joys of daylight once more.

Then my father fell.

A Dr. Scheinfeld lived in the building.

Someone ran to call him. He arrived immediately.

"Get your father to the hospital!"

An ambulance came speeding down Uziel Street and I watched as the EMTs maneuvered my beloved father onto the stretcher. In the hospital he was examined by a team of professionals.

"Rabbi Gold, your father has broken his hip." Terrible news. He was eighty-seven at the time and they couldn't operate. They did their best and tried their hand at a minor quasi-surgical procedure, but his fall kept him in the hospital for the next seven months.

My days and nights were spent at his bedside. Morning ran into night, and days passed wholly unaccounted for. Time ceased having any meaning in my state of constant exhaustion. I looked at my dear father and realized that I had a lump in my throat that just wouldn't go away. This was my father and he meant the world to me. How had our sabbatical year changed so drastically, so beyond measure?

My brother Rav Shmuel Yehoshua, who lived in Petach Tikvah, visited often, and when I realized that the end was near, I called my oldest brother in the States and told him to take the next flight to Eretz Yisrael. My father passed away surrounded by his three rabbi sons, all educators and Torah scholars, a legacy that any man would be proud of. We sat shivah together at 107 Uziel Street, the closure to a year of sadness and pain for our family. This was May 1981 and the entire year had passed in an uneasy alliance between the joy of being in Eretz Yisrael and the sadness of a parent's demise.

But the message was clear.

Eretz Yisrael is acquired through suffering, and if we were intent on eventually moving here, we were being given a taste of what to expect. G-d was showing us that the move would not be an easy one and that we should be prepared for challenges along the way. G-d was asking me, *Sholom, are you still ready to say "Eileich," I will go? Because it's not going to be an easy ride!*

That was our year. In many respects, it was a sabbatical completely at odds with what a sabbatical is supposed to be like. But our children got used to the Land and were excited about coming there to live. My father was buried in Yerushalayim on the Mount of Olives and we knew that this was the place for us as well, in sickness or health, in wealth or poverty.

Just a matter of time.

ى

During our sabbatical year, I arranged to spend a number of Shabbosim at fledgling communities around the country affiliated with the Young Israel movement.

We spent a freezing Shabbos at a hilltop community called Elon Moreh. They very graciously put us up in a caravan with walls so thin it felt like the wind was coming right through them. We traveled the Land, getting to know our beautiful country in every direction. We went out for about six or seven Shabbosim all told, and received modest remuneration from Young Israel which allowed us relative financial freedom. Besides helping us monetarily, my connection with Young Israel also provided me with a network of influential people who would serve as future liaisons with the Jerusalem officials in charge of assigning plots of land for future shuls in Har Nof.

All this meant that I had set the ball in motion for our future return and the shul that I hoped to build.

ى

Soon enough we were back in West Hempstead trying to make a decision regarding our future. Were we going to remain in suburbia? Was I going to remain the rabbi of West Hempstead, or were we going to follow our hearts and return to the Land of our ancestors? It was a very tough decision for us to make. What about finances? What about schooling for the children? What about jobs? We had a million and one questions and doubts. I had been offered a promising job while in Eretz Yisrael, which I was seriously considering. I owed my community another year at least, and during the course of that year, I had to make up my mind about the position. To accept or not to accept. Back and forth like a ping-pong ball.

It was November 1981 and I was being called upon to make the most difficult decision of my entire life.

I'll never forget having to make that painful decision. Here I was, living in a truly beautiful community, granted the opportunity to do what I loved most, to teach Torah to Jewish people. On the other hand, Eretz Yisrael... To move there was the chance of a lifetime! I found to my dismay that I wasn't able to make the decision.

What to do?

I wanted so badly to go. Bayla was very sure it was the right thing to do, but I couldn't stop asking myself all the "what ifs." Bayla said we were educated, we were willing to work hard and do whatever it would take to make it.

There had been a family of *baalei tshuvah*, the Cooperbergs, who had moved into our community. They lived five houses away from our home on Colonade Road. They were optimistic and searching and full of questions. We went through the entire process together, kashering the kitchen, answering all their questions, and so on. They were very nice people and we became extremely close with one another.

The Cooperbergs had a dog named Charlie.

A few years earlier, the Cooperberg family had decided to make aliyah. But though they took all family members with them. Charlie the dog was left behind. Charlie was very down in the mouth when his "parents" left him, but he made the best of it. He still lived on Colonade Road with "foster parents."

I used to run into Charlie almost every night. You see, I had developed a tradition over the years of going out every night for a walk at about eleven o'clock in the evening. I picked this up from the Brisker Rav in Eretz Yisrael twenty years before. I'd think over a class, grapple with a new concept, work out an original idea. The cold air was invigorating and it woke me up. The night was mine. Many times Charlie was also taken for a stroll before bedtime, and we would run into one another.

Charlie always looked thrilled when that happened. He'd come trotting over and stick his head between my coat and arm. He was the sweetest collie you ever saw, aside from the fact that he always looked like he needed a tissue. Listen, nobody's perfect. We had a relationship. After all, here was a dog with a lot of *derech eretz*, a dog who understood what a *rav* is. A dog fully cognizant of the holy work a rabbi does.

It was the night of the big decision. Were we going or staying? I had to decide that night. I went out for a bit, my nightly constitutional, bundled up in my overcoat, shivering slightly in the November chill. And behold, Charlie was bounding toward me, eagerly anticipating a pat from my gloved hands on his head. His adoptive parents said to me, "Rabbi, you'll never believe this. We just received a phone call from Israel, and the Cooperbergs have just purchased an airline ticket for Charlie!"

A pause.

"Charlie is going on aliyah!"

The words burst from my mouth.

"That *farshluggene* dog is going to Eretz Yisrael and I'm not? Not a chance in the world." I turned around, went into the house, looked my wife and kids in the eye, and said, "Gold family, we are going on aliyah!"

If there is a heaven for dogs, Charlie is there.

*Zachor oso kelev l'tov.* May that dog be remembered for the good. Charlie was a messenger from G-d, Who knew that I needed something to tip the scales. The lesson of Charlie is that G-d is constantly sending us messages. But if you're not tuned in, you miss the point.

The story of Charlie cannot be told without bringing in the story of the snowstorm for an encore.

After we had already lived in Eretz Yisrael for many years, my wife and I used to enjoy getting away to the Galei Tzanz Hotel in Netanya for a Shabbos every once in a while. It was a Shabbos of rest and relaxation, usually among perfect strangers, because this wasn't the normal haunt of our Har Nof crowd. It was the perfect escape for a busy rabbi and rebbetzin. On one particular "vacation" Shabbos the hotel was full; a bar mitzvah was being celebrated in one of the halls and we were acquainted with one family of visitors who were from Har Nof. Other than the Sapsowitzes, we knew not a soul. Minchah time rolled around. The Sapsowitzes approached us.

"Rabbi Gold, I have to tell you a story. There's a family making a bar mitzvah this Shabbos who came on aliyah about thirteen years ago."

It seems that the father of the bar mitzvah boy used to work out on Long Island. The family lived in Brooklyn, and he'd commute to work every day in Suffolk County, quite a long drive. The family was in turmoil at the time because the wife wanted to go on aliyah and the husband was agreeable in theory, but he just wasn't sure. Would he be able to support his family? Would it work out for the best? He didn't feel ready to commit to such a tremendous move.

A fateful snowstorm took place one Friday morning in late November or December 1982. It wasn't snowing when he left home earlier that morning, but by ten or eleven o'clock in the morning, it was coming down pretty heavily. He looked out the window and realized that the way things were heading, he probably wouldn't be able to make it back to Brooklyn for Shabbos. By twelve o'clock the radio reported that the roads were almost impassable. By twelve thirty it was clear that he was stuck on the Island for Shabbos. The first thought that entered his mind was "Where am I going to stay for the next day and a half?" He made a few phone calls and heard about a town called West Hempstead, where a certain Rabbi Gold lived. A bunch of people suggested that he call that rabbi. He dialed the number. The phone rang and rang and rang, but nobody answered. Now what?

He made some more phone calls and heard the name of another rabbi who lived in West Hempstead, Rabbi Meyer Fendel. He called the Fendel home. Goldie Fendel answered the phone.

He told her of his predicament.

"I'm stuck here in Long Island for Shabbos. There's no way I can get back to New York in time for candle lighting. But if I start driving now, I can still reach West Hempstead before Shabbos. Is there somewhere I can stay in your vicinity?"

"I'd love to have you stay with us," Rebbetzin Fendel told the man, "but my husband isn't home this Shabbos and I'm alone. He's actually in Eretz Yisrael right now, finalizing the final details for our move to Israel in a few months."

The stranded man listened to this bit news with major interest.

"Drive over to West Hempstead," she concluded the conversation, "and I'll find you a place to stay for Shabbos."

Before they hung up the man said to Goldie Fendel, "By the way, I've been trying to reach Rabbi Gold. I called a few times but nobody picked up. There must be something wrong with his phone. Maybe you can let him know."

"The Golds aren't living in West Hempstead anymore," Rebbetzin Fendel replied. "They made aliyah a few months ago and are now living in Yerushalayim."

A profound silence from the other side of the phone.

Then the man erupted, "I don't believe this! I called Rabbi Gold. He went on aliyah. I called Rabbi Fendel. He's preparing to go on aliyah. I'm arguing with my wife about going to Eretz Yisrael every day. She wants to go and I'm hesitating. Well, here's my answer. G-d is sending me a clear message. That's it, we're going!"

They went on aliyah a short while later. They had a baby boy after their arrival in Eretz Yisrael. They celebrated his bar mitzvah thirteen years later at the Galei Tzanz Hotel in Netanya, precisely on the Shabbos that I happened to be staying there.

How's that for coincidence?

Motzaei Shabbos after Havdalah, I went downstairs to the hall. The happy family was lined up, posing for family portraits. They still didn't know that I was staying in the hotel with them. Truthfully, they didn't know me at all. I entered the room, a stranger in their midst.

"Who's the father of the bar mitzvah boy?" I asked the assembled.

"I am," said a middle-aged man. "Can I help you with something?"

"My name is Gold," I said, "Sholom Gold."

And then there was sheer and unbridled bedlam, as he began hugging me, and then the entire room went crazy when they realized that the catalyst for their moving to Eretz Yisrael was there with them.

I only wish I had introduced myself with the words, "My name is Sholom Gold. I heard that you were trying to reach me." The fact is, you can't always come up with the perfect line at the right time.

And besides, in this situation, the perfect line had been the fact that there was no line, that I hadn't been there to answer his call. Bottom line, G-d is sending us messages every single day. "Come home, My children, come home."

༄

Charlie was a messenger sent to me straight from above and I knew it. It was time for us to leave. It was time to take things to the next level.

Before I resigned my post in West Hempstead, however, I decided to confer with those wiser than myself. I sent a letter to the Lubavitcher Rebbe asking him for a *brachah* on my upcoming life change. It's important for me to stress here that I *did not ask* the Rebbe whether he thought my going on aliyah was a good idea. All I asked for was a *brachah*.

The Rebbe wrote back as follows: "Anybody serving in the rabbinate or as an educator who leaves the States in order to go on aliyah is a deserter from the front lines for the struggle of the survival of Klal Yisrael. And even if you manage to hire somebody who is as talented as yourself to take over your position, it still doesn't make any difference, because we need hundreds more like you."

He also said that I could do more for aliyah if I stayed in America.

That was the gist of the letter.

But I had already committed to going to Israel. I had a job lined up. I was all set to go. I had only been asking the Rebbe for a *brachah*, and here I got a response telling me not to desert my post. I really and truly wanted to go to Eretz Yisrael. I had been dreaming of this moment for so long. Suddenly I was very worried. I felt that I couldn't go ahead with my plans without having another leading rabbi on my side, promising me that everything would be okay.

I decided to approach Rav Yaakov Kamenetsky for advice. He was in Toronto right then visiting with his second wife's family. I was in West Hempstead but I had to see him immediately. I called and made an appointment to see him as soon as I could get there. Then I boarded a plane and flew to Toronto.

I spent an extremely fascinating hour and a half with Rav Yaakov.

I told him the Rebbe's exact words.

"Sholom," Rav Yaakov responded, "the Rebbe is saying *dvarim shel taam*, things that make sense. The Rebbe is making a very good point."

He repeated those words four times in the course of our conversation. "The Rebbe is a *gadol b'Yisrael* and he's making a very good point."

"I understand that," I responded, "but this is something I've wanted to do for years. If I don't do it now, I'll never do it. The idea that I will never live in Eretz Yisrael is causing me a great deal of pain. What if I wrote another letter to the Rebbe explaining how much moving to Eretz Yisrael means to me? Is that a good idea?"

"The Rebbe is a *gadol b'Yisrael*," he said for the second time, "and you have to remember that you're not allowed to argue with a *gadol b'Yisrael*. And if he gives you the same answer after your second letter, don't ever dream of setting foot in Eretz Yisrael for the rest of your life!"

He was deadly serious.

That shook me up.

"That's exactly why I'm here," I told him. "I want you to give me permission to go to Eretz Yisrael, despite the fact that the Rebbe wrote me this letter."

He then told me the following words, which are inscribed on my memory and heart forever.

"*Sholom, zolst vissen, ich halt az es iz a mitzvah haint vi es iz allemol gevein tzu voinen in Eretz Yisroel. Un volt ich gekent, volt ich yetzt gegangen tzum airport arof oif a flugtzoig un geforen in Eretz Yisroel. Uber ich ken nisht* (Sholom, you should know, I believe that it's a mitzvah today as it always was to live in Eretz Yisrael. And if I could, I would go to the airport right now and get on a plane to Eretz Yisrael. But I can't).

I had another point in my favor to bring up. I quoted the Gemara that states how Rav Zeira wanted to move to Eretz Yisrael, but his *rebbe*, Rabbi Yehudah, was opposed, being that he held that anyone who moved from Bavel to Eretz Yisrael was disobeying a positive commandment.

So I said to Rav Yaakov, "Rav Zeira's *rebbe* was opposed to him moving to Eretz Yisrael, yet he disobeyed him and moved there anyway. He defied his *rebbe*, so why can't I go as well?"

Rav Yaakov started to laugh.

"Sholom," he said, "Rav Zeira had more *seichel* [intelligence] than you. He never asked Rabbi Yehudah for a *brachah*."

Rav Yaakov also told me another cryptic comment during the course of our meeting.

"You should know something, Sholom – it's easier to marry off children in Eretz Yisrael."

I couldn't understand what he was talking about but I maintained silence.

The truth is, the whole marrying off children thing had been one of my greatest worries about moving to Eretz Yisrael, and here was Rav Yaakov addressing the issue without me even bringing it up. (Although I didn't really understand what he was talking about at the time.)

Now he had given me another reason to move.

At the end of our meeting, I laid the question on the table.

"Rebbe, after everything we discussed, may I go?"

He was quiet for a second, and then he said, "Yes, Sholom, you can go." I had been granted the permission I so sorely needed.

I informed my congregation that they should initiate the search for another rabbi while we began putting our American affairs in order.

꙲

My conversation with Rav Yaakov and his subsequent declaration that he would have taken the next flight to Israel were he able to do so reminds me of a story that I heard told over in the name of Rav Shlomo Zalman Auerbach. It seems that a certain individual had been learning the halachic background pertaining to one's obligation to reside in Eretz Yisrael. When he finished going through all the opinions on the matter and had formulated a fairly clear picture, he came to the conclusion that he had a major question that he needed to discuss with a *gadol*.

What exactly was a Jewish person's obligation to live in Eretz Yisrael?

He flew to Israel and was driven through the narrow streets of Shaarei Chesed until he reached Rav Shlomo Zalman's simple apartment. He was greeted warmly and then proceeded to get to the point. He began by reviewing the opinions of the major commentators. The Rambam. The Ramban. How they looked at the obligation to live in Eretz Yisrael.

A few minutes into his oration, Rav Shlomo Zalman said a few words in his quiet voice: "*Es iz nit vichtig*" (It's not important).

The man couldn't understand what Rav Shlomo Zalman was talking about. What did he mean, it wasn't important? Was he not being clear? He carried on with his prepared remarks on the topic of Eretz Yisrael and the obligation of living there.

Once again, Rav Shlomo Zalman spoke up.

"*Es iz nit vichtig*" (It's not important).

The man couldn't control himself. "What does the Rav mean, it's not important?"

Rav Shlomo Zalman explained. "You're telling me the Rambam, the Ramban. But you don't need to go that far to get the point. All you need to do is open up a Chumash. On almost every single page, through every section of the Torah, we see that the will of G-d is that we, His chosen people, live here in Eretz Yisrael. Is it a *d'Oyraisa*? A *d'rabbanan*? A *mitzvah chiyuvis*? A *mitzvah kiyumis*? It matters not. The only thing that matters is that living here is what G-d wants from us. That's it."

That is how I came to explain Rav Moshe Feinstein's opinion regarding one's obligation to live in Eretz Yisrael. Because he clearly states that living in Eretz Yisrael is a *mitzvah kiyumis*, not *chiyuvis*, that there's no real obligation for a Jew to live in Israel. It's almost as if it's a suggestion from G-d and not more. For years I couldn't understand what Rav Moshe was saying. Until I finally tuned in to what I feel is the idea behind his ruling.

I feel that Rav Moshe is basically saying that living in Eretz Yisrael is not about a Jew's obligation to live in Eretz Yisrael. Living in Eretz

Yisrael is not like the other *mitzvos* in the Torah. It's a separate concept completely. It stems from a totally different place – from trying your best to carry out the will of G-d. The entire mitzvah is about wanting to accomplish the will of G-d. That's why there's no coercion. Because this is something that should be done because you want to do Hashem's will, not on account of being forced into anything. That's why you don't have to come here. But you should want to come. If you care about G-d and what He wants of you, then you should *want* to come! And that should be sufficient reason.

I have since adopted this explanation for myself. I once shared this insight with Rav Moshe's son Rav Reuven. He listened, nodded his head, smiled, and said, "This was probably the *hashkafah* behind my father's ruling."

And so my understanding was vindicated: Rav Moshe was simply saying that we should all *want* to come to Israel.

# PART TWO
# ERETZ YISRAEL

# 16

# FOR GOOD THIS TIME

I left for Eretz Yisrael on August 30, 1982, with the younger children, and Bayla came ten days later. We had had a policy all the years not to travel all together. It gave her time to take the exam for New York State certification in social work and to empty out the house. We hadn't been able to sell it, so we had put it up for rent. She gave away the last of the 110 V appliances – we wouldn't be using those any more – moved in with the Fendels for the last few days and left America on September 10.

The flights to Eretz Yisrael were uneventful. But it wasn't long before any semblance of routine came to a swift and decisive conclusion. There were a few hundred Americans who came on aliyah that summer. The vast majority were sent to the *mercaz klitah* (absorption center) in Mevasseret Tzion, a short distance from Yerushalayim and my new job in Bayit Vegan. I was probably the only one out of all those *olim* who actually had a job lined up. I arrived in the country on August 30 and was sitting at my desk on the first of September.

However, instead of arranging for us to move into living quarters in Mevasseret, the Sochnut informed us that we had a choice of two different locations of state-sponsored living: in Ashkelon or in Kiryat

Arba, both quite a commute from Yerushalayim. We tried explaining that the traveling would wreak havoc with our schedules and the children's schooling, but our pleas and explanations fell on deaf ears.

Mevasseret was out of the question because it was "full," and that was that. (We found out later that it was actually half empty.) We chose Kiryat Arba and even made some good friends there who took good care of us: Chaim and Irit Reichman, formerly of Toronto, and Andrea and Gary Cooperberg. But we didn't stay there very long; the commuting was just too much. This was before the government constructed the new highway from Yerushalayim to Kiryat Arba, and the winding, narrow, bumpy road through every Arab village along the way was difficult. In the end we left the *mercaz klitah* in Kiryat Arba and rented our own apartment in Yerushalayim.

But everything seemed to be falling apart.

The apartment that we rented was a disaster. The landlord was argumentative and unhelpful. The place was neglected and it was not in a good location for our children.

The job that I had naively imagined would be so perfect for me turned out to be unsuitable. I had to leave after about a year. A good friend of mine who had made aliyah earlier, Rav Emanuel Forman, told me very wisely, "Sholom, there is the job that brings you to Israel and there's the job that keeps you in Israel." The ultimate fiasco, however, and what nearly broke us, was the fact that we had purchased an apartment in Har Nof that had sounded great on paper and would have probably been a truly wonderful home for us, if the contractor hadn't gone bankrupt, leaving us with no funds, no home, and almost no hope.

That first year was a truly difficult time for the entire family. Our teenagers were in crisis. They were languishing. They were apathetic and completely stressed out by the adjustment.

Bayla and I looked at our family and we were fearful of what we were seeing.

The rabbi of a flourishing and growing congregation in the United States was now simply walking the streets of Yerushalayim without a plan, without the ability to support his family, and depressed beyond belief as he saw his lifelong dream of living in Eretz Yisrael slipping out of his grasp. It was very bad. Bayla had just earned her MSW in social work in America, but being that she wasn't sufficiently fluent in Hebrew she couldn't work in her field. Together with a partner, Tova Silverstein, she decided to open a retail business. They began selling women's hats and head coverings of all kinds. They called the store Headlines (that was my idea). It was there that snoods were revived from the 1920s. The truth is, Bayla saved us. She was the rock of the family in those trying days, and the money she brought in with her business went a long, long way. It gave me breathing space.

We reluctantly sent one of our children for counseling, and then another. And then the counselor spelled it out for us as follows: "One kid," he said, "not a big deal. Two kids? You've got problems. It's time for some family therapy."

We were mortified. The rabbi and his social worker wife – those who helped others with their family problems – having to go for family therapy? How the mighty had fallen! We were referred to an experienced and warm family therapist, Dr. Ron, who met with the entire family several times. At our final meeting he said, "You're a strong family. You're a healthy family. I'm not going to deny that you've been through a difficult time, but I know that you're going to pull through it."

But it would yet be a while before we actually pulled our way through. I was still trying to retrieve the money we'd lost from our apartment. I attended meetings along with others who'd lost just like us. A terrible feeling of dread filled my stomach. Would we ever have our own apartment? And underneath it, the agonizing fear that we'd have to leave Eretz Yisrael, because how could we remain without any money, any job, any way of supporting ourselves? Headlines was a wonderful business, but it wasn't enough. We needed more, and the more was just not forthcoming.

In the end, the government lawyers would end up renegotiating a deal with the banks whereby those who lost their money ended up having to add additional money to the purchase price. But at least we eventually received our apartments. Until then, however, it was pure suffering.

Meanwhile G-d was laughing the entire time. He knew the future. But we are not prophets. We couldn't see the future. We didn't know how well things would turn out in the end. Right then we were suffering and it seemed like it was never going to end.

&

During our sabbatical year there had been lots of talk about the future shuls of Har Nof. There were forms to fill out for those who wanted to organize minyanim. A group of thirty people could apply for a piece of property on which to construct a shul. So I put together a group of thirty people, some from the *mercazei klitah* in Mevasseret and Beit Canada, some from the people I was teaching, some who had moved to Israel from West Hempstead.

Rabbi Moshe Rose of the Young Israel movement of Israel, a good friend of mine, proved to be an invaluable source of assistance. He introduced me to key people in the Jerusalem municipality and helped me every way he could. I had numerous meetings with influential government people who were already unofficially helping to smooth the path for my eventual shul building.

Now that we'd returned, however, talk of shuls was starting to resurface. I was the first rabbi to be offered a shul. The municipality did more than offer me the land. I was taken on a personal tour of the four units under construction. They showed me the building that would eventually be known as "Boston" and three others. But I had other ideas. I contacted the person in charge of Jerusalem shul allocation, Yosef Gavish, and told him that I wanted to make a deal.

"My future congregation is for the most part not yet living in Har Nof. They will be moving in over the course of the next year, year and a half. Once my people have arrived I will set about creating a community with a certain character, color, and complexion. At that point I will want to build a shul. Let's make a deal. I will forgo what you're offering me now, but I want you to provide me with a letter on the stationery of the Jerusalem municipality, in which you promise me that when the next group of shuls will be built, I will be offered first choice of those shuls." Gavish couldn't understand me. Nobody had ever turned down an offer for a shul before. It was unprecedented.

I understood his reluctance to involve himself with a dreamer like myself who was willing to look a gift shul in the mouth while turning it down. This kind of odd behavior made people such as Gavish nervous. I knew that I would have to paint an even more coherent picture of my dream community for him. And I did. I talked about the kind of shul I hoped to build and what I envisioned for the future. And eventually, Yosef Gavish smiled in silent cooperation, because he understood what I was saying and was agreeing to work with me on this. And he gave me the letter, a commitment for the future.

~

Those were the best of times, those were the worst of times.

The worst of times because we were barely holding our heads above water and had no idea what the future held. And the best of times because we were living in G-d's Land, and relying completely on His kindness to survive.

The Torah tells us that Eretz Yisrael is acquired with hardships and challenges, and I can personally attest that those words are one hundred percent true. Whatever could go wrong did go wrong. Murphy's Law must have been invented after the Gold family made aliyah.

No job. No home. Our teenage children were struggling to cope with their new environment socially, academically, linguistically, and financially. The rabbi of West Hempstead, the man who had arrived from his spacious three-floor West Hempstead home on Colonade Road, ended up walking the streets of Yerushalayim trying to understand how he had ended up in his present predicament. (There are still people living in Kiryat Yovel today who recall me pacing up and down Shmaryahu Levin Street.)

Our life seemed to be in tatters and disarray. I was in a very low place emotionally right then. My life had fallen apart and I couldn't see any way to paste it all back together. Like Humpty Dumpty. It would take more than all the king's horses and all the king's men to make it all right again.

And then everything changed from one second to the next.

We were in Toronto to take care of my dear mother-in-law, Sarah Rubinoff, who was undergoing major heart surgery. While we were there, the OU (Orthodox Union) tracked me down.

Rabbi Bert Leff had been an invaluable member of my shul in West Hempstead. During the campaign to rally the community in favor of building a *mikveh*, Bert promised and indeed gave a magnificent *shiur* on the vital importance of having a local *mikveh*. His carefully crafted and masterfully presented *shiur* changed the balance in favor of the *mikveh*. I have always been grateful to him for that.

"The position of rabbi for the Fifth Avenue Synagogue has just become available," he told me. "We would like to present you, Rabbi Gold, as the OU's candidate for the position. Is this a position you'd be interested in?"

I couldn't speak. I almost couldn't breathe. Here was a ray of light streaking out of the darkest corner. Here was an opportunity to redeem myself from where I'd fallen. G-d loved me. He was granting me another lease on life.

"Sholom, are you there? Are you interested in applying for the job?"

My mind was whirling with thoughts. Here I'd finally made it to Eretz Yisrael. I'd sacrificed much to get there. And now it seemed as if it had been but a temporary stop on the road back to New York. I didn't want to go. I loved Eretz Yisrael. On the other hand, what choices did I have? None. Nothing. No job, no home, no money. How was I supposed to raise a family like this?

"Sholom, are you there?"

"Yes, I'm here."

"And?"

Very reluctantly, I said, "Okay, put my hat in the ring as a candidate. I'm in."

Later on that day I told my wife about the epic phone call I had just received.

Her response has to go down among the greatest responses of all time. Very calmly, and I mean very calmly, she looked me in the eye and said, "This is the best thing that could have ever happened to you now. It's very good."

Pause.

Then, "Just remember to send us a check once a month."

The shock of that response shook me to the core. Because she was utterly right.

I called the OU then and there and I told them to take my name out. I would not be moving to Fifth Avenue. I would not be moving to the Upper West Side. I would be returning to Eretz Yisrael where the Gold family belonged, and that was that. My wife knew from the moment we stepped onto the soil of Eretz Yisrael that this was the best place for a Jew to live and raise a family and she wasn't worried about me finding a job. "The cream always rises to the top," she liked to say. She believed in me and knew that everything would fall into place when it was supposed to.

And it did. Just like she knew it would all along.

History repeated itself. The women of our nation save their husbands in much the same way as the wife of On Ben Peles did for him, just as my mother did for my father when she forbade him to go to a job interview on Shabbat. My mother saved my father and my wife saved me.

I will never cease to thank the One Above.

Things were about to turn around, just like Bayla foresaw.

୪

I had gotten to know Rabbi Chaim Brovender during my sabbatical year. He was a kindred soul and I shared some of my dreams with him, knowing that he would be able to grasp the concept I envisioned.

"You know what I want to do?" I told him. "I'd like to build a center in Yerushalayim where adults can come and learn. There are so many people living in this city who are thirsting for Torah learning and don't have any place to get the nourishment they need."

He listened to my dream and tucked it away in his brain to be retrieved at the perfect, most opportune moment.

That moment had arrived. I was languishing away in what amounted to early retirement. I was way too young to retire. I had so much to contribute and nowhere to do it. When Rabbi Brovender found out that I was out of a job and without structure in my life, he called and asked me to come to his office. He wanted to discuss something with me.

Of course I agreed. It wasn't like I had anything better to do.

"Do you remember the dream you shared with me a few years ago, about adult education, back when you were on sabbatical?" Rabbi Brovender asked me when we met. "Are you still interested in turning that dream into a reality?"

I replied in the affirmative.

"Well," he went on, "I have two classes here at my school geared toward adults. Would you perhaps be interested in taking over those classes? Begin with that nucleus and build up a school."

With that sincere offer, Rabbi Chaim Brovender put me on the road to my goal.

I did it. I accepted his kind invitation, started teaching once again, and immersed myself in the task of creating a school for adult education. People came once and returned for more. Soon enough I began thinking of ways to expand the two classes into something bigger. Here was where my good friend Rabbi Moshe Rose of the Young Israel stepped into the picture once again. The offices of the Young Israel were then located in the basement of the Yeshurun Synagogue, and since there was nothing happening there at night, he offered me the use of the premises.

I thanked him for his kindness and took out a few ads in the *Jerusalem Post* advertising a number of classes on assorted topics at the Jerusalem College for Adults (JCA). Then I waited to see the result. I began with three or four people per class. My Gemara *shiur* built up to about ten regulars. The classes started seeing more activity as people told their friends and new people came to try it out and see if what we were offering was for them. It wasn't long before I had to hire another teacher to handle the overflow.

I needed financing to get the operation off the ground, so I left Eretz Yisrael for my first fund-raising trip to Toronto and returned with fifteen thousand dollars, a very generous amount of money in those years. It kept the programs going for the next four months.

❦

One day I gave a class on *geirut* (conversion) to my students. At the end of the class, one of the students, Dr. Avraham Schwartzbaum, who had been a university professor before becoming religious, spoke up.

"Rabbi Gold," he said, "I want to tell you a story."

There were ten people in the room when he began telling us the story. All of us were still sitting there spellbound an hour later. We didn't know what hit us. What a story it was! The Schwartzbaums were a young couple who couldn't have children. While spending a year in China for academic purposes, he found a baby girl who had been abandoned on a bench in a train station. The little Chinese girl changed their lives. That hour of storytelling eventually became the nucleus of his runaway best seller *The Bamboo Cradle* (which I jokingly referred to as "The Bamboo *Maidel*"), a book that has touched hearts everywhere around the world.

Josh and Linda Rettig were also special students. He was a radiologist from Dallas, Texas, and she was his chief assistant. Constant travelers, they took off two years to study Torah in Yerushalayim, ending up at the Jerusalem College for Adults. They were very interested in learning and developing intellectually. They later came on aliyah and built a house in Caesarea. They were fascinating, wonderful people, and insightful and involved students.

Josh and Linda were people who dabbled in all sorts of pursuits, one of which was art. One day they called me up excitedly to inform me that they had met a very talented Israeli artist, sculptor, and glass worker named Dani Kafri who lived in Yemin Moshe.

"Rabbi," they said, "you should really check this guy out. Knowing an artist can come in handy."

I followed their advice and met with Dani Kafri and viewed his art. It was very inspirational stuff. I was impressed by his talent and spirituality. Eventually, when my shul was ready to build our magnificent *aron kodesh*, it was Dani Kafri whom I hired for the job.

If ever you find yourself strolling through Har Nof and want to see a beautiful *aron kodesh*, come on over. The stained glass window, the delicate woodwork, the impressive height… Dani Kafri did himself proud, as did our architect Yeshayahu Ilan. Men of true talent and hard work mixed with idealism – the best combination.

~

Once when I was back in Toronto for a short visit, my two brothers-in-law informed me that a group of Torontonians were chartering a plane for a Sunday trip to New York – just a flight in and a flight back – to visit the Lubavitcher Rebbe in Crown Heights on a "Sunday Dollar Day." Feeling like I had developed a connection with the Rebbe over the years, I was more than happy to go along for the ride. When we landed in New York we drove out to 770, where lines of people waited for their dollar and blessing.

The line moved quickly and soon enough I found myself standing before the Rebbe, who handed me a dollar, which I accepted gratefully. Someone standing there turned to the Rebbe and said, "This man is a *rav* in Yerushalayim."

That got me a little nervous, as I couldn't help but recall the Rebbe's opposition to my move in the first place. The Rebbe met my gaze and without blinking an eye gave me a beautiful *brachah* which I cherish until this very day: "*Yaaroch yamim al mamlachto*" (You should reign long over your kingdom)!

I appreciated that *brachah* immensely. I still do. All in all, that Sunday commute to New York turned out to be a most special moment in my life. You don't receive such blessings every day!

There were other special moments during fund-raising trips back to North America. On one such trip I ran into Rav Binyomin Kamenetsky, the son of Rav Yaakov, at a wedding.

We spent a few minutes catching up and then he said, "You know something, Sholom, I owe you a debt of gratitude. Remember that fund-raising breakfast for the Yeshiva of South Shore that we did a few weeks before you left America? You were the guest speaker that morning. Well, after your speech, somebody came forward and donated a quarter of a million dollars to the school."

"It must have been quite a speech."

"It was, and I owe you something in return."

I sat there waiting to hear what my reward was going to be.

"I'm going to tell you a story," Rav Binyomin said, "and then we'll call it even."

I smiled at that statement. A story for a quarter of a million dollars. Pretty good tradeoff, no?

"A number of years ago, my father, Rav Yaakov, and his wife were in Miami for his birthday. Being that he was an older man and that celebrating a birthday for someone of such advanced years was a significant milestone, the entire family flew down to celebrate it with him. After the meal," Rav Binyomin went on, "we all went for a walk on Collins Avenue [the main street in Miami Beach]. There we were, just walking along the avenue, when we came to the end of the first block. It was at that point that Rav Yaakov looked around and said a few extremely cryptic yet powerful words.

"'*Men vet unz shmeisen*' ( –We're going to be beaten).

"Like all good *litvishe* stories this cryptic statement had to happen three times. And so, when we arrived at the next corner, Rav Yaakov looked around again and repeated the same frightening words, '*Men vet unz shmeisen.*'

"We didn't know why he had said those words in the first place and certainly not why he had repeated himself, but nobody was ready to ask him yet for an explanation. However, when we arrived at the end of the third block and Rav Yaakov repeated himself yet again, with his prophecy of us being beaten, someone had the guts to speak up and inquire, '*Vos meint der Tatte, men vet unz shmeisen?*' [What does our father mean by this talk of future beatings?]"

Rav Yaakov looked at his children and replied, "All my life I've been in *chinuch*, in education, teaching young people. Shmuel [Rav Shmuel Kamenetsky] is in Philadelphia teaching young people. Nosson is in Eretz Yisrael teaching young people. Binyomin is in South Shore teaching young people. But I look around the streets and there are so many adults. Who's going to teach Torah to all the adults? *Men vet unz shmeisen*, we're going to be punished for not teaching Torah to the grown-ups."

And then Rav Binyomin Kamenetsky said to me with a twinkle in his eye, "And that's exactly what you're doing. You're the one teaching Torah to the adults. My father taught me very decisively that teaching adults is a real obligation."

I guess if a story was all the reward I was going to get, then this was a pretty good story to be repaid with, containing as it did the very good tidings that I, at least, was not going to be beaten. I've used this particular anecdote on a few fund-raising trips and it's gone over well.

Truthfully, as much satisfaction as I received from the shul over our decades together, it was a completely different type of fulfillment from my teaching at the Jerusalem College for Adults. It may have started out on a very small scale (to the point where I used to open the doors of our original premises in the basement of the Yeshurun shul and sit in the empty, dank classrooms and wonder if anybody would come that night), but it grew quickly and it wasn't long before we needed more classrooms. Although we had an attendance of seven to thirteen people per class in the first year, by the time our second year had rolled around the school was taking off and I had already hired more staff.

For about ten years, we were located on Shalom Aleichem Street, a block away from what was the Laromme Hotel (now called the Inbal), and classes were full. Hundreds of people were attending classes on numerous subjects in Torah and growing spiritually, becoming more religious, and learning how to learn. There were classes on so many topics – Gemara, Navi, Chumash, Jewish philosophy. At one point we even branched out to Ma'ale Adumim and when that program became successful it eventually merged with a local program.

Rebbetzin Malka Bina, who today runs her very own successful learning program for women in its very own beautiful campus, began her career teaching with us. Some of the students wanted her classes in Hebrew. I told her it was a wonderful idea but there were already many classes available for Hebrew speakers and I wanted to focus on the English speakers. I encouraged her to go out on her own with the students from JCA who were interested and thus began Matan. I even sat on the board at the outset. We've taught Torah to thousands of Jews for the past twenty-five years and it's been a tremendous experience for so many people who would have otherwise not been exposed to Torah on a regular basis.

Max Weil was a *talmid* for a year, after which he came to the realization that a *kollel* framework of advanced Talmudic learning for

English-speaking working men was needed in Yerushalayim, and so, after many back and forth consultations, he initiated Kollel Sinai. I myself have been giving a *shiur* there once a week for the last fifteen years. So much learning, so much Torah – and it all began at the JCA.

And that was what Rav Binyomin Kamenetsky was talking about when he specifically repaid me with this story.

Who knows what I would have received for half a million dollars?

I can't even imagine.

# 17

# BEHIND THE IRON CURTAIN

December 1983, I received the offer of a lifetime.

Starting in 1967, the Israeli government sent two people to Russia every month. This was due in great part to the Six-Day War. After the monumental defeat experienced by the Arab armies, in what could only be described as a lightning victory handed to Israel by the One Above, Russia found itself on the receiving end for once. Their clients Egypt and Syria had suffered terrible losses. Thousands of soldiers had been killed and taken captive, Egypt's entire air force had been demolished, and millions of dollars' worth of Russian military weaponry and equipment had been destroyed by the Israelis. Russia was very unhappy with its situation in the Middle East.

The result was a move on the part of the USSR to cease their official recognition of Israel. This of course was coming on the heels of De Gaulle's decision to have France abandon Israel to its fate. The Iron Curtain that had descended after the end of the Second World War had suddenly become that much more formidable. And so, Israel began clandestinely sending in two people every month just to keep contact with the Jews living in that gigantic prison cell.

There were a few requirements for such an undertaking if you wanted to be part of the team. You needed a passport that had never seen the stamp of an Israeli customs or immigration official. Arriving in Russia with a compromised passport could mean being sent back on the first plane if the Russians were in a particularly foul mood that day.

My passport was of course full of Israeli entry and exit stamps.

What to do? I was confident that I'd come up with something.

I was slated to go in December and my partner was to be my old friend Rabbi Mallen Galinsky, administrator of Yeshivat Sha'alvim for thirty years. A mysterious individual, Aryeh Kroll, stood behind all this cloak-and-dagger stuff. Almost nobody mentioned his name and if you had to refer to him, you did so by calling him "The Boss." He ran the entire Russian operation. The most important stop before leaving the country was to meet with Kroll to receive instructions from the master.

His office was straight out of an espionage classic: a nondescript office in a dreary, gray building in Tel Aviv, guaranteed to be forgotten the moment you left it. He had nothing on his desk. Not a thing. This was the man who would give you instructions where to go, who to see while you were there, and what to bring along with you. Aside from the Chumashim and *siddurim* that we carried in our luggage to be given out, there was always something of great monetary value that the visitors brought along with them and somehow managed to leave behind, so the Russian Jews could sell it and have some money to support themselves for the next few months. We were provided with a very sophisticated camera to take along and given instructions exactly whom to give it to.

"The Boss" would then walk you figuratively through your entire trip, describing streets and communities and trees and buses which he'd never seen in his entire life. And his descriptions were always – but always – correct. Everyone who traveled to the USSR reported back to him. He collected all that information and put together a map of Russia in his mind, to the point where he was familiar with every street and statue, every store, every bridge and tunnel. It was uncanny how the man absorbed all this material and kept it at his fingertips.

Meanwhile, I needed to provide myself with a "clean" passport and proper cover story. For a passport, I needed a US post office. I happened to be going back to the States for a short visit, and I went into the post office in Hempstead. I had a little bit of a problem. When you ordered a new passport, the US government wanted to know if you had ever possessed a passport before and if so, what happened to it. Small but powerful questions. I entered the post office knowing that I was in for a hard time. Most people would have just said that they had lost their passports and that would have been the end of it. But I didn't want to lie.

There was an older African American gentleman behind the counter. He gave me a bunch of forms to fill out. I was thinking of my mother, a"h, who always said, *"Der bester lign iz der emes"* (The best lie is the truth). I stopped, looked him in the eye, and said the following.

"I was the rabbi here in West Hempstead for many years, but I moved to Israel a few years ago. Here's the thing."

I took a deep breath.

"I'm being sent on a mission to the USSR and I can't travel there with my passport as is, because it's full of Israeli stamps, which means I will be stopped when I land and sent right back to where I came from. That's why I need a clean passport."

It was the truth. The unadorned truth.

"Rabbi," he said to me, "I want to tell you something. Today at five o'clock, I'm retiring. I worked for the post office for thirty-five years and I'm hanging up my jacket for the last time in a few hours. But you're going to get your passport. I'm going to make sure that you get your passport!"

I received my new passport within a day. A spanking clean American passport – a final good deed by a man with deep beliefs.

Now for my cover story. I went to see my old friend Leon Gross, who'd been president of the shul when I arrived in West Hempstead. He was a man with a special soul. Leon owned a printing business on the Lower East Side. I approached Leon and asked him what he could do to help me create a cover for myself.

"Well, the name on your passport is Sidney Gold," he said. "That's a start. You won't go by Sholom on this trip. You're Sidney until you return from behind the Iron Curtain."

"With what position? I want a nice cushy job."

"Don't worry, Rabbi Gold, I'm going to set you up with something commensurate with your greatness."

In the end I assumed my new position as sales rep at ACE Printing, with business cards to prove it. Now I had my passport and cover. Mallen Galinsky took care of his as well. Things were coming together and we were ready to go. Were we spies? Well, I don't think you could call us that. I would go with the term "operatives of a foreign country entering enemy lands under false pretenses." Doesn't sound too good, does it?

The plan was as follows. We would leave Israel for London and go from there with our new passports to Russia. Here we ran into a slight problem. The Russians were going to examine our passports and would no doubt expect them to show that we had left America; only those passports were empty. This posed a slight challenge, yet nothing that couldn't be handled by a little Jewish ingenuity. Upon arrival in London, we were taken to the Israeli embassy, where a man named Tzemach went about preparing us for the next stage of the operation. First he combed through everything we'd brought from Israel to ensure that we were not carrying anything in our luggage that would have given away that we were not in fact from New York, but rather from Jerusalem. This was kind of crucial. For example, he examined our clothing, shirts and pants, to see whether there were any remaining tags from the last time they'd been dry cleaned. We were completely stripped of anything that would identify us as having come from Israel.

Our passports – those brand new, perfectly clean passports – were then stamped by someone in the embassy with US exit stamps, thereby proving that we had left the States earlier that same day, and we were handed two perfectly valid boarding passes from a flight that had left New York early that morning with a stopover in London. Every detail was taken into consideration, everything covered. These people were pros and they knew what they were doing. As I watched the meticulous care with which they were going through my luggage, a little voice screamed inside my head, "Sholom, it's not too late. You can still get out of this. Maybe traveling to Russia under false pretenses is not the smartest thing in the world for you to do?"

I quieted the voice. We were going. The time for regrets or even introspection had passed. Action. Not worry or fear. What would be, would be.

∞

The flight to Moscow was uneventful.

My stomach churned as the Aeroflot plane took us through one air pocket after another. It was a very bumpy plane ride. The Russian stewardess offered me water – or was it vodka? I declined. And then roughly four hours later we were coming in for a landing at Moscow's Sheremetyevo International Airport. This was it. We were landing in the cradle of Communism, land of the Siberian gulag, Lenin, Stalin, and more misunderstood and tortured geniuses than anywhere else in the world. A land stripped of all freedom or pretense of freedom.

Welcome to Russia. Know that someone is always watching you. You are never alone.

It was scary.

The first thing we noticed was that for such a world power, something was very wrong. Most of the electricity in the airport was off. The cavernous rooms were shrouded in darkness. We followed the signs to passport control, eight booths in a row – take your pick – each occupied by a stone-faced Slavic man in army uniform, hat on head, no smiles in evidence.

I placed my passport under the glass and my ordeal began.

The officer, face completely inscrutable, picked up my passport and looked at it for long, endless minutes. His reptilian eyes flickered between the passport and my face, the passport and my face. I wanted to scream out, to ask him what on earth he was looking for in the clean, blank pages of my nice, crisp American passport, but my throat had all but dried up.

Everyone else had already passed through passport control.

Even Mallen Galinsky.

From where I stood, I could see the uniforms opening his luggage, picking through items. Meanwhile, I was still standing there under intense scrutiny by Igor Goborov of the Apparatus of State Security. I began to sweat.

He kept on looking at me. Must have gone on for five straight, interminably long minutes. All of a sudden, by my side were two men of husky build in drab green uniforms, hats on their heads, blank expressions on their faces.

"Follow us."

I dared not disobey.

The Russian Bear had just yawned and swallowed me alive. My heart was pounding as we began walking out of the room and I took one last glance at a helpless Mallen, who gazed forlornly back in my direction.

The corridor was endless, the sound of our steps barely muffled by the thin carpeting on the floor. A bleak sun shone from the occasional window. Finally we reached the interrogation room. A bare table. Cement floors. A window in the side wall. A naked bulb hanging from the ceiling. A squat Russian interrogator sat squarely across the table from me, with an additional two big guys standing along the walls. I could feel a drop of sweat beginning to roll down the back of my neck. It was that kind of place.

They began to question me.

"Why have you come to Russia?"

"To see your beautiful country."

"What are you doing here? Who have you come to see?"

Question after question. These guys were pros.

"I came to see the country. To visit the museums in Leningrad. To meet the wonderful Russian people."

I was scared out of my wits. I kid you not. The interrogation lasted for the longest three-quarters of an hour in my life.

But I stuck to my story.

"My name is Sidney Gold. I work for ACE Printing on the Lower East Side of New York."

The underlying feeling in the chamber was one of disbelief on their part, as if they were saying, *We know everything about you. You're no printer from New York. We know who you are. You're a rabbi from Jerusalem. Coming to make trouble with our Jews here in Russia. We know. We know everything.*

I was an amateur up against the KGB. They had seen my kind before.

They knew all the moves. My knees were knocking together. My head swam. I felt the panic closing in on me. Was I having a heart attack? Where was Mallen while all this was going on? Were they interrogating him as well?

Next thing I knew they let me go and I proceeded to pick up my baggage for inspection. They opened my suitcases and took out every single item. And there was a lot of stuff. It didn't daunt them. These guys had all the time in the world. Time was about all they had.

Lots of food and books. I watched as they removed everything from the bag. The same bag that had been cleaned so meticulously back in London. Suddenly my eyes caught sight of something I hadn't noticed until then. None of us had seen it, including Tzemach back at the London embassy. I felt like I was going to faint. Literally. We'd brought along plates on which to eat and cutlery. The cutlery. That was the problem. It was wrapped in an Israeli newspaper from two days earlier. This was it. The game was up!

The KGB man looked at the newspaper for a second, the wheels turning in his mind.

Then, "*Yevri!*" (Hebrew!). Within seconds about five of these monsters had me surrounded. How ironic. I hadn't caught the newspaper. Tzemach in London hadn't caught it. But they had. They'd caught me red-handed.

I recalled a *shiur* I had given long before about Yehoshua and the spies he sent to Jericho. "*Va'yishlach Yehoshua Bin Nun min hashitim shnayim anashim meraglim cheresh, leimor lechu re'u es ha'aretz, v'es Yericho, va'yelchu, va'yavo'u...*" (And Joshua son of Nun secretly sent two spies out of Shittim, saying: "Go see the Land and Jericho," and they went and arrived...; Yehoshua 2:1).

In the next *pasuk*, we are told that the Jericho secret service informed their king that two spies had arrived in their city. Rashi tells us that the spies posed as pottery salesmen. A cover story as good as any other, no? They arrived at Jericho loaded down with pots and pans. They clearly weren't known for their prowess at the spying trade, however, because their cover didn't last five minutes.

That's exactly the way I felt. Me, the big spy, caught in the first hour of my arrival. To my intense relief and surprise, they suddenly replaced my belongings in my suitcases and motioned me to come along. The interrogation was over. Mallen and I were escorted through customs and given official permission to leave.

"You can go. Have a good time."

Obviously once it had been ascertained that we were not in fact from the States, but had arrived from Israel like they'd thought, the Russians were now allowing us to go off on our own with the hope that we would then lead them to the "criminals" (refuseniks) we were planning on making contact with. We were free to head out into the freezing, drab streets of Moscow.

I remember saying that the KGB probably possessed the biggest tape library of Torah *shiurim* in the world, because every rabbi that arrived in Russia gave Torah classes to the Russian Jews and the KGB doubtless recorded them all.

~

Traveling in Russia didn't just happen. There was one official tourist agency in Russia. It was called Intourist. There was no competition. Upon arrival in Russia, one was placed in Intourist's efficient hands and hoped for the best. Next thing we knew, Mallen and I found ourselves in a taxi driving through the snow-swept streets of Moscow toward our hotel, called – you guessed it – "The Intourist."

It was December, and the temperature was way down below zero. Absolutely freezing. Snowstorms everywhere. If I close my eyes, I can still recall stomping and crunching through the snow and ice of the numerous parks throughout Moscow and Leningrad, as the KGB agents followed us over hill and dale, not even trying to remain unseen. The weather was so abysmal that later on when we flew to Leningrad on one of Aeroflot's rickety propeller planes, I seriously thought that we were going to either have to make an emergency landing in the middle of nowhere or be lost forever in the dark and snowy Russian night.

Every team from Israel visited three Russian cities. Our three were Moscow, Leningrad, and Riga. Others went to Kiev or Odessa. Kroll was intimately familiar with every single one of them. It was now time to make contact with the people we had been told to see. There were many Jews waiting anxiously to meet us, to talk with us, and to learn from us. There was much work to be done.

It was the first night of Chanukah and we lit our menorah in the hotel room, closing all the curtains so nobody should see the burning lights, and then went out to visit the first home on our list. These were people who were studying Hebrew against the wishes of the regime, people who were thumbing their noses at Mother Russia.

Every Russian hotel had floor ladies back then. Their job was to report on the coming and going of every guest, and they carried out their task meticulously. It was almost a given that we'd be receiving visitors when we went out. But that was all part of the game.

We arrived at the home of our hosts.

It was time to light the candles there. Whereas we had made certain the curtains of our hotel room were tightly closed before lighting, they shoved their curtains as far apart as possible, lighting the menorah in a way that was guaranteed to show it off to the entire street. They were not afraid of anyone or anything. It was Chanukah and they were lighting their menorah. The battle of Jew versus Greek took on a whole new meaning there. Fear. Bravery. Courage. We had begun to really understand what those terms meant.

Chanukah is a time for singing, and I who love to sing took advantage of this special opportunity to teach them all sorts of songs. In addition to all the normal tunes that everyone sings like "Al Hanisim" and the regular "Maoz Tzur," I also taught them the Modzitzer "Maoz Tzur." As I stood in the middle of a Russian living room, surrounded by Jews who knew what self-sacrifice meant, I couldn't help but choke up.

To visit Russia was to descend into another world completely – a parallel universe, as it were, or as Rav Mallen put it, "*planetah acheret*" (a different planet). Take the Russian subway system, for example. We went down to the subway on what seemed like the longest escalator in the world. What were they trying to prove? You didn't look down when you rode that escalator. You just couldn't. It was too steep.

Two things struck me immediately.

Not a word was being exchanged by anyone riding the subway. Not one word among hundreds of people. People just sat there silently.

The second thing was that nobody was smiling. Nobody. Not even the babies. I watched the faces of the people riding the ascending escalator. Nobody was willing to meet my eyes. Later on during our trip, we came in contact with a group of tourists from Romania. They were laughing, drinking, merry. What a stark contrast to the Russians with their dour, silent ways, going about their monotonous lives in a world veiled with fear.

Our refusenik friends served as our guides through the complexity of the Russian subway. While we looked around us in mute anxiety, our guide was decidedly uninhibited by the silence surrounding us. The scene was unreal. Picture this. There we were, holding on for dear life in the rapidly moving subway car, while our guide, whose group had been studying tractate *Baba Batra*, turned to me and asked me to clarify a certain Tosafot that he didn't understand. Are you getting this? I was being asked to explain a Tosafot in the middle of the Russian night, in a subway car filled with silent Russians. My guide was discussing the *sugya* enthusiastically, at the top of his lungs, in Hebrew, while I tried my hardest to respond with the right answer to this Tosafot. It was a bizarre situation, to say the least. But what bravery! What courage! I was utterly humbled by the refuseniks' spirit.

There were two miracles that took place in the subway car that day. One, a Jew talking Torah on the Moscow subway at the top of his lungs. Two, the fact that I remembered that Tosafot and was able to answer him. These Jews just weren't afraid. They had made a decision. Took a position, a complete stand, and then lived like real men without blinking or even paying attention to the authorities.

We would be speaking at a Shabbat meal on Friday night. We had been given instructions to go to the Pushkin train station late Friday afternoon. Someone would be waiting to meet us. There were actually two people waiting.

We boarded a train, and the closer we got to our destination, the more young people boarded our car. When we arrived at our stop, we all got off that train together. We found our way to one of those endlessly long apartment buildings with twelve entrances that had been favored by postwar Russian architects with imagination issues. There was still not enough space for the burgeoning population, who had to sometimes share their apartments between two families. Religious Jewish families were forced to share their apartments with Russian non-Jews. Huge buildings. Hundreds of apartments. Thousands of people all living together under one roof.

We arrived at the home of our hosts, Slava and Mark Shifrin, and discovered that the tiny living-dining room, built for four, was occupied by a good twenty or thirty young Jewish students, gathered together to study their heritage. This was a Shabbat meal that we would never, ever forget. Not much to eat. Just enough. No fancy kugels. No fancy anything. A little bread. Some herring. Simple fare. But it wasn't about the food. Not at all. Who cared about feeding their bodies, when they could finally feed their souls?

These were university students, young people standing poised on the cusp of life, trying to choose a path. Would Torah be the one?

Davening plus the Friday night meal took about six hours. Minchah and Kabbalat Shabbat were said by the assembled, all together, word for word. The davening alone took about two hours. Then came the meal. What singing! What dancing! What words of Torah. Rabbi Galinsky spoke. I spoke. They listened closely, drinking it in. It was an intense religious experience taking place surrounded by darkness. One of the highlights of the evening was when they sang a popular song written by Shlomo Carlebach, "Uva'u Ha'ovdim." The high part of the song, over and over again, "Yerushalayim, Yerushalayim…," and they're crying, the tears gushing forth as their souls cry out for Yerushalayim, yearning to be reunited with the city of their dreams. Clearly the fact that a Jewish country existed in Eretz Yisrael was giving these people the ability to carry on.

The previous Friday night, I'd spent the evening with a group of American students in Yerushalayim. They too had sung that song, clapping and "shticking" it up. Yet now as I watched my newfound friends pining and begging to visit our ancient holy city, the contrast between the two groups was glaring. And I knew which of the two groups was singing the song the way Shlomo Carlebach had meant it to be sung.

Such heart. Such feeling. Such poignant grace and desire. Their eyes told the story of their souls' fervent wish to make it to the city of gold. The contrast tore me apart.

The meal was over in the middle of the night. And then we all left the Shifrins' home together. We walked back to our hotel, accompanied by many fresh-faced youngsters. It was bitterly cold outside and the Moscow streets were utterly deserted. But none of these young Jews cowered inside their long woolen coats. No, they sang and danced their way through Moscow, as if it were Simchat Torah. What a night. Who can forget the sound of those pure voices piercing the heavens with their music?

Morning dawned. A gray, leaden Moscow sky greeted us when we exited our hotel on that Shabbat morning, headed for the grand shul on Archipova Street, where hundreds and sometimes thousands of proud young Jews gathered, challenging the state by virtue of their mere presence. It all began one Simchat Torah, when a few hundred kids showed up and before anyone knew how or why, the group had swelled and there were thousands. With time, the shul on Archipova Street had become the hub of the Jewish community. Every Friday night and Motzaei Shabbat this was a place for the Jewish kids to come and talk and give each other internal strength just by being there.

On Motzaei Shabbat we went to meet with Yuli Edelstein, today Israel's Speaker of the Knesset. That was such a simple and easy sentence to write. But looking back, the situation was so different. The year after we had that Melaveh Malkah with him, he was arrested by Soviet authorities, for alleged drug possession. He spent three and a half years in a labor camp in difficult conditions and was seriously maimed. He was finally released in 1987 and allowed to go on aliyah.

This is what Dovid Hamelech meant when he wrote, "*Mekimi me'afar dal me'ashpot yarim evyon l'hoshivi im nedivim im nedivei amo*" (He raises the poor from the dust and the needy from the refuse heap, giving them a place alongside princes, the princes of His people; Psalms 113:7–8).

It was a wonderful Motzaei Shabbat. Consciously and knowing the risks, Yuli was one of the great teachers of Hebrew. He'd taught himself

Hebrew and spoke it well, to the point where conversing with him was a real pleasure. That was how we talked to one another. This was always an embarrassing problem for the American and English *rabbanim* who arrived and tried to communicate with the Russian Jews. The Russians couldn't comprehend how Jews who lived in free societies didn't know how to converse in fluent Hebrew! Here they were, exhibiting self-sacrifice to the point of risking their lives to learn and speak the language of the Jewish people, and yet Jews who had the ability to learn Hebrew as much as they desired couldn't carry on a decent conversation. The refuseniks couldn't grasp it.

༶

We spent three or four days in Moscow and then flew to Leningrad, where we were fortunate to spend Shabbat at the home of Rav Yitzchok Kogan, known to one and all as "the *tzaddik* of Leningrad." I will never understand how the Russians allowed such a holy, holy Jew to survive. A swirling snowstorm accompanied us throughout our stay in that town, turning all clothing damp and wet and making our throats scratchy and our eyes red. While staying at the Kogan home, we met someone who had just flown in from Sweden. He had some extremely shocking and disturbing news to impart: "The number 18 bus was blown up yesterday in the streets of Jerusalem!"

Mallen and I looked at one another in silent despair. We were consumed with worry. Our families rode that bus. My wife took that bus every day. My kids rode that bus home from school. My entire life was inextricably intertwined with the 18 bus. The same was true for the Galinsky family. We were both beside ourselves. Hours passed. Hours in which we imagined the worst. The fact that it had been bus number 18 was confirmed by a number of people. But we had no way of knowing who had been on that bus. The anxiety we felt was driving us over the brink.

The worst part about it was the fact that we had no way in the world to find out any details, as we were cut off behind the Iron Curtain. I discovered later on that my wife had taken the kids on a trip out of Yerushalayim for a few days. It was only when we landed outside the Soviet Union that we were able to ascertain the facts, but the next few days were pretty torturous. Yet despite the cloud of anxiety hanging over our heads, we went on with the program and made the best of the situation. We were in Russia for a reason and were determined to carry on. So we did.

While in Leningrad we had to keep up appearances; we were ostensibly there as tourists and were consequently forced to make the rounds of the more famous tourist sites. I don't recall being particularly impressed by anything Intourist had to offer until we arrived at Leningrad's famous Hermitage Museum, host to countless works of the most precious art in the world. I'll never forget entering the "Rembrandt room," a chamber dedicated to the master artist from Amsterdam. What colors! The depth, the scope, the talent of that man's brush. Unbelievable. Truly unbelievable. One scene depicted in a giant painting was entitled "The Sacrifice of Isaac," and I could only stand staring in wonder at the artist's vivid portrayal of our forefather's tenth test. It was a thing of absolute beauty.

જે

There was one man teaching Talmud in all of Riga. I walked in on his class. They were learning the second half of tractate *Pesachim*, the section dealing with *kodshim* – the Pesach offering, the Todah offering. Pretty technical stuff, not so easy for beginners.

I asked him a silly question.

"Why don't you teach these men something a little easier? Maybe *Brachot* or *Megillah*?"

He replied that there was only one Steinsaltz Gemara in all of Riga: *Pesachim*, part two.

I had my answer.

I think I smiled.

Someone had smuggled in that Gemara and left it there and that's all they had to learn from. It was a long, arduous process. First teaching yourself how to speak and read Mishnaic Hebrew and Aramaic, then educating yourself further in the intricacies of ancient Talmudic terminology. All for one reason alone: you're burning with a desire to grow in spirituality.

It was this strength of character that stood behind everything these heroes did. We were shown their shuls, saw them learning and davening. We went to a clandestine kindergarten for three- and four-year-olds. I stood in the center of a small, hidden room somewhere in the city of Leningrad and witnessed the purity of small Jewish children studying the *alef-bet*, because their parents knew that one day soon, the gates were going to open up and they would be granted their freedom. When that day arrived, their children were going to know how to read. And it was dangerous – being caught for teaching children Hebrew could mean five years in Siberia. I guess five years in Siberia is a small price to pay for the privilege of teaching Jewish boys and girls how to read the holy letters of our heritage.

We had become pretty close to some of these Jews over the ten days or so that we'd been in Russia. We'd already handed out all the goods we'd brought. All we had left was some kosher food – whatever we hadn't eaten. On the morning of our departure, in a burst of generosity I handed one of our hosts all the nonperishable items we had brought along with us. It meant little to Mallen and me, but to him it would be a huge, huge deal.

I'd forgotten one thing, however.

We hadn't eaten breakfast yet.

No matter. We'd survive a few hours of hunger until we returned to Israel and the free world.

On the plane the stewardess brought around apples and offered them to the lucky passengers. My stomach rumbled. For a moment I was tempted to accept an apple or three. But when I caught sight of the apples on the tray I changed my mind. They were pathetic. Tiny. Wrinkled. Full of blemishes. And then I made a prediction.

"Mallen," I said, "do you see these apples? Can you imagine finding such apples in the States? Can you imagine such apples growing in Eretz Yisrael?"

"Not a chance!"

"The USSR calls themselves a superpower," I went on, "but they can't even grow a decent apple. No superpower can survive if they can't even develop some apple trees. There's something rotten in Russia. I give them a few years and then it's all over. I'm telling you, Mallen, a few years and it's all over."

That was my prediction. Amazingly enough it came true.

☙

The Aeroflot plane came down for a landing in Germany, of all places. It was the first time in that hateful country for both of us. The moment we entered the arrivals hall in Frankfurt Airport, we felt such a rush of relief. Mallen gave out a shout of thankfulness at having escaped the grasping Russian arms. "*Hodu lashem ki tov, ki l'olam chasdo!*" (Praise G-d for He is good, for His kindness endures forever! Psalm 136:1).

Now it's decades later. Everything's different. People come and go. They do business with Russia. No big deal. Then, however, it was an accursed place and our trip was a very big ordeal.

We landed in London in the middle of the night and were taken to the home of an Israeli who fed us (we were pretty hungry by then), after which came a debriefing that lasted a couple of hours. They wanted to know everything about our trip, every detail – who we met, where we'd gone, whether anything surprising had transpired along the way. A couple of hours later we were done. Time to go back home. To Jerusalem of Gold.

☙

Our trip took place in the winter of 1983. At the end of that decade the Iron Curtain came tumbling down, and the Jews of Russia began leaving en masse for the State of Israel. Finally I was able to get together with many of those individuals whom I had met once before. Every so often I'll run into someone who took part in those historic Shabbat meals and we'll recognize one another and they'll get a faraway look in their eyes and begin quoting to me from the class that I delivered in that tiny living room in the heart of Moscow. It brings back memories.

When Yuli Edelstein was finally released after those punishing years in the gulag for teaching Hebrew, he made his triumphant way to Eretz Yisrael, where he resettled in Gush Etzion, later on becoming a member of Knesset and minister in a number of Israeli governments. I consider myself a lucky man to have been present at the celebration held in his honor when he arrived in Israel. Seeing him at last in Eretz Yisrael felt like a circle had been completed.

And that was my trip to Russia.

Never to be forgotten.

I will never forget those heroes either – Eliyahu Essas, Pinchas Polanski, Zev Dashevsky, and others of their caliber. It was a *zechut,* a real honor, meeting them.

༄

Sadly, while I was writing this book, Rabbi Mallen Galinsky passed away. He was a *rav* of note and an outstanding educator who stood at the helm of Yeshivat Sha'alvim for thirty years. Prior to his aliyah, in his position as director of the Torah Department of the Jewish Agency in New York, he was very successful in encouraging young *yeshivah* students to spend a year in Eretz Yisrael.

*Yehi zichro baruch.*

Tanya Edelstein, wife of Yuli, with whom we shared that Melaveh Malkah in Moscow in December 1983, recently passed away. Bayla and I went to be *menachem avel* Yuli at his home in Neve Daniel. When he saw me entering the room he stood up and we embraced. Rabbi Yisroel Meir Lau, who was sitting next to Yuli, wondered how he knew me. Yuli took a photo album that was on the table in front of him and showed a picture of me sitting with him thirty years earlier in Moscow. He passed the album around the room. Rav Mallen had taken that picture.

# 18

# BUILDING THE SHUL AND THE FAMILY

We had already moved out of Bayit Vegan by then to a rented apartment on Brand Street in Har Nof, and every day I looked out my window and saw people rushing to catch a minyan at what had become the "Boston" shul and I thought to myself, "Why didn't I take that shul when they offered it to me?"

It hurt. What can I say, it really hurt. I decided that I had to take matters into my own hands. After all, a little *hishtadlut*, a little personal initiative, never hurt anyone. I picked up the phone and dialed the head of the religious council of Yerushalayim, Rav Yitzchak Ralbag.

"Rav Gold!" he screamed when he heard it was me calling, "we're going to build you a shul. We want to meet with you." While I was still recovering from the shock of that welcome surprise, he continued, "Tomorrow morning at eight o'clock."

I arrived at their building on Chavatzelet Street the next morning.

Six or seven people were sitting there.

"Rav Gold," the spokesman said, "we're building a shul in Har Nof. It's yours."

Just like that, I had been granted a stunning gift. But the gift was going to cost me money. The Jerusalem municipality required you to provide a percentage of the cost of the building.

We made a quick calculation and arrived at the conclusion that my share would cost me over $300,000. The figure reverberated through my mind. I didn't have two nickels to rub together. How was I going to come up with $300,000?

I looked them in the eye and spoke with what I hoped seemed like complete confidence. "No problem. I will go on a fund-raising trip and return with the money."

To the people sitting in that room, my statement made perfect sense. After all, everyone knew that Americans and Canadians were rich. Certainly Gold should be able to raise that kind of money without a problem. And meanwhile I'm thinking, *Where on earth am I going to get this much cash?*

Then came the hammer blow.

"We need ten thousand dollars, Rabbi Gold, to seal the deal."

My world came crashing down all around me. How was I to come up with ten thousand dollars right then?

"Give me till tomorrow," was what I heard that cool, calm, and collected voice say to the assembled, and we adjourned, me on the verge of a crazy panic attack, not knowing what my next move was going to be, but not doubting that I was, with the help of G-d, going to pull this off. I left them and walked the streets of Yerushalayim. I had not a clue from whence would come my salvation. I went to teach my Gemara class that night and the boys at the center could tell that things weren't right. I was very, very agitated, very edgy.

"Rabbi, what's wrong?" they finally asked me.

I brought them up to date on my plan to build a shul in Har Nof, my meeting that morning, my false bravado, and the clincher: no ten thousand dollars, no deal. I told them that I planned on traveling to Toronto to raise the funds, but without ten thousand dollars it would be over before it began. "There's no way I can deliver on my promise. I have no money. It's that simple."

By the end of the class, they came over to me and presented me with a collection of checks to the tune of ten thousand dollars, made out to the Religious Council of Jerusalem. They had put it together for me. And I was able to walk into the building on Chavatzelet Street the next day and place that bundle of money down on the table, after which I told them, "Now I am leaving for Toronto."

Needless to say, I was deeply moved by my students' noble gesture.

I had but one stop in mind, one person whom I wanted to see. Avrom Silver had been a student of mine when I'd taught high school during my final year in Toronto. He was the reason, in my opinion, that G-d had sent me to teach at that school – it was a setup for later. I flew to Canada and everything went smoothly. I made an appointment to meet him at his office, where I told him the whole story. How I'd been offered the deal of a lifetime, to build a shul in Yerushalayim.

It took him under sixty seconds to make a decision.

"Rabbi Gold, I indeed want to dedicate a shul in Yerushalayim in my father's memory." Yosef Silver had been one of Toronto's prominent *baalei batim*.

I can't truly describe how I felt. A rare opportunity to finally accomplish something worthwhile in Eretz Yisrael. I now had hope, a goal, a holy objective, and the financial wherewithal to realize my dream.

I flew back to Eretz Yisrael a few days later via New York. I stayed in West Hempstead overnight at the home of Dr. Myron and Sandra Sokal, and in the morning when I awoke, my hostess informed me that Rav Yaakov Kamenetsky had passed away. I had to be at that *levaya*. I hurried to Flatbush, to Torah Vodaath. Rav Yaakov was the one who had stood behind me and wanted me to succeed. He had supported my decision to go on aliyah and he had seen it through until I was on the way. What awesome timing that I was there now to pay him this final honor.

I ended up giving the Jerusalem Religious Council the money in three installments. I watched as our building went up and was filled with joy as it grew and grew, until it stood proud, towering over the Har Nof skyline like a sentry on patrol, dwarfing the apartment buildings around it. My soul was filled with praise to Hakodosh Baruch Hu for all the good that He'd done for us.

We moved into the shul in time for Rosh Hashanah 1987. Kehillat Zichron Yosef (KZY) had been born. A new shul for a new year. I'm not sure it gets any more beautiful than that.

∽

Our shul was built by a committee of extremely dedicated people who stood by my side throughout the years and were always ready to do whatever it took to make things happen. The minyan began in the lobby of 50 Shaulson Street for Minchah Erev Rosh Hashanah 1986. There was a serious shortage of shuls in Har Nof at the time. Most people were davening in makeshift premises – apartments, lobbies, or bomb shelters.

I was grateful for the hundreds of fine Jews who came to pray with us every Shabbat and at the daily services throughout the week. For many years, Friday night at the shul was standing room only. And since everyone in the world has relatives in Har Nof, the shul became known throughout the world.

There were some superb events in those exciting days. An inaugural dinner to celebrate the shul's auspicious start. A cornerstone-laying ceremony and a Chanukat Habayit. Our shul was off to a grand start.

Everyone knew about KZY and many, many people were attending classes at JCA. Between those two vital parts of my life, I had become mentor and guide to a very large group of individuals. I remember when Avrom Silver decided to build my shul, I knew in some deep, instinctive way that Hashem had decided that it was time for our family's suffering to come to an end. We had managed to acquire Eretz Yisrael through suffering.

Of course we needed to mark the grand occasion of the shul's opening with a dinner. It was held at the Renaissance Hotel and attended by hundreds of people. People from the shul. People from Jerusalem College for Adults. People from the neighborhood. It really was a memorable evening. We kicked off the festivities at the shul – still empty with no permanent furniture yet – where a number of individuals spoke. Then we continued on to the hotel ballroom for the second installment of the program.

Avrom and Bonnie Silver were the guests of honor and we were appreciative to see that Avrom's mother Nancy had flown in as well. The Silvers have been the best of friends over the years and having them at the dinner cemented something that I could have never conveyed with mere words. My good friend and congregant Dov Rubin served as master of ceremonies and Rav Yitzchak Ralbag and Rabbi Moshe Rose gave *divrei brachah*, as did quite a few others who had been instrumental in bringing us to this point. Yosef Gadish and Efraim Shilo from the Jerusalem municipality were there, as was Alex Grossman, who had been one of Yosef Silver's partners. Aaron Bleeman represented his father, the third partner of Yosef Silver, Avrohom Bleeman. Also present were Tzvi Sand and his father Emanuel, and Harvey Douglin, manager of the Renaissance Hotel, all good friends over the decades.

The man who put the whole event together was a member of the shul, Paul Shaviv, who would go on to make major contributions of his talent and wisdom to Jewish education as the headmaster of major educational institutions.

Ezzy Hornfeld flew in from Toronto for the grand occasion.

Ezzy was a sweet man who never had children and managed to amass a nice amount of money in his life. With no offspring to leave his money to, Ezzy did *chesed* instead. He was always searching for a good cause, and many times I received a check from that fine fellow. After he passed away, I was stunned to learn that he had bequeathed a very significant amount of money to the shul to be used for a free loan society.

The fund was faithfully managed by Menachem Miller at the outset, then for years now Sholom Hershko has overseen its operation with Moshe Atlas and David Krumbein. We called it the Ezzy Hornfeld Gemach, and it is in operation until this very day and has been the address for thousands of families who have needed its services through the years. Ezzy was a special man and I remember him fondly. He brought happiness to many hearts when they needed it most.

As I gazed at that packed ballroom, filled with smiling and proud faces – the faces of people who knew that they were on the verge of building a wonderful new community in Eretz Yisrael – I couldn't help but remember how things had literally turned around in but a few years. I couldn't help but recall pacing up and down the street in Kiryat Hayovel, asking myself over and over why I had relinquished my position as rabbi of West Hempstead and given up everything in my life.

Now I knew why.

I was building a shul, a community. I had a school for adult education in Yerushalayim.

Every single bit of pain and suffering had been worthwhile to make that a reality. I could never have written the script myself.

༄

The phone rang one morning.

Eliyahu Avidan, a member of my shul who was working for the Foreign Ministry (he was later to become Israel's ambassador to Sweden), was on the phone.

"Rabbi Gold, Prime Minister Shamir is traveling to Madrid for a conference and would like to quote the following verse: *'Shalom, shalom la'rachok v'la'karov amar Hashem u'refativ.'* Do you know where that *pasuk* is written?"

I knew it was located in Yeshayahu but wasn't sure of the exact *perek*. But I remembered that this verse was part of the Yom Kippur *haftorah*, and my Yom Kippur *machzor* was sitting right there on the table.

"Hold on a second," I said, as I began flipping through the pages. A moment later I found the chapter and verse and quoted it to him: Yeshayahu 57:19, "'Peace, peace, to him who is far away and to him who is near,' said the Lord, 'and I will heal him.'"

The next day in class I made a prediction to my students that Shamir was going to quote a certain verse from Yeshayahu in his upcoming speech in Madrid.

Lo and behold so it was.

I confessed the following week and told them all how Eliyahu Avidan had asked me for the *pasuk*'s source. I didn't want them to think I was a prophet. I figured that I would leave the prophecy to Yeshayahu.

༄

From time to time events happen that serve to shake people awake and knock them out of their complacency – at least for a short while. One such incident occurred in Har Nof's early years and still haunts me when I think of it all these years later.

An American family relocated to our neighborhood. I think they were trying to decide whether they should move to Eretz Yisrael for good. At any rate, a week before Rosh Hashanah, their son stepped off a city bus and began crossing the street while the bus waited at the stop. The moment he stepped out past the bus, however, a car hit him head on, fatally wounding him. He was rushed to the hospital, his family thrust into crisis. The entire neighborhood began praying for his recovery. The situation was desperate and his condition critical. He hung on for a week, but much to the sadness of all, he passed away on Rosh Hashanah. The next day, the people of Har Nof escorted his body to its final resting place in a sea of tears and agony.

A *kinus hitorerut*, a gathering of reflection and awakening, was planned for a week later, in the middle of the Aseret Ymei Tshuvah, the Ten Days of Repentance between Rosh Hashanah and Yom Kippur, to take place at the Boston Shul. I was slated to be one of the speakers.

The shul was packed that night. I remember the scene like it happened yesterday. The first speaker arose.

"What do you expect will happen if there's a lack of modesty in our streets?" he thundered.

The second speaker arose. "If there's no Torah learning at night," he said, "how can we expect protection? I have a night *kollel*. We must ensure that Torah is studied at night!"

Things continued on in a similar vein. Every additional speaker found another reason why we had been thusly punished. Finally it was my turn.

I began by relating an incident recorded in the Talmud in *Yoma*.

I explained how the *kohanim* in the Temple used to race each other up the altar's ramp and whoever won the race would be chosen to carry out a certain part of the morning service. One day while racing, one *kohen* pushed another off the side of the ramp, causing his friend to break his leg.

The Sanhedrin's response was that from now on there would be no more running up the ramp.

I looked around at the packed shul and deliberately phrased my next question.

"Here's something I don't understand," I said. "After one of the *kohanim* was pushed off the side of the ramp, why didn't they make a gathering of reflection and awakening in the Temple to address the issue? Why didn't they blame the incident on a lack of modesty on the Temple grounds? Why didn't rabbis tell us that it had come about due to a lack of learning in the Temple at night? Or because of all the other reasons stated here tonight as theoretical possibilities?

"The answer," I said, and here I paused, "was that for hundreds of years there had never been an accident. But the moment there was an accident, our rabbis stepped into the picture and forbade what had become a dangerous practice.

"You can claim this terrible tragedy happened for a million reasons," I concluded, "but that would be missing the point. I feel the accident happened because people don't know how to drive properly and are careless in the approach they take when on the road. Driving is a serious business and it's time thought was given to teaching people how to drive in a way that doesn't endanger those around them. And," I concluded, "pedestrians have to know how to cross streets! This is the lesson of this tragedy."

When I finished speaking I left the shul.

About half a year later someone wrote an article in the *Jewish Observer* on the topic of the correct approach to dealing with tragedy, basically paraphrasing my entire speech in the Boston Shul, without citing me by name as the person who had given the speech in the first place, although the article did attribute it to "a rabbi in Har Nof."

No matter. As long as the lessons were learned.

That was the important thing, after all.

Today there are speed bumps spread out very liberally all over the roads in Har Nof to slow drivers down and inhibit recklessness. Yet there are those who still manage to turn a means of transportation into a weapon. *Rabbanim* and *roshei yeshivah* should devote sermons and *sichot* to the responsibility to drive safely. I see people every day crossing the street without looking both ways, not at a designated crosswalk, and worst of all, while talking on a cell phone. Chances are that the inattentive driver is also speaking on a handheld mobile phone. I am at a loss to understand how people can be so irresponsible.

☙

While Bayla and I were helping establish the community in Har Nof, my older son Menachem was developing into the fine *talmid chacham* and educator that he would later become. He loved to learn and was constantly pushing himself harder and harder.

The kids were all growing up and turning into adults. It was time to start worrying about *shidduchim*.

We had made aliyah in the summer of 1982. Our daughter Daphna became engaged three years later on a Motzaei Shabbat in 1985. We had had the good fortune to host a fine *yeshivah* student for occasional Shabbat meals. Yehudah Goldreich, son of Rabbi Avraham (Bumie) and Brenda Goldreich from Toronto, was learning at Yeshivat Kol Torah in Bayit Vegan at the time. We lived on Rechov Epstein then, a few minutes from the *yeshivah*, making our home an opportune place for a *yeshivah bochur* in search of a warm family atmosphere to come visit.

At eleven o'clock on that fateful Motzaei Shabbat there was a knock on the door and Daphna walked into the room with Yehudah at her side. From the look on their faces it was clear what was on their minds.

"Abba, Imma," Daphna said, "Yehudah and I want to get engaged."

Daphna was still very young at the time, all of seventeen years old. I had never dreamed that she'd get engaged at such a young age or that she'd be the first of her siblings to do so. But the truth was, she was a very mature girl. There was only one reason to ask her to wait until she was older and the reason was not her age.

It was her older sister Chavi.

I had always expected Daphna to wait for her sisters to get engaged before becoming a *kallah* herself. Still, we were overjoyed by her choice.

The words of Rav Yaakov from a few years before were suddenly playing in my mind: "You should know something, Sholom – it's easier to marry off children in Eretz Yisrael." Wow, was it easier! It seemed we had only moved to Eretz Yisrael yesterday, and already Daphna was getting engaged. I was overcome with joy at this exciting development.

A short time later there was another knock on the door.

Daphna's older sister Chavi walked into the room, accompanied by another *yeshivah* student whom we didn't yet know very well, Daniel Koenigsberg. They'd been going out for a little while and from the look on their faces, it seemed like this was to be the big night of reckoning.

"Abba, Imma…"

We waited expectantly.

"Daniel and I have some big news for you. We have decided to get engaged!"

"Mazel tov!"

Two sisters engaged on the same night. The house was hopping. It was wonderful. It was a joyful moment for the Gold family.

Chavi and Daniel got married first.

Daphna and Yehudah got married three months later.

And through that entire period of intense joy and celebration, the words of Rav Yaakov kept reverberating through my mind.

"You should know something, Sholom – it's easier to marry off children in Eretz Yisrael."

It was just as he had predicted.

After they married, Chavi and Daniel moved up to Nazareth Illit, where a friend of Daniel's, Pinchas Goldschmidt, was opening a *kollel*. (Rav Pinchas Goldschmidt is the *rav* of Moscow today, as well as president of the Conference of European Rabbis.) After a few years there, they relocated to Migdal HaEmek, where they became an integral part of Rav Nachman Bulman's community, and Daniel served as president of the *kehillah*. Eventually they returned to Yerushalayim, where Daniel works as an accountant.

Daniel is an interesting mixture of the American Midwest (Detroit), Ner Yisroel of Baltimore, all sorts of Chassidic influences, topped off by *Nesivos Shalom*. He and Chavi rule over quite a roost. Chavi is a Michlala graduate as well, and teaches *bagrut* English in high school in Jerusalem. Chavi's in-laws, Itamar and Phyllis Koenigsberg from Detroit, weren't living in Eretz Yisrael at the time of the wedding, but they do now.

Daphna and Yehudah's wedding took place during her final year in high school, which even hosted *sheva brachot* for her. Yehudah has transcribed a number of my *shiurim* about Eretz Yisrael that I hope will soon be published, and he faithfully maintains my website with over a thousand audio and video *shiurim*. He is a *masmid*, a *talmid chacham*, and the members of the family refer to him as "Google" because of his wide knowledge.

A number of years ago we worked together on a project very close to my heart. The *Haggadah Leil Shimurim*, written by the author of the *Aruch Hashulchan*, Rav Yechiel Michel Halevi Epstein, had been out of print for some time. Yehudah retyped the entire *sefer*. I wrote an introduction and we published it. It has been my favorite Haggadah for years.

Daphna works as an administrator in a post-high-school *yeshivah* in Ramat Beit Shemesh. Yehudah's parents, Rabbi Avraham and Brenda Goldreich from Toronto, subsequently came on aliyah and reside in Har Nof as well, much to our delight.

☙

Two years later we experienced a replay of the same beautiful situation all over again: our son Menachem and our daughter Libi also got engaged at the same time, in a scene that was uncannily reminiscent of their siblings' actions of some years earlier. The two couples got married six weeks apart from one another. At the time of the engagement, my daughter Libi, the glowing bride, turned to me and said, "Abba, do you remember what Rav Yaakov said when you went to Toronto to see him? How he told you that it's easier to marry off kids in Eretz Yisrael?"

"Indeed I do, Libi," I responded. "Indeed I do."

Within two years we had married off four children. *Hodu l'Hashem ki tov*. Menachem Mendel Mordechai was our third child to get married. He married Dina, daughter of Rabbi Boruch and Esther Katzman, who live in the Sanhedria Murchevet neighborhood of Jerusalem. They had made aliyah from Seattle, Washington. I never figured out how he did it, but Menachem learned for many years after he and Dina married, on what amounted to no budget at all. They didn't need much and lived with utter simplicity. Menachem is kind of a walking wonder. A big *talmid chacham*, he gives multiple classes in the institutions that he founded and everywhere he can help spread Torah to Klal Yisrael.

Menachem had decided on his life's mission a long time before. The idea first came about in 1983 when he went to Kiryat Shmona with Hillel and Bina Fendel on a *kiruv* assignment. He fell in love with the beauty and serenity of the north and decided then and there that one day he would return and build his own *kiruv* organization there. He was twenty-one at the time. Ten years later he followed his dream.

First he spent six months scouting the north: Acco, Nahariya, Yokneam, Atlit, Tirat Hacarmel, Nesher, Kfar Yona, Afula, and Hadera. He was looking for a place where there was room for growth and where he could make a difference. His goal was the transformation of a nonreligious town into a city of Torah. He made his decision. It was to be Afula, a medium-sized city in the Lower Galil, forty minutes south of Tveria.

Menachem didn't have two cents to rub together, but money (or the lack of it) had never stopped him before and he wasn't going to let it stop him now.

One day we were discussing his upcoming plans. "Menachem," I said to my son, "you can't do this without financial backing. How do you expect to make this a reality? How are you going to create an entire infrastructure without funding?" That was me. The voice of reason.

"Abba," he said with complete confidence, "it's going to work. I'm telling you." Complete trust in G-d. And why not? He was doing this for one reason only: to bring the residents of Afula back to their Creator. He had G-d on his side.

One Friday morning, he came over to the house and announced that they were moving to Afula in a few days.

"How are you going to make a living?"

"How are you going to pay your first months' expenses?"

"How are you going to pay rent, buy food?"

"It's okay," he said, "we'll figure it out." Then he walked out of the house. It was Friday afternoon and he had to get ready for Shabbat.

Fifteen minutes after he left, there came a knock on my door. I answered it and let an elderly gentleman, who said he was looking for me, into my living room.

He told me the following story. He used to live in Williamsburg and remembered me from when I was growing up. "They used to call you Shuly."

"That's right."

He had come to Eretz Yisrael to bury his wife. She had died about two weeks previously. I expressed my condolences. He'd been here since then and he had to see me.

Why did he have to see me?

"My wife put away money throughout her life, the idea being that after she died, the money should be given to a *yeshivah* for children in Eretz Yisrael."

A light bulb went on in my head.

"Really?" I said. "You came to the right place."

It seemed that he had been very fond of me when I was a little boy. They had had no children of their own and perhaps he had looked at me as some type of surrogate son. I took out a map of Eretz Yisrael and showed him Afula on the map.

"My son Menachem is moving here," I said, pointing to Afula, "with his family. He is going to start a school for precious Jewish children in a city where Torah is pretty much unknown."

This ninety-year-old man, Moshe Ber, took out his checkbook, wrote a check, and handed it to me.

I looked at the check.

It was for fifty thousand dollars.

It seems that my son's *bitachon* was far more effective than my rational parental doubt. Needless to say, I was deeply moved.

After good wishes and handshakes were exchanged all around, Moshe Ber left for Meah Shearim, where he was spending Shabbat, and I raced to the phone to call my son.

"Menachem," I said, "I just raised fifty thousand dollars for you!"

The guy I had been grilling mercilessly about funding had just received a heavenly advance on his building plans. He didn't have a penny to his name and suddenly he had fifty thousand dollars. Menachem was pretty excited, as you can well imagine.

"Just go build Torah in Afula," I said.

And he went. It was very difficult at the beginning (as most important things are). He took sick and couldn't move for a few months. It reminded me of what it had taken to bring me to Eretz Yisrael. Menachem went through a terrible time in the beginning as well, but eventually things started to fall into place for him.

And he started a school. How does one start a Torah school in the middle of a spiritual wasteland?

Menachem built it from the ground up. He went from door to door in Afula. Sometimes they let him in, sometimes not. If they allowed him over their threshold, he'd ask the parents if any member of the family needed to study for an upcoming bar mitzvah. If they did, he offered to teach them. He checked *mezuzot* and tefillin. He used any excuse he could think of to get a foot in the door. And let me tell you, he got in a lot of doors. Then he went to the playground and the big learner from the *yeshivot* of Yerushalayim began challenging the Afula teens to basketball games until he became friends with them on the courts. Eventually he opened a day school.

The Novominsker Rebbe came to Eretz Yisrael a while back with a group of Agudah supporters. They traveled around the country checking out different Torah institutions. They visited Afula because Menachem's school was officially a Chinuch Atzmai institution. When the Rebbe returned to Yerushalayim, he came in to see me and said the following words: "There's only one person in this country that's really doing the job that needs to be done – your son in Afula. He's taking kids from completely nonreligious homes and turning them into true Torah Jews."

But that wasn't enough for Menachem. He started a *kollel* in Afula. He started a *midrashah* for girls to give them a place to go to enrich themselves. Then he started a *yeshivah gedolah* there as well. And Afula has suddenly become a popular destination for young Charedi couples who see it as a wonderful location to begin their lives. Dina is also involved in education; she teaches computer skills and English in the Ulpana high school in Tveria. Menachem and Dina are a genuine example of people who have dedicated their entire lives to G-d and His Torah.

ے

My daughter Libi married Rav David (Dudu) Nadav, a close *talmid* of Rav Shlomo Zalman Auerbach, and in fact, Rav Shlomo Zalman graced us with his presence at their engagement party. I'll never forget the scene. We were sitting and celebrating their *l'chaim* when suddenly there was a knock at the door. Someone went to answer it and next thing we knew the *gadol hador* was walking into the room. Seeing Rav Shlomo Zalman was shocking – in a good way. The connection between Rav David and his *rebbe* continues, because he now has a special relationship with Rav Shmuel Auerbach, Rav Shlomo Zalman's son, as well.

Little did we know back when we used to listen to Yigal Calek's London School of Jewish Song that the star soloist of so many of their classic hits was Dudu Nadav, who would grow up to become our son-in-law. He is the kind of person from whom you learn to expect the unexpected. He has started outreach organizations in the most unlikely places, and brought some incredibly influential Israelis back to their roots. Recently he opened a new *yeshivah* for young teens with a completely original program. He is a person who thinks way out of the box, a fascinating individual who is constantly coming up with new projects and programs with which to bring people closer to Hashem. Libi is his anchor, inspiration, and full partner in all his undertakings. She herself holds a BEd from Michlala and a master's degree in Jewish history.

ے

Our youngest son Yirmi has an interesting story as well. While riding on a bus one day when he was fourteen, he met a young man called Yitzchak Rosenbluth, whose friendship he would always treasure. When he spent some time learning in New York several years later, Yitzchak found him a summer job so he could earn some spending money. Yitzchak worked for a company called Bodek, and one of their clients needed a truck driver. At Bayla's insistence he told his boss, Shaya Semel, that he couldn't drive the delivery truck in Brooklyn, but could only make deliveries up to the mountains. His mother said, "It wouldn't be good for *shidduchim*." His boss said he understood and agreed to his conditions. Hashem must have chuckled knowing Yirmi would one day marry the Semel daughter and bring her to live in Eretz Yisrael. People said she wouldn't "make it" here but Rochelle has thrived and blossomed. Her encouragement and faith in Yirmi's abilities have been invaluable in his becoming the man he is. He is very involved in the Ramat Beit Shemesh community and has an insurance agency there.

So those are our kids. We're very proud of them. The big miracle, in my opinion, is that not only did they survive but they stayed in Eretz Yisrael and all of our grandchildren and great-grandchildren were born in this country. Out of all our *mechutanim*, four sets already reside in Eretz Yisrael, and the fifth set of in-laws plans on eventually relocating here.

Thank G-d.

❦

One year, my wife Bayla and I agreed to be honored by the Young Israel of Israel as their guests of honor at their annual dinner in Jerusalem. This was a rarity for my wife, who shuns the limelight. I myself try to avoid accepting honors such as this, for one simple reason: they are a ton of work. Being honored translates into many phone calls, as the honoree frantically tries his best to ensure that all his friends and acquaintances will be attending "his" dinner, which is, after all, the reason the organization is honoring him in the first place, so that his friends will come and give them money.

That said, we accepted the honor for the Young Israel's tenth annual banquet because Rabbi Rose had been very helpful to me and instrumental in assisting in both the shul (KZY) and the school (JCA). The banquet was to be held on March 3, 1991, and once we had accepted the honor, we went full speed ahead trying to get a record number of guests to attend.

Preparing for this historic event was made much more difficult by the fact that the radio was spewing forth all manner of bad news from the madman in Iraq, Saddam Hussein. Not content with having just emerged from a long and protracted battle with neighboring Iran in which thousands of his countrymen had been killed, the Butcher of Baghdad had gone ahead and invaded Kuwait, heading straight for the oil-rich country's energy supplies, thereby incurring the wrath of the West, most notably the United States, who threatened to go to war with Iraq over the matter.

Saddam's response was to threaten that he had a host of Scud missiles aimed and ready to attack Israel, which he would not hesitate to use if he found himself under attack by the Americans.

This of course was more than a little worrisome.

As you all know, America did of course choose to go to war with Saddam. And Saddam did of course send a grand total of thirty-nine Scud missiles over our way. And Bush the father did not end up finishing the war in any decisive way, thereby leaving something over for Bush the son. But that would all play out in years to come. Meanwhile, we were just trying to plan our dinner.

You can see how that might have been a little difficult with all this Scud missile business hanging over our heads.

We persevered. Nobody even considered canceling the dinner, though we all nursed the fervent hope that there should be enough healthy people to attend the dinner when the time actually arrived.

I penned a piece in the (now-defunct) religious Zionist newspaper *Hatzofeh* two weeks before war broke out in the Gulf.

I quoted Yechezkel 38:8: "*Mi'yamim rabim tipaked*" (after many days [that you have sinned] you're going to be punished). Yechezkel is referring here to the final war at the end of days, the war of Gog and Magog.

"And at the end of years," the prophet continues, "you will come to a land [where there are three types of Jews: those who have] returned from the sword, [those who have been] gathered in from amongst many peoples, on the mountains of Israel that have always been desolate [but which are no longer so]." And now there is a third group of people who are arriving here as well, "*v'hi me'amim hutzaah*."

The Malbim says that this third group is referring to people who have only now been granted permission to leave the places in which they have been living until that point and are coming to settle in Eretz Yisrael.

I wrote as follows: "The first group that Yechezkel is referring to consists of those who came to settle in Eretz Yisrael after World War II. The Sh'erit Hapleitah – survivors of the Holocaust who were saved from the sword. The second group consisted of the numerous groups that followed. They came from all over, from many countries, specifically Arab countries. They are described as '*mekubetzet me'amim rabim*,' gathered in from many nations.

"But now," I wrote, "something new is happening. There is a large group of Jews who have up until this point not been permitted to leave, but have just been granted their release. The Jews of Russia, who are streaming into Eretz Yisrael." And this was in the months leading up to the Gulf War, and even as the Scud missiles were winging their way into the country on a daily basis. As they descended from the plane they were handed gas masks, and they continued to come.

"And the *pasuk* ends as follows: '*v'yashvu la'vetach kulam*,' and all of these three groups are going to live in this country safely and with tranquility."

And what does Rashi write? "*V'hamotzium min ha'amim lo yaazvena b'yadecha*" (And G-d Who saved them and gathered them in from the nations won't abandon them to you).

And you, Gog and Magog, what are you thinking? Don't you realize that the G-d Who rescued all these Jews didn't do so to abandon them in your hands? You should have thought of that. Did you really imagine that after saving the Jewish people with so many miracles, that G-d would transport them to Israel to be harmed over there?

And that's why you (Gog and Magog) are going to be destroyed.

This is clearly what Rashi means to say.

"This verse," I wrote, "is making a statement. We will survive the Gulf War. Hashem didn't protect us for thousands of years, didn't gather in all the exiles back to Eretz Yisrael, just so the mass murderers of the world should have an easier time destroying us. Not at all. We will survive this war!"

ಲ

The first Scud missiles hit Israel on January 15, 1990 with minimal damage. And miraculously, the same went for the rest of them. Thirty-nine Scuds and only two people killed. Just to put this in the right perspective, when Iraq attacked Iran with Scuds some years before, every one of them caused many deaths. This was a clear miracle.

My prediction in the paper had come true.

An interesting detail: It was the morning after that first terrifying night of sheer horror in which we huddled in our sealed rooms and felt vulnerable in the extreme. A woman member of my shul called me after Shacharit beside herself, seeking something to calm her down.

"Rabbi, please give me a verse for comfort, for something to hold on to."

I didn't hesitate. A verse in Yeshayahu (26:20) came to mind: "*Lech ami bo ba'chadarecha u'sgor delatecha baadecha; chavi kimat rega ad yaavor zaam*" (Go, My nation, into your rooms, and close the doors behind you; hide for a moment until the anger is past).

Twenty minutes later I started receiving the phone calls from people who wanted to know if I'd heard about this monumental verse that so clearly predicted our current predicament. I found that amusing.

The right verse for the right moment.

It spread like wildfire. Like all good things do.

As days went on, people were already getting used to the situation. Many of them decided that there was no reason to enter their sealed rooms any longer. It was sufficient to have *emunah* and *bitachon*, they posited.

To this I quoted a conversation between the One Above and the prophet Shmuel. G-d instructed Shmuel to go to Beit Lechem and anoint one of Yishai's sons as future king of Israel.

Shmuel protested that such an act would enrage King Shaul and endanger his life.

"What's going on with Shmuel Hanavi? What kind of behavior is this?" I asked. "G-d told him to go. Why is he even worried? Where was his faith?"

And you probably expected G-d to reply, "Shmuel, trust Me. Just trust Me." But G-d didn't say that. Instead Hashem said, "Take along a heifer and say, 'I have come to bring an offering to Hashem.' This will be your cover story."

What happened to Shmuel's belief, and what happened to G-d just telling him, "Don't worry, I'll take care of you"?

The answer is that faith in G-d does not mean taking unnecessary risks. Man is required to do everything possible to protect himself and Hashem is indeed confirming to Shmuel that that's the correct way. Not relying on miracles. It does not mean "Though I walk through a valley of Scuds I will fear no evil, for Thou art with me."

In the end, the Gulf War was a miracle to remember. Thirty-nine miracles to be exact. And though we feared an empty turnout on the big night in the Ramada ballroom, the war was over a scant few days before the dinner and that ballroom was simply jammed to the rafters. The war ended on Purim, Thursday 14 Adar, February 29, and the dinner was held three days later on Sunday, March 3. What an evening it turned out to be. It was a celebration of life and thanksgiving to Hashem.

# 19

# Oslo, or, What Were They Thinking?

On Thursday, September 9, 1993, an announcement was made that shocked the entire country. An agreement had been worked out between Yasser Arafat, world-class terrorist, and Yitzhak Rabin, prime minister of Israel, which stated that the PLO and the State of Israel were now going to make peace. In an act of supreme shortsightedness, Israel would be bringing the banished Arafat (who had been sinking into oblivion) back from Tunis to Israel along with thousands of his PLO henchmen.

As is often the case, the country became hopelessly divided between those individuals who were filled with euphoria at the "peace" that would soon be ours and everyone else, who wanted Arafat as far away as possible.

Monday, September 13 was to herald a new dawn for Arab/Jew relations in the Middle East. A historic signing ceremony took place on the White House lawn hosted by American president Bill Clinton, and attended by the guests of honor Rabin, Peres, and Arafat.

On Shabbat morning, two days before the White House ceremony, I stood up in front of the holy ark in my shul on Agassi Street and delivered my first anti-Oslo speech.

"If you take a look at the end of Parshat Chukat," I began, "the Torah depicts the struggle taking place between the Jewish nation and Sichon, king of the Emorites. Sichon refuses to allow the Jews passage through his land, and not content to stop there, dispatches his army against the fledgling Jewish nation, who then beat Sichon's army in a series of epic battles. This culminates with the nation of Israel in control of every part of Sichon's country. The Torah goes into great detail here, making sure to inform us that the Jews conquered Cheshbon and its satellite cities as well.

But how in fact did Sichon first take control of Cheshbon way back at the beginning his career? Well, the Torah tells us that he captured it from the king of Moav. Cheshbon originally belonged to Moav, but Sichon managed to grab hold of it. And he eventually managed to conquer the entire land of Moav until Arnon. The Torah then tells us: "Therefore, the bards sing, 'Come to Cheshbon, let the city of Sichon be rebuilt, because fire came out of Cheshbon, and flames emanated from the metropolis of Sichon, which consumed all of Moav and Arnon'" (Bamidbar 21:27).

I looked at the sea of faces sitting before me and asked them the following question.

"Why does the Torah feel that we have to know about Cheshbon? Why do we have to know that Sichon waged war with the first king of Moav and that he managed to conquer his cities ?And what difference does it make that flames of fire came spewing out of Cheshbon ?What does this have to do with Torah and the Jewish people"?

Then I quoted a Gemara in *Baba Batra* 78b.

Says Rav Shmuel Bar Nachmani in the name of Rav Yonatan, "*Mai dichtiv 'al ken yomru hamoshlim*' [therefore, the bards sing]" Why do we have to know about the bards and their songs of victory? Why do we need to speak of how the fire of Sichon left Cheshbon and spread through the lands of Moav?

Rav Shmuel Bar Nachmani answers in the name of Rav Yonatan. "Do you want to know who the *moshlim* – the rulers, not bards – really are? Those are the people who are in control of their evil inclinations."

What does it mean to "come to Cheshbon"? That means let us come and make a calculation (*cheshbon*) what you gain from the *mitzvot* you do and what is lost when you allow a mitzvah to escape your hands.

And you must also work out the "benefit" you'll gain from the sins that you do and the losses you will incur from those sins. Everything must be worked out in mathematical terminology. Because this is the *cheshbon*, the calculation of our lives.

Rav Ruderman, my *rosh yeshivah* in Ner Yisroel, once asked what connection there is between Sichon's conquest of Cheshbon and the great *cheshbon* of life. What is this Gemara telling us?

He answered as follows. Cheshbon was a city on the border of Moav. A flea-bitten, one-horse town with a local lockup, a saloon, and one dusty street (my description, not the Rosh Yeshivah's). When Sichon began his assault on Moav, all the military commanders of Moav were faced with a tough decision.

Should they commit their forces to the defense of Cheshbon, a little nothing town, or not? They decided that they were not going to fight for Cheshbon. Instead they made a strategic withdrawal in the spirit of Neville Chamberlain's invitation for Hitler to help himself to the Sudetenland in the name of "peace in our time."

The result? Sichon entered the tiny, strategically insignificant town without shooting a single arrow. And you know what he did? He bided his time. He began bringing in men, materials, weapons. He started building fortresses and digging defenses against the enemy and he turned that one-horse town into a stronghold called Cheshbon. From there he struck out against Moav and conquered it.

The Gemara is teaching us the following, said the Rosh Yeshivah. "The evil inclination never sucks a person into his trap by telling him to desecrate Shabbos. That's much too big of a sin to begin with. No. He tells him to do something small. He bides his time and convinces the person to do another little sin, and then another, and before one knows it, the *yetzer hara* has established a foothold, a beachhead in one's heart and from there goes out the flame to consume the entire individual."

That's the way Rav Ruderman explained the Gemara. Cheshbon is the evil inclination's beachhead in every Jew.

I looked around my shul on that Shabbat morning, took a deep breath, and made a prediction.

"The Israeli government is about to give the terrorists a beachhead in Eretz Yisrael. Ultimately, *aish* – fire – will emerge from Gaza and flames from Jericho! How can the Jews of Eretz Yisrael be doing something so mad?"

At the time there were people who became extremely angry at me for speaking so negatively about such an incredible dream. But looking back, tragically, I was correct from day one. Sichon took a tiny one-saloon, one-sheriff outpost and turned it into Fort Sichon, and that's exactly what the world-class architect of terrorism was planning on doing as well. And it was our fault, because we brought him right through the door. And it was all a tragic, tragic mistake.

How could our leaders contemplate the possibility that a terrorist organization dedicated by its charter to the destruction of the Jewish state would now become those who would protect us? What blindness had descended upon them? What manner of madness motivated them to make what Yeshayahu 28:15 calls "a covenant with death and a contract with the grave"?

༈

All this took place in Elul. As we prepared for the Yamim Noraim, the government of the State of Israel prepared to make the greatest mistake in its short history. The deal hadn't yet been done. But the government was so certain of being able to convince their citizens that they announced the Oslo Accords before they were in fact official. The prime minister went to Washington, DC, and stood on the White House lawn before the accords were even legal, before the agreement had been ratified by the Knesset. Which meant that we still had time to change their minds and bring it down. Petitions were circulated and signed by thousands of people stating that we, the citizens of Israel, were unequivocally against the Oslo Accords. They were then delivered to key players in the government, so they could see that the people were not on their side.

We in Har Nof called a communal rally in our shul, Kehillat Zichron

Yosef, just a few weeks after the shocking announcement of the Oslo Accords. The shul was packed to the rafters. The guest speaker was MK Benny Begin, who analyzed the Declaration of Principles and revealed its numerous weaknesses that would endanger the lives of many Jews. He spoke about the fact that Israel had relinquished the "right to hot pursuit," which meant that terrorists could perpetrate acts of violence and flee back into PA territory with Israel unable to pursue. In fact, that's exactly what happened.

But our protest was all to no avail.

How on earth had the democratically elected leaders of Israel even entertained the thought of standing together with the worst terrorist in the world on the White House lawn before the agreement was even ratified in the Knesset? And yet it happened. We watched it happen and a feeling of fear for the future took hold of us. We were stunned.

In the end, the Oslo Accords were passed in the Knesset.

If you think about it, how could the government have allowed their great plan to get derailed?

They couldn't.

There was too much on the line. The President, the Prime Minister, and the Terrorist had already shaken hands with one another. It mattered not that a possible majority of the country was vocally against such a move, because the country had too much at stake to back down. Even then. They had no choice but to move forward, which they did, while millions wept in sheer terror of what the future held.

അ

Peace would not come to the shores of the Holy Land. Instead of peace, the opposite arrived. Terrorist attacks began taking place in the country on a regular basis. People would be taking the bus to work on a regular Sunday morning, just sitting on a bus on the congested Jerusalem streets, when suddenly an explosion would rip through the quiet neighborhood, shattering any illusion of peace. Bus bombings were the terrorists' big weapon and they used them masterfully. People simply became afraid to ride the city buses.

And it wasn't only the buses. There would be stabbings in crowded marketplaces and shooting at innocent Jewish civilians as they went about their business.

I had feared for this scenario.

And so, we began to demonstrate.

There was still a chance to slay the monster that had arisen. There were so many more steps that had to be taken before the accords would be completely implemented. This was only the beginning. If the government fell, the whole insane plan would be shelved, put on hold. There would be a respite.

At that point in time, as terrorist attacks increased almost daily with wild abandon, even a temporary reprieve would have been very welcome. We demonstrated outside the offices of policy planners in the government, the top politicians, the president, the ministers who had the power to pull their parties out of the Knesset. Actions such as those would have caused the government to topple and fold like a hastily constructed house of cards. Arafat and his band of bloodthirsty murderers had still not arrived from Tunis. The fire was still somewhat contained. There was still time to place a lid on it, to retake the beachhead.

I will never forget the moment I heard the news that the Oslo Accords had been ratified and passed in the Knesset plenum. The accords were now legal and had become the law. In slow motion, I reached down to my shirt and ripped it, tore *kriah* on my clothing much the same way I had done when my father passed away years before. Then I sank down to the floor and began to cry for my beloved Eretz Yisrael and the horror that had descended on our lives.

☙

And so the country found itself divided once more. It was like we had returned to the days when the Haganah and the Irgun were at loggerheads with one another. Now too, there were two sides. The Left, in favor of making peace at any cost, euphoric at what they perceived as "the opportunity of a lifetime." And the Right, who were almost all vehemently against making "peace" with a sworn enemy, a terrorist, a global outlaw, appalled by the idea of believing that he would protect us from terrorism.

The slogan of those against was "*Eretz Yisrael b'sakanah!*" Eretz Yisrael is in danger! They held a vast demonstration which attracted upwards of a quarter of a million people to stand and express their fear for the future of the country while listening to inspiring speeches by rabbis, community leaders, and elected officials deeply concerned about the unfolding events. The government had set out on a march of folly unparalleled in Jewish history. The generation of the Holocaust placing trust in a band of evil gangsters and agreeing to give them parts of Eretz Yisrael was unfathomable. Although the numbers of those attending the demonstration had been large, the government, concerned by such a high turnout, sought to downplay the gathering.

Something had to be done.

I did the only thing I could think of.

I began getting in touch with every rabbi I could find, the goal being the establishment of an organization that would fight this terrible decree with every weapon at our disposal.

One day, the phone rang at midnight, quite past the usual time for calls.

It was Rav Nachum Rabinovitch, the much esteemed *rosh yeshivah* of Yeshivat Birkat Moshe in Ma'ale Adumim and one of the first *rabbanim* whom I asked to join my organization.

"Sholom," he said, "Someone else is trying to put together an organization of *rabbanim* just the same as you. Rav Avraham Shapira, *rosh yeshivah* of Mercaz Harav, has been calling up rabbis everywhere, trying to spearhead a movement to combat the accords. You should be in touch with Rav Shabtai Zelikovitch as soon as possible. He's coordinating things for Rav Shapira. Joining forces would be the best thing to do."

I called Rav Zelikovitch and told him everything I had been doing up until that point.

"Let's all meet," he said simply. And that's how the first meeting between Rav Avraham Shapira and myself came about.

I went to Rav Avraham's home. The Kiryat Moshe neighborhood is home to Yeshivat Mercaz Harav, a world-famous institution of higher learning that would be the site of a terrible terrorist attack on Rosh

Chodesh Adar in years to come. But that was all in the distant future.

Yeshivat Mercaz Harav is the jewel in the crown of Kiryat Moshe, a neighborhood of mostly Dati Leumi Jews. Alongside the *yeshivah* building is a little path that winds itself back into the neighborhood and leads to Sirkis Street and the simple apartment of Rav Avraham Shapira. This apartment would become the symbol of the opposition to Oslo. I cannot tell you the number of times the TV cameras and journalists of the world press camped themselves outside that apartment waiting to hear what had been decided within.

Every few weeks for the next two years, Binyamin Netanyahu, future prime minister of Israel and then head of the opposition, came to report to Rav Avraham about any developments in the matter of Oslo. We hosted numerous members of the Knesset and actually planned many matters of opposition in that spartan, unadorned home. Of material objects there were few, but the shelves of *sefarim* stretched from ceiling to floor.

Our efforts might have been effective and successful were it not for the madness that had overtaken a huge element of the population, which firmly believed that the nation was on the path to salvation and that transporting an arch-terrorist and forty thousand of his bloodthirsty followers to Israel would bring about peace in our days.

And so, with no recourse, and in a world gone completely insane, we became the opposition. We held meetings every few weeks, constantly relating to the different issues that were arising. Rav Avraham Shapira was the leader, ably assisted by Rav Moshe Neria and Rav Shaul Yisraeli, the three great luminaries of the religious Zionist world.

There were a number of regulars who were involved on a constant basis: Rav Zalman Melamed, Rav Haim Druckman, Rav Dov Lior, Rav Meyer Fendel, Rav Yehoshua Magnes, Rav Chaim Shteiner, Rav Daniel Shilo, Rav Yosef Friedman, Rav David Chai Hacohen, and Rav Yosef Artziel. It was Rav Yosef Friedman who contributed his considerable organizational skills to get things going. Each one dedicated his time, talents, and professional abilities to the cause. And along the way we came up with a name for our group. It was called the Ichud Harabbanim l'maan Am Yisrael v'Eretz Yisrael, Rabbis United for Israel and the Jewish People.

This was the group that shook up the entire country when we ruled that soldiers should refuse to follow orders when called upon to remove Jews from their homes. This halachic ruling would reverberate through the country, its ramifications impacting on the very foundations of our society. Newspaper editors wondered whether this ruling would cause disintegration in the army, or in the social fabric of the country as a whole. This halachic ruling resurfaced in a big way during the disengagement from Gaza, when the question of disobeying orders was once again brought to the fore of public consciousness.

Our first act as an organization was to actually organize as many rabbis as possible under one umbrella. To this end, we held a mass meeting at the Renaissance Hotel in Jerusalem. Harvey Douglin, a member of my shul and close friend who is the general manager of this prestigious hotel, provided crucial assistance over the next few years, graciously allowing us the use of the hotel's magnificent ballroom for a very affordable rate. The gathering was a huge success, with at least a thousand rabbis in attendance.

Meanwhile, Oslo was a fluid monster, never standing still, constantly developing itself, like a hydra with seven heads. Monster it may have been, yet the government continued to support it, though Arafat's real agenda peeked through time and again. The government had staked its prestige on the so-called "peace process." In fact, it was all fiction. The much hailed "land for peace" was a deathly dangerous slogan, empty of all substance. No one was going to give us peace for any land unless it was all the land.

Arafat delivered his infamous Johannesburg speech around this time, and while this speech should have been sufficient for the Israeli government to shelve Oslo for good, it curiously did not have any such effect.

Arafat the terrorist in his trademark kaffiyeh, five-day stubble, and sunglasses had become Arafat the world traveler, feted by kings, queens, and dictators alike as the new hope for civilization. I assume such heady feelings of adoration affect a person to some degree and Arafat had become the lucky recipient of an aura of respectability. Maybe that's why he had the chutzpah to make the following remark during a speech given in Arabic at a mosque in South Africa.

*Do not fear that I am changing,* he said, calming his slightly agitated brethren who were no doubt wondering what had happened to their fearsome tiger. *Although I talk of peace for the sake of the West and Israel, it is of course not at all what I have in mind. We have not given up on our dream of reconquering the Holy Land, and none of you should have any fears on the matter.*

This was the gist of Arafat's mind-blowing Johannesburg speech.

Jewish people are very smart. This is a fact. Everyone knows it. Somehow a copy of the tape of Arafat's South African speech was obtained and made good use of. Our first step was to pay a visit to the office of Hebrew University's expert in residence on Middle Eastern affairs. Moshe Sharon, a good and reliable man, translated the entire Johannesburg speech for us and even honored us with a personal speech on the matter, delivered at one of the meetings of our organization at the Renaissance Hotel.

Our next step was to leak the contents of the tape to the newspapers, which should have caused an uproar and led to the rescinding of all and any agreements that had been reached with Arafat up until then. This, amazingly enough, did not occur, showing once again the blind madness that had overtaken so many in the land of the Jews. Almost nobody even felt the need to respond, and if they did respond, it was by claiming that Arafat was saying what he had to say to his people, but that he didn't really mean a word of it.

We, on the other hand, didn't believe for a second that he had changed. After all, can a leopard change its spots?

࿘

December 1993. We had a problem. People were immersed in the glamour of Oslo and simply didn't care about their brothers living in settlements. Yehudah and Shomron were considered outside the pale. We needed to get people to care. One way to do that, I felt, was with the twinning concept.

We'd find cities or neighborhoods that were sympathetic to the plight of those living outside the Green Line and twin them with cities like Ariel, Itamar, and Shilo, whose homes were proudly perched on the mountaintops of Yehudah and Shomron. In fact, the first twinning ceremony took place on Chanukah, between the town of Eli in the Shomron and our Har Nof neighborhood of Yerushalayim. Both ends of the twinning ceremony took place on the same day. I officiated in Har Nof, where over one thousand people filled our shul, after which we boarded nine buses for the second part of the twinning ceremony, which took place in Eli itself and which was hosted by Binyamin Netanyahu, then head of Israel's opposition in the Knesset.

This made a tremendous impact. Although it may not have accomplished much from a legal perspective, it garnered major results from a psychological point of view. The people who lived in all these settlements finally, for the first time in a while, felt that people cared about them, were identified with them, and most importantly, were on their side.

And feelings like those, feelings of solidarity for one's fellow Jew, cannot be underestimated.

The official kickoff of the twinning experiment took place the day before phase one of the Oslo disaster was carried out. Oslo I had a name. The masters of PR had obviously thought long and hard about how exactly to sell their terrible plan to the Israeli public and they came to the conclusion that it must be fed to them in small, palpable doses. That was why phase one was called *Aza v'Yericho Tchila* (Gaza and Jericho First).

This meant that Arafat would first be receiving Gaza and Jericho. And of course Peres was walking around saying, "If Arafat wants Aza, let Arafat have Aza. After all, who needs Aza anyway?" As to Jericho, it was a sleepy, backwater city with a few palm trees and not much else. What difference did it make to Israel if Arafat took control of Gaza, where every block of houses was another booby-trapped death wish for our troops, or Jericho, which was a nothing town with a few date trees and a mini-mart. Let them have those two places if that would make them happy.

And the people, never having heard about Sichon, Cheshbon, and the beachheads of life, agreed.

So it was that we stood in our shul in Har Nof on December 11,

1993, the day before the implementation of Oslo I, and commenced with the twinning ceremony.

≈

Four years later Binyamin Netanyahu was about to leave Eretz Yisrael for the Wye House plantation, where he would be subjected to intense pressure from President Bill Clinton for all sorts of things – none of them good for Israel. Before leaving, Netanyahu came to the home of Rav Avraham Shapira on Sukkot for a blessing. Rav Avraham asked me to be present, first for a private meeting with him, and after that for the meeting together with the prime minister which would take place in Rav Avraham's *sukkah*. We encouraged the prime minister to be strong. I asked Rav Shapira whether I might say a few words to the prime minister before we adjourned, and he graciously consented.

Looking Binyamin Netanyahu in the eye, I said: "There's a *midrash* which states that on the day of the destruction of the Beit Hamikdash, G-d said to Yirmiyahu, 'I feel today like a father whose only son just died on the way to the *chuppah*.' G-d then tells Yirmiyahu, 'Go wake the Avot, Avraham, Yitzchak, and Yaakov, because I want them to cry with Me.'

"Yirmiyahu hurries to the Me'arat Hamachpelah in Chevron. He calls out to the Forefathers.

"'You are being called to stand before the Master of the world.'

"'Why does G-d want us to come?' they ask.

"'I don't know,' the prophet Yirmiyahu answers.

"This is very strange. Yirmiyahu just uttered an untruth. He knew precisely why G-d was summoning the forefathers. Why then did he not say the truth to them? And the *midrash* ends by saying that the reason Yirmiyahu didn't want to tell them why they were being called to G-d's side was that he feared they would take him to task and reproach him, saying, 'How did you allow a tragedy like the destruction of the Temple to happen in your days, under your watch?' In other words, he was afraid of the judgment of history. In your days this happened to our children?"

I paused and looked at Netanyahu.

"Sometimes people make a big mistake," I said. "They think that the judgment of history is what their children will think of them or what their grandchildren will say about the actions they took. They worry how people will view their life and accomplishments.

"But with the Jewish people it's not like that," I told Netanyahu. "The moment you choose an action, you're judged now by everyone from the past, by all your ancestors from generations back. They are all watching you now from heaven, waiting to see how you will act and fare. And they will all judge you instantaneously. Our forefathers. All the people from history. It's not only how your sons will look at you. It's not how people in the future will look at you. It's how our ancestors will look at you! All of Jewish history is standing and watching you right now. You have to remain steadfast, strong, and courageous." It was said with great respect and was appreciated by the prime minister.

༄

Our group did not rest. After the huge gathering at the Renaissance in November and the twinning ceremony with Eli in December, our next step was to organize a trip of ten rabbis to the States to meet with their counterparts there. This was to take place in January 1994. We would be meeting with *roshei yeshivah*, rabbis, Chassidic Rebbes, heads of Jewish schools, key leaders of influential Jewish organizations, and the press, to inform them of the danger facing the Jews of Eretz Yisrael. We hired a representative in the United States to set up meetings for us.

We stayed in America over Shabbat and each one of us spoke in a different shul and community so as to alert as many people as possible to the severity of the situation. I stayed at the home of Rav Feivel Wagner, the *rav* of Young Israel of Forest Hills, and spoke at his shul among others. Rav Haim Druckman came along on the trip, as did Rav Yehoshua Magnes, Rav Nachum Rabinovitch, Rav Eliezer Waldman from Kiryat Arba, Rav Shabtai Zelikovitch, Rav Yosef Friedman, and Rebbetzin Shifra Blass. Important Torah scholars all of them. We attended meeting after meeting. It was very well organized. We wanted to meet with as many people as possible. Time was of the essence and we used it to the maximum. We stayed at a hotel in Manhattan, in the cold of winter, for about ten days, while meeting with people in the area.

There was one great man whom all ten of us went to see as a group: Rav Avraham Pam, the *rosh yeshivah* of Torah Vodaath, my alma mater. We explained to him the entire situation, describing the dangers that awaited the Jewish people if the government of Israel continued their insanity.

He listened very closely, true empathy in his eyes.

"You have to speak with Rav Moshe Sherer," he finally said.

Eventually the meeting wound its way to an end. As everyone started filing out of the room, Rav Pam stopped me.

"Sholom," he said, "wait a minute."

Everyone left the house, got into the cars, and turned on the heat. The cold was so bitter, so absolutely intense. Just like our mood.

He was standing there with his rebbetzin and he said, "Sholom, tell me, tell me the situation in Eretz Yisrael."

I told him the situation in no uncertain terms. I spelled it out in detail. How the government was bringing Arafat and his bloodthirsty murderers into our backyards and giving them large swaths of Eretz Yisrael. He listened to every word I had to say. And then I saw something that I had never seen before and would never see again after that day. As Rav Pam stood there, tears began streaming down his cheeks and running into his beard. The man was simply crying like a baby. His empathy was incredible.

When I left his home, I knew that I would never forget that sight.

The sight of Rav Pam standing there, crying, crying, crying.

After running around for ten days straight from rabbi to rabbi and from community leader to community leader, the ten of us returned home, tired to the bone. We were fighting an endless battle, and it didn't feel like we were winning in any way at all.

Many people just didn't grasp how much danger Oslo posed. On one of my visits to Toronto I found a kindred soul in the person of Herb Green. He was completely unaffected by what was considered politically correct. He was an independent thinker who saw the situation with great clarity. We became fast friends.

❧

I cannot tell you how many meetings there were.

I cannot tell you this because I lost count.

I cannot tell you how many plans we made.

I cannot tell you this because I lost track.

I cannot tell you how many demonstrations there were, because I just don't remember.

And every few weeks, there was another item in the paper that fed us false hope that the whole thing was going to fall through, that it would be sustainable no longer.

It wasn't long before our worst fears were realized and the City of Gold had become the city of fear. Buses were being bombed on an alarmingly regular basis. You'd hear one ambulance siren and tense up. If nothing happened, you knew things were still okay. But more often than not, that first siren would be joined by a second siren which would then merge with a third, and you knew, you just knew with a sinking feeling that another bus had been bombed and more Jews had been killed.

Instinctively we would put on the radio or television and there we would hear and see the first reports of a *pigua*, a terrorist attack. The very next move was to begin calling around frantically to all family members, hoping and praying that they weren't among the injured or worse. The phone calls went on back and forth until we found out that the immediate family was safe. Then began the interminable wait to hear the names of the dead and maimed, which always was the source of great pain.

My mind often went in silent prayer and hope to a *pasuk* in Yeshayahu (65:19): "For I (Hashem) will rejoice over Yerushalayim and exult with My people and there will no longer be heard in it the sound of weeping and the sound of outcry." And I thought to myself, "Not the sound of ambulances, nor the sirens of emergency vehicles speeding to the scene of a terrorist attack."

The number 18 bus was a target more times than I'd like to remember and that in particular was an extremely scary detail for me personally, because my wife and kids rode that bus all the time. Their lives, consequently, were in constant danger, as was the life of any person who lived in the city, took public transportation, or even walked the streets. There were bombings every week. Terrorists shot at random passersby. Stabbings took place on Ben Yehuda Street and in the Machane Yehuda Shuk.

The citizens of Israel were gripped with fear.

Just boarding a bus became an ordeal that required courage.

Still the "peace planners" pushed on, terming those who perished in the bus bombings *korbenot hashalom*, "peace offerings."

What made it all the worse was that we had predicted all this was going to happen and nobody had listened to us. How had things come to this? Hadn't we shouted ourselves hoarse warning everyone? Why wasn't anybody willing to listen?

# 20

# FIGHTING THE GOOD FIGHT

There was an empty apartment owned by Yeshivat Mercaz Harav in Kiryat Moshe which became our headquarters for working meetings. Planning meetings were all held at the home of Rav Avraham Shapira, but the actual work took place a few minutes away. By Pesach 1994, we reached the point where there was nothing left to do anymore. The scene and focus of all the activity was moving from Jerusalem to Washington, DC, because the United States Congress was slated to meet in June to vote over a possible allocation of money to the Palestinian Authority.

And so we decided to move our struggle to the United States as well.

Our group would spend its time on Capitol Hill lobbying senators to refuse to transfer money to the PA unless they complied with the Oslo Accords Declaration of Principles. We didn't want to openly disagree with the State of Israel or the president of the United States. Instead we focused on the fact that the Palestinians under Arafat were breaking the agreements each and every day and did not, consequently, deserve monetary reward for their behavior.

The agreements had been broken before the ink had dried on the paper. For example, there were supposed to be twelve thousand police and there were forty thousand police. They also possessed a tremendous amount of weaponry, much more than was allowed by the agreements.

Punishment for the PA was in order; financial reward, most definitely not.

Our goal was to present Congress with the facts. No more than the facts. And we called for compliance. Compliance by the PA with the Oslo Accords.

"You know who should be here demanding compliance?" I would ask the congressmen and senators whom I later met. "The Israeli Left. They're the ones who want this deal to work. But the only way this deal will work is if the Palestinians are forced to keep their side of the agreement."

꙳

For the next five weeks, through parts of May and June, I lived in the United States, during which time I, along with the other members of the planning committee, made two trips to Washington, DC. Three people came along with me from Eretz Yisrael: Yosef Friedman and Yedidya Atlas, both from Bet El, and Dov Kalmanovitch from Kiryat Moshe. Dov holds the dubious distinction of being the first person to be injured in the First Intifada. The four of us planned the trip to Capitol Hill. We prepared packets to be sent out to fourteen hundred rabbis across America. They included video footage, Arafat's infamous recording from the Johannesburg mosque, and lots of other vital pieces of information.

The travel arrangements and preparation of the packages cost a significant amount of money and we decided to approach Irving Moscowitz, the famous philanthropist, for some assistance. I had never spoken to Mr. Moscowitz before, but we knew of one another.

I called him up in Florida and told him what I was doing, explaining the situation and giving him a detailed breakdown.

He listened.

"Rabbi Gold, please send me a budget for your operation."

We sent him the budget. It called for seventy-two thousand dollars to undertake "Operation Capitol Hill." I called him up the next day and asked him for fifty thousand toward the seventy-two.

"Oh, no," he said to me, "oh, no. I'm paying it all. All seventy-two thousand. Don't ask anyone else for any money. You hear me? I want the whole thing!"

The logistics of our "March on Washington" were incredibly complicated. Just being in touch with all those rabbis was a full-time job for an entire office. Rabbi Pesach Lerner was our man. He opened his heart to everything we were trying to accomplish and lent us full usage of the Young Israel office building in Manhattan, which quickly became our New York headquarters. He was with us all the way and his support really helped pull everything together. Rabbi Steven Pruzansky of Congregation Bnai Yeshurun of Teaneck and Rabbi Neil Winkler of Young Israel of Fort Lee, New Jersey, were both also of incredible assistance to us, as was Rabbi Heshy Reichman of Yeshiva University.

On March 17, 1994, there was an executive meeting of the RCA. I was in touch with those friends of mine who were still a part of the organization and informed them that I would like to make a presentation. The meeting took place at the White Shul in Far Rockaway. It was a rainy, dreary day in the Five Towns and I missed Yerushalayim. Still, I did a pretty good job.

"We are not at loggerheads with the Israeli government," I explained, "but there has to be compliance and accountability on the part of Israel's partner for peace and we want you, members of the RCA, to stand at the forefront of this attempt to garner truth. We want you to head these efforts."

The idea was that we, the Israeli rabbis, would take a backseat in this case, and keep as low a profile as possible. We didn't want it to be perceived as an Israeli operation that would be vilified as meddling in American policy. We wanted the leadership to be American rabbis who legitimately petition their own government in a matter of great concern to them. The last thing we needed was to be accused of operating as a fifth column for the Israeli government. It was better for all concerned that the entire concept should at least appear to have originated with the rabbis of America.

It so happens to be that the same way we had formed our group of rabbis who were opposed to Oslo, another group of rabbis in the

American rabbinate had done the same thing, but these men saw things from the perspective of the Israeli Left. They put together an organization of their own, called Shvil Hazahav (the "Golden Path"), whose job it was to thwart our efforts. These men believed in Yitzhak Rabin and Shimon Peres and were determined to see the Oslo Accords through till the bitter end. (Which it was.) They truly thought that peace was at hand.

And therefore it came as no surprise that attending this meeting of the RCA was a rabbi who had been a protégé of mine at one point in his life, yet who now strongly identified with the Left. After I finished speaking, this man asked for the floor and tried his best to muddy the waters of truth and mask the urgency. He maintained that my group should not be helped and that the RCA should have nothing to do with us.

I had been warned about people like this, by other well-meaning individuals who advised me to forget about trying to obtain the RCA's support. But I did not heed their advice and it was a good thing, because after giving equal floor time to both parties, they took a vote where it was decided thirty to one to get involved and play a significant role on the big trip to Washington. In the end, my colleagues of the RCA concurred with my mission statement and came through with the goods.

※

The big day finally arrived. Rabbi Pesach Lerner arranged the buses for the rabbis who'd be traveling to Washington from New York. A very efficient and practical man, he also organized plenty of sandwiches to get us through what would prove to be an endless and arduous day. Meanwhile, other rabbis made their own way to Washington from cities across the length and breadth of the United States. Lots of old friends of mine were coming to join us that day. Great men, one and all. Builders of Torah in America and people who truly cared about Eretz Yisrael.

Yossi Friedman and I had gone to 770 Eastern Parkway to meet with Rabbi Yehuda Krinsky, personal secretary to the Rebbe and a key leader in the Lubavitch movement. He was extremely enthusiastic about helping us and promised to send his emissaries down to Washington. In the end, there were quite a few rabbinical delegates representing Chabad on that historic day. They rolled in from Philadelphia, Baltimore, and New York. They arrived with their typical fire and charm. They were amazing (as they always are).

I took Amtrak into Washington on the night prior to the big day. My son Yirmi (who has been a welcome addition on many of my adventures) accompanied me. He always takes care of me. Upon arrival, we took a cab to the home of a cousin, Sidney Meyers. His mother was one of my father's sisters.

Mordechai Twersky, our man in Washington, had been working furiously, setting up appointments with as many senators and congressmen as he could for the over one hundred rabbis who came to lobby Washington that day. We paired off with one another. Then began our rounds from early that morning, and as the day wore on everyone on Capitol Hill soon found out that we were there and why.

The press was there too.

Gershon Jacobson, legendary journalist for the *Algemeiner Journal* (the famous Yiddish newspaper), told me later that all the press had received a call from Shimon Peres that morning, requesting them not to cover our arrival and subsequent lobbying of Capitol Hill. This request was of course completely ignored by all. We would later find out that Peres had called Senator Gillman and asked him not to meet with our representatives due to his fear that our activities would cause great harm to the "peace process." (If only they had. If only they had.) Senator Gillman paid no attention to Peres's plea and not only met with our rabbis in his office, but even joined us for a press conference.

We began our long-awaited day with an open-air demonstration in front of the Lincoln Memorial. All of us were there. A number of us spoke, including me. One of the Chabad rabbis spoke, as did Rabbi Faskowitz, the president of the Council of Young Israel Rabbis.

We then adjourned to a nearby park where we all ate breakfast together. And then we saw the congressmen and the senators. Forty, fifty of them. We met them in their offices and sat with them over lunch. We explained our position and argued the merits of our case. We demanded that Arafat and the PA should have to prove they had changed for the better if they wanted to receive a share of the American citizens' money: compliance with the accords, accountability for their actions, and financial transparency. Big words, with important meaning. We also begged the senators to demand an accounting – and the records to go with it – of what exactly had been done with past monies that had been received by the PA. Until these goals were accomplished, the PA should be considered a terrorist organization and treated as such.

We were a vocal, articulate bunch who answered and cajoled and badgered and discussed. The hours passed like minutes and too soon it was time for everyone to meet in one of the Senate hearing rooms, a chamber large enough to hold us all, where we sat face-to-face with a number of highly influential members of the Senate and Congress. Some of them addressed us personally and Rabbi Moshe Tendler and Rabbi Hershel Schachter, *rosh yeshivah* at YU's Rabbi Isaac Elchanan Theological Seminary, represented us with speeches of their own.

During the meeting, Yirmi and I had to leave to catch a flight to Chicago. Bayla's sister and brother-in-law, Honey and Alan Aaron, were making a family *simchah* that evening.

No, our efforts did not stop Oslo.

Our operation didn't derail the pursuers of "peace."

But at least we caused the Senate and Congress to sit up and take notice of what was going on in Israel's backyard. We called for accountability, a sentiment most American senators heartily agreed with. We found them very sympathetic to our plight. And that was a welcome change from the many who disagreed with our cause.

We let it be known that we would not cease to oppose this spurious "peace." I was later informed that on Israeli TV that night, I was described as a well-known extremist and enemy of peace.

൞

I received the phone call a short time later.

"Rav Gold, this is Galit Ben-Zakai, the producer of *Popolitica*."

*Popolitica* was probably the most popular television show at that time. With millions of viewers and an exciting cast of panelists, headed by Tommy Lapid and Dan Margalit, it was *the* draw of the day.

The producer told me that *Popolitica* wanted to devote a segment to discussing a controversial statement that had been made by an American rabbi regarding the Rambam's view of punishment for a *moser* (a person who informs on a fellow Jew to secular authorities), and they wanted to have me on the show as a guest.

This came as a major shock. Not that a rabid anti-Charedi journalist like Tommy Lapid would devote an entire evening to shredding the religious yet again. That came as no surprise. No. The shock was that they were actually inviting a religious rabbi to respond and to present the other side of the picture. An appearance on the show would actually allow me to do some damage control.

I thought it over for a while, debating the pros and cons in my mind. The pros? I could turn the whole thing around and explain how the words of the Rambam were being misinterpreted.

The cons? I would be up against men who were experts at shredding people like me.

After much thought, I decided to take the risk. I would get on the show with a carefully crafted statement and would convincingly present my position.

Morning arrived. I was slated to appear on the show that night. I was filled with a terrible kind of tension. As the hours wore on, I became increasingly nervous. If their entire agenda was my destruction, what chance did I have? Maybe I was making a terrible mistake?

My phone rang a few hours before I was to leave for the studio.

"This is Galit from *Popolitica*. I'm sorry to have to cancel on you, but an emergency has just come up and tonight's show will be devoted to that instead."

I asked what had happened.

"Someone tried to kill Hosni Mubarak in Egypt. Once again I apologize for the inconvenience and hope that we will be able to have you on the show some other time."

"No problem," I said.

I meant it.

Looking back, I realize that G-d saved me that night. Agreeing to go on that show was a tremendous error on my part, because they would have roasted me alive. They were experts at that kind of thing, while I was a novice. They would have managed to elicit some statement from me that they would have intentionally misinterpreted, and it would have come back to haunt me for the next twenty years. G-d saved me that night in a big way. And Mubarak almost lost his life because of my mistake.

☙

The Jewish Agency was holding a meeting for its foreign members and the keynote speaker was Shimon Peres. He would be addressing some five to six hundred of the Jewish Agency's wealthiest supporters at the Crowne Plaza Hotel in Jerusalem.

At that time, I had a group of people who were my "right-hand men," always ready to drop anything for the cause: Moish Kempinsky (if you needed something done, he was your man), David Stahl, Moshe Halevi and Yehudit Spero.

Our group decided that we were going to infiltrate that meeting, our goal being to put Peres on the spot and question him in the middle of his speech.

Security was checking everybody who came in.

I'll never figure out how they did it, but twenty of the women got in and were dispersed throughout the crowd.

I arrived at the black-tie affair dressed appropriately for the occasion. I didn't look like a right-wing extremist. In fact, I was dressed very well. But I didn't have my invitation card.

"Did you leave it in your room?" the young, well-meaning security guard asked me.

I smiled slightly. He took that for a yes.

"Go on in," he said. Just like that, I was inside.

Peres avoided the truth from the beginning of his speech to the end. I began heckling him about Jerusalem, because there were reports about a secret letter he had sent promising to give away half of Jerusalem.

People began yelling at me to be silent.

Peres stopped them. "Let him talk," said the big peacemaker, in an elegant gesture of gallant statesmanship.

So we went at each other for a few minutes.

He held a question-and-answer period when he finished, more stretching of the truth from start to finish. There was going to be peace and everything was good and fine and wonderful.

A woman supporter of the Jewish Agency then asked the following insightful question (truthfully it was a pretty good question and I commended her in my mind for asking it): "Mr. Peres, what do you think we should do, what steps should we take, so that our children will feel as connected and loyal to Israel as we do?"

You could see his legendary brow furrowing in intense thought as the big man pondered the question. And then, as everyone was waiting in breathless anticipation for the brilliance that was sure to come, he came up with this jewel of thought: "Your children – teach them Hebrew!"

I almost burst out laughing and I said, "Every terrorist speaks Hebrew." I should have said it louder, but at least everyone around me heard. That was his brilliant idea? Educate your children, your future generations by teaching them Hebrew? That's it? How sad.

After the event was over, three people approached me in quick succession and made the following comment: "Rabbi, you're a zealot and the zealots destroyed the Temple!"

I hadn't known that. I thought it was the Romans.

I ignored the first two. But when a woman from Boston came over to deliver the same line, I had to ask her a few questions.

"Who said so?" I asked her. "Where did you hear this novel idea? Who said that the zealots destroyed the Temple?"

"The prime minister spoke to us last night. Rabin. And he ended his speech by saying, 'You should know that the zealots destroyed the Temple.'"

That was the bottom line. Anyone who disagreed with the men in charge was a zealot. They turned anyone who had a different opinion into a zealot. They smeared their characters. They made them persona non grata. They carried out an outstanding campaign of muddying tactics. They knew exactly what to say to convince the world that they, and only they, had the country's best interests in mind. And they succeeded to a great degree.

# 21

# THE WAGES OF "PEACE"

When the news item first appeared in the papers, I read it over and over, shocked at how much it bothered me, even after so much time. On December 10, 1994, Yitzhak Rabin, Shimon Peres, and Yasser Arafat were slated to receive the Nobel Peace Prize at an exclusive ceremony attended by the Who's Who of Western civilization in the city of Oslo, where it all began. The actual award-giving ceremony was to take place on a Motzaei Shabbat, a year and a half after they had signed the accords in the first place. The brave soldiers of peace were off to Oslo to reap the benefits of their labors.

Meir Indor put together a group of about 150 people who had lost family members due to terror attacks and flew them out to Oslo to demonstrate against the peace process. I was invited to join this august group, an invitation I accepted on the condition that my son Yirmi accompany me.

We landed in Oslo on Friday and arrived at our hotel at about two thirty in the afternoon. Shabbat started early in that northern city. The hotel was a fifteen-minute walk from the hall where the ceremony was being held and a fifteen-minute walk in the opposite direction from the shul where everyone – Rabin and Peres included – were davening that Friday night.

It's extremely cold in Oslo.

In the month of December it's like a freezing version of Gehinnom. Smoke pouring out of every mouth.

We arrived at the one shul in Oslo a few minutes after the services had already begun. Rabin and Peres being in attendance meant that the security team had already locked the door of the shul and wouldn't allow anyone in. The fact that we were not granted access to the shul, if anything, stirred us up even more. We held an incredible Friday night prayer service outside in the frigid Oslo night – a service like Oslo had never seen before. I would not care to repeat the experience, but I will never forget it either.

We were a few hundred people demonstrating outside the shul on the famous Friday night lockout in Oslo. The majority were people from Israel, but there were quite a few there from the United States as well and even a small number from Europe. We lined the side of the barricaded road and waited for Rabin and Peres to emerge from the shul and to commence their walk through the icy cold back to their hotel.

Despite the fact that I disagreed with their policies regarding Oslo with every fiber of my being, part of me could not help but respect the two of them for a demonstration of Jewish pride. Rabin and Peres walking through the streets of Europe on a Friday night so as to avoid desecrating Shabbat. A fifteen- or twenty-minute walk, in bitter, bitter cold.

The next morning on the way to shul we couldn't help but notice the headlines on the Oslo newspapers. There were large pictures of Peres with his face covered in blood. He'd slipped on the snow and ice the night before and had been lucky to escape with a bloody nose and nothing more. I guess that's worth something in heaven.

Rabbi Michoel Melchior, the rabbi of Oslo, having heard that I was extremely upset about what had occurred at the previous evening's services, apologized publicly to us all the next day at the *kiddush* following the davening. We ate the morning meal together at our hotel. The day passed extremely quickly; Oslo in the winter has a lot more darkness than daylight. All told, Oslo is a pretty depressing place. On Motzaei Shabbat we drove over to the Grand Hotel where the big three were staying and greeted them with a fresh burst of jeers when they left to the Oslo City Hall, a short distance away, for the Nobel Prize Awarding Ceremony.

There we were standing outside the town hall for hours, as the festive lights twinkled in the brightly lit building and the media personalities and politicians were escorted out of their fancy cars and into the town hall to watch two Jews and one Arab terrorist share a prize that was a mockery and a sham and might have been the worst prize ever handed out in the Oslo world of unethical hypocrisy. We were so emotional, so worked up – screaming for hours without letup, answering questions thrown at us from journalists and yelling some more – that I don't even remember being cold.

And so, the freezing streets of Oslo are clearly the closest I will ever get to a Nobel Peace Prize.

And when I asked myself why I felt the need to stand in the freezing cold of an unsympathetic Oslo and scream myself hoarse, while Rabin and Peres stood inside surrounded by the warm adoration of the nations of the world, I answered the question thusly. If no Jews protested the travesty in Oslo that night, it would have been a tremendous desecration of G-d's name. No. Someone had to go on record protesting the injustice of it all. And I was proud to be one of those people, with Yirmi at my side. There were some close encounters with big horses and Viking-tall police. We stood our ground while our hearts were breaking.

We went home the next day. I did not tour Oslo. And If I never see that accursed city again, it will be perfectly fine with me.

☙

On the Sunday morning of January 22, 1995, there was a catastrophic terrorist attack at a bus stop in Beit Lid, right outside Netanya. Soldiers had been congregating around the bus stop, waiting for the buses that would transport them back to their bases. The terrorists exploded one bomb, instantly killing and maiming many, and then when the victims' comrades rushed toward the site of the explosion to help them, the terrorists detonated a second bomb. They exploited the soldiers' natural instinct to come to their fellows' aid in order to increase the kill rate by striking down many of the would-be rescuers. Twenty-one soldiers were killed in the brutal attack. It was a terrible, terrible attack and the outcry rose toward the heavens.

What usually occurred after a terrorist attack was that people would instinctively begin to drift together all over the country to city squares to demonstrate against the government, whose policies were on a collision course with the nation's collective sanity. In Yerushalayim, the gathering place for demonstrations was at Zion Square, at the corners of Jaffa and Ben Yehuda Streets in the center of town. Without any announcements or signs advertising the event, people began streaming toward Zion Square that evening in masses, filling the square and pouring onto the surrounding streets.

The people were angry and they wanted to tell the world that they were unwilling to put up with this any longer.

They were fed up with their crazy government.

Within half an hour there were so many people in Zion Square that you could barely move. Thousands were already there and more were arriving. Dozens of police had taken up positions alongside the edges of the crowd and were waiting.

I was standing at the edge of the crowd just beside a police van that was serving as the police force's impromptu headquarters when I heard the commander order to his team of police to "rush the crowd and get them out of the square."

Nobody was doing anything wrong. There was no reason in the world to cause them harm. The police would be attacking innocent civilians for no reason. I turned to the police commander and said, "Excuse me, nobody has done anything illegal here. The whole country is in pain. Everyone here is just sharing in that painful suffering. Twenty boys were killed today. What do you want from them?"

"GET AWAY FROM HERE!" he bellowed at me while reiterating his instructions to the police to get ready to rush the crowd.

I began going from policeman to policeman, saying, "They are our brothers and sisters. We're all in pain here. Don't listen to him!"

The commander got very upset with me. He began pushing me, yelling at me to get away from there immediately. Before I knew it, he had maneuvered me into the hands of some policemen who began shoving me forcefully away from Zion Square, up Ben Yehuda Street, the roar of the crowd in my ears, me screaming at them the entire time to leave the crowd alone, them paying me no attention, no heed.

Eventually the commanding officer grew fed up with me and delivered the following ultimatum: "Either you leave now," he said, "or I will be forced to arrest you."

"I'm a rabbi," I replied, "and my responsibility is to make sure that there is no violence between Jew and fellow Jew. I'm not going to stop until I make sure that nothing happens."

"Arrest the rabbi!"

Two policemen surrounded me on either side and a third joined them from behind, and together they began attempting to manhandle me forcefully toward the back of a far-off paddy wagon. Not that I was going peacefully. No. I was fighting them off and yelling the entire time, "Don't hurt those kids in the square. They're in pain, just like you!"

All of a sudden, who should come marching down the street? None other than my son Yirmi, who took one look at the three policemen arresting his *abba*, and throwing caution to the wind began grabbing the cops off me – an illegal act in anyone's book.

The commander took one look at the new developments and, pointing at Yirmi, yelled, "Arrest him too!"

The next thing I knew, we both were being pulled through the crowd in the direction of the vehicle that would transport us to jail. The roar of the crowd was deafening by now, voices chanting endlessly, raised in spirited shouting, when the police made the mistake of shoving me right through all those thousands of people. The moment we entered that gigantic crowd – that hollering, angry, surging sea of people – a silence descended on the thousands of yelling, shouting people in that endless mob. A silence so thick as to be almost tangible. They looked on in quiet wonder at the sight of the policemen shoving and pushing a white-bearded rabbi who didn't stop struggling and resisting the entire time while screaming at the top of his lungs that the crowd should not be harmed, that they were in pain too!

They pulled me past the sport shops and the shoe stores and the jewelry businesses and restaurants, past the numerous establishments that would normally be doing a brisk business, paying no attention to my screams and shouts. But even they couldn't ignore the silence of the crowd. Because that silence spoke infinitely louder and more powerfully than words could ever have.

I could hear the people whispering, "They're arresting the *rav*, they're taking the *rav* to jail!"

I didn't know that these Israeli kids even knew that I was a *rav*.

There was a paddy wagon on Jaffa Road and they dumped me and Yirmi into the jail-like enclosure in back, locking the door with a resounding clatter.

It was at that point that my wife Bayla came running up to the side of the paddy wagon and said to me with urgency in her voice, "Sholom, the car keys – you have the car keys!"

And I was thinking, "Your husband has just been taken away, you may never see him again, and all you can think of is the car keys?"

The truth is that she wanted those car keys so as to go for help, but far be it from me not to enjoy a little bit of humor in this otherwise extremely depressing situation.

Next thing we knew, someone got into the cab up front and drove us the few blocks to the Russian Compound for processing and booking. The Russian Compound was a mob scene. People were milling about in every direction, everyone talking at the top of their lungs, policemen everywhere. It was a wild scene on a cold, damp, dank night, and Yirmi and I were going to prison. On the way into the Russian Compound I caught sight of Uri Ariel, today a member of Knesset, then a political activist. He was yelling into one of those old-fashioned cell phones, the kind you needed a crane to lift.

"I just found out that they arrested Rav Gold," he was yelling.

I tapped him on the back. He turned around, looked at me in surprise.

"It's true," I said. "I'm here."

They took us in for processing.

They wanted to book Yirmi too, but I explained to them that Yirmi really had had nothing to do with the entire scene, that he'd just come along to help his elderly father.

It wasn't the first time I had pulled the "elderly father" routine. The cops went for it. These weren't the same police who had arrested me and they didn't know what was going on. I mean, the complete disarray in that police station cannot be described. Yirmi was free to leave, but he wasn't going anywhere. He was planning to remain with me until this crazy nightmare wound its way to the bitter end.

They booked me for disturbing the peace.

"This," I quipped, "is a peace that should be disturbed. This is not peace."

I turned to Yirmi. "Aren't I supposed to get one phone call? Isn't that the way it works? Where's my one phone call?"

He told me that as we were being pushed through the crowd, one of his friends had handed him a phone. "You don't need your one phone call, Abba, you can have as many phone calls as you want."

Now I had a phone, but for the life of me, I couldn't figure out who I should call.

So we waited.

We waited on a hard wooden bench in a dismal hallway in some corner of the Russian Compound, while the sounds of yelling began to evaporate and abate and the dead silence of the Jerusalem nighttime started filtering through all the noise. Peace was about to descend on Jerusalem's jail. Still we waited to find out what they were going to do to me. Honestly, the waiting was worse than anything else. It was absolutely nerve-racking.

It was about two hours later when a policeman approached.

"Follow me," he said, his tone and demeanor stern. Tough. Playing the part of the big, unapproachable cop. My heart began beating faster in my chest. He led me along a dark, dimly lit corridor.

"Gold," I'm thinking to myself, "this is the big moment. You have to be strong. The Chinese torture is about to commence. Think of Yosef Mendelevich in the Soviet gulag. Be strong. Just stand there and be strong!"

At the end of a corridor that seemed to last forever, he deposited me in the classic interrogation room.

A bare little bulb was hanging over the table.

The original officer who had booked me was sitting there.

"Sit down."

I sat, waiting for my interrogation to begin.

The officer lifted his head, met my eyes.

"*Kvod harav*" (honorable rabbi), he said, and my head whipped up in surprise at these respectful words, "my father passed away a month ago. I have a lot of questions regarding the laws of mourning. Can you answer my questions, please?"

He delivered this line like a lost sheep, desperately seeking reassurance.

We sat there, I answered every last one of his questions, and the entire time I'm thinking to myself, "*Mi k'amcha Yisrael?*" (Who is like Your nation Israel?).

When we finished talking, he shook my hand and said, "Rabbi, you're free to go."

A few minutes later, at a quarter to one in the morning, Yirmi and I danced out of the Russian Compound into a quiet Yerushalayim and a night that seemed much less dismal all of a sudden. The air was bracing. All in all, it was a night of pain, anguish, and that great feeling that *amcha*, the people, are precious, caring, and know the truth.

❧

The next few years were filled with endless tension and moments of tremendous sadness. Ambulance sirens were familiar acquaintances by then and little children had gotten into the habit of dressing up like members of Zaka on Purim. Nobody was safe from the suicide bombers. Israeli security forces were on constant alert as they attempted to foil the never-ceasing flow of terrorist attacks. It was a truly untenable situation.

Some of the more gruesome attacks made even the stone-hearted world take notice.

The attack outside the Dolphinarium in Tel Aviv in which twenty-one teenagers were killed and 132 wounded.

The gut-wrenching attack at a Netanya hotel that killed dozens of people who were sitting down to their Pesach Seder, bringing new meaning to the timeless words of the Haggadah, "*B'chol dor va'dor omdim aleinu l'chaloteinu*" (in every generation, they rise up to destroy us).

There would be the incredibly painful attack on Yeshivat Mercaz Harav later, in which an Arab terrorist killed eight of the *yeshivah*'s pure, talented students in cold blood while they were sitting and studying in the *yeshivah*'s library.

The list went on and on.

The Sbarro pizza shop bombing.

The triple bombing on Ben Yehuda Street.

The bombing at Machane Yehuda.

The list seemed to stretch on to infinity. Sometimes it felt like it was never going to end.

Many were the times we demonstrated at the intersection at the entrance to Yerushalayim. There we stood, holding placards, yelling slogans, showing the world our displeasure at the craziness that had taken control of the country. Once a bunch of *yeshivah* students on their way to the bus stop across from where I stood passed me by and a few of them stopped for a second and said to me, "Why are you even wasting your time? It's not going to help. Nobody's listening."

I think they felt bad for me.

I took a break from calling out to passing motorists and spoke to those boys from the heart.

"I'm surprised that *yeshivah* students such as yourselves aren't familiar with the Brisker Rav's famous *vort*."

That caught their interest.

I explained.

"The Brisker Rav asked a question. We all know about Pharaoh's three advisers, Bilaam, Yisro, and Iyov. Bilaam advised the king to decimate the Jewish nation. Iyov remained silent. Yisro objected and fled. Iyov was afflicted with incredible suffering in the years to come. The commentators attribute that suffering to the fact that he remained silent in the face of the Jewish nation's tribulations. But why was he punished, asked the Brisker Rav, when there was nothing that he could do? When he didn't do anything wrong?

"The answer, said the Brisker Rav, lies in this idea: Sure, there was really nothing for Iyov to do. He was truly powerless. Not only that, but were he to have protested it would not have helped the Jews at all. It would have been a complete waste of time. Sort of like what I'm doing right now. But G-d expected something from Iyov. G-d demanded of him to care enough to give a *krechtz* or two. To sigh. To ask 'What will become of the Jewish people?'

"Because even if you can't stop something, even if you know that Pharaoh is going to go ahead and carry out the final solution, basic humanity demands that you give a *krechtz*, a groan, a sigh. Do you see what's happening to Klal Yisrael? Jews are being killed, there's a terrible process taking place even as we speak, and people don't have the time or inclination to offer up a *krechtz*. No '*oy vey!*' *Az es tut vey, shreit men*. When it hurts, you scream!"

They had nothing more to ask of me.

ஃ

A vital meeting took place at the home of Rav Avraham Shapira on July 12, 1995.

The topic at hand? A halachic ruling for the soldiers of Israel.

The question? The government was planning on dismantling a number of military bases in Yehudah and Shomron. What was a soldier to do, in the event that he received an order to assist in the dismantling of an army base in the State of Israel? It was a thorny and explosive question, and many people in the Dati Leumi world were waiting to hear how their rabbis were going to rule. A loaded situation.

At the end of our discussion, a ruling was rendered. It was as clear a ruling as possible. No ambiguity. *Seiruv pekudah*! One was obligated to disobey the order. A soldier must go to jail rather than obey those orders. The reasoning behind our ruling was that dismantling an army base in Yehudah and Shomron was a matter of life and death. It would leave the area open for terrorist infiltration.

Someone leaked word to the press that the rabbis were meeting to discuss the hottest topic of the day: disobeying a direct order. The very essence of the fabric of the army. Just walking into Rav Avraham's house meant wading through an army of video cameras. The entire street was filled with media trucks and journalists. We knew exactly what was going to happen when we released our ruling. We knew that we were going to be denigrated and vilified by the entire establishment.

I remember an interview that I gave for one of the big media corporations. They sat in my living room and the interviewer asked me, "Rabbi, how can you condone such a thing? This could destroy the army!"

"We are the post-Holocaust generation," I replied. "Is an Israeli soldier ever going to be able to say 'I was only following orders'? Is this what we expect of ourselves or did we learn differently from bitter experience? We lost six million in order to learn that we don't follow orders blindly. Any order that will leave Jews in grave danger is not an order that should be carried out simply because it is an order.

"I'll tell you something else," I went on. "I come from the United States and everybody there understands that there is such a thing as a conscientious objector. Sometimes there are things I cannot do because I don't believe in them. And nobody can force me to go against my most basic and fundamental beliefs."

I once read an interview with a soldier who was part of the team sent by David Ben-Gurion and Moshe Dayan to deal with the *Altalena* (the boat full of weapons that had been brought by Menachem Begin, then commander of the Irgun). He had refused to obey those orders. Yitzhak Rabin, then a young commander in the Haganah, gave the order to shoot the *Altalena*. The soldier who had been ordered to shoot the canon refused the order. He later claimed that "the greatest decision I ever made in my life was to disobey that order. And," he continued, "I know the soldier who obeyed the order and ended up killing sixteen men and wounding many others. He hasn't had a moment of peace in his life because of that decision."

Sometimes the greatest thing a person can do is to disobey a wrong command.

One year, I was asked to chair a session of the Israeli news station Arutz Sheva's Jerusalem Conference at the Hyatt Hotel.

The journalist Yedidya Atlas told me that I would be privileged to introduce Dr. Bernard Lewis, the world-famous expert on the Middle East. Yedidya chose me because he knew that I had read Lewis's books and was an avid fan. Before the session, he introduced me to the distinguished guest. I asked Dr. Lewis, "How is it possible for the government to continue the Oslo process in view of your explanation that jihad in Muslim belief leaves no place for compromise but stipulates that war must be waged against the infidels until victory?" He answered simply with the words of the prophet Yirmiyahu (5:21): "*Einayim lahem v'lo yir'u*" (They have eyes but do not see).

When the time came for the final session to begin and I was preparing to ascend the dais, someone came running over to me and said that Dr. Lewis pronounces his first name, Bernard, with emphasis on the first syllable. I thanked him. A moment later, a second fellow came running over, out of breath, and told me that Dr. Lewis insists that his first name be pronounced with clear emphasis on the second syllable. I now had a problem. I had these two options that I had to choose from. I could simply introduce him as Dr. Lewis. I chose a different approach. While everyone was waiting in the silent hall, I walked over to our guest and asked him, "Do you have a Hebrew name?"

"Yes. Dov," he told me.

I approached the microphone and said, "It makes no difference to me how the professor's name is pronounced throughout the world, but here in Yerushalayim he is our own Reb Dov. Ladies and gentlemen, the world's expert on Islam and the Middle East, Reb Dov Lewis." Dr. Lewis was beaming from ear to ear.

※

The BBC called me up for a comment after the signing of Oslo II, the Israeli-Palestinian Interim Agreement on the West Bank and the Gaza Strip, on September 28, 1995.

They wanted to know my opinion on the matter.

"In ten years from now," I told them, "it won't be worth the paper it's written on. It's useless and valueless. And it will eventually be relegated to the garbage dumps of history. I'll give you an example of a worthless piece of paper," I told my BBC interviewer. "In May 1939, His Majesty's government issued an infamous White Paper, setting a limit of seventy-five thousand Jewish immigrants for the five-year period of 1940 to 1944. After that date, further Jewish immigration would depend on the permission of the Arab majority. What happened to that White Paper?" I asked my BBC interviewer rhetorically. "There are five million Jews in Israel today despite your White Paper, which currently finds itself consigned to the garbage heaps of history. That will be the fate of Oslo II."

    I enjoyed that interview very much.

～

Of course, all anti-Oslo activism ceased on one Motzaei Shabbat that will go down in Israeli history as the night that changed the country. I am referring to the evening that Prime Minister Yitzhak Rabin was assassinated by Yigal Amir at a peace rally in Tel Aviv. His death served as a fatal blow to the Israeli Right, as the Israeli Left, its journalists and media personalities all condemned the Right for having caused the assassination. We were all being accused of murdering the prime minister, Charedim and Dati Leumi alike. The Likud. Settlers. Netanyahu. All tarred with the same brush. The brush of the killer.

～

The *Mesillat Yesharim* identified two types of moral blindness. The first is when darkness covers one's eyes so that he simply does not see what danger lurks before him. The second kind of blindness is more severe. Man is deceived to the point that he sees a man and thinks it's a pillar, or sees a pillar and thinks that it is a man.

    Intellectual blindness stems from a distortion rooted in one's mind, a strongly held belief or philosophy that is false.

    This blindness can be of two kinds. One, when a person is unaware of what is happening around him. He is blind to the evils of the world. The more serious syndrome is when one sees evil and thinks it is good.

    Both types of blindness descended upon Israel on the day of the infamous handshake. How could a sane, rational, and intelligent people invite into their homeland the architect of global terrorism and tens of thousands of his terrorist killers and hope to make peace with them? How could our government do something that no other nation has ever done? How could they begin a headlong rush into folly? Blindness, willful blindness, turning a blind eye. Even the *Mesillat Yesharim* could never have imagined such blindness.

We stood at the intersections of Israel's major highways with placards and signs in our hands reading "Don't Give Them Rifles!!!" We did this over and over. But it didn't help because the people were blind. We demonstrated. Petitioned. Faxed. E-mailed. Wrote. Spoke. Argued and debated. All to no avail. The keepers of the state knew better than we what was good for us.

The man on the street mistakenly saw killer as man and murderer as partner. That was the first kind of blindness. Far more dangerous were those who suffered from the second kind of blindness. Those who were intellectually convinced that we would be able to make peace with our neighbors. Those who believed that a man like Arafat had turned into a peaceful dove in his old age. Those who believed that we had "stolen the land" from the Arabs.

Moral blindness. It's a terrible thing.

It was the blind leading the blind.

☙

Eighteen years later in February 2013 I received a call from a friend who told me, "Rabbi, you're in the movie." For the next two weeks nearly everyone I met said, "You're in the movie." The movie they were all talking about was *The Gatekeepers*, a documentary built around interviews with the six living heads of the Shin Bet, Israel's security service. Their dialogue is accompanied by film footage spanning some thirty years of clandestine activity that is quite impressive. For the Oslo years, they chose films of a number of demonstrations in Zion Square in Jerusalem. That's where I appear speaking before the thousands assembled to express opposition to the ill-conceived and ill-fated accords.

I was transported back in time to relive the pain and the fear that gripped us. In the planning stages of these gatherings I would usually insist that we prepare signs and placards in English so that the world press would have something to show globally, carrying our message. I would also suggest that it would be a good idea to have someone address the gathering in English for the benefit of the press and for many of the protesters who were English-speakers. The usual response was, "Well, you do it." So I did. So there you have it. Eighteen years later, making a film to be shown all over the world, they chose me speaking in English and not Netanyahu, Sharon, or Landau.

*The Gatekeepers* was nominated for an Oscar. The thought did cross my mind that it might have been because of my powerful and eloquent twenty-five-second appearance, but ultimately I concluded that perhaps it was because of the other hour-and-a-half of the film.

It didn't receive an Oscar and that was a relief. The tone and tenor of the dialogue was classic Left. "Settlements are the obstacle to peace." "Yigal Amir killed the peace process." No mention of Palestinian refusal to make peace. In 1948 they were opposed to partition and remain so today. Don't they realize that Herzliyah and Kiryat Arba, Netanya and Tapuach are all "settlements" in Palestinian thought? It was pitiful. They still don't get it. They agonized about protecting Arab civilians to the point that it seemed that they might have lost sight of the fact that their prime purpose is to protect Israeli civilians. Why don't they let the Hamas "heroes" who cower behind women and children protect their own civilians.

In my brief appearance in the film I spoke of the promises made to the people at the inception of the Oslo Accords. "You promised us peace and we got war, you promised us life and we got death, you promised us tranquility and we got terror!"

The film did strengthen my conviction that Hashem is watching over us. Israel's security service pulled off masterful strikes against the enemy. Hashem does not slumber nor sleep.

When I finally did go to the theater to see the movie, in the lobby afterwards, a woman came over to me and asked, "What did you think of the assassination?" So many thoughts flew through my head. Should I ask her if she meant in comparison to the Kennedy and Lincoln assassinations? But I understood what she was getting at. She really expected a religious Jew to say that he approved of the assassination. Rabin had it coming. She believed, eighteen years later, that more than half the country killed Rabin. I was enraged. My response was pained and defiant: "In all my life I have never been asked such an ugly question. A profound tragedy occurred and you ask what do I think about the assassination?"

The woman literally ran away from me. Her escort explained that her father was a leading political figure and he suffered from "them." I assume that means the religious, the Right, the settlers. I was very saddened by this brief exchange. They still believe we are all guilty. To top it all off, in the movie they showed quite prominently the infamous picture of Rabin in an SS uniform, the surefire sign that we incited the masses against him. But we all know that the despicable picture was the work of one of the Shabak's own agents, Avishai Raviv, in order to stain the entire Right.

We were opposed to Oslo and we were right.

༒

It was February 1996 when the bus bombings began in earnest. Day after day we were faced with exploding death in the streets of Yerushalayim. It was a heavy-hearted routine. Those never-ending sirens. Ambulances rushing past.

This went on for years.

There's a sign near Aza Street in the Rechavia neighborhood of Jerusalem in memory of Chezi Goldberg. He was on a bus that blew up. Chezi was a *tzaddik*. I know we say that about a lot of people, but in his case, it happens to be true. Originally from Toronto, he was a social worker and special ed counselor who never stopped trying to think of new ways to help people, especially kids. He was killed at the end of January 2004. I remember this clearly, because he had made an appointment to meet with me a few days into February, but he never made it to that appointment. He left behind a wife and seven beautiful young children. Chezi Goldberg – may he be remembered for the good.

༒

Erev Rosh Hashanah 2000, the Second Intifada erupted. Hostilities intensified from day to day. Rav Avraham Shapira called a meeting of a small group of *rabbanim* in his *sukkah*. Some were regulars like Rav Yehoshua Magnes, Rav Yosef Artziel, and Rav Menachem Felix, and some were people I was meeting for the first time. One *rav* in particular made a deep impression on me. He spoke with such passion and sincerity about Yerushalayim and Har Habayit and the guilt that we must bear for not having done enough to guard the sanctity of the holy places. After the meeting I went to make his acquaintance and learned that he was Rav Binyomin Herling. A *talmid chacham* and a *rosh yeshivah*, he was a resident of Elon Moreh and involved with his whole soul in the struggle for Eretz Yisrael. An aura of sanctity enveloped him.

Later that week, on the night of Hoshanah Rabbah, I gave the opening *shiur* of the all-night Torah study in the OU Israel Center. Phil Chernofksy, the director of educational activities, made certain every year that I opened the proceedings. Phil, a good friend, is the creator of *Torah Tidbits*. That day, a Thursday, was fraught with great tension. A group of hikers, attacked by terrorists, had been pinned down on Mount Eval near Shechem.

Following the *shiur* I returned home, put on the radio, and heard that on Mount Eval, Rav Binyomin Herling was killed. Rav Binyomin, who was a *tzaddik*, brutally murdered on the land he loved so much.

ۿ

It was just another demonstration on Highway 1. We were stopping traffic across the main artery leading into Jerusalem. Denying vehicles entry to Jerusalem can heat things up pretty quickly, because there are numerous cars entering the holy city on a minute-to-minute basis and a human chain across that particular stretch of road ensures a traffic jam that will last for miles. If you're trying to make a point, this is an effective way to do so.

The police responded quickly. Their task was to get the protesters out of the avenue immediately. Within moments they were swarming everywhere, wielding their batons liberally. I got shoved to the ground by a burly officer, my *kippah* fell off, and I couldn't see it anywhere.

The policeman hoisted me up off the ground and requested that I move back to the side of the road.

"I need my *kippah*!" I told him emphatically.

It was almost nighttime by then and the lighting was of the dim variety that obscures and blinds. You couldn't clearly see where anything was.

"I'm not moving!"

While this was going on, I saw a number of policemen out of the corner of my eye pushing someone else. Another glance and I realized to my utter shock and dismay that they were shoving Yosef Mendelevich to the ground. Yosef Mendelevich! The man who had looked the Russian bear in the eye and had not been afraid. Being shoved to the ground in Eretz Yisrael, by the very people he had so longed to join. The irony was incredible, indescribable.

I ran over.

"*Zeh gibor Yisrael*" (this man is a hero of Israel), I told one of the policemen, "a prisoner of conscience. Don't hit him!"

The cop got scared. They hoisted Yosef up from the floor. He had lost his glasses and couldn't see a thing.

The commanding officer gave an order. "Everyone is to look for Yosef Mendelevich's glasses." They searched for his glasses, found them, and returned them. They also searched for my *kippah*, found it, and returned it. I grabbed hold of Yosef Mendelevich and we both moved to the side of the road.

I could see how bad those young cops felt for having mistreated such a hero.

That's what it was like back then.

From one end of the human spectrum to the other. In a matter of moments.

ܐ

We celebrated the *aufruf* of Chanan Sand in our shul one Shabbat. His parents, Tzvi and Tamara Sand, were longtime members of the shul, good friends and wonderful people. The parents of the *kallah*, Dr. David and Debbie Applebaum, came walking in from Rechavia. After davening we held a *kiddush* and David Applebaum came over to me.

"Rabbi Gold, I haven't heard a *drashah* of such passion since the last time I heard you speak."

Those were the final words we exchanged with one another.

The wedding had been called for Wednesday night. Before I went to sleep that Tuesday night, I knew that there had been an attack at Cafe Hillel but I still didn't know who the victims were.

At seven o'clock the next morning, I found out. The phone rang. My daughter Chavi was on the line.

"Abba," she said, and there was a quality in her voice that I had never heard before. "Do you know who was killed in that *pigua*?" My heart dropped to the floor. Who would it be this time?

"Dr. David Applebaum…and the *kallah* Naava." The walls closed in on me. The room swam before my eyes and I gave a scream from the innermost depths of my soul. I don't think I have ever given a cry like that in all my life. It woke my wife.

This was the worst tragedy I could think of.

A bride on the eve of her wedding! Sitting with her father, full of joy, brimming over with happiness. Her whole life to look forward to. All snuffed out in the flower of youth. Over. Finality. Tragic doesn't sum it up. There are no words.

Dr. Applebaum. What a great man. A Torah scholar. A student of Rav Ahron Soloveichik. He put out Rav Ahron's *sefer* on the Rambam. A specialist and innovator in the field of emergency medicine. A revolutionary in the concept of the emergency room and how it should operate for key results. He revitalized the concept of emergency care.

And he was a brave man in addition to it all.

I remember an attack on Jaffa Road. There was shooting everywhere. Bullets were flying around people's heads. And there was David Applebaum, working on someone who was injured and paying no attention whatsoever to all the firing. Bullets whistled around his head and he didn't even notice. He was too intent on saving another life. There was a picture of it in the newspaper. Unbelievable. A prize-winning picture.

That week he'd been out of the country leading a seminar in the field of emergency care. He had returned just in time for the wedding.

Naava's wedding dress was later sewn into a *parochet* for the holy ark at Kever Rachel.

I don't get to the Shaare Zedek hospital that often, thank G-d, but whenever I'm there and I see the large portrait of Dr. David Applebaum hanging in its prominent place of honor right at the entrance to the emergency room, I stand for a few minutes and cry like a baby. The last time I was there, I was standing before the picture when I noticed the date of his death...and then I realized that his *yahrtzeit* was that day. And I cried and I cried... Great, great people.

And there were others. May 13, 1996, Dovid Boim, a student at the Mateh Binyamin High School in Beit El, was waiting for a bus when he was killed by Hamas terrorists. He was only seventeen years old. Dovid from Har Nof, the son of Joyce and Stanley Boim. And there were others: Aharon Gross, Nachshon Wachsman, Alisa Flatow, Rabbi Hillel Liberman, Samuel Berg, Sarah Blaustein, Shoshana Greenbaum. Yaron Ungar and his wife, Rav Binyamin Kahana and Talia, Malka Roth, Dr. Moshe Gottlieb, Judith Greenbaum, Allan Beer, and the list goes on... *Hashem yinkom damam.*

Lists are so cold and impersonal but this one is searing with pain. A country stopped for a week praying for Nachshon. Friday night in Har Nof, as in many other places, we congregated in the streets to pray – and then after Shabbat the sad news and the funeral at Har Herzl. Aharon Gross in the middle of Chevron, Dr. Gottlieb on a bus... All holy *neshomot*, all pure, all cut down by a hatred that knows no end, a Lethal Obsession (the title of Robert Wistrich's magnum opus that chronicles anti-Semitism through history).

Whenever I speak about these terrible happenings, about the never to be forgotten experiences in those months of terror, I end my speech with the following verse from Yeshayahu 65: "Only rejoice and be happy forever, for what I am creating. For behold, I am recreating Jerusalem as gladness and its city as joy. For I will rejoice over Jerusalem and exult with My people and there will no longer be heard in it the sound of weeping and the sound of outcry."

# 22

# OF CLASSES, TRIPS, AND TRAVELING

I was asked to deliver a class to an outstanding group of women at the old Israel Center on Strauss Street, one Motzaei Shabbat. This particular group was completely dedicated to Kever Rachel and my speech would have to reflect that element. It was an extremely busy night for me. After the Israel Center speech, I had another affair to attend – a seventieth birthday party for Irving Maisel (he who had stood at my side and confronted Yossi Beilin at the Dead Sea a few years earlier). After that I had a flight to catch at Ben-Gurion Airport. And as usual I had a busy Shabbat of *drashot* and *shiurim*.

Yes, it was a busy night.

My wife basically forbade me to drive. "You're under a lot of pressure right now and it's not a good idea. You have too many places to go and you can't do it on your own. Yirmi is driving you."

The order had been given and I acquiesced gracefully. It happened to be that she was right. Motzaei Shabbat rolled around and Yirmi drove me to the old Israel Center. As I sat there in the car, I realized that I simply did not know what to say. I had spent time preparing a speech for that Shabbat morning and a Torah thought for Friday night and a class for Shabbat afternoon and that was all besides my set of regular weekly classes. I simply hadn't had the time to prepare anything.

We drove past Binyanei Hauma and I looked heavenward and said, "Master of the world, please help me!"

As we drove up Agrippas Street, the kernel of a thought flew into my mind. We turned from Agrippas onto Haneviim Street. We were almost there and I still needed a little time to develop my tiny thought into an appropriate speech. At the corner of Haneviim and Strauss Streets there is a traffic light which was then red, thereby providing me with another few precious minutes to think. As the light turned green, Yirmi made a left turn and parked in front of the center, while I got out of the car, the final touches of the speech still crystallizing in my mind.

I spoke about one of the most painful conversations in all of Torah: the one between Rachel and Yaakov Avinu, regarding Rachel Imeinu's state of childlessness (Bereishit 30:1–2).

Rachel says to Yaakov, "Give me children and if not then I am dead!"

"*Va'yichar af Yaakov b'Rachel*" (Yaakov got angry at Rachel), and he said, "*Hatachas Elokim anochi asher mana mimech pri vaten?*" (Am I the One Above Who is withholding children from you?).

In effect Yaakov is asking, *What do you want from me? Am I G-d? Do I have the power to grant a person children?*

Let's examine this scenario for a second. What does Rachel want from Yaakov? "Give me children and if not then I am dead!" That's irrational. It's illogical. It makes no sense.

And shouldn't Yaakov understand that Rachel is a woman who is crying out from the very depths of her pain? Her sister Leah is bearing child after child while she has none? Doesn't he comprehend the enormous pain of a woman who has no children? Doesn't he realize how terrible it is? She has no children. Doesn't he feel bad for her? She is the one he loves so deeply. Why does he reply to her in such a harsh manner? It seems unfeeling, cold, and distant.

Here I looked around at my audience, who were listening intently, and then I continued as follows.

The *Mesillat Yesharim* in the fourth chapter tells us that G-d reprimanded Yaakov Avinu with the following words: "*Kach onin et hame'ukot?* Is this the way you answer a woman in pain?"

Indeed, G-d gave Yaakov Avinu reproof over his choice of words.

Yet if so, what was the correct way to speak? What should Yaakov Avinu have said? What would have been the proper way for him to have addressed his wife?

Why didn't Yaakov turn to his wife and say, "Rocheleh, let's say another chapter of Tehillim together, let's storm the gates of heaven"?

"After thinking things over," I told the assembled, "I have to conclude that there is a lot more to this exchange than meets the eye."

Fast forward. It's the day of the Temple's destruction. Yirmiyahu has been sent by G-d to rouse the forefathers and together they stand before Hashem, interceding with Him not to carry out the terrible decree.

Avraham's plea is rejected.

Yitzchak's plea is rejected.

Yaakov's plea is rejected.

All of a sudden, Rachel Imeinu comes walking in. And Yaakov is standing there, watching intently.

The prophet Yirmiyahu (31:14) tells us the following: *"Rachel mevakah al baneiha...ki einenu"* (Rachel cries for her children...for they are no more).

Rachel is crying out for her children. Pleading with G-d for her children who are being sent into exile. Yaakov is waiting with bated breath. What will G-d reply to her anguished cries? Will He cite the multiple sins of the Jewish people? Will he muffle her screams with countless tales of idol worship and unforgivable behavior?

Yaakov waits. Will G-d turn her down? If He does, Yaakov will be able to say, "Master of the world, *kach onin et hame'ukot?* Is this the way to answer a woman in pain? Is this the way one replies to a woman whose children are being banished?"

Rachel is in effect saying the same thing she said all those many years before: "Give me children and if not then I am dead!"

Yaakov watches to see what G-d is going to do. G-d, after all, can't say, "Am I the One Above Who is denying you children?" He *is* the One Above! What's Hashem going to do? How is He going to reply to the distraught mother pleading before him?

It is as if G-d has no choice and replies, *"V'shavu banim li'gvulam"*

([I promise you that] your children will return to their homes [Yirmiyahu 31:16]).

Now that we know what transpired on that fateful day, I'm going to share a little secret with you.

Yaakov Avinu wasn't nervous. Wasn't waiting tensely for G-d's reply to Mama Rachel. He knew that G-d was going to give her a favorable reply. You want to know why, and how I know this? I'll tell you. Because if G-d reprimanded him so forcefully for speaking to a woman in pain in such a way, there is no doubt that G-d would have demonstrated to Yaakov Avinu, the choicest of the Avot, how one *should* answer a woman in such a state of mind.

Now I'm going to take this idea one step further.

The question is when and where G-d actually showed him.

Toward the end of his life Yaakov Avinu is speaking to his son Yosef when he utters this famous verse: "*Va'ani b'vo'i mi'Padan, metah alai Rachel*" (And when I was traveling from Padan, Rachel died on the way).

And Rashi says something absolutely incredible about this verse.

Yosef, viceroy of Egypt, stood before his ailing father. Yaakov looked his beloved son in the eye and said, *Yosef, I know that you were upset at me all these years for burying your mother on the side of the road, for not even bringing her into the city for a proper burial, and I am asking you to take me all the way to Chevron for burial in the Me'arat Hamachpelah. Now that I'm approaching the end of my life, I'm going to share with you my reasons for acting this way.*

*Yosef, you want to know why I did this? Why I buried your mother whom I loved with all my heart on the side of the road?*

*Because G-d instructed me to do so.*

*Do you want to know why G-d instructed me to do such a thing?*

*Because one day in the distant future, the nation of Israel will sin to the point of no return and they will be sent into exile and the weeping nation will pass alongside Rachel's grave on the way to Beit Lechem. And at that point Rachel will rise up and intercede before G-d to save her children and G-d will acquiesce and accede to her request.*

And why did G-d tell Yaakov all this? If it was all to come about in the future? When it would only occur in generations to come?

Because G-d gave Yaakov reproof. He rebuked him for talking to Rachel in such a sharp manner. And it stands to reason that G-d then explained to Yaakov exactly how one *should* address a woman in that state of mind. How one *should* act when someone is suffering such acute agony.

To sum it up, G-d's disapproval of Yaakov's actions was genuine. And the fact is, when G-d used those exact words to reprimand Yaakov, He knew that they would return to force Him into saving Klal Yisrael in generations to come and He used them precisely for that reason. Because we are His children and He wants the best for us.

That was the *shiur* that I told those women in the Israel Center fifteen years ago.

And recently I had occasion to say it over again. But this time I had something to add. A story I heard. Something that brings me to tears every time I think of it.

When the government was about to sign the first Oslo Accords, Rav Hanan Porat (Torah scholar, member of Knesset for ten years, founding father of the movement to settle Yehudah and the Shomron and one of the paratroopers who broke into the Old City of Jerusalem in the Six-Day War) was laboriously going through the numerous maps of the terrain to be handed over to the Arabs, when he realized that according to what he was seeing, Kever Rachel was slated to be included in the transfer of lands to the Palestinian Authority and would no longer be under Israeli control. *Kever Rachel!* This find shocked Porat and spurred him into immediate action. He attempted to set up an appointment with Prime Minister Rabin for that day, but only succeeded in receiving an appointment for two days hence.

And so it came to be that Hanan Porat found himself walking purposefully through the Knesset two days later, a sheaf of maps under his arm, when he happened to meet Rabbi Menachem Porush, veteran member of Knesset and as Yerushalmi a Jew as one could possibly be.

Porush saw the look on Porat's face. It piqued his curiosity. Maybe it was the thunder where a good-natured look normally resided.

"Where are you going, Chanan?" the elder spokesman of the

Orthodox community wanted to know.

"I have an appointment with the prime minister right now. Did you see the maps?"

"What maps?"

"The maps that delineate what we're giving those Arabs. The maps clearly show that Kever Rachel is going to end up as Arab property."

"*Chalilah v'chas!*" Porush exclaimed, "That can't happen! I'm coming with you."

So the two of them continued on together to see Rabin.

Entering the prime minister's office, Hanan Porat spread the maps out on the prime minister's desk for him to get an accurate picture.

"Here, Prime Minister, take a look. According to the way the maps were set up, Kever Rachel is going to end up in Arab hands."

Rabin removed his glasses and studied the maps. He appeared noncommittal. He didn't seem that concerned.

All of a sudden, a primeval scream pierced the tranquility of the prime minister's office. Menachem Porush was screaming with all his might.

"DI MAMME RUCHEL, DI MAMME RUCHEL!" he screamed, and started crying like you wouldn't believe. Tears flowed down into that long white beard. He grabbed Rabin, placed his arms around him, and gave him a bear hug.

"YITZCHOK, *di kenst dus nisht tun!* You can't do this!"

Rabin, as soon as he managed to extricate himself from Porush's arms, called for the army chief of staff, and gave orders to change the maps to include Kever Rachel in the final agreement. Kever Rachel was staying in our hands.

Kever Rachel was saved in that meeting. Because sometimes, a five-minute meeting is all it takes. Or even just a cry. As long as it's from the heart.

༄

On Rosh Chodesh Tammuz 1998, we were scheduled to travel to Toronto on what turned out to be the day of my grandson's *brit*. David Chai Gold (Yirmi's oldest), today a strapping young man in his teens, was entering into the covenant and I was lucky enough to be present at this auspicious occasion. David Chai has always been a thoughtful guy, and this character trait was visible even back then, seeing as he made sure to be born early enough to allow me to make the *brit* before leaving for the airport.

I entered the shul on that morning during the first minyan, just as they were opening the doors of the *aron kodesh*, our beautiful and impressive ark, filled to the brim with numerous Torah scrolls, some belonging to the shul, others on loan to us from assorted individuals.

The next scene is indelibly inscribed on the parchment of my mind. The ark was completely empty! It was a shocking sight, to say the least. Thieves had broken into the shul and stolen our Torah scrolls in the middle of the night. I was heartbroken. The joy of the *simchah* merged with the sadness and loss. Six Torah scrolls were gone. Just like that. People stood there transfixed in their places. Nobody uttered a word. The shock was absolute as we tried to come to grips with what had happened, to assimilate that some wicked person had stolen all of our Torah scrolls.

I attended that *brit* with a lump in my throat the entire time – a smile on my face and tears coursing down my heart as my grandson became a full-fledged Jew.

There was one hero in the story: Shmuel Weinstein, the insurance agent who covered our shul, got the insurance company to pay in record time and in full. In full. A few hundred thousand shekel. But even after we received the money, the pain and shock still remained. It was as if we had lost our children with no clue to where they had been taken. I don't wish this on anyone. The police never solved the crime and never recovered our Torah scrolls. There was no sign of breaking and entering, no way to determine whether the crime had been committed by Jew or Arab, old or young. I couldn't even remain in the shul to deal with this emergency because we had a wedding in Toronto the following night. We left the scene of the crime to the *gabbaim* and disappeared right in the middle of the crisis. Maybe it was better for me to get away for a while. Having my empty ark stare me in the face was too painful.

In the end, some of the people who had lent us their Torah scrolls wanted the money back. Others took the money, purchased a new scroll, and lent us the new one as well. Everyone did what was right for them, but the bizarre devastation of that day never faded completely.

֎

We flew to Toronto a while back for the wedding of our niece Dena Rubinoff to Moshe Weinstock. We flew El Al as usual because we trust the national carrier. We were coming in for a landing at Toronto International Airport – we were almost down on the runway, in fact – when the aircraft suddenly reversed course and instead of continuing in the landing pattern, lifted upwards and began taking us farther and farther away from Toronto.

Seconds later the pilot was on the intercom.

"Ladies and gentlemen, this is your captain speaking. Due to some technical difficulties, we will not be landing in Toronto right now. We will be diverting this flight to Montreal instead. Thank you for your understanding and cooperation."

The plane was suddenly abuzz with conjecture and conversation between passengers, crew, and one another.

"Maybe there's a fire in the airport?"

"Maybe there's a terrorist attack?"

Nobody knew what was going on.

We landed in Montreal about an hour later. When the plane rolled to a stop and we were allowed to use our cell phones again, Dov Rubin (a close friend of mine and a member of our shul for many years), who was flying on to Los Angeles, called another close friend of ours, Tzvi (Howie) Maisel, in Eretz Yisrael for an update.

Had he heard about any emergencies in Canada on the news that would have caused a plane to be diverted from Toronto to Montreal?

Howie Maisel was on it. Thirty seconds later he had an answer for us. "I've checked on my computer and your plane was the only one diverted from the Toronto airport."

"Any idea why they flew us to Montreal? What was so special about our flight?" Dov asked our friend.

"No idea. Everything else is fine – all other departures and arrivals are operating on time. Yours was the only flight with issues."

In the meanwhile all the passengers on our flight were herded into a large chamber in the Montreal airport, big hulking Canadian Mounties keeping guard at the doors. It was disconcerting to say the least.

Suddenly a rumor began spreading through the room. The flight we'd been on had been targeted by terrorists who had been planning to bring it down as it landed in Toronto. Terrorists operating on Canadian soil! Supposedly there had been a truck parked right off Highway 401, with a mini missile launcher ready to be used.

Why us?

Nobody knew.

Had they been caught?

Nobody knew.

One thing we did know. The Canadian government never denied the rumors. And if they were true, we had been a hair's breadth away from being blown up on the runway of Toronto's Pearson International Airport.

But how did the pilot know about this? Slowly clarity began to emerge. The tip-off had arrived from Tel Aviv, from an Israeli security agent who had been monitoring the radio frequencies in Toronto and had stumbled upon a terrorist attack waiting to happen.

We remained in Montreal for a few hours. When we were finally in the air again, we were informed that we would not be landing in Toronto, but would continue on to Hamilton, Ontario, instead. From there we were bussed into Toronto, helicopters of the Royal Canadian Air Force hovering over our buses. What a voyage this was turning out to be. In the end, a three-bus convoy took the highway into Toronto, helicopter overhead.

We sat down on the bus. A Jew from Boro Park sat one row in front of us. A Jew from Flatbush took the seat on the other side of the aisle. A Gentile woman and her daughter sat two seats ahead. Of course, when a few Jews sit down next to one another, they can't resist a conversation.

"What's your name? Where are you from?"

"Hungary? Poland?" You know how it is. Jewish geography.

We talked for a few minutes and I picked up on the fact that these men weren't speaking English like typical New Yorkers. In fact, if my antenna was guiding me correctly, their accents sounded Israeli.

"Are you from Eretz Yisrael?" I asked the two of them.

"Bnei Brak," one volunteered.

"Meah Shearim," the other admitted.

"You're visiting the States?"

"No," Flatbush replied, "I live here now. Like it better here." Boro Park concurred. Did they want to return? They did not. Did their decision to live in the States have to do with making a living? It did not. They just liked life in America.

These statements hit me hard. I was about to respond when someone beat me to it. The young Gentile woman sitting a few rows ahead turned around in her chair, gave them a scathing look, and said, "I don't understand you people. You have the most beautiful country in the world, the Holy Land, and you don't want to live there? You left Jerusalem to go live in America? Do you have any idea what you've given up?"

I turned to my wife and said, "If I was ever happy that I made aliyah it's now! To be told off by this girl would be a terrible embarrassment. Can you imagine – a Gentile girl dressing down Jews for not living in Eretz Yisrael."

Then the girl's mother turned around. Fire smoldered in her eyes.

"Isaiah 49:22."

I actually knew which verse she was referring to: "*Ko amar Hashem Elokim...* (so says the Lord G-d): I'm going to lift My hands to tell the Gentiles, and I will raise My banner toward all the peoples. And the Gentiles are going to bring the Jews back to Eretz Yisrael in their arms and your daughters on their shoulders."

She was telling them off. Boy, was she telling them off!

"I'm a non-Jew," she was saying. "And I can't relate to how nonchalant you are about trading in the country of your heritage for foreign lands."

It was pretty powerful reproof. Although I did have to explain to those two "New Yorkers" what she meant with her quote. I guess they had never studied Isaiah 49:22.

We eventually arrived at the Toronto airport, and were herded inside, hot and disheveled as one can only be after such a long international flight with so many interruptions. As we stepped off the bus, a Canadian Mountie who seemed to stand at about seven feet looked down at the two of us and said to my wife, "Lady, you're safe now. Lady, you're safe now."

"Safe from what?" she asked.

But that's all he would say, no matter how we pressed him for details.

Of course reporters from Canadian national television were waiting to interview us when we exited the building and the faces of all the intrepid passengers were shown across the width and breadth of Canada that evening. All in all, it had been a fairly exciting trip, but the most interesting moment for me by far was watching the five-minute interchange between the Jewish and Gentile passengers. It had been enlightening to say the least.

How is it that the Gentiles know so well that which we don't?

಄

As you can deduce from the last few stories, my wife and I used to travel on a fairly regular basis. Having served in the past as president of the Council of Young Israel Rabbis in the States, I was invited for a number of years to fly in to America for Young Israel's annual conference of rabbis, where I presented the current state of affairs in Israel to the assembled. One particular conference took place deep in the middle of the winter. February. Worse than freezing, cold as America can get. On one of these trips, my wife and I landed at Newark Airport and after passing through customs, we headed over to the rental car office.

To my surprise and joy, the rental company representative informed me that I was entitled to an upgrade. Which is how we found ourselves loading our luggage into a brand new, fully appointed Lincoln Town Car, with leather seats, sunroof (not that we were going to be getting much use out of that) and dazzling music-playing device. It was quite a vehicle. We settled in, I flexed my wrists, turned on the ignition, and pulled smoothly out of the airport, toward Boro Park.

Minutes later we were cruising along the New Jersey Turnpike. I recall enthusiastically exclaiming about the utter bliss of finding myself in the driver's seat of such a beautiful car.

Was it just a car?

Far from it.

A marvel of human technology, a tremendous blend of science and uncompromising standards. Like I said, the upgrade really was a pleasant surprise.

We had been driving for about twelve minutes when I heard an unfamiliar sound. In fact, I had never actually heard this particular sound before while driving, but I had a sinking feeling that I knew exactly what it was.

A flat tire. That's what I was hearing and feeling. It had to be. Pretty ironic, all in all. Thing is, I had never changed a flat tire in my life. I was kind of clueless when it came to changing tires. Now what?

We were approaching an exit ramp and I pulled off to the side, trying to decide what we were supposed to do next. The one streetlight at the end of the exit barely lit up the wind-chilled darkness. I got out of the car and examined the tire. It was shredded. No way to drive with such a tire. It was bitterly cold. Barely any cars on the road. The few cars whose drivers were out braving the elements sped by, ignoring me completely. I began to feel sorry for myself.

And then I had a mind-blowing epiphany.

G-d was waiting for me to make a move. He helps people who try to help themselves. It was up to me to begin the process.

"Bayla," I said, the decisiveness and backbone returning to my voice, "I'm going to change this tire."

"Not that I doubt your capabilities in any way," she replied, "but you've never done this before. You don't know how."

"Open the glove compartment," I said, "and you'll find a manual published by the car company with clear instructions for pretty much any situation that can arise. I'm sure there will be directions for changing a flat. I am going to teach myself right now."

I took that manual and got out of the car, where I went to stand under the solitary streetlight to read the instructions by the dim light shining down at me. I was reminded of a story, a legend I'd been told when I arrived at Ner Yisroel so many decades before. Every *yeshivah* has its own brand of stories about its *rosh yeshivah* and Ner Yisroel was no exception.

When the *Ohr Sameach* on the Rambam was first published, a single copy arrived in Slobodka and was passed around among all the students, each one taking a chance to take a swim in its holy waters. Rav Ruderman received the *sefer* in the evening hours and as legend has it, he slept that night not at all. Instead, continues the story, he stood under a street lamp in front of the *yeshivah* and studied the *Ohr Sameach* the entire night through. By morning he'd memorized the *sefer* cover to cover.

"How the generations have fallen," I mused to myself as I stood shivering in the intense cold under that dim street lamp on the edge of the New Jersey Turnpike, *sefer* in hand just like my *rosh yeshivah* of many years before, except that he'd been committing the *Ohr Sameach* to memory and I was desperately perusing "The Guide to Changing a Flat" and didn't get it.

When I finally got the picture to some degree, I realized that I'd need to find the jack to begin the process.

"Where's the jack?" I asked myself.

I was informed by the book that the jack was located in the trunk. I opened the trunk, my brain and stiffening fingers warning me that I was looking at possible frostbite in the not-too-distant future. It took me a while to find the jack under the carpet in the trunk and even after I finally located it, I still had to maneuver it out of its place with a special wrist action that took me a while to master. I wrestled with the jack until I got it out of the trunk and then, following along with the instructions line for line, I set up the jack beneath the car. There. Never done this before, but it's really happening.

As I began jacking up the car, something happened.

A huge truck pulled off the highway and came to a stop not far from where I crouched working the jack. A giant African American man emerged from the cab. He was a tough-looking guy and I was suddenly very afraid.

"Excuse me, sir," he said, "do you by any chance need some help?"

The question was asked in the most polite, sweetest way imaginable.

"I'm going to help you."

Seconds later a car painted a fire-engine red pulled up alongside the truck. Another man emerged. This man was a blond. Blond hair to the point of being almost white. My two saviors. Black and white. It was kind of cute.

"I'm an off-duty policeman," the blond guy said. "I was driving on the other side of the highway when I caught sight of you stranded. It took me a while to get around here. Sorry it took so long. Can I help? And in the meanwhile, why don't you have your wife take a seat in the front of my car. My wife's there as well and it's nice and warm."

We didn't say no to that offer.

As she was getting into the car, Bayla turned to me.

"I know you. You're going to make a *drashah* or a class out of this, aren't you?"

"You're wrong," I replied, "I made it already."

It didn't take the two of them more than ten minutes to change that tire. I offered the truck driver a tip, but he didn't want my money. I removed a fifty-dollar bill from my wallet and shoved it into his hand, ignoring his protests. He'd done a really big mitzvah and deserved a reward. The policeman made it very clear that he'd just been doing his job and didn't want a tip. Bayla returned to the Lincoln, the policeman drove off, and the truck driver climbed back into the cab of his truck.

At this point in the story, my wife and I have a disagreement as to what came next. I claim that the driver started the engine, drove a little bit, and disappeared into thin air. She claims that he drove down the exit ramp and got back on the highway like any normal truck.

She says he was a regular man.

I say he was no ordinary truck driver; he was an angel in disguise.

As soon as we reached our hosts Tzvi Meyer and Chaya Neuberger in Boro Park and settled in (Tzvi had been a *chavruta* of mine in Ner Yisroel and his home was always open to me), I found a copy of Megillat Esther and flipped through it rapidly. I had to determine whether the idea that had flown into my mind while standing in the freezing wind on the New Jersey Turnpike had been correct. There are 167 verses in

Megillat Esther, which means that there's a swing verse in the middle. Eighty-three verses on one side, eighty-three verses on the other.

The verse in the middle is "*Va'tomer Esther la'melech*" (and Esther said to the king), "*sh'elati u'bakashati*" (this is my request, this is my desire). This is where Esther officially begins the process of pleading for the Jewish people.

But what does that have to do with me, with us? I explained it like this.

There we were, stranded on the highway, on a freezing, frigid, bone-numbingly cold evening. Not knowing what to do. I'd never changed a flat tire in my entire life. No cars were willing to stop for us. Now what?

There was an uproar in heaven. The angels stood before G-d.

"Master of the universe," they pleaded, "Sholom and Bayla Gold are stuck in a car with a shredded tire. They can't drive. Nobody cares. Can we please help them?"

G-d did not agree. The angels were not being allowed to send us salvation.

A few minutes later another angel came charging into the heavenly courtroom.

"You know what just happened? Gold just removed the manual from the glove compartment. He's trying to do it on his own!" The excitement in heaven was palpable.

"Can we help him now?"

G-d's response: "It is not yet time."

A few minutes later: "Master of the universe, it's so cold outside; please allow us to help him."

No reply.

A few more minutes pass.

"Gold just opened the trunk. He's looking for the jack. I think he's really going for it. Can we send someone now?"

The response is still no.

Five minutes later: "Look at him, he's about to jack up the car. He's doing it all by himself! Can we help him now?"

Finally the King of the universe inclines His head in the affirmative. They are being allowed to help us.

A mighty cry is unleashed through the heavens. "Send in the rescue forces!" Seconds later they arrive. The truck driver and the off-duty policeman come to our rescue. Just like that swing verse in the Megillah where everything changes when Esther takes matters into her own hands. Because that's exactly what G-d is waiting for. That's when the *siyata di'shmaya*, the heavenly assistance, arrives.

Verse 84 in the Megillah is where Esther has to jack up the car. She does it. And everything begins to unravel for Haman and Achashverosh right after that.

Because she was willing to get out into the cold and start to change her own tire.

&

Aloh Naaleh was an organization whose time I felt had come. Its goal was to educate and encourage Jewish youth to make aliyah. It lasted for a few years. We held an annual gala event in the Renaissance ballroom to which we invited the American students from about fifteen *yeshivot* around the country. About nine hundred students used to show up to that event. We'd hold another evening in the ballroom for American seminary girls a few weeks later that would draw close to six hundred participants.

We'd deliver pep talks to these great kids and explain how incredible it would be for them to move here. I was a keynote speaker and there were a number of others who spoke as well.

We held fairs at assorted locations where foreign students were able to learn about their options in adult education, the Israeli job market, making aliyah, and housing options. Aloh Naaleh was a much-talked-about organization among the American youth studying in Israel. It's not uncommon for me to meet people even now, years later, who remind me that they heard me speak about making aliyah at Aloh Naaleh and decided that what we were saying made sense.

We organized speaking tours for our staff in the States as well. I myself traveled in America and spoke at shul after shul, explaining, answering, and describing the incredible beauty that awaited Anglo Jewry in the Holy Land. Not only that, but any time we heard of a rabbi or well-spoken businessman who was traveling to America on business or pleasure, we'd set them up at different speaking venues.

The man who worked with great self-sacrifice and wisdom to make it all happen is Rabbi Yerachmiel Roness, formerly of Har Nof, now in Ramat Beit Shemesh. He still keeps it alive by producing a weekly *dvar Torah* that encourages aliyah and *ahavat Eretz Yisrael*. The founding group included David Hollander, Rabbi Chaim Luban, and Rabbi Meyer Fendel.

Unfortunately Aloh Naaleh did not last very long, but it managed to do a lot of good in the few years that it remained alive. I'm proud of the Aloh Naaleh initiative and know that if someone were to approach me today with an infusion of cash and goodwill, I would be glad to reignite the spark and bring that organization back to life.

*∾*

Through the years I've been invited to be a guest speaker and scholar in residence at numerous locations around the globe. The Jewish community of South Africa in particular has invited me for a number of special occasions. In an ironic turn of events I was invited to spend Yom Yerushalayim one year in Johannesburg, the next in Los Angeles at a city-wide celebration, the next in Toronto, and so on – basically a different city every year. It seemed like I was never actually *in* Yerushalayim on Yom Yerushalayim. But I considered those trips crucial, for they allowed me to act as a roving ambassador to communities across the Diaspora while stressing the importance of Yerushalayim and Eretz Yisrael for every single Jew.

On one particular trip to Johannesburg, I arrived at my destination all fired up to speak but with a flaming sore throat. It hurt to swallow, it felt positively murderous to cough, and as for laughter – forget about it.

"I have an extremely bad cold and sore throat right now," I began, "but I'm going to deliver my speech to you in spite of it.

"This morning President Bush said in a speech that 'a window of opportunity has opened up in the Middle East.' Well, you know something, friends, every time they open up a window of opportunity in the Middle East I get a really *farshluggene* cold."

That line brought down the house.

Since we'd gotten quite friendly during the course of my sojourns in South Africa, when the community opened a new *kollel*, I was invited to deliver classes there for about a week. It was a wonderful experience for Bayla and me. There is really no comparison anywhere in the world to the type of hospitality exhibited by the South African community. The graciousness, charm, and warmth shown to us were outstanding. They even took us on an unforgettable trip to the famous Kruger Park. Our wonderful hosts and guides were Joe and Phyllis Simon.

A childhood friend from Williamsburg, Avraham Tanzer, is a very prominent rabbinic leader of Glenhazel, Johannesburg, and *rosh yeshivah* of Yeshiva College.

Those days of traveling are sort of behind us now (not completely, but the volume is definitely reduced), but the memories of our visits to Jewish communities around the world will never be forgotten.

# 23

# Israeli Innocents Abroad

For a number of years now we have been traveling to Europe for a week in the summer. One of these trips was an in-depth roots study of Jewish communities that once were and are no more, that were utterly destroyed during the Shoah. Among other place we visited Kovno, Slobodka, Vilna, and Ponevezh in Lithuania; then it was on to Poland where we saw Warsaw, Lublin, Lizhensk, Kotzk, Krakow and the death camp Majdanek, in addition to stops at other sites of Jewish interest. I had for years resisted joining these groups because I didn't want to tread on that accursed earth, but Bayla finally prevailed on me.

It was a painful, emotional, and profoundly moving experience.

Upon our arrival in Vilna we were given little paper flags of Lithuania with a note attached. The following is the text of the note:

> We wish to congratulate all Lithuanians and country's guests on Lithuanian National Day!
>
> On 6 July 1253 the coronation of Mindaugas, Lithuania's first and only king, took place.
>
> The coronation of King Mindaugas and his wife Duchess Morta is one of the most significant events in Lithuanian history.

> The Papal Bull issued on this occasion established Lithuania's placement under the jurisdiction of the Bishop of Rome which means recognition of the state of Lithuania.
> Since 6 July 1991 this date is celebrated as Lithuanian National day.
> Vilnius International Airport

That note triggered so many thoughts and feelings that I saved it and pasted it into one of my notebooks so that I could refer back to it. I began to think about the independence days or national holidays of as many countries as I knew and arrived at the conclusion that none possess the power, the drama, the pathos, the profound meaning, and the majesty that our Yom Haatzmaut holds for Am Yisrael. How dare anyone trivialize or make fun of so great a gift from Hashem to His people. I read about "one of the most significant events in Lithuanian history." I respect a people that venerates its past. I am utterly baffled by those who can't see the majesty of their present.

I was asked to say a *dvar Torah* on Friday night in Vilna, once one of the jewels of world Jewry, known for its scholarship and the towering spiritual growth that made Vilna known and respected worldwide, now reduced to nothing more than memory, glorious past, insignificant present, and absolutely no future.

My *dvar Torah*, which I never dreamed that I would ever say in Vilna itself, was based on a Gemara in *Sanhedrin* 94a. "R. Yochanan said: Why was that wicked one, King Sancheriv, referred to in the Book of Ezra by the exalted title of Asnapar, the Great and Venerated (Ezra 4:10)?" He had destroyed most of Eretz Yisrael and sent the Ten Tribes off into exile and it was only at the gates of Yerushalayim that his army was destroyed in one night by the angel sent to protect the city. The Gemara's answer is fascinating: "It is because he did not speak derogatorily about Eretz Yisrael," as the verse states, "Until I [Sancheriv] come and take you to a land that is like your land (II Kings 18:32)." He did not say that he was going to exile them to a better land than theirs. That would have been considered speaking ill of Eretz Yisrael.

The Gemara goes on to show that, on the other hand, the Ten Tribes whom he exiled were indeed guilty of this sin. They felt that their places of exile were worthy replacements for Eretz Yisrael. "When they came to the land called Shosh, they said this land is equivalent to our land. And when they came to a placed called Almin, they said that this land is like our world (*almin*), our homeland Eretz Yisrael." Rashi here states that *almin* is in particular a reference to Yerushalayim, which is referred to as Beit Olamim (the Eternal House). It is quite clear from the Gemara that calling any other place Yerushalayim is in effect a blow to the dignity and sanctity of our Holy City. Therefore, I don't believe that the description of Vilna as "Yerushalayim of Lithuania" is permitted, and that it must be rooted in some foreign source. I was always opposed to pizza parlors, restaurants, communities, or cities referred to as Jerusalem II or Yerushalayim of America.

A while later, after I had said this in my shul in Har Nof, one of the members, Hyman Flax (formerly from Saint Louis, where he served for many years as the executive director of the Vaad Hoeir), came into shul and said to me, "Rabbi, I just read that when Napoleon conquered Vilna and was taken through the ghetto, he exclaimed, 'This is just like Jerusalem.'" The mystery was solved. That was that. Napoleon was the one who coined that term "Jerusalem of Lithuania." It did indeed not come from Jewish sources.

☙

Yerushalayim figures in another one of our European adventures. The summer after our roots tour we traveled to southern France. There was a one-day trip I wasn't going to miss: a visit to the city of Worms in Germany, a city steeped in Jewish history. For a number of years Rashi lived there, and his seat in the shul in which he studied is preserved. The Jewish presence in Worms dates back at least to the tenth century. The city, known in medieval Hebrew as Vermayza, was a prominent center of Jewish learning. It was also the site of two terrible pogroms – in 1096 when Crusaders on their way to the Holy Land massacred some eight hundred Jews there, and again during the Black Death epidemic of 1348 when Jews were accused of poisoning the wells and were killed there in great numbers. Worms is also known for its Jewish cemetery dating from the eleventh century, believed to be the oldest in Europe, and for its eleventh-century shul.

The cemetery is truly a peaceful, beautiful place, with many shade trees and grass carpeting the landscape. Many great rabbis are buried there, the most famous of all being Rabbi Meir of Rothenburg, the Maharam. Next to him is the grave of Alexander Suskind Wimpfen, who ransomed Rabbi Meir's body fourteen years after his death. Rising anti-Semitism had convinced the Maharam that the only haven for Jews was Eretz Yisrael, and he attempted to travel there but was captured on the way by the archbishop of Mainz. Great sums of money were raised and offered by the Jewish community for his release, but he refused to be ransomed because of the exorbitant demands.

Kristallnacht in 1938 marked the end of the Jewish community of Worms.

Well, there we were on a tour bus to Worms. A rest stop was made at some big convenience store on the highway. We were told to leave everything on the bus and return as quickly as possible. Bayla and I went inside for a few minutes, and when we came out we couldn't find our bus among all the tour buses there. After a little while it dawned on us that the unthinkable and unforgivable had indeed happened. We had been left behind. Our cell phones and food were all left on the bus. We didn't even have the phone numbers of the bus driver, the guide, or the hotel at which we were staying. And we didn't speak the language. We were going into a state of panic. We met a fellow with a *kippah* who tried to help us get in touch with our hotel, but to no avail.

About half an hour into our odyssey, I saw someone getting into a car, a thirtyish blond fellow, so I approached him and learned that he understood English. I told him our story and he responded that he was on his way to Mainz and he could go by way of Worms; he told us to get in. As we entered the car Bayla whispered to me anxiously, "Don't tell him where we are from." Europe is not such a friendly place to Jews, so she was concerned. Sure enough, about ten minutes into our journey the driver asked us where we came from and without hesitation I answered, "Jerusalem!"

We got to know Derek Kuhn and his companion Dominique.

About an hour later we arrived in Worms and I asked Derek to drop us off in the center of town. There was no response. He was telling me without saying it that he would not drop us off until he succeeded in uniting us with our group. Derek and Dominique had hand-held computers, a GPS, and who knows what other newfangled twenty-first-century contraptions. They had a list of sites of Jewish interest in Worms. Derek asked me if I would have a guess about where the group might be. I said, "The old Jewish cemetery." Within seconds they had the street, it was entered into the GPS, he made a U-turn, and off we went through Worms.

In no more than perhaps ten minutes, as we made a turn, Bayla exclaimed, "There's our bus." It sure was, parked in front of the old Jewish cemetery. We had arrived just in time because the bus driver was giving instructions to a young Israeli-born rabbi from Mainz who had accompanied our group. He was on his way to find us.

Everyone was quite happy to see us. Maybe other people would have come back storming and shouting at the guide, "How could you leave us behind?" Not us. We didn't want to upset anyone, we liked the guide, and I thought to myself that I could get a story out of this adventure. Furthermore, I enjoyed playing the role of the macho tough guy. Don't you worry about the Golds. Drop them anywhere and they will find their way. The women surrounded Bayla, and the men, who had already been through the cemetery, took me to the grave of the Maharam, Rabbi Meir of Rothenburg, and his ransomer, then to the Maharil and a number of other greats. It is a truly strikingly beautiful cemetery, said to be the only one not destroyed during the Second World War.

During our visit to Worms I was keenly conscious of a tradition quoted in the *Seder Hadorot* that says, "The reason evil decrees befell the holy community of Vermayza more than other places is because after the seventy years of the Babylonian exile, Jews returned to Eretz Yisrael and Yerushalayim, but those in Vermayza did not return." It would seem from this that there was a Jewish community there long before the tenth century – in fact some fifteen centuries earlier. The *Seder Hadorot* continues: "The people of Yerushalayim wrote to the community of Vermayza that they too should come home and settle in Eretz Yisrael so that they should be able to come for the Three Festivals to Yerushalayim…and they paid no attention and they responded, 'You live in the big Yerushalayim and we will dwell here in the little Yerushalayim.'" Because of this there were more decrees against them than against other cities.

Their mistake was twofold. They refused to return to Eretz Yisrael and they saw themselves as Jerusalem II. At that time Jews in Vermayza held positions of prominence and power and were very wealthy. Apparently they did not want to leave their comfortable situation in order to return to the land from which they had been exiled, even though return was now possible. Worms is the tragic story of a city that produced great Torah scholars yet suffered death and destruction.

I wondered and still wonder whether my quick, proud response to Derek, "Jerusalem," may have been the key to our salvation.

࿔

Our visit to the concentration camp Majdanek was marked by a cloudy, overcast sky. It set the mood for that accursed place. Only soon after we left did the sun begin to shine.

It brought to mind what someone told me soon after our aliyah in 1982, that Rav Meir Chodosh, the *mashgiach* of Chevron Yeshiva, said that he watched the skies over Yerushalayim for sixty-five years and even during the stormiest days the sun always broke through the clouds at some moment. I have been watching now for over thirty years from our *mirpesset* and can also testify that the sun shines every day over the Holy City.

࿔

The most significant point of interest in our visit to Lublin was, of course, the huge and impressive yet tragic Yeshivas Chachmei Lublin, built by Rav Meir Shapiro, the originator of the *daf yomi*. In May 1924, the cornerstone-laying ceremony took place in the presence of approximately fifty thousand people. The decision to build the *yeshivah* was taken at the Knessiah Gedolah of Agudas Yisroel in Vienna the year before, in August 1923.

The *yeshivah*'s opening ceremony took place in June 1930. Thousands arrived from all over Poland and abroad. The *yeshivah* building was unlike any other in Europe. It provided for all of the students' needs – dormitory, dining rooms, and a massive Torah library that eventually held twenty thousand volumes.

Nine years later the Nazis marched into Lublin, gutted the inside, and burned the contents of the library in the town square. The cries of Jews watching the books being burned were so loud that the Germans ordered the army band to drown out the cries of desperation.

Two significant facts are, I believe, not so commonly known. The first is that Rav Meir Shapiro, toward the end of his life (he died in 1933 at age forty-six), said that he never regretted any decision he made in his life except one: that he should have built the *yeshivah* in Yerushalayim. The second is that Rav Avraham Yitzchak HaKohen Kook, who was a member of Agudas Yisroel and could not attend the Knessiah Gedolah, sent a letter proposing that a central *yeshivah* for European students be built in Yerushalayim. The letter was never brought before the plenum.

⁂

The last forty-eight hours of our roots journey became a most fitting and totally unplanned conclusion to that painful journey. We had seen the tragic fate of once proud, thriving communities pulsating with life, intellectual and spiritual creativity – the birthplaces of great *talmidei chachamim*, Chassidic Rebbes, and a plethora of "*pashute Yidden*" who lived, created, and were expelled, rebuilt, and left indelible impressions for over a thousand years before being brutally extinguished.

Our return home to Eretz Yisrael was supposed to be by LOT Polish Airlines from Krakow to Vienna and then Austrian Airlines to Tel Aviv. But it just didn't work out that way. Bad weather delayed our departure from Krakow and we knew that we would not make our connecting flight. We arrived in Vienna quite late and were put up in a hotel. The airline had us booked into a hotel far off the beaten path and nowhere near the Jewish area of Vienna. I insisted on a hotel where we would be close enough to kosher shops. We finally were checked in to the Vienna Hilton. We were hungry when we arrived and we were a group of about thirteen people. Faygie Heiman called her family in Israel who, being in the travel business (Ben Zvi Travel), contacted a caterer in Vienna. Sure enough, Mr. Berenholz appeared at about midnight with sumptuous meals for all of us. He refused to accept payment.

Thursday the odyssey continued when we boarded an Austrian Airlines flight to Tel Aviv, but never took off. A heavy downpour and a loud crash shut down the electricity. The air-conditioning was not working and it was hot. We remained on board until the pilot announced that the plane had been hit by a bolt of lightning and we would have to wait for another plane. We went back to the airport lounge and after about an hour, we were notified that a new aircraft had arrived but a bird had hit the engine and it would take time to repair.

We boarded again ready for takeoff but there was no movement at all. By then it was nearly 1:00 a.m. and the captain announced, "Ladies and gentlemen, this Austrian Airlines flight is cancelled. All passengers please return to the lounge." So began a forty-eight-hour adventure that included one night in the Hilton Vienna (not bad) and a second night in the airport (pretty bad).

We were supposed to be home Wednesday night but found ourselves, early Friday morning, after a terrible night in the airport, tired, exhausted, grubby, and with no way to get home for Shabbat. We all lined up at the Austrian Airlines counter, which was the carrier responsible for the connecting flight.

Friday morning wore on with no progress. We wanted desperately to get home but there seemed to be no way. Some *chassidish* fellows reported about a flight to Bucharest with a connecting El Al flight to Eretz Yisrael. Some members of our group flew back to Warsaw and got onto El Al to Israel. People were frantically searching for any route or airline that would get them home. Then we discovered that there was a flight from the Vienna airport, the last El Al plane to Israel before Shabbat. We hurried over and got on line. All they could tell us was that they would try their best to get as many of us on as possible. This was our only hope. El Al told us to be patient, but patience felt very elusive by this point. We were already thinking of how we would go about making alternative arrangements for Shabbat. To put it mildly it had not been a pleasant two days. Every minute that passed was like an eternity.

With only a few minutes left to the scheduled departure time, an El Al official approached me and silently and swiftly handed me what were obviously two boarding passes and whispered, "Board the plane now." The feeling was indescribable. We hurried onto the plane and started looking for our designated seats. It seemed we had gone too far so we turned around and proceeded toward the front of the plane. A stewardess saw us checking, bewildered, took our boarding passes, and with a smile directed us to Business Class. We couldn't believe our good fortune. We were going home to Eretz Yisrael for Shabbat, and in Business Class.

Exhausted but exhilarated, we collapsed into our wide, comfortable, cushiony seats, and then my imagination took over. I thought about hundreds of thousands of Jews wandering through Europe after the Shoah, with no place to go. Back "home" was no longer an option, elsewhere they were unwanted, so they turned toward Eretz Yisrael. They walked across Europe hoping to get onto a crowded, unseaworthy boat that would bring them to the only place on earth they saw as their own. They knew that they would come up against His Majesty's Royal Navy, which would attempt to deny them their only haven.

Over seventy thousand survivors of the Shoah braved the high seas and made their way home against all odds. The study of the illegal immigration is one of the greatest chapters in the history of our history-laden people. For them there was no one handing out a boarding pass onto an El Al flight in Business Class to get home for Shabbat. El Al has an outstanding record of bringing Jews home.

Since our arrival would be late Friday afternoon, we made arrangements to stay with our children in Ramat Bet Shemesh, Rochelle and Yirmi and Daphna and Yehudah. Landing in Eretz Yisrael was a truly joyous moment.

# 24

# Dreams, Nightmares, and Memories

I had a dream for many years. I wanted to build my very own campus for the Jerusalem College for Adults. I could picture the building in my mind – a stream of people entering and leaving, dozens of classes taking place every week, hundreds of students in attendance, a garden surrounding and encircling, the calming feel of nature lending peace to all who entered our grounds. The school had moved a few times too many over the last few years, and I wanted to settle down in one place without ever thinking of having to move again. It was a lifelong dream. And then my dream suddenly became attainable. I was about to receive a very impressive contribution from Mrs. Bonnie Silver of Toronto, who wanted to dedicate the school in memory of her husband Avrom, my former *talmid* and dear friend and dedicator of our shul in Har Nof.

But along came a friend, Rabbi David Cohen, who had an idea that changed everything; he wanted to meet to discuss it.

Rabbi David Cohen had served as my executive director back when I served as *rosh yeshivah* in Ner Yisroel of Toronto. I still remember the day in 1966 when he entered my office on the *yeshivah* campus.

Though young in years, he was full of confidence and secure in his abilities. I asked him what he wanted.

"I want a job."

"What do you want to do?"

"I would like to serve in an executive capacity."

I like to consider myself a fairly good judge of character. I hired David Cohen and still feel that it was a very good decision on my part.

Even though he was all of twenty-one at the time.

You could say that he cut his teeth on our *yeshivah*, learned the ropes of management, and garnered lots of life experience. All in all, it was a good thing for everyone.

Now Rabbi Cohen wanted to meet with me again. Much water had flown under the bridge since we'd last worked together. We were decades older. Rabbi Cohen had gone on to work for the OU in a key management position. He had become quite an influential individual over the years. We used to go out once in a while for dinner. This time, I could tell that he had something particular in mind. I wondered what it was.

We had ourselves a nice meal and after some catching up on both our parts, Rabbi Cohen said, "Sholom, I would like to make you an offer. A merger. I want you to move your Jerusalem College for Adults into the Israel Center. This will be great for you. You will have the kind of facilities you have always wanted, for as many people as you need. You will also have complete financial backing from the OU. You will never have to fund-raise again. For our part, we would like to fill our center with Torah learning and since your students are our natural clientele it makes sense from every direction."

I listened.

At first I was inclined to turn down his offer. After all, my mind had been set on my dream of a brand new campus for many years. The campus was finally in my grasp, and merging with the Israel Center would mean waving goodbye to that dream forever. On the other hand, I would be joining the Israel Center, rather than being in competition with it. The expanded staff and student body would make more varied and creative programs possible, and I wouldn't have to raise money ever again. It was a tough call for me. I needed to discuss the offer with people who would understand all the ramifications, both legally and financially. So I set up a meeting with Larry and Marsha Roth.

I had met Marsha Roth eighteen years earlier when she walked into one of my classes in the Jewish Quarter of the Old City. She'd seen an ad in the paper, decided on a whim to give it a try, and the rest is history. She became a frequent student of the Jerusalem College for Adults and has been with us since that first chance class. The Roths have come through for me at moments of financial crisis through the years and we have grown very close with one another. Unfortunately, Larry was hit by a bus and killed in a tragic accident in February 2011. A tremendously charitable individual, he is sorely missed by all who knew him.

I trusted Larry's judgment. He was a successful businessman who knew the ways of the world.

I told the Roths about my offer for a merger.

I also told them how I finally had the chance to build a campus of my own.

"Take the OU's offer, Rabbi Gold."

Larry was very serious.

"This is the best thing that could have happened to you. You'll never have to fund-raise again. This is incredible!"

Larry changed my way of thinking. That was all I needed.

I called back Rabbi Cohen and told him I was in. It was time to merge.

My next step was to talk to Bonnie Silver. My big donation was coming from her, and I needed to know that she'd be on board with this move. I explained that going this route meant receiving an instant building and that the OU would put her husband's name on the building (which they did). I told her that having the OU on our side meant that the Jerusalem College for Adults would remain in operation for a very long time to come. Mrs. Silver agreed that this was a very good idea, on condition that I should be dean of the Avrom Silver Jerusalem College for Adults at the Israel Center. Bayla was to be employed by the center as well, as were our entire staff who had been with me for so long:

Rabbi Aaron Adler, Rabbi Macy Gordon, Aviva Gottlieb Zornberg. Everyone transferred over with us.

For twenty years I had been forced to travel to Toronto to raise funds. My brother and sister-in-law Mendel and Judy Rubinoff's home was my home during the years of my traveling to Toronto. They are like brother and sister to me. I can't say enough about their graciousness, *hachnasat orchim*, and kindness to me during all those years. Mendel's advice has stood me in good stead on many occasions.

However, now my fund-raising trips would become a thing of the past. I was finally free of that tremendous responsibility and could teach and learn with a much lighter heart. Avi Berman manages the center today and we have a wonderful relationship. G-d truly protected me and I recognize that fact, because I could have never managed my dream by myself.

୭

People don't usually make really close friends in their older years. Most of our good friends are made during childhood or in our teenage years. But I have met someone who not only became a dear friend of mine but even calls himself my brother.

"My only brother was killed years ago," he told me; "I need a brother. You're my brother now."

Rabbi Nachman Kahana and I met at the Israel Center. Rabbi Kahana sits upstairs in the Israel Center boardroom, with its magnificent view of Yerushalayim, and learns Torah (he's a phenomenal scholar) and writes his original thoughts. He has written a series of more than fifty *sefarim* on Tosafot, entitled *Mei Menuchot*.

We have become best friends and love each other with all the fondness of a youthful friendship. And that's so uncommon. I can meet up with someone I studied with in Ner Yisroel fifty years ago and the feelings of closeness and kinship are so strong that it's almost as if the intervening years have never even been there. But how often do you meet someone when you're sixty or seventy and hit it off in a way that's reminiscent of the friendships of youth? Both Rabbi Kahana and I have gained tremendously from one another. Not only that, but when I was considering retirement a few years ago because I wanted to devote my days to learning all the things I hadn't yet managed to cover, Rav Nachman made two comments that made me throw that plan out the window.

"Sholom," he said to me, "people with your talents and abilities are not allowed to stop teaching." While I was still reeling from that line he added, "And who says that G-d doesn't want you to teach any longer? Maybe what He really wants is for you to continue delivering classes for years to come?"

I had no reply to these sentiments, so I carried on teaching. He was right for saying it, and as for me, all I can say is thank You, G-d, for making me smart enough to listen to him. And I plan on teaching for as long as I can.

Rabbi Nachman Kahana is a real friend and we are lucky to have found one another.

࿇

If the Oslo Accords came into being because of an intellectual kind of blindness, reinforced by the hope that the olive branch had replaced the gun, that the lamb and the lion were finally joining in friendship, that a new day was dawning, by 2005 all those illusions should have been shattered. The terrorism and intifadas that had been unleashed should have convinced all that there was no peace process. So it was infinitely more confounding when Prime Minister Sharon concocted the antiseptically benignly named "Disengagement from the Gaza Strip." In fact it was expulsion, exile, for ten thousand Jews who had turned Gush Katif into a veritable Garden of Eden with the encouragement and assistance of successive governments. And Sharon had once stated, "Netzarim is like Tel Aviv."

The Oslo Accords were a shambles, never taken seriously by Arafat or his successors. It was obvious to all that the Arabs could not be trusted and would continue to relentlessly pursue their objective of taking all of Israel.

So a new and different form of blindness appeared upon the scene, so irrational it defied definition. It was a blindness that was self-imposed, carefully planned and executed with a strange and eerie kind of perfection. I call it "turning a blind eye," or willful blindness. The Disengagement from Gush Katif, we were told by its advocates – and with a straight face – would make Israel a more democratic and more Jewish country. I don't know how they figured, but that's what they said. Of course, there would be no fear of terrorist activity because the Gazans would worry that once we had no more settlements in the area, if they attacked us we would just go back into Gaza and solve the problem unilaterally once and for all.

We were going to become the darlings of the world. The nations of the world would shower us with love and affection.

What a fantasy.

We voiced our vigorous opposition. Gush Katif would become a staging ground for terror attacks and rocket barrages in our cities in the south. We knew that the brave residents of Gush Katif were our first line of defense – while the Left portrayed them as obstacles to peace. We railed against the destruction of great institutions of Torah that had been built there, of the agricultural miracle that was the hallmark of Gush Katif. We demonstrated on the highways and in city squares, we joined hands in a human chain from Gaza to the Kotel, we wore orange bracelets, and so much more. But to no avail. Tens of thousands of soldiers and police were trained for months in advance to carry out the expulsion. It was madness plain and simple.

When all the protests had failed and the great act of insanity was actually about to be carried out, Bayla and I headed for the Gush to show our support for the beleaguered expellees. We arrived at the checkpoint too late. The army had sealed it shut. So we went to Ashkelon and took a room in a hotel in the hope of making it in or at least to wait out the terrible expulsion there. We remained for two days, watching it on television and crying all the time. The horror of men, women, and children, Jews, being cast out of their homes by fellow Jews – and in Eretz Yisrael – was unbearable. In history we know of countless expulsions of Jews perpetrated by non-Jews. This expulsion, by our fellow Jews, was a painful first.

Of course, exactly what we had predicted came true; it couldn't be otherwise. The Gush became a launching pad against us, the magnificent agricultural infrastructure was immediately destroyed, holy places were demolished, and the world didn't start loving us. But even we who opposed it all could not have predicted that Hamas would win the elections in Gaza, raising the confrontation level considerably.

Attacks from Gaza intensified until Israel was left with no choice but to go to war. The flight from southern Lebanon in 2000 also led to war.

Finally, on December 27, 2008, Israeli troops went back into Gaza. The three-week operation was named Oferet Yetsukah, Cast Lead.

Our grandson Benyamin Goldreich was one of the combat soldiers. It was our first direct experience with the front lines of a war and it was difficult for us. We became Israelis during those three emotionally draining weeks. The worry, the praying, and – thank G-d! – the relief when it was all over and he arrived home safely connected us to all the other families with children who had gone off to war.

Before Benyamin went into Gaza he called one of his *yeshivah bochur* cousins and told him, "I am going to do my job. Now you do yours and learn Torah with all you've got."

In the middle of the war Benyamin's younger brother Efraim Yosef got married; the wedding date had long been set. It was the first child of our daughter Daphna and her husband Yehudah to get married. Benyamin, the *chatan*'s older brother, was deep in Gaza and could not leave his unit to come to the wedding. It was too dangerous to get him out.

To think our children were celebrating the first wedding in their family without their oldest son! My grandson would have called his brother on his cell phone, but all the soldiers' phones had been collected by the army upon entrance to Gaza. A few hours before the wedding started, his commanding officer lent my grandson his own phone so that he could make a brief call. He spoke to his brother for a couple of seconds, wished him mazel tov, and promised that they'd be reunited shortly.

I officiated at that wedding. The groom, Efraim Yosef, was also serving in the army during that period and there must have been about a hundred soldiers clustered around the *chuppah*. It was Parshat Miketz. Gripping the microphone in hand, I began to speak.

Rashi in the *parshah* relates an emotional conversation that took place between Yosef, ruler of Egypt, and his brother Binyamin, who does not yet know that the stranger before him is really his brother.

"Tell me about your family," Yosef requests of his younger brother.

"I have ten sons," Binyamin replies.

"What are their names?"

"…Achi, Rosh, Mupim, Chupim…"

Very interesting and uncommon names, to say the least.

"What do these names mean?" Yosef asked his brother.

"I had a brother," Binyamin sadly replied, "and all of my children are named after events in the life of my brother."

Yosef was moved. Extremely moved. "Why did you name your son Chupim?"

"Because I didn't merit to stand under the *chuppah* when my brother got married…and he missed my wedding as well. We are two brothers from the same mother. Very close. Yet neither of us merited to be at the other's wedding. That's why I named my son Chupim."

I looked around at the crowd, met the eyes of soldier after soldier, gazed on their youthful countenances with love.

"Efraim Yosef is standing under the *chuppah* right now with his *kallah*, Pazit," I said, "but his brother Benyamin hasn't merited to be here, standing at his side. *Im yirtzeh Hashem,* G-d willing, when Benyamin returns safe and sound from war and gets married, Efraim Yosef will be there, and he will dance and sing and rejoice."

Then I recited the prayer for the well-being of the soldiers of Israel. I was told that there was not a dry eye in the house. I can't really tell you about that myself, because it was kind of difficult for me to see through the tears that were blinding my own vision. In this "blindness" I sensed a feeling of brilliance and clarity.

Four years later Benyamin married Naamah, and again I was the officiating rabbi – Efraim Yosef was there!

ತಿ

For several years now, I have been serving as the rabbinic director of JewishIsrael (jewishisrael.ning.com), an organization that takes a critical look at Israel's burgeoning relationship with evangelical and fundamentalist Christian entities.

Due to the numerous political, economic, and security hardships facing Israel, large sectors of the Jewish community in both Israel and the Diaspora have become dependent upon evangelical Christian political influence and charity. And, at the risk of losing "friends," there has been great reluctance on the part of rabbinic and Jewish community leadership to draw red lines or issue guidelines to govern this interfaith relationship. The lack of accountability is exacting a severe cost on all sectors of Israeli society, which has seen alarming growth in the numbers and influence of so-called "Jewish believers in Jesus."

Evangelical Christians have gained a serious foothold in Israel and JewishIsrael is the only organization in Israel that addresses this complex issue with clarity and with a passion to safeguard Torah and tradition. The staff at JewishIsrael cares to thoroughly examine and address the type of challenging and painful subject matter that few care to deal with in earnest.

JewishIsrael has assembled an advisory team of community leaders and activists, rabbis, counter-missionary specialists, and prominent academics in the field of Christian history and millennialism. I would like to acknowledge a few of the JewishIsrael board members, with whom I work most closely.

Avraham Leibler and his wife, Shulamit, direct JewishIsrael. They draw from their experience as philanthropists and activists for numerous Zionist causes, including Shulamit's extensive work with victims of terror.

Anita Tucker serves as JewishIsrael's community affairs advisor. Anita is the recipient of the Moskowitz Prize for Zionism. Anita was also one of the earliest pioneers of the Gush Katif settlement enterprise, becoming a leading spokesperson for the residents during the long and intense struggle against the "Disengagement." She has had extensive dealings with a number of evangelical leaders and church groups.

Ellen Horowitz is JewishIsrael's content and research director. More Jewish mother and artist than scholar, she found herself compelled to become a writer during the upheaval and tragedy brought on by the Oslo Accords. Years ago, after working with numerous Christian groups and leaders in Israel, Ellen became alarmed by the unrestrained and irresponsible approach to the Israel-evangelical alliance and pored over the halachic dissertations on interfaith relations by Rav Joseph B. Soloveitchik. After consulting with those closest with Rav Soloveitchik, Ellen decided to dedicate her time and efforts to pursuing this issue.

The process of reestablishing the Jewish people in Eretz Yisroel means going from one crisis to the next, overcoming obstacles, forever facing new challenges. The years of standing behind police barriers demonstrating against the folly of Oslo, thousands holding hands in a human chain from Gush Katif to the Kotel, prodding and pleading with Members of Knesset and the US Congress are over. I feel now that together with my friends and colleagues of JewishIsrael we are involved in a significant struggle far from Zion Square or the entrance to Jerusalem. A struggle for the sanctity and soul of Israel. I fervently pray that we succeed.

꙲

After living in Har Nof for quite a few decades, my wife and I decided that we could use a change of pace and scenery. Since we love the Galil and Golan, we came to the conclusion that a temporary move up north would be just the thing for us at this particular juncture in our lives. But we needed to wait for the right time. After giving the matter much thought, we decided that the perfect opportunity had arrived after Pesach 2009. We settled on Migdal – a picturesque town of four shuls, limited shopping, a *makolet* (small grocery store) and incredible views – as our destination. We were shown a number of apartments and fell in love with one. There was a porch on one side of the house blessed with a glorious view of the Kinneret and on the other side an additional porch where one could sit and stare in endless fascination at Mount Arbel.

Kinneret on one side.

The Arbel cliffs on the other.

Scenery doesn't get much better than that. Yes, other countries possess the Grand Canyons and Niagara Falls, the Alps and Black

Forest. We however have the Kinneret and the Arbel and they, in the words of Rav Kook, "speak to us."

We weren't there full-time (I still have teaching obligations every week), but come the weekend, we'd hop in the car and a few short hours later, we'd arrive at our "country home near Tveria." There was nothing like it. Jump in the car, drive up to Migdal, and next thing you know, you're on the porch with a *sefer* and a drink, relaxing in the afterglow of Tveria's sun setting on the Kinneret. Sometimes I took off a week or two, sort of a mini-sabbatical, and then I was able to study in peace and solitude, write down my thoughts and speeches, and just appreciate the beauty and awesomeness of living in a place that resounded with echoes of the past and dreams of the future. We became well acquainted with the Galil and Tveria and got a feel for the towns and villages that our ancestors called home.

Our children and grandchildren loved our country home. They couldn't stop visiting. They even brought their friends. Suddenly everyone had an address in the Galil. It was an absolutely wonderful experience for us.

One Motzaei Shabbat we drove into Tveria and parked adjacent to the Tayelet (promenade). The walkway is situated across the street from Tveria's ancient cemetery. Great men of the past are buried in that cemetery. We parked the car, got out, and were about to begin walking the Tayelet when I heard someone screaming and shouting for dear life in the cemetery. It sounded serious.

"Bayla, you can continue walking while I find out what's happening," I said.

Upon entering the cemetery I bumped into a *chassidishe* boy who was just standing there minding his own business.

"What's going on here?" I inquired.

"The Stoliner Rebbe's *yahrtzeit* is taking place in a few days and a group of Chassidim have come up to Tveria to daven at his *kever*."

"Which Stoliner Rebbe would that be?" I asked him.

"Rav Yochanan," he replied.

Memories of my relationship with Rav Yochanan flooded my mind with a biting intensity. Rav Yochanan was my Rebbe. And here I'd merited to stand by his graveside a few days before his *yahrtzeit*. I was overcome by a sense of sanctity and nostalgia for days gone by. There were a few hundred Stoliner Chassidim clustered around Rav Yochanan's grave. I watched the scene in silence for a few minutes. Then I turned to the Chassid standing beside me and muttered almost to myself, "I don't think there's anyone here tonight who even saw the Rebbe besides me."

The Chassid stared at me in surprised shock. "What? You were acquainted with the Rebbe?"

"I davened in his shul in Williamsburg for seven years."

The place went crazy. Word spread through the crowd like wildfire. There was a man here who'd actually known the Rebbe back in the early years.

I was propelled to the center of the crowd, and they demanded that I recount all the *mofsim*, the miracles I had witnessed at Rav Yochanan's court. I told them anything I could remember from my time spent in his lofty presence and spoke about our relationship at length. They listened with appetite. This was rare. Being with someone who had actually spoken with – who had known – the Rebbe.

I went back again the following year. I kept track of the date and made sure to be there when the Chassidim arrived. It was the least I could do for "my" Rebbe.

Last year the current Stoliner Rebbe put in an appearance. I stood there staring at him. Just watching him gave me the shivers, because the Stoliner Rebbe of today resembles his grandfather in almost every way. A replica. The build of his body, the color of his beard, his eyes, the color of his skin. Like two drops of water. It was uncanny. I felt like fifty years had just slipped away, and I was back in the Stoliner *shtiebl* standing in front of the Rebbe, watching him with admiration just as I'd done so many decades ago.

I mentioned my observation to a group of people standing around. They were very excited. It seems they had heard this bit of information from additional sources as well. Knowing that their Rebbe shared his grandfather's looks touched a chord deep within their hearts. It was like the circle had been closed.

There were a few more surprises awaiting me in that Tverian cemetery – people who had served as crucial influences on my life.

The Kopycznitzer Rebbe was buried there.

And Zishe. His son. Remember what the Rebbe used to call us? Zishe's Chassidim. I'd learned so much from those glorious souls, lessons that have remained with me for all time. I'm so grateful to them all. Here they all were, transported from America, to their eternal resting places near my home.

It seemed like all my experiences connected with the cemetery in Tveria occurred on a Motzaei Shabbat. Zishe's *yahrtzeit* fell out on a Motzaei Shabbat and I drove over to the cemetery, parked, and began searching for his grave. I knew he was buried adjacent to his father, the Kopycznitzer, but I didn't recall where either grave was. A man entered the cemetery, an aristocratic individual accompanied by his family. I approached.

"Do you by any chance know where the Kopycznitzer Rebbe is buried?" I asked.

The question hung in the air, in the utter silence of the cemetery.

The man studied me for a while. I could see that he was wrestling with something. An indecision of some kind.

Finally, "SHOLOM!" he yelled out. "Is this Sholom Gold?" Next thing I knew, he was hugging me.

It was Professor Aaron Twerski. I hadn't recognized him. But when he said my name, there was no mistaking that voice. I had gotten to know both him and his twin brother way back in 1957 when they came to learn in Ner Yisroel. Two *chassidishe* boys stranded in the frigid coldness of the classic Lithuanian atmosphere.

Next thing I knew, Rav Ruderman had wanted to see me.

"Sholom," the Rosh Yeshivah said, "these two students, Aaron and Michel, just came from Milwaukee to study at Ner Yisroel. I want them to feel at home here in Baltimore."

I waited to hear how I fit in to all this.

"Since you hail from Williamsburg and have all that *chassidishe* blood coursing through your veins, I'd like you to take care of them."

I took my job seriously. I began organizing a weekly Melaveh Malkah for boys who felt connected to the *chassidish* way of life. We sang and danced until all hours of the night. Our meal was simple, but the food was accompanied by a healthy dose of Torah from the *chassidishe* giants of yesteryear. I served in this counselor/older brother/mentor role for about a year, during which time we developed an extremely close connection with one another.

It seemed every time I visited that cemetery, there was another trip down memory lane waiting to happen.

Our stint in Migdal lasted for about two and a half years, at which time the drive up north began exacting a harsher toll on me than previously. I was getting older and the things I'd once found easy to do were getting a little more difficult.

Thank G-d.

Getting old sure beats the alternative.

# 25

# Family Reunions

During our stay in Migdal, we hosted a Shabbaton for the entire family. We rented a guest house called Nof Kinneret that had enough room for everyone – children and grandchildren included – and enjoyed a wonderful Shabbat together. Shabbat afternoon before Minchah, Sabba (that's me) had a talk with his grandchildren. With the majestic Mount Arbel rising to the north and the glistening Kinneret and the Golan to the east, I shared some thoughts with them. It seemed like it was just yesterday that I was playing punch ball in Williamsburg on Wilson Street, enjoying those who could hit three sewers, and "Johnny on the pony" in front of 616 Bedford Avenue, the Agudah. Now, a lifetime later, having reached the stage when one wonders what one has really accomplished in life, I was facing a fine group of young people eager to hear Sabba…or maybe just humoring him. Well, we'll see.

This is what I told them.

My father died in 1981 in Yerushalayim when we were on sabbatical here. He had lived with us for the last years of his life. He is buried on Har Hazeitim. He left very few material possessions. He didn't own a home or an apartment, nor a car (he never drove), no stocks, bonds, or monetary instruments of any sort, no significant savings. He was a factory worker his whole life. He cut leather for shoes. His job didn't define him nor in any way capture his essence.

So when he passed away in Yerushalayim he left nothing – or so it seemed. He had a little orange-colored suitcase with not much in it that accompanied him for many years. I once had a peek in it. There were old invitations to his three sons' weddings, newspaper clippings about us (all three were rabbis), and nothing much else.

I had forgotten about his little suitcase until I came across it some while after he died and decided to go through it. It was in fact full of the expected yellowing, browning papers and photographs, but then I came across an envelope. I opened it and took out a letter in an advanced state of aging, holes at the folds, and read it. I remained silent for a long time after reading it. *Nechadim*, my dear grandchildren, today I want to tell you the story of the letter, because it has had great impact on your family and has formed the structure and essence of your lives. This letter may even explain to you a great deal about your Sabba (me) and Savta. So here goes.

The letter was from Dr. S. Bernstein, Director, Palestine Bureau of the Zionist Organization of America, to Mr. Gold, 91 Lee Avenue in Williamsburg, Brooklyn.

Dr. Bernstein informs my father that "We are in receipt of a letter from the Immigration Department of the Jewish Agency in Palestine in Jerusalem (dated July 30, 1946, ref. # 10474/G), wherein they inform us that you and your family have been duly registered for Palestine certificates."

The letter continues: "However, they state further that owing to the complete lack of certificates at the present time, there is no possibility for them to do anything in your case now.

"Let us hope that in the not too distant future an adequate number of certificates will be at their disposal, so that all of those wishing to go to Palestine will be enabled to do so.

"Sincerely yours, Dr. S. Bernstein."

The letter is dated August 9, 1946.

To fully comprehend the meaning and message of the letter we have to analyze it step by step.

Let's begin with the date. What was happening in the world in general and in Eretz Yisrael in particular in 1946? The Second World War ended in 1945, leaving Europe in ruins and revealing the horrible truth of the systematic destruction and planned extermination of six million Jews. The worst crime in history had been perpetrated by Germany, aided and abetted by most of the rest of the world. The nations of the world did not want the Jews, neither before, during, nor after the War. The cruel story of American and Canadian anti-Semitism has been extensively documented. The British ruled in Palestine.

In 1939 His Majesty's government issued a White Paper limiting Jewish immigration to a total of seventy-five thousand over five years and henceforth – listen to this – no Jew would be permitted into Eretz Yisrael. At the precise moment that millions of Jews were desperately clamoring, begging, pleading for a place to flee to and escape the impending doom, Eretz Yisrael was closed before them. From our perspective it is near impossible to understand such cruelty, such hearts of stone, such despicable inhumanity.

Even after the war, when the broken survivors desperately wanted to leave the giant cemetery that was Europe in those days, the British continued to refuse entry into Palestine. The mighty British fleet was stationed in the Mediterranean to make certain that no Jews would reach Eretz Yisrael.

Hundreds of thousands of Jews remained homeless in Europe, wandering from place to place. Then began one of the great dramas of history. A homeless people with nowhere to go began walking across Europe, from country to country in order to reach the Mediterranean seashore. Word was out that hardly seaworthy boats were leaving to make the dangerous run through the British blockade in the hope of reaching the shores of Eretz Yisrael. A people on the brink of despair became inspired with the mission of going to the one place on earth that was home.

It is so important to know this history so that you can appreciate the dramatic changes in our world.

Since 1948, any Jew anywhere in the free world can get onto a plane and move to Eretz Yisrael with no need for any other country's certificates.

I want you to remember this well. Anyone who trivializes Yom Haatzmaut has no knowledge of Jewish history, is not tuned in to the pain and suffering of a whole generation of Jews in Europe and Arab lands, and denies the great outpouring of Hashem's kindness to His people in giving them Eretz Yisrael.

What was happening in Eretz Yisrael-Palestine in 1946? Jewish underground groups had decided that Britain must go. They took on the mighty British Empire, upon which the sun had not yet set, just as Jews had risen against other great empires that no longer exist. It was a classic modern-day example of the few against the many.

On July 22, 1946, six days before the communication from Jerusalem, the southern wing of the King David Hotel was blown up by the Irgun. That section housed the offices of the British Mandatory forces. They were the ones who issued the pitiful number of "certificates" to enter Eretz Yisrael.

With Eretz Yisrael erupting into battle, how many American Jews do you think had applied for aliyah? They must have thought that the Golds had taken leave of their senses. What could have moved an economically lower middle class *baalebatishe* family in Williamsburg to apply for aliyah at a time of such upheaval?

I know the answer but I'm not sure that many people today will understand – *ahavat Eretz Yisrael*! Love of Eretz Yisrael. That was an integral component of the spiritual baggage of any Jew through the long exile. It is so sorely lacking today and in such short supply that it seems a bit quaint, archaic, far out, a relic of a previous era. But my parents had it.

The letter's final paragraph expressed the "hope" that there will be sufficient certificates to allow all who wish to come to do so. Dr. Bernstein couldn't have imagined that less than two years later, the British would be gone, thrown out by Jewish resistance, and a State of Israel would come into being. No certificates, no blockades, no unseaworthy boats. But a flood of Jews flowing from all over the world – going home. This was the outpouring of Hashem's great kindness and the fulfillment of the promise to Rachel Imeinu – the children shall return to their boundaries.

I concluded by urging my children and grandchildren to remember the letter and its significance. I told them to never ever lose sight of a great Rashi that sums it all up. It says in Shmot 13:11, "And it will be when Hashem will bring you to the land of the Canaanites as He swore to you and your forefathers and He will give it to you." Rashi comments on the last words of the *pasuk*, "and He will give it to you": "The Land should be considered in your eyes as if it has been given to you on that very day (i.e., every day) and it should not be considered in your eyes as an inheritance received from ancestors." The Land should never ever be taken for granted.

Not only were Sabba and Savta Gold great lovers of Eretz Yisrael but in equal measure, so were Sabba and Savta Rubinoff – your Savta's (Bayla's) parents. Your Savta had an uncle (her father's younger brother), Yeshaya Rubinoff, H"yd, who in 1948, at age twenty-two, left Toronto to help defend Eretz Yisrael.

When the UN voted to partition Palestine, on November 29, 1947, the Jewish administration asked for volunteers to help fight in the war that was already beginning. Shaya had served in the Canadian army and had been sent overseas, seeing firsthand the remnant of the Jewish communities in Europe emerging from the concentration camps. He was one of the first of the group of Macha"l (Mitnadvei Chutz La'aretz, volunteers from abroad) who came to Eretz Yisrael. The training he had received with the Canadian army stood him in good stead.

He joined the Palmach's Yiftah Brigade, which first fought up in the north. After securing that area, the soldiers made their way to wherever they were needed. Shaya ended up in the Latrun area, which was sorely in distress. On Shabbat in Barfilia, today just outside of Modiin, a bomber plane strafing everything in its path found a target in this beautiful young man. He died in the ambulance on the way to the hospital and is buried in Tel Aviv.

Back home, Savta and her family were in the bungalow in Pontypool, Ontario. It was the tenth of Tammuz when the telegram came. Savta was only six years old but she will never forget her mother screaming, "Oh, no!" and her Aunt Jennie fainting. The family was devastated. Not long afterwards, Savta's parents received a letter Shaya had written just a few days before his death in which he said that that it was a beautiful Land and he was never coming back.

To this day he is a hero in the Rubinoff family, and his ultimate sacrifice is part of our heritage of love of the Land. If he was willing to die for it, the very least we can do is live for it. That is the true *mesirut nefesh* – self-sacrifice for his people and his Land. He will never be forgotten. May his blessing be a memory.

I urged my children and grandchildren to remember their heritage on both sides, and the dedication and heroism their ancestors showed for Eretz Yisrael. I told them I prayed it would stay with them for the rest of their lives, and I left them with this closing thought: My father, *a"h*, didn't leave stock, bonds, annuities, savings, nor land. He left the Land as an eternal inheritance.

∽

We recently celebrated my wife Bayla's birthday. She was seventy years old.

The Gold family very much enjoys getting together to celebrate the milestones of life and this was no exception. Everyone was there. Of course I had to say a few words. Truthfully, I had prepared well for the occasion. I looked around at my children, grandchildren, and great-grandchildren, my beautiful family whom I love so much, and I shared with them what was on my mind.

"You all know," I began, "that my hero is Rabbi Akiva. Always has been, always will be."

Heads were nodding all around through my opening line. They know me.

"You all know his fascinating story," I went on, and I proceeded to tell them about how Rachel, the wealthy and beautiful daughter of one of the richest men in Yerushalayim, met Rabbi Akiva and recognized the immense potential hidden beneath the shepherd's exterior. Not only did she marry him, thereby rendering herself penniless, she sent him off to learn Torah in a *yeshivah*, far, far away. The years passed. Five years. Ten years. Twelve years later, when he returned home, he heard her say that she'd gladly grant him twelve additional years of learning, and he turned around and retraced his steps to the study hall for twelve more years. Twenty-four years in all. It was finally time for the tremendous scholar to return. But he did not return alone. He stood at the head of an army, thousands and thousands of students all calling him *rebbe*. What an entourage.

And Rachel came to see him.

She made her way resolutely through the tangle of students to prostrate herself before the man whom she had believed in so many years before. The man for whom she had sacrificed her fortune, her relationship with her father – basically everything. The students did not want to allow her into the inner circle. But Rabbi Akiva saw her.

"Let her in," he commanded the students, "for all the Torah I have learned and all the Torah you have learned is hers. She is responsible for it all!"

What does Rabbi Akiva mean by this statement?

Rachel possessed a tremendous talent, an uncanny ability to look at an ostensibly simple man – a shepherd, an ignoramus, someone who was already forty years of age – and to see the glowing jewel that lay within. Never for a moment did she falter. She believed in him with all her heart and soul. And it was this power that propelled Rabbi Akiva to his high level of greatness. The ability to discern what lay within became his hallmark also. He is the great teacher who was able to see beyond the here and now.

The rabbis looked down on the Temple Mount from Har Tzofim and saw a fox running out of the Holy of Holies and they cried, but Rabbi Akiva laughed. He was able to discern the future, even through a hazy veil of tears. He was always taking it one giant step further. He foresaw a day when old men and women would sit in Yerushalayim while children scampered through the joy-filled streets. He was able to see redemption. Even then. By using Rachel's abilities and strengths.

Rabbi Akiva was once giving a *shiur* when he saw that people were falling asleep. To wake them up, he related the following cryptic line: "Let Queen Esther, the great granddaughter of Sarah Imeinu who lived for 127 years, come and rule over 127 states."

What's Rabbi Akiva telling us here?

I'll tell you what it doesn't mean. People weren't falling asleep during the *shiur*. No, there was something else wrong. Rabbi Akiva was living under the brutal, cruel heel of the Roman oppressor, the Temple had been destroyed – the Jewish people were reaching the point of despair.

The Aruch Hashulchan writes in his work on the Haggadah, *Leil Shimmurim*, that Avraham Avinu and Sarah Imeinu were physically incapable of having children. The very birth of Yitzchak was an open miracle. "That birth," he continues, "is referring to the Jewish nation, which will only survive the next six thousand years with open miracles."

This was what Rabbi Akiva was telling his people. If our matriarch Sarah, who wasn't capable of bearing children, did in fact have a child, while living 127 years, anything is possible. And her granddaughter Esther, who ruled over 127 states, would win the day with her own spate of open miracles as well.

Rabbi Akiva is famous for another statement as well (*Yoma* 85b): "*Amar Rabbi Akiva: Ashreichem Yisrael. Lifnei Mi attem mittaharin, u'mi metaher etchem?*" (Says Rabbi Akiva: Praised be you Israel. Before Whom are you purifying yourselves and Who purifies you?).

"*Avichem she'ba'shamayim*" (Your Father in heaven).

"*Shene'emar: Mah mikveh metaher et hateme'im, af Hakadosh Baruch Hu metaher et Yisrael*" (As it says: Just as a *mikveh* purifies the impure, so too does G-d purify Israel).

"*Mikveh Yisrael Hashem*" (G-d is the *mikveh* of Israel).

What is Rabbi Akiva saying here?

This was the first Yom Kippur after the Temple's destruction. For hundreds of years, the Jewish nation gathered on the Temple Mount on Yom Kippur and watched the priests carrying out their holy tasks. Sacrifices on the altar. The high priest offering the *ketoret*. Throwing the goat down the razor-sharp side of the craggy mountain where it landed in a million pieces at the bottom. All this was something to see and experience, something looked forward to by the entire nation.

And now it was no more.

Said Rabbi Akiva, "*Ashreichem Yisrael*" (how fortunate are you people of Israel), because ultimately, purity comes from G-d. Even if there is no high priest and no two goats and no Temple and no spicy fragrance of *ketoret*.

*Lifnei Mi atem metaharin? Lifnei Avichem she'ba'shamayim.* Before Whom are you purifying yourselves? Before your Father in heaven. G-d will purify you, with or without a Temple.

The Aruch Hashulchan poses the following question: Why did so many influential rabbis come together at Rabbi Akiva's Seder in Bnei Brak? Rabbi Eliezer and Rabbi Tarfon and Rabbi Yehoshua and Rabbi Elazar Ben Azariah. What were they all doing there?

The answer, says the Aruch Hashulchan, is that all these great rabbinical authorities wanted to show their gratitude to Rabbi Akiva for everything he did and represented. Because he was the one who comforted them. As they said, "*Akiva nichamtanu, Akiva nichamtanu*" (Akiva you have comforted us, Akiva you have comforted us).

That's why they were gathered in his home – as a token of their appreciation to the man who was able to see and appreciate the entire picture. To the man who never got depressed because he knew that G-d had a plan and that His nation would be redeemed. And this strength of Rabbi Akiva is what has kept the Jewish nation strong for thousands of years.

After extolling Rabbi Akiva and the woman behind the man, I then returned to my wife.

The type of foresight exhibited by Rabbi Akiva and his wife Rachel is very much the kind of foresight shown by *my* wife through our more than fifty years of marriage. She always knew what was right for our children and she always knew what was right for me. Although she had been born in Toronto and her entire family lived there – parents, brothers, sister – she encouraged me to leave the city of her youth, because she felt I needed to move on and would be able to use my abilities with more powerful results somewhere else. It was very difficult for us to leave, but she knew that I needed to move, to gain more experience, to grow in all sorts of ways. She didn't think twice and she made it happen.

And she was right. One hundred percent right. Because sometimes you have to start over in life. And West Hempstead turned out to be a wonderful experience for us. But it was all because of her!

After we moved to Yerushalayim and things were extremely difficult, she didn't throw up her hands and concede defeat. She decided to open a business, her hat store, Headlines, which became a famous spot to purchase women's head coverings in the center of town. Women would travel long distances to buy a hat or *tichel* at Rebbetzin Gold's store. She and her partner Rebbetzin Tova Silverstein managed the store for ten years. A successful business, run by women with no business experience but plenty of drive. She typically downplays the importance of her contributions, but don't let her tell you otherwise: it was crucial and she simply pulled us through.

Not only that, but she started a volunteer organization called Nechama, together with her friend Tova Reish who hails from Toronto, an occupational therapist for many years and wife of Rabbi Moshe Reish, *a"h*, a *talmid chacham* and beloved *rebbe*. They gathered a group of women together to study and to train as bereavement and trauma counselors. Her social work degree from the States was being put to use to help comfort those whose lives had been irrevocably altered.

There was a period of time when the phone calls coming into our home read like the headlines of the newspapers. She met with and guided counselors who comforted victims from the many terror attacks. Nechama volunteers were always ready to meet with those who needed counseling. It was a wonderful service. After ten years she handed over the reins to her head counselors, Thea Givati and Adina Rakoff, because as important as it is to know when to develop a brand new idea, it's just as important to know when to bring in new strengths. It was time for her to move on.

Like I said, my hero has always been Rabbi Akiva. Well, my wife Bayla has been my Rachel from day one and please G-d, for many years to come.

# 26

# Retirement

In 2006 I decided the time had come to retire from my position as *rav* of Kehillat Zichron Yosef of Har Nof. My friends in the Israeli rabbinate have never forgiven me for this decision, since in their collective minds a rabbi remains at his post until he no longer can. For example, if you're a *rav* in Har Nof, you remain *rav* in Har Nof until you pass away and the burial society maneuvers you onto Har Hamenuchot. They believe that a *rav* should never voluntarily relinquish his position, elderly, feeble, and infirm though he may be.

I decided, however, that it was time for me to channel some energies to other parts of my life that I hadn't had time to focus on as much as I may have wanted to.

I had been a devoted *rav* for forty years, and being constantly available for the community and congregation automatically meant being less available for the family. I was rarely able to go to my children for Shabbat. I had a position and commitments. I had to give a *drashah*. My family had been relatively understanding about having to share me with the congregation. But I felt that they deserved to see more of me. I wanted to become part of their lives, to be there for their milestones.

So I retired from the shul. And I feel that I made the right decision.

I had another incentive as well. Something happened a few months before that pushed me to make that tough decision. The Second Lebanon War. Thirty young men from my shul had been sent to the front during that war. I was very nervous and tense. I couldn't stop thinking about "my boys" out there. The phone would ring and I'd be afraid to answer it, wondering if it heralded bad news. August 2006 was a nerve-racking month.

I remember being out shopping when a member of my congregation called me with the terrible news that his nephew Yonatan Einhorn had fallen in Lebanon. I went to see him that night. The funeral was the next day. It was a heartrending sight. Such a special, wonderful young man. They showed me a *sefer* that the young soldier had put together – a compilation of all the halachic laws pertaining to a soldier's life. The laws of prayer, Shabbat, *yom tov*. He'd had it printed up in a tiny volume so he could carry it with him wherever he went.

His death was a real loss for our nation as well as for all who knew him.

And it wasn't only him. My stress and agony increased by the day. I couldn't help it. I cared for those boys like my own children and feared for their lives, the way a father wants to protect his family.

When that war finally came to an end, I told myself that I had done my best and that it was time to step down. It was time for someone with younger nerves to step into my shoes and take over the pulpit.

After it was official and there was no turning back, I felt the awesome responsibility of the rabbinate leaving my tense shoulders like a physical weight, slipping, slipping away…and I felt so much lighter.

It was time for other people, younger than I, to take up the torch. Kehillat Zichron Yoseph was most fortunate to find Rav Moshe Leventhal to serve as *mara d'atra*. Rav Leventhal is graced with many great qualities: *talmid chacham*, *darshan*, man of halacha, who, together with his wife Batya, is involved fully in the life of KZY. For the first time since I became a *rav*, I have one, and Bayla has a *rebbetzin*. I wish them what the Lubavitcher Rebbe wished me.

Thursday, November 8, 2008. Bayla and I had spent the day with our *mechutanim*, Rabbi Avraham and Brenda Goldreich, visiting our grandson Benyamin Goldreich, son of Daphna and Yehudah. He was receiving his *kumtah* (beret) as a soldier in Sayeret Givati. It had been a wonderful day and I was about to deposit the Goldreichs outside their home at the bottom of Har Nof. I parked on Nissim Street, right up against the curb. It was getting dark, around six or seven o'clock. We were saying our final goodbyes when a taxi cab appeared from nowhere and hit our car with tremendous force, sending us flying. The taxi continued along on his own momentum, completely out of control, to the point where it ended its journey upside down on a pile of rocks. We were dazed and shaken up, while my wife, who had received the brunt of the impact, was screaming, screaming – her leg caught under the driver's seat – she was in terrible pain.

I emerged from the car swaying alarmingly, walking like a drunk, unable to find my balance. The car had been totaled. A bus pulled up beside us and came to a stop. I guess the driver had witnessed what happened. Hachovesh of Har Nof arrived at the scene a few minutes later. Akiva Pollack, Yirmi's childhood friend, had everything under control. It felt good to be in such capable hands. The rest of the team performed flawlessly as well.

Bayla had to be dislodged from the car and was in excruciating pain. We were all transferred to the hospital in record time. I was in pain; our *mechutanim* were suffering as well. But it could have been much worse. In the hospital they told us that Bayla had to go into surgery immediately. Her hip had been dislodged from its socket. According to her doctor, this kind of pain ranks up there with some of the worst pain imaginable. I was given pain killers and remember things through a hazy curtain. What an evening it had turned out to be!

Bayla had to remain in the hospital over Shabbat while I was tanked up on pain killers and sent home. I went to shul Shabbat morning to recite the blessing of Hagomel, but overall it seemed to me that I had managed to escape the brunt of the accident.

Sunday morning I awoke in agony.

A delayed reaction. But when it hit, it hit hard. For the next month,

I couldn't even get dressed by myself. The two of us, Bayla and I, sat in our home like two invalids and barely moved. Our bodies had undergone such trauma, they had entered emergency mode and almost completely shut down in protest. In the end, it took about a year before Bayla was back to herself.

There's a point I'm trying to get to.

Right after the accident, people from the shul called us.

"Rabbi Gold, do you need anything? Can we help you with anything?"

"No, we're fine. Thank you very much."

Apparently my protestations of self-sufficiency hadn't been convincing because the packages of neatly wrapped and beautifully prepared meals began arriving at our door daily soon after. They were delivered complete with instructions on what needed to be warmed up and for how long, and with a detailed list of *hechsherim* attached. It was simply beautiful to see the community swinging into action as they dedicated themselves to helping us recover. It was the perfect way for me to get to know my community in a way that I never had before. They were magnificent. Simply magnificent. The phone didn't stop ringing. Everyone was davening for us. We felt extremely loved by those around us. And we appreciated it.

I'm pretty sure that being so loved helps a person recover quicker. The *gemilat chesed* of Kehillat Zichron Yosef was impressive. We get choked up when we think of it.

∽

During the last few years, I have been fortunate to be present at several fifty-year anniversary celebrations. Ner Yisroel of Toronto was the first to celebrate fifty years since its establishment.

They invited me and sent tickets for both me and my wife to attend the dinner in Toronto. We were accompanied by our son Yirmi, who was there because he's always there. I was handed a plaque which read as follows: "In appreciation to Rabbi Sholom Gold in recognition of his major contribution in the founding of the *yeshivah*. His selfless dedication and outstanding accomplishments in the *yeshivah*'s first decade will always be remembered."

Being at that dinner was a real trip down memory lane. Originally, the dinner's organizers asked me to speak for a few minutes only, a benediction of sorts.

"I'm going to need at least five minutes," I told the man who called. He had to go back to the committee on that because they had that dinner planned down to the second. In the end, however, when I began speaking, reminiscing to the packed ballroom about the *yeshivah*'s early days, the room hushed and people grew still, eyes moist as they recalled the humble beginnings of a *yeshivah* that had grown into a venerable Toronto landmark in education.

Simply put, they didn't want me to stop talking.

I was reminding them of how it all began fifty years before. I was the only person in the room who had actually been there, who had known all of them and their parents and grandparents. I had sat in every one of their homes and met with their parents and convinced them to send their children to learn by us and they had agreed reluctantly.

I went through the room, person by person, face by familiar face, relating anecdotes and humorous incidents that had occurred as I traversed Toronto, fulfilling Rav Ruderman's request that there be a *yeshivah* in their great city. I spoke of the Kuhl family, and the Gasners, Hershel Rubenstein, Saul Sigler, and the Lebovics. I gave honorable mention to the Hofstedters and the Reichmanns and Joe Tenenbaum and Mrs. Gryfe (whose wonderful son Hershey, one of our first students, tragically passed away at the prime of his life) and all the venerable Toronto rabbis who showed me the ropes and gave me my start.

I told the story of Ner Yisroel of Toronto.

I described the Rosh Yeshivah's request and how I hadn't known what I was getting into, and how scary yet exciting an endeavor it had turned out to be. I found myself being drawn into the narrative, remembering little details from the long-gone past, from the days when I'd been young and confident and ready to breach new frontiers. The crowd smiled and laughed and grew nostalgic and pensive in turn as the poignant beginnings of their *yeshivah* were being described. It was one of my finest speeches ever.

It was very important for me to acknowledge that there had been rabbis and educators of great stature who, with much self-sacrifice, had brought Toronto to the stage where it was ready for a *yeshivah*. Ner Yisroel was not born in a vacuum. It represented the next frontier to be conquered, and it was my good fortune to be entrusted with that challenge and, with Hashem's help, to carry out the mission successfully.

The dinner was in honor of two special *baalei batim* – Avrohom Bleeman and Sandy Hofstedter – and I depicted the broadness of their endless contributions in a way that opened the eyes of the crowd to the depth of their generosity. They came running over to hug and kiss me when I finished the speech. It was a real moment of *nachat*. I had started something fifty years before and was granted the priceless opportunity of seeing the fruits that had grown and sprouted on the branches of a tree that I had nurtured and tended with love, care, and affection.

I ended off with the following words.

"When Rav Ruderman sent me to Toronto in 1959, he didn't know that I had been planning on moving to Eretz Yisrael. I figured that I'd spend a year or two in Toronto and then revert to my original plan to make aliyah. In the end, my plans were pushed off for about twenty plus years…but we made it in the end. Thank G-d we made it in the end."

The entire ballroom broke into thunderous applause.

❦

The next fifty-year milestone celebration was for my former shul, Congregation B'nai Torah of Toronto.

The shul that had once been housed in a shack.

The shul that had been put on the map with the help of a ten-thousand-dollar donation from Joe Tenenbaum, later to become one of the most famous philanthropists in the world.

The shul where I had delivered my debut speech on Shavuos morning.

B'nai Torah.

Instead of them inviting us in for the big day, they made a surprise move and decided to celebrate their fiftieth anniversary in Eretz Yisrael with a well-planned and beautifully executed Shabbat. The guests all stayed at the Jerusalem Plaza and the meals were held at the Israel Center. On Motzaei Shabbat a gathering was held for all the people who had been part of B'nai Torah in the past and had since made aliyah. I'm talking about a good five to six hundred people.

It was a night to remember.

~

West Hempstead was the next fifty-year reunion on the list.

They called well in advance of the dinner and sent two sets of plane tickets. One set for Rabbi Sholom and Bayla Gold and the other for Rabbi Meyer and Goldie Fendel. What a beautiful celebration. It took place over an entire Shabbat. I spoke. Rabbi Fendel spoke. We stayed at the home of Aryeh and Yaffa Silverberg and enjoyed every minute of it. There was a magnificent *kiddush* that Shabbat morning and an extremely enjoyable dinner in the ballroom of the Sands a few days afterwards.

What can I say? Fifty-year reunion celebrations are very satisfying as parties go.

~

This past year we celebrated one additional fifty-year milestone. I'm referring of course to the fifty-year anniversary of Rabbi and Mrs. Gold, the most important fifty-year celebration of all. From time to time we've taken the family away for a weekend at some point during the year. What can I say? The extended Gold family likes to get together. It's a tremendous blessing. Yeshivish, Dati Leumi…everyone gets along. The smiles, the friendship, the harmony, the warmth and delight at being in one another's company are as special as can be. We try to save the get-togethers for when we're celebrating something.

One year we got together in honor of it being twenty years since we made aliyah.

One year we got together to celebrate a special birthday.

Every time a different happy reason.

Our fiftieth wedding anniversary. What a Shabbat that was! What a feeling of togetherness. The speeches commemorating our fifty years together, the poems and songs, the jokes and laughter, the davening and learning, and best of all, the communal *zemirot* and singing, the downtime and great food all served as a reminder of how lucky both Bayla and I are. We know it and thank G-d every single day for the bounty with which He has showered us.

# Epilogue

And so I arrive at the end of my narrative. My life has been a long and sometimes exhausting ride, and I have experienced turbulence at numerous moments throughout. Yet it's been consistently exhilarating and full of heavenly assistance from day one. As I stand on my porch overlooking a view straight out of the Tanach, I can see the endless mountains surrounding Yerushalayim. Countless communities, millions of individuals all living the dream of the end of days.

I can't help but recall the names and memories of years and decades gone by. My mind is filled with memories. Memories of my parents. Of my brothers, the Einstein debater and the one known as "Rashi." Of my wife (what would I have done without her?!) and children. The times we shared and share. And so many more people, places and experiences.

Memories of Rav Yaakov Kamenetsky. Rav Moshe Feinstein. Rav Yaakov Yitzchok Halevi Ruderman. Rav Avraham Pam. Torah Vodaath. Ner Yisroel. Williamsburg. Chaim Gelb. The Kopycznitzer Rebbe. Zishe's Chassidim. Stolin. Eretz Yisrael. Chevron. Ponevezh. Rav Shach. Rav Chatzkel. The Brisker Rav. Rav Tzvi Pesach Frank. Rav Tzvi Yehuda Kook. Rav Yitzchak Isaac Halevi Herzog. Rav Yosef Shalom Elyashiv. The Belzer Rebbe. The Ponevezher Rav. Rav Amram Blau. Chaim Herzog. Shlomo Carlebach. Rav Yisroel Gustman. Rav Dovid Kronglass. Congregation B'nai Torah of Toronto. The Lubavitcher Rebbe. Rav Shlomo Heiman. Ronnie Greenwald. The Tchebiner Rav. Rav Nosson Scherman. Rabbi Linchner. Rav Shloime Freifeld. The Tyrell mansion. West Hempstead. The *eruv*. Rav Shimon Eider. The *mikveh*. The OU. The Debreziner Rav. The Young Israel. Rav Avraham Shapira. Rabbi Naftali Neuberger. Rav Nota Schiller. Rav Shlomo Jacobowitz. Bibi Netanyahu. The twinning with Eli. P'eylim.

Charlie the dog making aliyah. The Satmar Rebbe. Rav Aharon Kotler. Mike Tress. Rav Pesach Lerner. Venice. Gateshead. Freezing Oslo. The accords. Russia. Aryeh Kroll. The Bostoner Rebbe. Demonstrations. Moscow. Leningrad. Riga. Kehillat Zichron Yosef in Har Nof. The Russian Compound. Undergoing questioning in the Moscow airport. Rabbi Mallen Galinsky. Irving Maisel. Rabbi Meyer Fendel. Rav Nachman Kahana. Being followed by the KGB. Answering Tosafot difficulties on a Moscow train. Losing jobs. Opening schools. Julius Kuhl. The Hofstedters. Meyer Gasner. Hershel Rubenstein. Harold Vogel. The devoted members of my shul. Rav Avraham Schwartzbaum. Meir Lebovic. Tveria and the Rambam's grave. Rav Eliezer Silver. The Twerski brothers. Migdal. Joe Tenenbaum. Moshe Reichmann. The Jerusalem College for Adults. Rabbi Moshe Rose. Prime Minister Menachem Begin. The trailer trip across the United States. Avrom and Bonnie (may she live a long and happy life) Silver. Mendel and Judy Rubinoff. Rav Nachman Bulman.

The list and the memories go on and on and on.

It's been a long journey and thank G-d it's not over yet. I have no doubt that much still awaits us. There are still countless *shiurim* waiting to be given and numerous stories whose time has not yet come. And I know that one day (may it happen soon) I will find myself standing under the bridge at the entrance to Jerusalem and Rabbi Akiva will step out of the smoke and fog and he will smile in silent wonder when he sees that his prediction of long, long ago has finally come true. Because the dreams are coming true. Now and in our days.

Mashiach is almost here.

All we need to do is *ibberhippen der brik* for a short while more, until the shofar sounds and the dream has become a reality.

# INDEX

Aaron, Alan, 292
Aaron, Honey, 292
Acco, 262
Adler, Chavi (Gold; niece), 22, 159
Adler, Mordechai, 22
Adler, Rabbi Aaron, 346
Afula, 262–64
Aharon, 190–91
Akiva, Rabbi, 52–54, 362–65, 366, 376
Alon Moreh, 209
Amir, Yigal, 308
Applebaum, Dr. David, 313–14, 315
Applebaum, Debbie, 313
Applebaum, Naava, 314
Arafat, Yasser, 194, 271, 279–80, 284, 287, 296, 347
Ariel, 280
Ariel, Uri, 301
Artziel, Rav Yosef, 278, 312
Ashkelon, 221, 348
Ashkenazi, Yossele, 45–46
Associated Hebrew Schools (Toronto), 124, 127
Athens, 196
Atlas, Moshe, 255
Atlas, Yedidya, 288, 307
Atlit, 262, 263
Auerbach, Rav Shlomo Zalman, 216–17, 265
Auerbach, Rav Shmuel, 265

Avidan, Eliyahu, 256
Avraham Avinu, 364
Avraham, Avraham, 43
Avrom Silver Jerusalem College for Adults at the Israel Center, 345. See also Israel Center

Bais Yaakov of Toronto, 138
Baltimore, 35, 36, 39, 103, 104–9, 110–11, 114–17, 118, 174, 182, 199, 291
Barfilia, 361
Bartenura, Rav Ovadia Mi-, 49, 50
Batsheva Hotel (Jerusalem), 192
Bechoffer, Robbie, 189
Begin, Benny, 275
Begin, Menachem, 198, 200, 201, 204–6, 306, 376
Beilin, Yossi, 194–95
Belarus, 131
Belzec (concentration camp), 6
Belzer Rebbe. See Rokeach
Benghazi, 197
Ben-Gurion, David, 306
Ben-Zakai, Galit, 292, 293
Ber, Moshe, 263
Berenholz, Mr. (caterer), 341
Berg, Samuel, 315
Berlin, 21
Berman, Rav Avi, 346
Bernstein, S., 358

Bet Lid, 298
Bina, Malka, 232
Blass, Rebbetzin Shifra, 283
Blau, Amram, 54, 75, 76, 77–78, 103, 375
Blaustein, Sarah, 315
Blech, Rabbi Benjamin, 173
Bleeman, Aaron, 255
Bleeman, Avrohom, 121, 255, 372
Bloch, Rav Elya Meir, 34
Bnei Brak, 63, 65–67, 70, 71, 76, 101, 112
Boim, Dovid, 315
Boro Park, 329
Boston Shul (Har Nof), 251, 257, 258
Bostoner Rebbe, 376
Bovna, Ghetto, 6
Branover, Herman, 195
Brisker Rav (Rav Velvel). See Soloveitchik, Yitchok Zev
Bronx, the, 10
Brovender, Rabbi Chaim, 227–28
Bulman, Rav Nachman, 185, 186, 260, 375
Bush, George H. W., 267

Calek, Yigal, 265
California, 158–59
Camp Aguda, 166
Camp Kol Rina, 166
Carlebach, Shlomo, 33–34, 83, 244, 375
Carter, Jimmy, 204
Chazan, Rav Elya, 38
Chazon Ish, 66
Chernofksy, Phil, 312
Chevron, 59, 382, 315, 319, 375. See also Yeshivas Chevron
Chodakov, Rabbi, 158

Chodosh, Rav Meir, 59, 102, 339
Cleveland, 6, 35, 137
Clinton, Bill, 271
Cohen, Rabbi David, 150, 343–44, 345
Community Hebrew Academy of Toronto, 138
Congregation B'nai Torah (Toronto), 146–48, 157, 372–73, 375
Cooperberg family, 210, 211
Cooperberg, Andrea, 222
Crown Heights (NYC), 32, 230
Cyprus, 46, 101

Dashevsky, Zev, 250
Dayan, Moshe, 306
De Gaulle, Charles, 234
Dead Sea, 81
Debreziner Rav. See Stern, Rav Moshe
Dessler, Rav, 112
Detroit, 260
Dimona, 87–89
Doliner Rebbe, 32, 38
Douglin, Harvey, 255, 279
Dovid Hamelech, 245
Druck, Zalman, 83, 278, 283
Druckman, Rav Haim, 278, 283

Edelstein, Tanya, 250
Edelstein, Yuli, 245–46, 249–50
Egypt, 66, 84, 149, 150, 151–52, 153, 154, 187, 188, 189, 190–91, 234, 293, 319
Eider, Rav Shimon, 165, 167, 175, 375
Einhorn, Yonatan, 368
Einstein, Albert, 19, 20
Eitz Chaim School (Toronto), 127, 145, 146

Eli, 281, 283, 375
Elizabeth (NJ), 106
Elyashiv, Rav Yosef Shalom, 95, 96, 97–98, 99, 102, 156, 188, 375
England, 9
Entebbe, 197–98
Epstein, Rav Yechiel Michel Halevi, 261
Eretz Yisrael, 15, 24, 25, 30, 40–41, 86, 87, 88, 102–3, 136, 180, 186, 207–9, 213–18, 221, 244, 276–77, 284, 335–36, 338–39, 342, 359, 360–62
Essas, Eliyahu, 250
Eytan, Rafael "Raful", 152–53

Far Rockaway, 177, 185
Faskowitz, Rabbi, 291
Feinstein, Rav Moshe, 33, 137, 154, 164, 167, 173, 203, 217–18, 375
Felder, Rav Gedalia, 124, 148, 202
Felix, Rav Menachem, 312
Fendel family, 221
Fendel, Bina, 262
Fendel, Dovid, 189
Fendel, Goldie, 193, 189, 199, 212–13
Fendel, Hillel, 262
Fendel, Rabbi Meyer, 163, 180, 189, 193, 194, 199, 212, 278, 332, 373, 376
Finkel, Rav Leizer Yudel, 39
Flatbush, 253
Flatow, Alisa, 315
Flax, Hyman, 336
Forman, Rav Emanuel, 222
France, 9, 234, 336
Frank, Rav Tzvi Pesach, 61, 102, 375
Freifeld, Rav Shloime, 138, 375

Friederwitzer, Moshe, 165
Friedman, Rav Yosef (Yossi), 278, 283, 288, 290
Fulda, Leo (Yehuda), 69, 102

Gadish, Yosef, 255
Galinsky family, 246
Galinsky, Rabbi Mallen, 235, 237, 238, 241, 242, 244, 246, 248–49, 250, 376
Gasner family, 371
Gasner, Meyer, 122, 376
Gateshead (England), 42–43, 376
Gavish, Yosef, 224, 225
Gaza Strip, 307
Gaza, 281, 348–49
Gelb, Chaim, 4, 13–14, 34, 375
Germany, 9, 249
Gertzlin, Rav Nosson Elya, 37
Gillman, Senator, 291
Givati, Thea, 366
Glatzer (yeshiva student), 93
Glencove (Long Island), 195
Goborov, Igor, 238–39
Golan Heights, 188
Gold family, 199–203
Gold, Ariel, 58
Gold, Bayla, 52, 117, 119, 130, 131, 155, 159, 160, 163, 170, 199, 200, 210, 221, 222, 223, 226, 227, 250, 266, 292, 301, 327, 329–30, 333, 334, 337, 338, 345, 348, 353, 361, 362, 366, 368–69, 370, 373, 374
Gold, Chava Bayla (Sandhaus), 5, 24, 102, 112, 113, 361
Gold, David Chai, 321–22
Gold, David (nephew), 6, 196
Gold, Dina Katzman, 261–62, 265
Gold, Rav Doron, 22

Gold, Efraim Fishel, 5, 6
Gold, Esther, 6
Gold, Gittel Leah Bernbaum, 6
Gold, Hindele, 6
Gold, Rav Menachem, 159, 188, 261–63
Gold, Miriam, 19
Gold, Naphtali, 5
Gold, Pinya Rochel, 5
Gold, Rochelle (daughter-in-law), 342
Gold, Rochie, 19
Gold, Sandy, 22
Gold, Sara, 22
Gold, Sarah, 5, 6
Gold, Rabbi Shaul (Sholie), 19
Gold, Rav Shmuel Yehoshua (Stanley), 19, 20–22, 112, 113, 136–37, 208
Gold, Yaakov, 6
Gold, Yehoshua, 5, 6
Gold, Yehuda (father), 5–6, 17, 23–28, 207, 208–9, 357–58, 362
Gold, Yehuda (grandson), 202
Gold, Yehudit, 6
Gold, Yirmi, 159, 163, 199, 201, 265, 291, 292, 296, 298, 300, 301–2, 303, 316, 317, 342, 370
Gold, Yona, 5
Gold, Rav Yosef Yoel (Joe), 19, 20, 196
Goldberg, Chezi, 311
Goldberg, Mr., 17
Goldberg, Yankel, 42
Goldreich, Rabbi Avraham (Bumie), 259, 261, 361
Goldreich, Benyamin, 349, 350, 361
Goldreich, Brenda, 259, 261, 361
Goldreich, Daphna Gold, 5, 159, 259, 342, 349

Goldreich, Efraim Yosef, 349, 350
Goldreich, Naama, 350
Goldreich, Pazit, 350
Goldreich, Yehudah, 259, 261, 342, 349
Goldschmidt, Rav Pinchas, 260
Golombeck, Rav Avrohom, 69
Gordon, Rabbi Macy, 346
Gordon, Rav, 157
Gorelick, Rav Moshe, 124
Gottlieb, Moshe, 315
Grafstein, Liba, 132
Grafstein, Yirmiya, 132
Graubart, Rav Yehuda Leib, 163
Green, Herb, 284
Greenbaum, Joey, 127–28
Greenwald, Reb Yankel, 166, 167
Greenwald, Ronnie, 35–36, 375
Griffel, Rav Yaakov, 113, 115
Grodzinski, Rav Chaim Ozer, 112
Gross, Aharon, 315
Gross, Leon, 236–37
Grossman, Alex, 255
Grozovsky, Rav Reuven, 32, 38
Gryfe, Hershey, 123–24, 371
Gryfe, Ruth, 123–24, 371
Gush Katif, 347–49
Gustman, Rav Yisroel, 112, 113, 375

Hacohen, Rav David Chai, 278
Hadera, 262
Haifa, 47, 48, 100
Halberstam, Rav Yekusiel Yehudah, 28
Hamilton (Ontario), 324
Hammer, Esther, 19
Hebrew Academy of Nassau County (HANC), 175, 187
Heiman, Faygie, 341
Heiman, Rav Shlomo, 12, 31, 375

Heinemann, Rav Moshe, 174
Hempstead, 236
Herling, Rav Binyomin, 312
Herzliyah, 310
Herzog, Chaim, 84–85, 102, 375
Herzog, Rav Isaac Halevi, 83–85, 94, 95, 100, 102, 105, 375
Heschel, Rav Avrohom Yehoshua (Kopycznitzer Rebbe), 31, 34, 55–57, 354, 355, 375
Heschel, Rav Moshe, 31
Heschel, Rav Zishe, 31, 354
Hofstedter family, 371, 376
Hofstedter, Rav Dovid, 202
Hofstedter, Sandy, 121–22, 372
Hollander, David, 332
Hollander, Rabbi David, 206
Hornfeld, Ezzy, 255
Horowitz, Ellen, 351

Ilan, Yeshayahu, 229
Indor, Meir, 296
Iraq, 86, 267
Israel, 15, 25
Israel Center (Jerusalem), 312, 316, 320, 344, 372
Italy, 9
Itamar, 280

Jacobowitz, Rabbi Shlomo, 145–46, 375
Jacobson, Gershon, 291
Jakober, Dr., 124
Japan, 8, 9
Jennie (aunt), 362
Jericho, 281
Jerusalem, 41, 22, 90, 92. 96–97, 107, 111, 129, 156, 162–63, 246, 256, 294, 312, 332, 336, 338–39, 340

Bayit Vegan, 40, 48, 54, 58, 89, 192, 207, 221, 259
Ben Yehuda Street, 286, 304
Geula, 54–55, 59, 61, 76
Har Habayit, 312
Har Hazeitim, 357
Har Nof, 209, 224, 251, 253–54, 257–58, 261, 274, 281, 282–83, 322–23, 336, 369
King David Hotel, 360
Kiryat Moshe, 277–78, 287, 288
Kiryat Yovel, 225, 256
Kotel, the, 50, 156, 348, 352
Machane Yehuda, 286, 304
Meah Shearim, 76
Old City, 49, 111, 129, 150, 345
Ramat Eshkol, 92
Russian Compound, 301–3
Temple Mount, 150, 363, 364
Zion Square, 299–300
Jerusalem College for Adults (JCA), 228, 229, 232–33, 254, 266, 343–44, 345, 376
Johannesburg, 332

Kadishai, Yechiel, 206
Kafri, Dani, 229
Kahana, Rabbi Nachman, 346–47, 376
Kahana, Rav Binyamin, 315
Kahana, Talia, 315
Kahaneman, Rav Yosef Shlomo (Ponevezher Rav), 66, 70–71
Kahanov, Rav Luzer, 18
Kalmanovitch, Dov, 288
Kamenetsky, Rav Binyomin, 230–31, 233
Kamenetsky, Rav Nosson, 231
Kamenetsky, Rav Shmuel, 231
Kamenetsky, Rav Yaakov, 38, 115,

117, 148, 166, 215–16, 231, 253, 259, 261, 375
Kanotopsky, Rabbi Zvi Dov, 163
Kaplan, Rav Naftali, 36, 37, 38, 39
Karp, Rav, 18
Katz, Rav Mottel, 137
Katzman, Rabbi Boruch, 261
Katzman, Esther, 261
Kehillat Zichron Yosef (KZY; Har Nof), 157, 254, 266, 274–75, 367–68, 370
Kelemer, Rabbi Yehuda, 170
Kempinsky, Moish, 294
Kerem B'Yavneh, 180
Kesselman, Bernie, 177
Kever Rachel, 315, 316, 320
Kfar Yona, 262
Kiev, 241
Kiryat Arba, 221–22, 310
Kiryat Shmona, 262
Koenigsberg, Chavi Gold, 186, 260, 314
Koenigsberg, Daniel, 186, 260
Koenigsberg, Itamar, 261
Koenigsberg, Phyllis, 261
Kogan, Rav Yitzchok, 246
Kolbishev, 5
Kook, Rav Avraham Yitzchok HaCohen, 111, 340, 353
Kook, Rav Tzvi Yehuda, 60, 103, 375
Korolnek, Harry, 146
Kotler, Rav Aharon, 33, 34, 48, 48, 106, 130, 134–35, 143, 376
Kotler, Rav Shneur, 139, 143
Kotzk (Pol.), 334
Kovno (Lith.), 334
Krakow (Pol.), 334, 340
Krinsky, Rabbi Yehuda, 290
Kroll, Aryeh, 235, 241

Kronglass, Rav Dovid, 22–23, 37, 39, 82–83, 375
Krumbein, David, 255
Kuhl family, 371
Kuhl, Julius, 120, 121, 376
Kuhn, Derek, 338, 339
Kulefsky, Rav Yaakov Moshe, 112
Kushelevsky family, 58
Kushelevsky, Rav Tzvi, 58
Kushelevsky, Rav Elya, 89, 102

Lakewood Kollel (Toronto), 138
Landesman, Avrohom, 42
Lapid, Tommy, 292, 293
Lau, Rabbi Yisroel Meir, 250
Lebanon, 349
Lebovic family, 371
Lebovic, Avram, 131
Lebovic, Meyer, 120, 121, 123, 376
Lebovic, Minnie, 120
Lebovic (Weitz), Ruth, 130
Leff, Rabbi Bert, 226
Leibler, Avraham, 351
Leibler, Shulamit, 351
Leibowitz, Boruch Ber, 32
Leipzig, 21
Leningrad, 241, 246–47, 248
Lerner, Rabbi Pesach, 289, 290, 376
Levenstein, Rav Yechezkel (Rav Chatzkel), 72, 375
Leventhal, Batya, 368
Leventhal, Rav Moshe, 368
Levovitz, Rav Yeruchem, 39
Lewis, Dr. Bernard (Dov), 307
Libel, Chaim, 42
Liberman, Rabbi Hillel, 315
Lichtenstein, Josh, 176
Limasol (Cyprus), 46
Linchner, Rabbi, 40–41, 48, 54, 375
Lior, Rav Dov, 278

Lithuania, 334–35
Lizhensk (Pol.), 334
London, 43, 102, 249
Los Angeles, 332
Luban, Rabbi Chaim, 332
Lubavitcher Rebbe. *See* Schneerson, Rav Menachem Mendel; Schneerson, Rav Yosef Yitzchak
Lublin (Pol.), 334

Ma'ale Adumim, 232
Madrid, 256
Magnes, Rav Yehoshua, 278, 283, 312
Maharil, 338
Mainz, 338
Maisel, (Howie) Tzvi, 323
Maisel, Irving, 194, 316, 276, 316
Majdanek, 334, 339
Malbim, 268
Manchester, 102
Manhattan, 195, 283, 289
    Lower East Side, 10, 17, 31
Margalit, Dan, 292
Meir of Rothenburg, Rabbi (the Maharam), 337, 338
Melamed, Rav Zalman, 278
Melchior, Rabbi Michoel, 297
Menachem Mendel of Kotzk, Rav (Kotzker Rebbe), 206
Menachem Mendel of Shklov, Rav, 50
Mendelevich, Rabbi Yosef, 195, 302, 313
Mendlowitz, Rav Shraga Feivel, 4, 6, 38, 111, 112
Meron, 52, 100
Mevasseret Tzion, 221, 222, 224
Meyers, Sidney, 291
Migdal, 52, 352, 356, 357

Migdal HaEmek, 186, 260
Miller, Dr. Bert, 174
Miller, Menachem, 255
Mintz, Rav Chaim, 126
Montreal, 127, 323–24
Montreux (Switzerland), 101
Mordechai Hayehudi, 143–44
Morocco, 41, 86
Moscow, 238, 241–46
Moscowitz, Dr. Irving, 288–89
Moshe Ben Maimon, 60, 217, 293, 314, 328
    grave, 75–76, 103, 376
Moshe Ben Nachman, 49, 50–51, 60, 216
Moshe Rabbeinu, 24, 135–36, 137, 189–92
Mount Eval, 161, 312
Mount Gerizim, 161–62
Mubarak, Hosni, 293, 294

Nachman of Breslov, Rebbe, 50
Nadav, Rav David (Dudu), 265
Nadav, Libi Gold, 159, 261, 265
Naftali of Ropshitz, Rav (Ropshitzer Rebbe), 5
Nahariya, 262
Nasser, Gamal Abel, 149
Ner Yisroel (Baltimore), 35–40, 71, 81–83, 103, 104, 106, 110, 111, 115–16, 117, 195–96, 328, 346, 355
Ner Yisroel (Toronto), 117, 120, 122, 123–27, 134, 138, 145, 195, 199, 202, 343, 370–72, 375
Neria, Rav Moshe, 278
Nesher, 262
Netanya, 310
    Galei Tzanz Hotel, 212, 213
    Park Hotel, 303

Netanyahu, Binyamin (Bibi), 278, 281, 282–83, 308, 375
Netanyahu, Yoni, 198
Neuberger, Chaya, 329
Neuberger, Rav Naftali, 110, 114, 115, 158, 199, 375
Neuberger, Tzvi Meyer, 329
New York City, 102, 134, 198, 291
Newcastle upon Tyne, 43
Novominsker Rebbe, 264
Nussbaum, Rav Chaim, 122

Oceanside (NY), 173–74
Ochs, Rav Dovid, 124, 149
Ochs, Rav Mordechai, 124
Odessa, 241
Ohr Chaim (Toronto), 138
Oren, Michael, 151
Orlando, 199
Oslo, 194, 205, 296–98, 376
Ostrov, 132
Oxford, 21

Pam, Rav Avraham, 18, 32, 284, 375
Paris, 43–44, 102
Parshan, Rav Avraham, 135, 136, 137
Patterson (NJ), 58
Pechman, Bert, 164
Peres, Shimon, 194, 271, 281, 290, 291, 294–95, 296–97, 298
Perlow, Rav Yaakov (Stoliner Rebbe), 29–30
Perlow, Rav Yochanan (Stoliner Rebbe), 29, 30, 353–54
Philadelphia, 291
Pirchei Agudas Yisroel, 4, 10, 11
Poland, 334, 340
Polanski, Pinchas, 250
Pollack, Akiva, 369

Ponevezh (Lith.), 334. *See also* Yeshivas Ponevezh
Ponevezher Rav. *See* Kahaneman
Pontypool (Ontario), 361
Porat, Rav Hanan, 320–21
Porush, Rabbi Menachem, 320–21
Povarsky, Rav Berel, 70
Povarsky, Rav Dovid, 68, 69
Prestwick (Scotland), 42
Price, Rabbi Avraham, 149
Pruzansky, Rabbi Steven, 289
Purcel, Francis, 167–68, 170, 171
Pustkow, 6

Quinn, Rav Nesanel, 31, 48, 103, 160

Rabbinical Council of America (RCA), 179, 182, 185, 188, 192, 289–90
Rabin, Yitzhak, 152, 271, 290, 295, 296–97, 298, 308, 311, 320–21
Rabinovitch, Rav Nachum Eliezer, 148, 203, 277, 283
Rachel (wife of R. Akiva), 362–63
Rachel Imeinu, 317–20, 360
Rakoff, Adina, 366
Ralbag, Rav Yitzchak, 251, 255
Ramat Beit Shemesh, 261, 266
Rambam. *See* Moshe Ben Maimon
Ramban. *See* Moshe Ben Nachman
Rashi, 20, 22, 135–36, 137, 240, 268, 319, 336, 350, 361
Raviv, Avishai, 311
Rayatz. *See* Schneerson, Rav Yosef Yitzchak
Reichman, Chaim, 222
Reichman, Irit, 222
Reichman, Rabbi Heshy, 289

Reichmann family, 371
Reichmann, Moshe, 122, 138, 376
Reish, Moshe, 366
Reish, Tova, 366
Rettig, Josh, 229
Rettig, Linda, 229
Riga, 241, 247
Rivkin, Rav Moshe Dov Ber (Duber), 18, 32
Rokeach, Rav Aaron (Belzer Rebbe), 55, 102
Ron, Dr., 223
Roness, Rabbi Yerachmiel, 332
Roosevelt, Franklin Delano, 14
Ropshitz, 5, 6
Rose, Rabbi Moshe, 224, 228, 255, 266, 376
Rosenbluth, Yitzchak, 265–66
Rosenthal, Leslie (Akiva Chaim), 124
Rosenthal, Rabbi (Sudbury, Ont.), 124
Rosenzweig, Rav Berel, 124
Roth, Larry, 345
Roth, Malka, 315
Roth, Marsha, 345
Rubin, Dov, 255, 323
Rubinoff, Binyomin, 131, 361
Rubinoff, Dena, 323
Rubinoff, Judy, 346, 376
Rubinoff (Rubanovitch), Menachem Mendel, 131
Rubinoff, Mendel, 346, 376
Rubinoff, Sarah, 225
Rubinoff, Sarah Grafstein, 131, 361
Rubinoff, Yeshaya (Shaya), 361
Rubinstein, Hershel, 121, 130, 371, 376
Ruderman, Rav Yaakov Yitzchok Halevi, 36, 39, 41, 103, 104–5,
106–7, 110–11, 114, 115–18, 119, 126, 138, 196, 273, 328, 355, 371, 372, 375
Russia, 149, 234, 238–244, 248, 376

Sadat, Anwar, 204
Sand, Chanan, 313
Sand, Emanuel, 255
Sand, Tamara, 313
Sand, Tzvi, 255, 313
Sandhaus, Chana, 5
Sandhaus, Chava Bayla, 5
Sandhaus, Eunice, 6
Sandhaus, Feiga, 5
Sandhaus, Maryam Devoraḥ, 5
Sandhaus, Moishe, 6, 16
Sandhaus, Mordechai Duvid, 5
Sandhaus, Moshe, 6, 7
Sandhaus, Samuel K. (Sandy), 7
Sandhaus, Sunny, 7
Sandhaus, Tziviya, 5
Sapsowitz family, 212
Sarah Imeinu, 364
Sarna, Rav Chatzkel, 59, 102
Satmar Rebbe. *See* Teitelbaum, Rav Yoel
Schachter, Rabbi Hershel, 292
Scheinfeld, Dr., 208
Scherman, Rav Nosson, 42, 375
Schiller, Rav Nota, 130, 375
Schneerson, Rav Menachem Mendel (Lubavitcher Rebbe), 137, 158, 183, 214–15, 230
Schneerson, Rav Yosef Yitzchok, 32, 183
Schoenfeld, Rabbi Fabian, 19, 20
Schreiber, Max, 179
Schwartzbaum, Avraham, 229, 376
Seattle, 262
Semel, Shaya, 266

Sha'alvim, 180, 250
Shach, Rav Elazar Menachem, 66, 67–69, 102
Shamir, Yitzhak, 256
Shanghai, 157
Shapira, Rav Avraham Elkanah, 277–78, 282, 287, 305, 306–7, 312, 375
Shapira, Rav Avraham Yosef, 154–55
Shapira, Rav Yaakov, 202
Shapiro, Rav Avrohom Yeshaya, 18, 32
Shapiro, Rav Meir, 339, 340
Sharon, Ariel, 84, 347
Sharon, Moshe, 280
Shaviv, Paul, 255
Shenker, Bentzion, 34
Sherer, Moshe, 283
Shifrin, Mark, 244, 245
Shifrin, Slava, 244, 245
Shilo, 280
Shilo, Ephraim, 255
Shilo, Rav Daniel, 278
Shimon Bar Yochai, Rabbi, 52
Shmuel, 269–70
Shochet, Rav, 157
Shomron (territory), 280, 305
Shteiner, Rav Chaim, 278
Shwekey, Yaakov, 114
Siberia, 5, 248
Sigler, Saul, 121, 371
Silver, Avrom, 157, 253, 254, 255, 343, 376
Silver, Bonnie, 255, 343, 345, 376
Silver, Rav Eliezer (Rav Leizer), 42–43, 109–10, 114, 376
Silver, Nancy, 255
Silver, Rav Reuven, 127
Silver, Yosef, 253

Silverberg, Aryeh, 373
Silverberg, Yaffa, 373
Silverstein, Tova, 223, 366
Simon, Joe, 333
Simon, Phyllis, 333
Slobodka (*yeshivah*, Lith.), 328, 334
Sokal, Myron, 253
Sokal, Sandra, 177, 253
Soloveichik, Rav Ahron, 314
Soloveitchik, Rav Joseph B., 19, 352
Soloveitchik, Yitchok Zev (Rav Velvel), 54, 60–61, 62, 78–79, 102, 211, 375
South Africa, 279, 332–33
Spero, Dr. Moshe Halevi, 294
Spero, Yehudit, 294
Spinner, Rav, 166
Sprecher, Chavie, 19
Spring Valley, 38
Stahl, David, 294
Staten Island, 165, 174
Stavsky, Rabbi David, 179
Steipler Gaon, 66
Stern, Rav Moshe, 177, 180, 375
Stoliner Rebbe. *See* Perlow
Straits of Tiran, 149
Sudbury (Canada), 124
Swidler, Sonia, 177
Syria, 187, 234

Tanzer, Rav Avraham, 333
Tapuach, 310
Tchebiner Rav. *See* Weidenfeld, Rav Dov Berish
Teichtal, Rav Yissachar Shlomo, 186
Teitelbaum, Rav Yoel (Satmar Rebbe), 28, 29, 44–46, 47, 48, 102, 190, 376
Teitz, Rav Elazar Mayer, 70, 105–6
Tel Aviv, 55–56, 73, 87, 91, 235, 324

Dolphinarium, 303
Telz (*yeshivah*), 35, 118, 128
Tendler, Rabbi Moshe, 292
Tenenbaum, Joe, 145, 147–48, 371, 372, 376
Tirat Hacarmel, 262
Torah Academy for Girls (TAG; Far Rockaway), 163
Toronto, 117, 118, 119–133, 134–38, 145–49, 157, 163, 174, 202–3, 215, 225, 228, 230, 284, 324, 332, 346, 371–72
   Tangreen Village, 145, 148
   Tyrell estate, 122, 125, 127, 375
   Willowdale, 145, 159
Tress, Mike, 4, 10–11, 376
Truman, Harry, 15
Tzfas, 100
Tucker, Anita, 351
Turin, Rav Asher, 127
Tveria, 52, 75, 100, 265, 353, 355, 376
Twerski, Aaron, 355
Twerski, Michel, 355
Twersky, Mordechai, 291
Tzemach (Israel embassy, London), 237, 240

Ulpana (Toronto), 138
Ungar, Yaron, 315
USSR. *See* Russia

Venice, 21, 44–45, 101, 102, 376
Vienna, 21, 339, 340–41
Vilna (Lith.), 334, 335–36
Virginia, 199, 220
Vogel, Harry, 376

Wachsman, Nachshon, 315
Wachspress, Marvin, 164
Wagner, Rav Feivel, 283
Waldman, Rav Eliezer, 283
Wallin, Chaim, 182
Warsaw, 334
Washington, DC, 200–201, 204, 274, 287, 288
Wasserman, Rav Elchonon, 10, 11
Weidenfeld, Rav Dov Berish (Tchebiner Rav), 56, 103
Weil, Max, 232–33
Weinberg, Moe, 207
Weinberg, Rav Noach, 126
Weinberg, Rav Yechiel Yaakov, 101
Weinberg, Rav Shmuel Yaakov, 114, 115, 138
Weinstein, Shloima Yosef (Joey), 42, 55, 56
Weinstein, Shmuel, 322
Weinstock, Meyer, 125
Weinstock, Moshe, 323
Weiss, Rav Gershon, 36, 126
West Bank, 150, 307
West Hempstead, 159, 161–65, 167–72, 174–76, 177–79, 180–84, 193, 195–96, 203, 209–10, 253, 365, 373
   Young Israel, 154, 157–59, 187
Wexler, Rabbi Stanley, 177
White House, 200, 204, 271, 274
White Shul (Far Rockaway), 289
Williamsburg, 3, 4–5, 7–8, 10, 11–14, 16, 18, 28–30, 31, 40, 102, 166, 263, 357
Wimpfen, Alexander Suskind, 337, 338
Winkler, Rabbi Neil, 289
Wistrich, Robert, 315
Worcester, MA, 19, 196
Worms (Ger.), 336–39
Wortzman, Shea, 138

Wouk, Herman, 183
Wurzburger, Rabbi Walter, 124

Yaakov Avinu, 317–20
Yam Hamelach, 194
Yamit, 154, 155
Yehudah (territory), 280, 305
Yehudah Hachassid, Rav, 49, 50
Yemen, 86
Yerushalayim. *See* Jerusalem
Yeshiva Torah Vodaath, 4, 7–8, 15, 23, 25, 28, 30–31, 54, 70, 79, 80, 111, 149, 253, 254, 375
Yeshiva Yesodei HaTorah of Toronto, 138
Yeshivas Chachmei Lublin, 339–40
Yeshivas Chevron, 59–60, 62–65, 76, 93–94, 375
Yeshivas Ponevezh, 30, 63–64, 65–73, 76, 80–82, 101, 102, 103, 105, 375
Yeshivat Merkaz Harav, 277–78, 287, 304
Yeshurun Synagogue (Jerusalem), 228
Yirmiyahu, 22, 140, 282, 318
Yisraeli, Rav Shaul, 278
Yokneam, 262
Yosef, Rav Ovadia, 154

Zelikovitch, Rav Shabtai, 277, 283
Zivotofsky, Bernie, 164
Zoberman, Meir Yechiel, 130
Zornberg, Aviva Gottlieb, 346